D1806913

GOVERNANCE AND THE DEMOCRATIC DEFICIT

Governance and the Democratic Deficit
Assessing the Democratic Legitimacy of Governance Practices

Edited by

VICTOR BEKKERS, GESKE DIJKSTRA, ARTHUR EDWARDS
Erasmus University Rotterdam, The Netherlands
MENNO FENGER
Ministry of Social Affairs and Employment, The Netherlands

ASHGATE

© Victor Bekkers, Geske Dijkstra, Arthur Edwards and Menno Fenger 2007

All rights reserved. No part of this publication may be reproduced, stored in a retrieval system or transmitted in any form or by any means, electronic, mechanical, photocopying, recording or otherwise without the prior permission of the publisher.

Victor Bekkers, Geske Dijkstra, Arthur Edwards and Menno Fenger have asserted their right under the Copyright, Designs and Patents Act, 1988, to be identified as the editors of this work.

Published by
Ashgate Publishing Limited
Gower House
Croft Road
Aldershot
Hampshire GU11 3HR
England

Ashgate Publishing Company
Suite 420
101 Cherry Street
Burlington, VT 05401-4405
USA

Ashgate website: http://www.ashgate.com

British Library Cataloguing in Publication Data
Governance and the democratic deficit : assessing the
   democratic legitimacy of governance practices
   1. Democracy 2. Political planning 3. Political science
   I. Bekkers, V. J. J. M.
   321.8

ISBN-13: 978-0-7546-4983-0

Library of Congress Cataloging-in-Publication Data
Governance and the democratic deficit: assessing the democratic legitimacy of
   governance practices / edited by Victor Bekkers ... [et al.].
      p. cm.
   Includes bibliographical references and index.
   ISBN 13: 978-0-7546-4983-0
   1. Public administration. 2. Decentralization in government. 3. Public-private sector
cooperation. 4. Organizational change. I. Bekkers, V. J. J. M.

   JF1351.G678 2007
   351.73--dc22

2006025810

ISBN-13: 978-0-7546-4983-0

Printed and bound in Great Britain by MPG Books, Bodmin, Cornwall.

Contents

PART I   THEORETICAL FRAMEWORK

PART II   GOVERNANCE AT A DISTANCE AND MARKET GOVERNANCE

List of Figures

List of Tables

Notes on Contributors

Victor Bekkers is Professor of Public Administration at Erasmus University Rotterdam. He holds the chair on the empirical study of public policy and public policy processes.

Lex Cachet is Associate Professor in the Department of Public Administration at Erasmus University Rotterdam. His research interests include policing, public safety and crisis management.

Geske Dijkstra is Associate Professor in Economics, Department of Public Administration at Erasmus University Rotterdam. Her current research interests focus on the macro-economic effectiveness of aid and debt relief, and on the influence of bilateral and multilateral aid agencies on policy and governance of recipient countries.

Arthur Edwards is Assistant Professor in the Department of Public Administration at Erasmus University Rotterdam. His research focuses on the impact of ICTs on democracy.

Menno Fenger joined the Department of Public Administration at Erasmus University Rotterdam as an Assistant Professor. He is interested in the tension between institutional path-dependency and theories of policy change, primarily in the field of welfare policy. He currently works in the Netherlands Ministry of Social Affairs and Employment.

Michael Hill is a retired Professor of Social Policy at the University of Newcastle-Upon-Tyne. He continues to research and teach social and public policy. He has written extensively on policy implementation, British social policy and comparative social policy.

Peter Hupe is Associate Professor in the Department of Public Administration at Erasmus University Rotterdam. Central in his research is the theoretical-empirical study of the policy process, particularly matters of implementation and political-administrative management.

Evelien Korteland is a Ph.D. student at the Center for Public Innovation, Erasmus University Rotterdam. Her research is focused on the diffusion and adoption of innovations in the public sector.

Lieve Lodewijckx is currently affiliated with the Faculty of Law of the Catholic University of Mozambique at Nampula.

Peter Marks is Assistant Professor in the Department of Public Administration at Erasmus University Rotterdam. His research is focused on the application of complexity theory on public administration.

Frans van Nispen tot Pannerden is Associate Professor of Public Administration at Erasmus University Rotterdam. His research areas include the interface of policy analysis and fiscal policy, and public governance, notably the implementation of the Stability and Growth Pact within the ongoing process of European integration.

Johan Posseth is a Ph.D. student at the Department of Public Administration, Erasmus University Rotterdam. His research is focused on result-oriented budgeting and steering in the public sector.

José Ruano de la Fuente is Professor of Political Science in the Complutense University of Madrid. His main research areas are local government and multi-level governance.

Linze Schaap is Assistant Professor in the Department of Public Administration at Erasmus University Rotterdam. He founded the Centre for Local Democracy. His main research areas are local democracy and regional governance.

Arie van Sluis is Assistant Professor in the Department of Public Administration at Erasmus University Rotterdam. His main area of research is the police organization and the police system, the relations of the police with democratic institutions and public safety policy.

Koen Stapelbroek is a post-doctoral researcher at Erasmus University Rotterdam, specializing in the history of political thought.

Patty Zandstra joined the Department of Public Administration at Erasmus University Rotterdam as a Ph.D. student. She currently works in the Netherlands Ministry of Foreign Affairs.

Preface by the Editors

The 'governance' phenomenon has received substantial attention among scholars and practitioners of public administration and political science. Some even define it as a 'hype'. Yet we do see a fundamental change in the central role and position of government organizations in governing all types of societal problems and challenges. New mechanisms or instruments for producing semi-public goods and services with a political nature have emerged. Shifts of governance and new modes of governance have been introduced, and they can be assessed in different ways. One perspective is that of democratic legitimacy. Governance can be described as the emergence of a political order that may challenge the traditional role of representative democracy and its institutions. Some scholars refer to a democratic deficit. In this book we investigate this claim with a group of researchers, many who belong to the Center of Public Governance of the Department of Public Administration of the Erasmus University Rotterdam. We develop a line of theoretical reasoning for assessing the democratic legitimacy of governance practices, and we empirically examine governance practices in different countries and in various international contexts. What is the democratic nature of these governance practices? How does representative democracy deal with these practices? Does this lead to the rise of other democratic arrangements to compensate possible democratic deficits?

We would like to thank Julie Raadschelders who edited our non-native English and Susanne Groot for copy-editing the manuscript. We are also grateful to the anonymous reviewers who gave a number of thoughtful suggestions for improving the quality and coherence of the manuscript. Finally, we would like to thank the authors and all members of our research group who contributed to this collective undertaking.

Victor Bekkers
Geske Dijkstra
Arthur Edwards
Menno Fenger

Rotterdam, June 2006

List of Abbreviations

ADL	Agente de Desenvolvimento Local [Agents of Local Development]
BCUs	Basic Command Units
BEPGs	Broad Economic Policy Guidelines
BWIs	Bretton Woods Institutions
BZK	Ministerie van Binnenlandse Zaken en Koninkrijkrelaties [Ministry of the Interior and Kingdom Relations]
CDL	Commissão de Desenvolvimento Local [Local Development Commission]
CDRPs	Crime and Disorder Reduction Partnerships
CoR	Commmittee of the Regions
COSAC	Conférence des Organes Spécialisés dans les Affaires Communautaires et Européennes des Parlements de l'Union Européenne [Conference of Community and European Affairs Committees of Parliaments of the European Union]
DMCR	Environmental Protection Agency Rijnmond
EB	Executive Board
ECB	European Central Bank
ECOFIN	Economic and Financial Affairs Council
EDP	Excessive Deficit Procedure
EES	European Employment Strategy
EESC	European Economic and Social Council
EFP	Economic and Financial Committee
EMCO	Employment Committee
EMU	European Monetary Union
EP	European Parliament
EPA	Environmental Protection Agency
ESAF	Enhanced Structural Adjustment Facility
ESCB	European System of Central Banks
EU	European Union
FED	Federal Reserve
FY	Fiscal Year
GCA	Greater Copenhagen Authority
GDP	Gross Domestic Product
GIS	Geographical Information System
GLA	Greater London Authority
HICP	Harmonized Index of Consumer Prices

HIPC   Heavily Indebted Poor Country
HMIC   Her Majesty's Inspectorate of Constabulary
IBRD   International Bank for Reconstruction and Development
IDA   International Development Association
IEG   Independent Evaluation Group
IEO   Independent Evaluation Office
IFC   International Finance Corporation
IFIAC   International Financial Institutions Advisory Commission
IMF   International Monetary Fund
LDFs   Local Development Frameworks
LKNP   Landelijk Kader Nederlandse Politie [National
              Framework of the Netherlands' Police]
LPF   Lijst Pim Fortuyn [List Pim Fortuyn]
LR   Leefbaar Rotterdam [Livable Rotterdam]
MAMM   Mogovolas, Angoche, Mogincual, Moma
              [four districts in Mozambique]
Maraps   Management Reports
MD   Municipal District
MLG   Multi-Level Governance
NAPs   National employment Action Plans
NGO   Non-Governmental Organization
NHS   National Health Service
NICE   National Institute for Clinical Excellence
NPM   New Public Management
NPTs   Neighborhood Policing Teams
OECD   Organisation of Economic Co-operation and Development
OED   Operations Evaluation Department
OFSTED   Office for Standards in Education
OMC   Open Method of Coordination
PA   Police Authority
PPAF   Policing Performance Assessment Framework
PRGF   Poverty Reduction and Growth Facility
PRSCs   Poverty Reduction Support Credits
PRSPs   Poverty Reduction Strategy Papers
PSI   Policy Support Instrument
QMV   Qualified Majority Voting
RAB   Residential Advisory Board
RMO   Raad voor Maatschappelijke Ontwikkeling
              [Council for Social Development]
SAF   Structural Adjustment Facility
SAPRI   Structural Adjustment Participatory Review Initiative
SCP   Sustainable Cleveland Partnership
SCS   Steering Committee on Safety
SCSNDA   St. Clair Superior Neighborhood Development Association

SDRs	Special Drawing Rights
SDS	Strategic Development Strategy
SER	Sociaal-Economische Raad [Social-Economic Council]
SGP	Stability and Growth Pact
SNV	Netherlands Development Organization
SPO	Safety Program Office
TEC	Treaty Establishing a Constitution for Europe
TQM	Total Quality Management
UN	United Nations
UNDP	United Nations Development Programme
UNICE	Union des Industries des pays de la Communauté Européenne [Union of Industrial and Employers' Confederations of Europe]
WB	World Bank
WRR	Wetenschappelijke Raad voor het Regeringsbeleid [Scientific Council for Government Policy]
WTO	World Trade Organization

PART I
THEORETICAL FRAMEWORK

Chapter 1

Governance and the Democratic Deficit: Introduction

Victor Bekkers, Geske Dijkstra, Arthur Edwards, and Menno Fenger

In the 1990s, the public sector experienced a shift in the dominant 'steering' paradigm. The idea that government could effectively intervene in societal developments and solve societal problems from a centralized and hierarchical position, detached from society, and according to the goals laid down in policy programs, met with a lot of criticism. Traditionally, the government was placed in the center of societal developments and problems. Ineffective government interventions were primarily seen as flaws in the 'machinery of government', as the result of imperfect knowledge about the nature and effects of the problem, and as the product of a mismatch between the policy instruments that were used and the policy goals that were formulated. In the 1990s, we can observe the emergence of a new steering paradigm which is called the 'governance paradigm', in contrast to the classical 'government paradigm'. This shift from government towards governance implies that:

- Government is not an entity but a conglomerate of actors;
- Government is not the only actor that attempts to influence societal developments, and
- Government interventions are interventions in policy networks, in which power, resource dependency, and strategic behavior are vital elements.

Successful government interventions depend on the extent to which public, private and semi-public actors succeed in creating a shared understanding of the nature of the policy problems and how they should be handled. The idea of governance reflects the attention that should be paid to the processes themselves in which actors with different interests, resources and beliefs co-produce policy practices that they share. The paradigm shift from 'government to governance' gives government organizations a position in complex exchange networks, characterized by (inter)dependency and communication relations with relevant stakeholders in their environments (other governments, citizens, companies and societal organizations). In this book, the concept of governance represents the recognition of the limits of government and governmental steering and the shift towards central government's reliance upon other actors, sectors and levels of government. A key element in the governance concept is the ability of organizations to self-organize and self-regulate along with other organizations, sectors and levels of government, out of which new forms of coordinated or collective action may arise.

Governance has its impact upon the institutions that traditionally form representative democracy. In a network setting, it is much less clear who is accountable for what tasks than in a traditional hierarchical setting. Moreover, the idea of representative democracy is challenged by elected politicians and policy officials engaging in 'wheeling and dealing' with societal actors rather than doing what they are elected for: political decision-making. Furthermore, the shifts in authority from central government to other public bodies or levels of government are only democratically 'neutral' when democratic institutions also respond to this shift in an appropriate manner. These considerations lead to a hypothesis, which is often suggested but seldom empirically tested: governance leads to a democratic deficit. The central purpose of this book is to assess the impact of governance on democracy. Our investigation begins by assuming that the answer to this question is unknown as yet, but several positions on the impact of governance on democracy might roughly be distinguished.[1]

On the one hand, governance might be presented as a threat to democracy. A first argument for this point of view is that governance challenges the institutions of representative democracy. If one views representative democratic institutions as the primary means for collective decision-making, governance and democracy might be seen as incompatible (Klijn and Skelcher, *forthcoming*). However, a democratic deficit may also appear outside the model of representative democracy. It can be argued that, although governance practices include a wide variety of private and public actors, '[...] the incorporation of organized interests into the formulation and implementation of political decisions can hardly be considered a process of democratization' (Papadopoulos 2003, 478). Fundamental questions can be raised with regard to, for instance, the inclusion of weakly organized interests and communities, the quality of the representation of these groups, responsiveness and accountability (Benz and Papadopoulos 2006). On the other hand, there are authors who claim that governance, or more specifically, governance in networks represents a more advanced form of democracy than traditional representative democracy. Klijn and Skelcher refer to authors like Castells (1997), according to whom democracy becomes more a societal model of deliberation and multiple forms of accountability.

Several other positions can be formulated. Governance can be seen as complementary to representative democracy. In particular, it can be argued that while the shifts of collective decision-making outside the scope of direct parliamentary control pose the potential of a democratic deficit, governance practices also provide new arenas for democratic involvement (Sörensen 2002). In this case, a central question is how different sorts of democracy can be combined and what the proper

---

1   Klijn and Skelcher (forthcoming) distinguish four 'conjectures' about the relationship between governance networks and (representative) democracy: incompatible, complementary, transitional, instrumental.

position of representative democracy would be in such a model. Lastly, governance can be seen as instrumental for enhancing the functioning of representative democracy, especially by emphasizing steering on output rather than throughput.

By analyzing cases in different international, national, regional and sector contexts, this book tries to increase the knowledge on the impact of governance on democracy. The central question of this book is: What are the consequences of new forms of governance for the democratic legitimacy of public policies?

1. Unpacking the Concepts of Governance, Legitimacy and Democracy

Like so many other concepts in the social sciences, the key concepts of our book's title are 'fuzzy' concepts: concepts with no clear meaning and an inherently positive connotation. For who would be against 'democracy', or what arguments would there be to strongly oppose the idea of 'governance'? Since the key target of this book is to assess governance's impact on democratic legitimacy, the answer to this question is affected both by the interpretation of governance and the perspective on legitimacy and democracy that one takes. Therefore, this book starts off by unpacking and decomposing these concepts. In this introductory chapter, we present an outline of the basic arguments that are examined in the Chapters 2 and 3.

The starting-point for our arguments is that the answer to our central research question depends on the type of governance that is at stake, the idea of legitimacy that one uses and the perspective on democracy that one embraces. Let us briefly present the dazzling variety that is connected with each of these concepts.

Governance

In the discussion about governance, several shifts have been distinguished:

- From public towards private forms of governance.
- From public towards forms of governance in which the civic society plays an important role.
- From central forms to decentralized forms.
- From national forms to international and supranational forms.
- From geographical forms to functional forms.
- From vertical to horizontal forms.

In the conceptual framework on governance developed in the second chapter, we reduce these shifts to five different modes of governance. The first type is *governance at a distance*. In this mode of governance, the relationship between the organizations which steer and the organizations which are the object of steering is still hierarchical, but the organizations to be steered are given a (substantial) amount of discretion to develop and implement their own policies, based on the recognition of self-regulation. *Multi-level governance* is our second type. Multi-level governance refers to the upward and downward shifts of problem-solving capacity, responsibilities and competences from the nation state. The 'upwards shift' refers to supranational or intergovernmental authority bodies, the 'downwards shift' refers to the regional and local levels that increasingly gain importance in policy-making processes as well. *Market governance* is the third type of governance that we distinguish. The concept of market governance refers to the use of the market mechanism of supply and demand in governance processes. The fourth type is *network governance*. In this mode of governance, steering is focused on facilitating a shared understanding between the organizations or stakeholders in a policy network in order to create a common and trustworthy policy practice through interaction, communication, negotiation and exchange. *Societal self-governance* is the fifth type, and this mode of governance is about creating, facilitating and enabling policy initiatives developing within communities.

What all of these modes of governance have in common is that problem-solving capacity is transferred from the traditional state institutions towards other levels or institutions. The distinction of these five types is a first step towards the assessment of governance's impact on the democratic legitimacy of public policies.

Democratic Legitimacy

Legitimacy is the second concept that requires clarification. Like the other central two concepts in our framework, legitimacy is hard to define. Stone (2002, 285) argues that legitimacy might be regarded as the political scientist's equivalent of the economist's invisible hand: 'we know it exists as a force that holds societies together, but we cannot give very satisfactory explanations of how to create it or why it is sometimes very strong and sometimes seems to disappear.'

The concept of legitimacy is closely related to authority. A legitimate authority is one that is recognized as valid or justified by those to whom it applies. In this book we distinguish three aspects of democratic legitimacy, namely input-, throughput- and output legitimacy (cf. Scharpf 1999; WRR 2004). For each of these three aspects we define certain norms or criteria for assessing the legitimacy of governance practices. *Input-oriented legitimacy* emphasizes the normative idea of 'government by the people'. In terms of norms, this refers to the quality of representation, the opportunities that are available for citizens to participate in the political process and the openness of the agenda-setting process. *Throughput-oriented legitimacy* focuses on the quality of the decision-making process. Relevant criteria include the quality of participation by citizens and the quality of 'checks and balances'. Finally, *output-oriented legitimacy* emphasizes the normative idea of 'government for the people'. The criteria for assessing governance practices on this aspect include the effectiveness and responsiveness of policies and accountability.

Democracy

In addition to refining the ideas of governance and legitimacy, our research objectives also require a decomposition of the concept of democracy. The various modes of governance are embedded in different democratic arrangements or types of democracy. First, they are (more or less) loosely coupled to representative democracy. Furthermore, they might be embedded in other types of democratic arrangements. As outlined in Chapter 3, we distinguish the following five models of democracy:

- *Representative democracy*: a democratic regime in which the adult citizens elect their representatives who then form a legislative assembly with the function of controlling the government, and deciding on specific laws and policies.
- *Pluralist democracy*: a form of government in which the making of political decisions involves the steady trade-off and appeasement of the demands of numerous groups representing different interests.
- *Deliberative democracy*: a form of democracy that provides institutions for the resolution of problems of collective choice through free public deliberation
- *Direct democracy*: a form of democracy in which important policy as well as constitutional decisions are made by the use of the citizens' initiative and the referendum.
- *Associative democracy*: a democratic regime characterized by the direct participation of citizens in the regulation of 'non-political domains', including (semi-) public and private service organizations, the workplace and neighborhoods.
- *Consumer democracy*: a set of institutions in which the expression of needs and demands is channeled by the democratic organization of public service delivery.

Each model of democracy provides for specific institutions and devices for fulfilling the norms of input, throughput and output democracy. In chapter 3 we show, however, that because of the various normative orientations that underlie these models of democracy, they differ in how they can be expected to accommodate the legitimacy criteria. This consideration points to one of the central themes of the book, namely how different models of democracy can work together in ways than can be mutually supportive in terms of democratic legitimacy (Saward, 2001).

2. Research Questions

The roadmap for this book follows from the building blocks that have been presented in the previous section and will be elaborated in the chapters 2 and 3. We assess governance's impact on the democratic legitimacy of public policies by analyzing various governance cases. The central question is: *what are the consequences of new forms of governance for the democratic legitimacy of public policies?*

In each of these cases, the contributions to this book deal with the following questions:

1. How can the new governance practice be described and what expectations regarding the legitimacy of public policies underlie this practice?

Several developments, intentions or assumptions may have given rise to a governance practice. As far as legitimacy is concerned, these expectations may refer to the inputs, throughput or outputs of the governance processes.

2. What processes of collective will-formation and democratic feedback can be observed in the new governance practice and to which model(s) of democracy do they refer?

In traditional government steering the representative model was dominant. In the governance era, policy processes have become unleashed from representative democracy, while at the same time we may observe that other models of democracy emerge, in addition to the representative model.

3. What strengths and weaknesses in the governance practice can be observed with respect to input-, throughput- and output legitimacy?

A key question of this book is how the new arrangements can be assessed in terms of democratic legitimacy, and how the potential gap of legitimacy created by the introduction of governance in the public sector is filled.

4.To what extent do these (new) governance practices have a 'democratic deficit' and how can it be understood? What solutions may be advanced, in terms of which models of democracy?

Finally, we draw conclusions on the strengths and weaknesses of specific modes of governance with respect to democratic legitimacy and advance or discuss possible solutions. One important element in this discussion is a reconsideration of the role of representative democracy in relation to other types of democratic arrangements.

3. Outline of the Book

The book has four parts. In the first part, we develop our theoretical framework by elaborating on the key concepts of the central question. Victor Bekkers and Menno Fenger start by exploring the different meanings that can be attributed to the governance concept (Chapter 2). They identify the backgrounds that can possibly account for the emergence of governance in the public sector. Specific modes of governance are distinguished: governance at a distance, market governance, multi-level governance, network governance and societal self-governance. Finally, they argue that these governance practices can be understood as emerging political orders. This sets the stage for the discussion of legitimacy and democracy in the next chapter. Victor Bekkers and Arthur Edwards explore the concepts of legitimacy and democracy (Chapter 3). They decompose the general notion of legitimacy by distinguishing input, throughput and output/outcome legitimacy. They formulate a number of criteria for assessing the legitimacy of governance practices. This is followed by a preliminary problematization in terms of legitimacy of the various modes of governance distinguished in Chapter 2. Next, they introduce several models of democracy. They assess these models of democracy in terms of their strengths and weaknesses related to input, throughput and output/outcome legitimacy. This framework supports the assessment of governance practices on legitimacy and suggests possible strategies for democratization. The theoretical section concludes with a chapter by Koen Stapelbroek, who takes a 'snapshot' of the democracy debate in the 18th century (Chapter 4). The author shows that an eighteenth-century perspective helps one recognize the limits of what liberal-democratic regimes can be expected to do by showing how political thinkers of the time responded to the emergence of intensified political and economic competition between states. He concludes that rather than viewing governance as likely to negatively affect democracy, it might be argued that governance should be expected to enhance democracy.

In Part II the empirical part of the book begins by examining two types of governance, governance at a distance and market governance. Victor Bekkers, Menno Fenger and Evelien Korteland analyze the assumptions that lay behind the modernization programs at the national level in different European countries (Chapter 5). In these modernization agendas, the governance concept, and New Public Management ideas in particular, occupy a central place. The authors conclude that the major thrust of these modernization programs is focused on the empowerment of citizens as consumers. Complementary to representative democracy, a new democracy model has emerged that can be described as consumer or client democracy. Lex Cachet and Arie van Sluis assess the legitimacy of police governance in the Netherlands and the UK (Chapter 6). In both countries, the police system has undergone significant changes, with more centralized performance-based arrangements at the national level. At the same time, policing has undergone a process of pluralization, in partnerships between public and private actors (market governance) and between agencies and citizens (network governance). The authors argue that political steering of the police, within the representative model of democracy, shows serious shortcomings at the local level. While other democracy models are becoming relevant and useful, they are in addition to and not substitutes for representative democracy. Peter Hupe and Michael Hill deal with the issue of the autonomy of professionals in the implementation stage of public policies (Chapter 7). The authors discuss two cases of social policy in the United Kingdom, health and education. They focus on accountability. Horizontal mechanisms are observed as possibly compensating for deficits of both vertical steering and vertical accountability.

Chapters 8, 9 and 10 are devoted to network governance and societal self-governance (Part III of the book). Peter Marks analyzes the wide variety of actors that are involved in the city of Rotterdam's safety policy and local government's attempt to govern this network (Chapter 8). He shows how arrangements of representative democracy, deliberative democracy and consumer democracy work together and enhance the legitimacy of urban safety policy. Arthur Edwards assesses the legitimacy of local deliberative forums, in which residents, regulatory agencies and businesses discuss environmental issues (Chapter 9). He compares a 'Residential Advisory Board' in The Netherlands and an Environmental Committee in Cleveland (United States), focusing on the question of how the signaling and monitoring functions of these forums can be enhanced by embedding them in pluralist and representative democracy. Geske Dijkstra and Lieve Lodewijckx analyze governance in an entirely different institutional setting. Their chapter deals with a case of 'donor-induced participation' in Mozambique (Chapter 10). This study sheds new light on the issue of a possible tension between deliberative democracy and representative democracy as it is often posed in the context of established democracies. In stead, the authors suggest that the existence of a legitimately elected and representative legislative body is a necessary condition for the success of deliberative policymaking.

Finally, chapters 11 to 14 discuss the idea of multi-level governance and its impact on democratic legitimacy (Part IV). José Manuel Ruano de la Fuente and Linze Schaap examine practices of regional governance in four European countries, contrasting formal bodies of regional governance with forms of inter-municipal coordination (Chapter 11). They assess, in particular, the extent of input and throughput legitimacy in these different institutional settings. Frans van Nispen and Johan Posseth discuss the legitimacy of EU-governance in the field of economic policy, EU's best example of 'strong governance' (Chapter 12). Using recent Eurobarometer surveys, they assess input, throughput and output legitimacy of the monetary and fiscal policies of the European Union and discuss possibilities for enhancing democratic legitimacy. Patty Zandstra assesses the democratic legitimacy of the European Union's Open Method of Coordination (OMC) as a specific type of multi-level governance (Chapter 13). She formulates key requirements for an optimal functioning of the OMC from a democratic legitimacy perspective and then examines to what extent these are fulfilled for decision-making processes around the National employment Action Plans. Finally, Geske Dijkstra reflects upon the democratic deficit in supranational institutions such as the International Monetary Fund and the World Bank, showing how and why this deficit has increased over time (Chapter 14). She argues that the often-overlooked relationship between the lack of democratic control of the institutions' bureaucracies and the practice of ever expanding tasks and responsibilities must be taken into account when analyzing proposals for improving democratic legitimacy of these institutions.

In Chapter 15, the editors present their conclusions. In this final chapter, not only do we try to answer the central question on governance's impact on democratic legitimacy, but more specifically, we identify the relation between different types of governance and models of democracy in relation to the different aspects of legitimacy. Furthermore, we suggest some lines of thought for democratization strategies. This analysis might then contribute to a richer understanding of the relation between governance and democracy and provide relevant inputs to both the scientific and practical debate on the legitimacy problems in current governance practices.

References

Benz, A. and Papadopoulos, Y. (2006), 'Introduction: governance and democracy: concepts and key issues', in Benz and Papadopoulos (eds.), pp. 1–26.

Benz, A. and Papadopoulos, Y. (2006) (eds), *Governance and Democracy. Comparing National, European and International Experiences* (London, New York: Routledge).

Castells, M. (1997), *The Power of Identity* (Cambridge: Blackwell Publishers).

Klijn, E.H. and Skelcher, C. (*forthcoming*), 'Democracy and governance networks: compatible or not? Four Conjectures and their Implications for Theory and Practice'. *Public Administration.*

Papadopoulos, Y. (2003), 'Cooperative Forms of Governance: Problems of Democratic Accountability in Complex Environments', *European Journal of Political Research* 42, 473–501.

Saward, M. (2001), 'Making Democratic Connections: Political Equality, Deliberation and Direct Democracy', *Acta Politica* 36:4, 361–79.

Scharpf, F. (1999), *Governing in Europe* (Oxford: University Press).

Sörensen, E. (2002), 'Democratic Theory and Network Governance', *Administrative Theory and Praxis* 24:4, 693–720.

Stone, D. (2002), *Policy Paradox: The Art of Political Decision Making* (New York and London: Norton & Company).

WRR (2004), *De staat van de democratie. Democratie zonder staat* (Amsterdam University Press).

Chapter 2

The Governance Concept in Public Administration

Menno Fenger and Victor Bekkers

In the last decade, the concept of 'governance' has become a very popular theme in the theory and practice of public administration. The popularity of this concept even inspired Frederickson (2005) to rhetorically ask:'Whatever happened to public administration? Governance, governance everywhere'. It cannot be denied that to some extent, the booming popularity of governance is only a matter of semantics. Lynn et al. (1999, 2) state, 'The term "governance" is widespread in both public and private sectors, in characterizing both global and local arrangements, and in reference to both formal and informal norms and understandings. Because the term has strong intuitive appeal, precise definitions are seldom thought to be necessary by those who use it. As a result, when authors identify 'governance' as important to achieving policy or organizational objectives, it may be unclear whether the reference is to organizational structure, administrative processes, managerial judgments, systems of incentives and rules, administrative philosophies, or a combination of those'. The popularity of the governance concept partly explains why the Brookings Institution recently changed the name of its highly regarded 'Governmental Studies' program to 'Governance Studies' (Frederickson 2005, 4), the Twente Public Administration Department established the Institute for Governance Studies and, admittedly, this book has been published by Erasmus University Rotterdam's Center for Public Governance. The previous discussion illustrates the fuzziness that is connected with the governance concept. Frederickson (2005, 1) therefore concludes that in some cases governance is 'substantively the same as already established perspectives in public administration, although in a different language'. However, it is not the concept of 'governance' as such that is subject to fuzziness and vagueness, it is the extension of the concept to virtually every aspect of public administration.

The central purpose of this book is to assess the impact of governance on democracy. Are we able to assess the democratic legitimacy of governance arrangements in public administration? Is there a democratic deficit? Not surprisingly, the variety of interpretations of governance is reflected in the differing opinions on the impact of governance on democracy. On the one hand, governance is presented as a threat to democracy. For instance, Papadopoulos (2003, 473) argues that 'the democratic deficit of governance is problematic both for normative and for pragmatic reasons'. On the other hand, there are authors who claim that governance, or, more specifically, governing in networks, represents a more advanced form of democracy than traditional representative democracy (for instance Castells, 1997; see Klijn and Skelcher, forthcoming). What is lacking in these general arguments is a clear image of the two key concepts' meanings: 'governance' and 'democracy'. Therefore, in this chapter we elaborate the concept of 'governance' and in the next chapter we focus on the concept of 'democracy'. This enables us to develop more precise statements on the possible impact(s) of governance on democracy. In this chapter we start by exploring the different meanings that are commonly attributed to the 'governance' concept in public administration (section one). In section two, we identify the historical backgrounds that possibly account for the emergence of governance in the public sector. In section three, we try to pinpoint the practical implications of 'governance' by elaborating on the changes in processes of policy, politics and government that might be labeled as 'governance practices'. Section four focuses on the potential impact of these varying governance practices on democracy. If a governance practice can be understood in terms of an emerging political order, what is the legitimacy of the binding decisions that are made in these practices?

1. Defining Governance

According to Fredrickson (2005, 2), it was Harlan Cleveland who first used the word 'governance' as an alternative to the phrase public administration. 'In the mid-1970s, one of the themes in Cleveland's (...) speeches, papers and books went something like this: "What the people want is less government and more governance" (1972)' (Fredrickson 2005, 2). However, the use of the governance concept is not restricted to the discipline of public administration. On the contrary, Van Kersbergen and Van Waarden (2004) have identified nine uses of the governance concept, stemming from a wide variety of disciplines including politics, law, public administration, economics, business administration, sociology, geography and history. 'Good governance', 'corporate governance', 'multi-level governance', and recently even 'government governance' are word pairs that illustrate the disciplinary variety. Following Van Kersbergen and Van Waarden (2004, 151–152), we could argue that all these applications of the governance concept have three elements in common. First, the governance concept refers to pluricentric rather than unicentric systems. Second, 'networks, whether inter- or intra-organizational, play an important role. These networks organize relations between relatively autonomous, but interdependent actors. In these networks, hierarchy or monocratic leadership is less important or even absent. The formal government may be involved, but not necessarily so, and if it is, it is merely one – albeit an important – actor among many others'. Third, the focus is on processes of governing instead of the structures of government. These processes concern negotiation, cooperation and working in concert rather than the traditional processes of coercion, command and control (Van Kersbergen and Van Waarden 2004, 152).The governance approach assumes that the actions of a wide variety of public, private and semi-public actors affect social problems like organized crime or socially deprived neighborhoods in large cities. Successful interventions in these problems require the organized, concerted actions of all of these actors, thereby overcoming the problems of collective action that this variety of actors implies.

According to Rhodes (1997, 53), 'governance' has the following characteristics:

- Interdependence between organizations.
- Continuing interactions between all kinds of public, semi-public and private actors within several societal domains and at different levels.
- Game-like interactions, rooted in trust and regulated by rules of the game negotiated and agreed by the actors involved.
- A significant degree of autonomy from the state.

Similarly, Papadopoulos (2003, 476–77) states that a definition of governance should include the following five features:

- 'it results from the need to counteract the centrifugal dynamics of interest fragmentation between sectoral, territorial, class or lifestyle communities when they are caught in relations of mutual interdependence,
- it aims to enhance state resources in term of knowledge (...), organization (...), and authority (...);
- it involves networks (...) that usually include public actors (...) who can represent different territorial levels, experts and interest representatives (...);
- it presupposes an accommodative orientation within such networks, where participants are expected to demonstrate an inclination for compromise-seeking (...);
- it usually leads to less formal modes of decision-making within structures that are hardly visible from the mass public and that remain uncoupled from the official institutions of representative democracy'.

If we look at the discussion on governance and the characteristics that Rhodes has discerned, we are able to stipulate three striking elements that give us an indication about the essence of governance.

The first element is the notion of *self-regulation* in policy networks. Due to the organizational fragmentation of society and government itself, government is not able to control society and societal developments from one single, super-ordinate position. Governance implies that government has acknowledged the fact that organizations (and in a broader sense society in general, or specific societal actors) have self-regulating or self-organizing capacities. Collective action within society or within a policy sector can be seen as the outcome of self-regulation through negotiation, exchange and communication (Kooiman 1993).

Following the recognition of self-regulative capacities and the necessity to coordinate their activities due to the increased interdependencies between the organizations involved, the issue of *co-operation* is a second striking characteristic of governance. Governance can be understood as the way in which different actors or organizations with different interests, positions and views are capable of co-producing common or shared goals or outcomes. For this reason, governance arrangements can often be seen as co-operation structures. Governance is about 'sustaining co-ordination and coherence among a wide variety of actors with different purposes and objectives such as political actors and institutions, corporate interests, civil society, and transnational organizations' (Pierre and Peters 2000, 4).

Third, governance might be seen as a way of creating binding decisions for a collective entity, which implies that governance practice can be understood in terms of a political order or a political system. Through the co-operation and co-production of several actors or organizations, the collective decision-making that takes place is, in essence, *political decision-making*; the decisions refer to the allocation of public goods or public values for a community. This raises a number of questions that refer to the legitimacy of these governance arrangements For instance, who is responsible for the quality of this decision-making process and its output and outcomes in these governance arrangements? Or, who has access to these 'new' decision-making processes that go beyond the established decision-making processes of the traditional institutions of representative democracy?

Specific modes of governance, or governance practices might be distinguished on the basis of the specific mixture of each of these three characteristics. We illustrate these in the next section. However, before introducing specific modes of governance, we first try to explain the historical backgrounds of the shift from 'government to governance'. An important explanation for this shift, amongst others, is the much-acclaimed 'crisis of the state'.

2. From 'Government' to 'Governance'

The general argument in the governance literature is that a wide variety of developments have undermined the capacity of governments to control events within the nation state. Trends like the flow of power away from traditional government institutions upwards to transnational bodies and downwards to regions and sub-regions, the rise of global markets, the increasing importance of networks and social partnerships, greater access to information, and growing social complexity are usually held accountable for this. As a consequence, the state 'can no longer assume a monopoly of expertise or of the resources to govern, but must rely on a plurality of interdependent institutions and actors drawn from within and beyond government' (Newman 2001, 11–12). This trend is also referred to as a shift 'from government to governance'.

In the traditional 'government' perspective, government was put in the center of all kinds of societal developments and problems. Governments were supposed to be able to intervene effectively in societal developments and solve societal problems from a centralized and hierarchical position, detached from society, and according to the goals laid down in a policy program. Ineffective government interventions were primarily seen as flaws in the 'machinery of government', as the result of imperfect knowledge on the nature and effects of the problem, and as the product of a mismatch between the policy instruments that were used and the policy goals that were formulated. Since the 1990s, this idea has met with a lot of criticism, and some of these criticisms can be captured under the label of the governance paradigm. Key assumptions in this governance paradigm are:

- Government is not an entity but a conglomerate of actors.
- Government is not the only actor who tries to influence societal developments, and
- Government interventions are interventions in a policy network, in which power, resource dependency, and strategic behavior are vital elements.

As has been stated in the previous section, the governance approach emerged against the background of critics of the state's capacity to deal with societal problems. The persistence of crime, unemployment, poverty, and hunger in large parts of the world, created doubts about the problem-solving capacity of local, regional, national and supranational governmental institutions. More specifically, we can identify five 'crises of the state' that have contributed to the emergence of the governance paradigm: a financial crisis, a regulatory crisis, a rationality crisis, an implementation crisis, and a complexity crisis.

The Financial Crisis of the Welfare State

The economic recession, which started at the end of the seventies and lasted until the mid-eighties in many countries, brought about a crisis of the welfare state for almost every government in the Western world. This crisis can be understood as a financial crisis. The problem was not so much whether a comprehensive welfare system would be desirable, but whether it could be financed in a situation of increasing demands. Moreover, efficiency deficits in the implementation of welfare state regulations, in terms of bureaucratization, were also a major reason that questions were raised (Mayntz 1993, 9). As a result, a plea was made for a withdrawal of government.

The Regulatory Crisis of the Welfare State

The implementation of all kinds of regulations, through which rights, obligations and financial means were allocated among society, also led to a regulatory crisis. During the emergence of the welfare state, the main carriers of government intervention in society were legislation and planning. Hood (1986) talks about the rule and rote-approach of government intervention, while Van Gunsteren (1976) refers to the dominance of the central rule approach in government, in which command and control are seen as important characteristics of how government tries to influence societal developments, and in which policy making is seen as the development of regulatory policies. However, these regulatory policies failed. One reason is that rule-oriented interventions can only work under specific conditions. Hood (1986, 21–22) specifies these conditions. First, these rules must be knowable and discoverable by the participants before they make the decisions, which these rules govern. Second, the purposes served by these rules should be broadly acceptable and easy to discern. Moreover, the rules should in fact serve the purpose, for which they are intended – that is they should incorporate valid cause-effect assumptions. Third, these rules must be completely consistent with one another so as to avoid uncertainties bound up in 'umpiring' decisions about which rules get priority in conflict-of rule-cases. Fourth, the conditions in which rules apply should be completely specified in advance to limit uncertainty as to when or where the rules apply. Fifth, standards incorporated into rules should be capable of clear verification so as to limit the scope for subjective interpretation. Finally, where rules divide behavior or other items into categories, these categories should be robust and unambiguous. If you look at the practice of administration, you see that most of these conditions cannot be met. As a result, more detailed regulatory policies were developed with more detailed instructions of how to behave or how to implement the norms that have been formulated (Hood 1986).

The Rationality Crisis of the Welfare State

Effective government interventions presuppose that governments have insight in the causal relationships that are important for assessing whether a specific kind of intervention would produce the desired outcomes in terms of goals to be achieved (Mayntz 1993). From this point of view, the causal relations (cause-effect relations) as well as final relations (means-end-relations) should be known when regulatory policies are going to be drafted. The opening of a school in a new neighborhood will not lead to serious problems and can be seen as a routine matter, but the fight against juvenile crime in a neighborhood is more difficult because valid knowledge about possible causes, effects and side-effects is not available. We do not know what the outcomes of specific interventions would be, and at the same time, there is normative confusion. Moreover, we are unable to develop a hierarchy of norms and values that should be pursued. This is why most societal problems can be described as 'wicked problems'. In some cases this knowledge deficit was analyzed in terms of acquiring more information as well as improving the information-processing capacity of government.

Implementation Crisis of the Welfare State

Evaluation and implementation studies of public policies have shown that the process of implementation of regulatory policies do not evolve mechanically. Implementation encompasses much more than the simple setting in motion of the machinery of government through which the desired outcomes will be produced. Government agencies, but also citizens, societal organizations and companies that are confronted with various regulations, do not behave as powerless and willing cogwheels in an implementation machinery, which themselves behave according to the instructions that have been given. Policy implementation is not a technocratic and neutral issue – it is highly political. Moreover, implementation usually requires the involvement of multiple agencies, thereby reducing the probability of correct implementation, even if the agencies are willing to implement the policy (Pressman and Wildavsky 1973).

In addition, the idea of street-level bureaucracy (Lipsky 1980; Prottas 1979) argues that all kinds of decisions are made during the implementation stage that are, in essence, political decisions. This can be considered as a process of policy formation in the context of policy implementation. Moreover, implementation very often implies that tailor-made solutions have to be made because of specific or changing implementation conditions. This implies discretion on the part of the organization that has to implement a specific rule or program. However, discretion implies a transfer of tasks, responsibilities and authority from the center to the periphery in order to guarantee these tailor-made implementation (see also Fenger and Henman 2006).

The Complexity Crisis of the Welfare State

The emergence of the welfare state during the 20th century can be seen as the expression of an ongoing process of modernization. Characteristic for this modernization process is the process of functional differentiation and fragmentation, which produces highly specialized and rather autonomous subsystems and organizations that are, at the same time, highly interdependent. The complexity of functional interdependencies and causal networks has grown immensely. This results in unpredictable direct and indirect effects that originate in wide-ranging output-input relations between many actors. The network character of these relationships present cognitive and manipulative problems because we do not know the nature of this complexity while at the same time we do not know the desired and undesired outcomes of the possible interventions in these networks (Mayntz 1993,16).

Hence, the several crises of the welfare state have contributed to a shift in the dominant steering paradigm of the welfare state, in which government was perceived as the single actor responsible for the development of society and the attack of societal problems – an actor that has become more dependent from other public, private and semi-public actors. This has resulted in a number of shifts of problem solving capacity from the center of the state towards other public and private bodies. Moreover, it has resulted in the emergence of specific governance arrangements.

3. The Shifting Modes of Governance

In the previous sections, we dealt with the governance concept from a more or less descriptive perspective. We explained the backgrounds against which the governance paradigm has emerged. However, writing about governance and reflecting upon the consequences of governance for democracy requires the identification of empirical manifestations of governance. So how can we more clearly identify the empirical manifestations of governance? The emergence of governance practices in public administration can be observed in the shifts that take place in various existing policy domains or societal sectors on the one hand and in the emergence of new modes of governance on the other.

Shifts in Governance

The first way is by noting that what all of these practices have in common is the transfer of problem-solving capacity from the traditional state institutions towards other levels or institutions. According to Van Kersbergen and Van Waarden (2004) the following shifts in governance capacity can be identified:

- An upward vertical shift from nation-states to international public institutions with supranational characteristics such as the EU, the WTO, and the IMF. This upward vertical shift also can be observed within specific state functions, such as the judiciary and the police.
- A downward vertical shift from national and international to sub-national and regional levels. In part, this is related to the previous shift because international bodies rely on local agencies to implement and enforce their regulations. But there is also a growing tendency within states to decentralize tasks, authorities and responsibilities to the regional level and from the central to the decentralized level of government, in favor of other territorial bodies of government, such as municipalities and regions.
- A horizontal shift between the executive, legislative and judicial power. In many countries, the judiciary is assuming a more active role in rule interpretation, and also in *de facto* rule formation.
- A horizontal shift from public to semi-public, autonomous organizations and agencies. 'Policy-making, implementation, enforcement and control have become differentiated as separate functions. For reasons of efficiency and effectiveness in complex situations and political prudence or credibility, some of these sub-tasks have been delegated to more autonomous semi-public or even private institutions' (Van Kersbergen and Van Waarden 2004, 154).
- A horizontal shift from public to private organizations. For instance, in Dutch public administration, the reintegration of sick and disabled persons that were formerly the tasks of public organizations has now being shifted to private companies.
- A horizontal shift from the central public level to the civil society. In several countries, governments are trying to replace regulation by 'self-responsibility' of its citizens. The intellectual roots of this governance practice lie in notions like communitarianism, 'civil society' and 'the third way'. All of these notions deny the central importance of bureaucracies in the delivery of public services and instead look for means of 'co-production', personal involvement and citizen engagement as the way to make government perform better.

Bureaucracies may still be necessary, but the people themselves can play a larger role in helping themselves (Peters 1996, 62).

- A shift toward the withdrawal of the state from certain activities with the state being replaced by an appeal to the self-regulating capacity of citizens. In most instances, this appeal to self-regulation is inspired by the desire to decrease the number and complexity of state regulations that create a high administrative burden for citizens and organizations.

Modes of Governance

These shifts in problem-solving capacity can lead to the emergence of specific modes of governance. Therefore, several authors treat governance from a more normative perspective, and suggest governance-related modes of steering that might be used to deal with social problems more effectively (Snellen 1987; Kooiman 1993; Peters 1996). The following modes might be distinguished.

Governance at a Distance: Deregulation, Performance and Accountability

In this mode of governance, the relationship between the organizations that steer and the organizations that are the object of steering is still hierarchical, but the organizations to be steered are given a (substantial) amount of discretion to develop and implement their own policies, based on the recognition of self-regulation (Snellen 1987). The results (output and outcomes) that an organization produces become the objects of government intervention instead of the internal processes of an organization (the throughput). This implies a retreat of government, which only governs at a distance. For instance, in the Netherlands, this mode of governance can be observed in how sheltered working places are being governed by the Ministry of Social Affairs. In these sheltered working places, physically or mentally disabled persons are employed to carry out special tasks and services under rather normal production conditions. Since 1984, the Ministry of Social Affairs has recognized that these places possess self-regulating capacities that should be stimulated – within certain boundaries. The governance activities of the ministry have been directed toward formulating specific input criteria, for which a lump sum budget has been authorized and on formulating and monitoring specific output criteria, like the out-flow to regular work (Bekkers 1998).

As a result of this retreat of government, deregulation is an important instrument that can be used to reduce the administrative burden in order to provide the necessary administrative freedom or discretion (Peters 1996). The fundamental assumption of the move towards deregulation is that government could perform its functions more efficiently if some of the constraints on bureaucratic action were eliminated. The problem is not the people in government; the problem is the system, i.e. the rules and regulations inhibit swift and effective action (Peters 1996). Deregulation can be seen as a prerequisite for de-bureaucratization that in turn opens the door for public entrepreneurship.

Kooiman (1993) defines this mode of governance as 'hierarchical governance': giving more discretion in order to enhance the necessary flexibility of an organization to respond to, for instance, changing implementation conditions, but within a hierarchical framework. However, a super-ordinated framework of performance indicators limits this given discretion. These indicators are based on a specific scheme of parameters. The steering activities in this mode are focused on the definition of certain input and output or even outcome parameters to which the organizations have to comply. Input steering refers to the definition of specific parameters in an allocation model on which a budget or lump sum is distributed among organizations in order to fulfill specific tasks or to accomplish specific policy goals. Output and outcome steering are focused on the definition of certain indicators that reflect the desired output or outcomes of an organization. The organization is free in organizing how to achieve the desired output or outcomes, but it is held accountable for the results (output and/or outcomes) it has achieved in relation to the budget it has spent in trying to achieve these outputs. Monitoring systems and benchmark systems contribute to the transparency of the output or outcomes, and this can lead to corrective interventions of the steering organizations. Within this mode of governance, the agreements between the organizations that steer and the organizations that are steered can be outlined in a management contract that specifies what results should be achieved in relation to a specific budget.

It is in this mode of governance that the ideas about New Public Management (NPM) and governance meet. Both paradigms emphasize the shift from process accountability towards accountability in terms of the results that have been achieved (Hood 1986; see also Fenger and Henman 2006).

If we look at the accountability issue in this mode of governance, we see a shift in how accountability has been organized. Traditionally, accountability is organized in a vertical, hierarchical way in which, for instance, government agencies are held accountable by a minister or by Parliament for the results they have achieved. Nowadays, we also witness more public ways of accountability in which information about the results of an agency are also made accessible and transparent for societal groups other than administrative and political superiors, like citizens as consumers of public services or professional peers (Meijer and Bovens 2005). These public accountability arrangements are complementary to the more political, rather 'classical' accountability arrangements that recognize the fragmentation of the network society with its proliferation of stakeholders.

Multi-Level Governance

In the literature on governance, another type of governance has been described that is relevant for the goal of this study: multi-level governance. This type of governance focuses on the cooperation between several layers of government. Multi-level governance refers to the upward and downward shifts of problem-solving capacity, responsibilities and competences from the nation state. The 'upward shift' refers to supranational or intergovernmental authority bodies, like the European Union, the

World Trade Organization or the World Bank. The 'downward shift' refers to the regional and local level that is increasingly gaining importance in policy-making processes (see also Valadas 2006). The concept of multi-level governance therefore refers to the pooling of problem-solving capacity that is needed to counter the policy problems and risks that occur in the 21st century. The consequences of a worldwide trend such as the globalization of production processes, for instance, manifest themselves locally (like the closing of production plants in western countries). The same holds true for the issue of global warming, which is a worldwide trend with worldwide causes and effects. However, the consequences first appear at the local and regional level. Multi-level governance systems have emerged or should emerge to counter these problems.

Supranational governance can be described in terms of the emergence of centers of governance that involves a plurality of state and non-state actors on different levels who are concerned with coordinating activities around particular functional problems within a variable territorial geometry that cross the traditional boundaries of the nation state. The result is a continuous process of negotiation between nested governments at different levels (sub-national, national and supranational) in order to cope with growing economic, political, social and cultural interdependencies between these levels of government (Hooghe and Marks 2002, 4). Moreover, one can observe that in these emerging multi-level patterns of negotiation, not only state-like or governmental organizations participate, but that also non-governmental organizations, like associations of employers and employees or even environmental advocacy groups are involved (Bache and Flinders 2004).

Market Governance

The concept of market governance refers to the use of the market mechanism of supply and demand in governance processes. In this governance mode, government interventions are focused on the shaping of a level playing field, which facilitates self-regulation, like the development of a collective quality system within a policy sector or the sharing of information between different service providers in order to create a transparent market for privatized public services. One could say that a level playing field or an arena is created in which interdependent stakeholders meet and negotiate with each other in order to achieve co-operation or collective action (Snellen 1987).

Steering interventions can be focused on the allocation of (equal) positions in the arena, the process of inclusion and exclusion of actors, and the definition of the boundaries of the arena. Steering can also be focused on the definition of playing rules that the actors in the arena should comply with in the negotiation processes they undertake in order to achieve collective action. Government interventions are not related to defining the specific outcomes of the collective behavior within the arena or level playing field. The content itself is the product of self-regulation between the parties involved. Instead, government interventions are restricted to shaping the relations (stipulating interdependency) and defining the rules of the game, which could facilitate co-operation and stimulate self-regulation.

In the practice of public administration, we see that this mode of governance is rather dominant in the liberalization of traditional public monopolies as a result of EU legislation. The liberalization of the telecommunication sector in the 1990s and the recent liberalization of the electricity market, which should lead to a 'real' market, could only be achieved if a level playing field is created in which providers can compete which each other. A supervisory agency is needed to monitor the nature of the competition between them in order to prevent, for instance, the forming of a trust cartel. In the Netherlands, another example is the privatization of public health insurance. Public and private health insurance companies should compete with each other on the prices they charge for a specific package of health services. Government only deals with the definition of a basic package of health care services that should be offered to everyone. Government does not define the actual price setting in this market, it only insures that no one is excluded from basic public health services.

From this perspective, the introduction of market models into the public sector has been seen as a strategy of reforming government. Its primary intellectual roots lie in the belief that a market model or an analogous competitive model will contribute to a more efficient allocation of resources, like public health services, in society (Peters 1996).

Network Governance

In this mode of governance, steering is focused on facilitating a shared understanding between the organizations or stakeholders in a policy network in order to create a common and trustworthy policy practice through interaction, communication, negotiation and exchange (Snellen 1987; Peters 1996; Koppenjan and Klijn 2004). Kooiman (1993) defines this mode of governance as co-governance. The positions, tasks, interests and frames of reference of relevant (public and private) stakeholders are linked together in order to create competitive perspectives on the nature of the problem and possible solutions. In this mode of governance, the focus is on the active participation of a variety of interests involved that can be discerned around (rather complex and wicked) policy problems like the reconstruction of a urban area, in which private and public partners should co-operate, or the prevention of juvenile crime in which all kinds of public organizations and societal organizations should work together. Bringing together these stakeholders not only adds to the acceptance of the policy program (in terms of support) once it has been drafted, but it also enhances the quality of collective problem solving as a result of the possible new combinations of knowledge, information and experience. The fundamental concept behind this version of participation, which can be related to discursive democracy (Dryzek 1990) or 'strong democracy' (Barber 1984) is that the 'experts' in a bureaucracy do not have all the information, knowledge or even the right type of established policy answers to deal with a specific challenge. Therefore isolating important decisions from public and plural policy involvement could lead to policy errors. For instance, public agencies, which deal with the decline of neighborhoods, have a natural habit of defining this problem from their dominant frame of reference. The police will look for causes in relation to crime, public works will define the problem from the quality of the physical environment, like the quality of the streets, the presence of playgrounds for children or the quality of the houses in the neighborhood. Social workers will define these problems from the social quality of the neighborhood, like the degree of social cohesion and patterns of social inclusion and exclusion of specific group of inhabitants. From a governance perspective, it is important to bring these frames of reference together and integrate them to match the dominant frame of reference of the inhabitants of the neighborhood. Moreover, this implies that citizens should also have a say in how problems and solutions will be defined. Citizen's participation is another important characteristic of this mode of governance.

In this mode of governance, it is important that these stakeholders, who are actually rather autonomous, are able to recognize the interdependencies between them. Each actor depends on vital resources, such as competences, money, knowledge and information that are not completely at one's disposal. These resources are not free, but other actors control them, which implies that there is no central actor who unilaterally enforces his/her will. The result is a complex mixture of conflict, bargaining and co-operation. If these actors involved are capable of creating a shared understanding about the nature of the policy problem and possible actions to be taken, they are willing to exchange resources in order to organize collective action. It is important for each party to win to a certain extent, to minimize possible losses, or even to compensate an unequal distribution of costs ands benefits among the actors. For instance, the reconstruction of a shopping center in a city implies that all kinds of desires and interests have to be linked together and integrated in a concept that offers all of the parties involved a 'win-win' situation in order to be accepted. Real estate developers have to be convinced that it is worthwhile to invest in this shopping center. However, they will only participate in the project if local government and/or public transport organizations are willing to improve the quality of the transport infrastructure (bus, underground) so that people can easily reach the shopping center, that there are enough parking places for cars and that public safety within and around the center is guaranteed by the police. From this perspective governance relates to the process of co-operation in order to achieve some forms of collective action. In the practice of public administration, we see different forms of collaboration, for instance between public and private organizations (as has been described in the previous example), between different layers of government (for instance between local inspection and nation wide inspection agencies in order to deal with monitoring and enforcement of environmental protection legislation) or even between nation-state and supranational and international government bodies (like the co-operation between the national police organizations and other national security agencies in order to exchange information in relation to fighting terrorism).

Societal Self-Governance

Unlike the previous type of network governance that focuses on co-production of policies by public and societal actors, in societal governance the public actors disappear from the stage. Communitarianism and social capital are central in societal self-governance.

According to Pierre and Peters (2000, 147), the working assumption in communitarian approaches is 'that most socio-economic problems can be solved at lower levels of aggregation than those at which they are currently addressed. Further, there is an implicit judgment that with the proper social engineering, even large-scale cities and towns – if not nations – can be made into more communal decision-making systems. There is also a belief that people are inherently communal rather that individualist, so contemporary structures are failing to fulfill some basic needs of the public'. The communitarian answer to this is the 'third way' between the market and the state, or between the political ideologies of neo-liberalism and socialism (Etzioni 2000). Within the communitarian perspective, public governance merely is about creating the conditions for self-governance in communities.

To create effective, efficient and legitimate structures of self-governance, there needs to be trust among the members of a community. It even appears that 'high-trust' communities perform better economically than 'low-trust' communities. The concept of social capital is closely related to the concept of trust. Putnam (2000, 21) defines social capital as 'social networks and the norms of reciprocity and trustworthiness that arise from them'. Fukuyama (1999, 14) defines it as a 'society's stock of shared values' that serves as 'the prerequisite for all forms of group endeavor that take place in a modern society, from running a corner grocery store, to lobbying Congress, to raising children'.

Societal self-governance is about creating, facilitating and enabling policy initiatives developing within communities. Neighborhood Watch programs are examples of societal self-governance 'in action', and governments are increasingly appealing to societies' self-organizing capacity to deal with problems. However, it appears that self-governance requires a certain level of trust or social capital among society's members.

Governance and New Public Management

In the public administration discipline, there has been some debate on the nature of the relation between the ideas of the New Public Management (NPM) on the one hand and the governance paradigm on the other. Perhaps it is possible to define NPM as a specific governance practice. Developed in the late 1980s, the 'New Public Management' has evolved into a highly popular label for a wide variety of reforms in the public sector that have two common features: 'lessening or removing differences between the public and the private sector and shifting the emphasis from process accountability towards a greater element of accountability in terms of results' (Hood

1995, 94). In more detail, Pollitt (2003, 27–28) identifies the following eight key elements of the 'New Public Management' (NPM):

- A shift in value priorities away from universalism, equity, security and resilience and towards efficiency and individualism, defining the role of a citizen as a 'homo economicus'.
- A shift in the focus of management systems from inputs and processes towards results and outputs.
- A shift towards measurement and quantification, especially through the development of performance indicators and benchmarks systems.
- A preference for more specialized, 'lean', 'flat' and autonomous organizational structures.
- A substitution of formal, hierarchical relationships between or within organizations by contracts or contract-like relationships.
- A much wider deployment of markets or market-type mechanisms for the delivery of public services.
- An emphasis on service quality and a consumer orientation.
- A broadening and blurring of the frontiers between the public sector, the market sector and the so-called third or non-profit sector.

If we look at the list of characteristics of NPM, we see that there is some resemblance between NPM and governance. Although NPM and governance have different historical and intellectual roots, both stress the importance of performance and accountability and the creation of markets or market-type coordination arrangements for the delivery of services. Two perspectives on the relation between NPM and governance might be developed. First, the shift from NPM to governance might only be considered as a linguistic step in the evolution of public administration. In this perspective, governance is a mere continuation of NPM practices, but it is embedded in a theoretical body of knowledge about the changing role and position of government, while NPM as a reform movement has primarily been rooted in the practice of public administration. The theoretical framework of 'governance' could be seen as an ex post legitimization of a number of bottom-up practices which have been called NPM. Conversely, governance might be viewed as a necessary answer to the failures of the NPM movement. From this perspective, NPM's stress on privatization, performance management, out-sourcing and the introduction of market-incentives within state organizations has led to a rather dysfunctional degree of fragmentation and differentiation in the public sector organization. For instance, performance management can strengthen the internal focus of organization, in which all the energy (and other means) are directed towards the achievement of specific results. Co-operation with other organizations, for instance in attacking crime, can be seen as a possible threat to the realization of the organization's targets, especially if the realization of these targets are related to budgetary changes. Organizations that are submitted to performance management systems take the line of least resistance by putting forward those performance indicators, which they themselves can influence effectively. The emphasis that governance approaches places on coordination, cooperation, and negotiation can be seen as a necessary adjustment to the practice of NPM, which stimulates the maximization of self-interest.

4. In Search of Legitimacy?

In the practice of public administration a number of shifts of governance have occurred, and these can be understood as reactions of a failed central-rule approach of government interventions (Van Gunsteren 1976). New modes of governance have emerged in the slipstream of these shifts. Still, these shifts and modes are not neutral because in these emerging governance practices, binding decisions are being made in relation to how societal problems will be solved and specific target-groups will be addressed. The quest for the democratic legitimization of governance can be understood from three lines of reasoning. First, it is important to recognize that these shifts and modes of governance represent new political orders. Second, there is a tension between these governance practices and the dominance of the representative democracy model that could lead to potential 'democratic deficits'. Third, we have to look at the normative assumptions that lay behind the manifestation of governance practices in day-to-day public administration. Is there a hidden ideology? Let's explore these lines of reasoning.

Governance Practices as Emerging Political Orders

Many governance practices can be described as shifts of power from the central, state-level to other territorial layers of government (international, supranational, local, regional), functional layers of government (quangos) or to other societal spheres (private, public/private partnerships or non-profit). Because political systems have traditionally been organized around the state as the ultimate source of political authority in a specific territory, this raises legitimacy problems. It is the state and its bodies that claim to have the monopoly on the legitimate exercise of power within its territory. Its jurisdiction extends directly to all of the residents of that territory (Morris 1998, 105). Moreover, it is the state that constitutes a political order capable of making binding decisions for the residents in its territory. Demonstrating that a state as a political order is legitimate justifies its existence and (some of its) powers (Beetham 1991, 40). Or, to justify a state might be to show its powers to be just, right or reasonable (Morris 1998, 106). At the same time, we see that many states, especially in the western hemisphere, are democratic states. In democratic states, as Aristotle wrote in *The Politics* 'the people (or demos) is sovereign', which means that it is the people who rule. This implies that the state can be seen as the carrier of the sovereignty of the people, as the expression of the people's will (Easton 1965, 106). So, the notion of democracy adds a specific challenge to the legitimacy of the democratic state, seen as a political order. In the end the institutions of the state make binding decisions for the people within its territory.

Governance implies that new authority structures and arrangements emerge that go beyond the traditional jurisdiction of a state (for instance, international and supranational cooperation), or that within a state, new cooperative arrangements develop that cross the traditional jurisdictions of the intra-state public organizations (for instance, public private partnerships and regional co-operation structures between municipalities). Moreover, within these emergent governance arrangements, binding collective decisions are being made and power is exercised. The consequence is that governance arrangements can be seen as a political order, but what is the legitimacy of these new political orders that go beyond the traditional political order that is represented by the classical institutions of the state?

Governance and Representative Democracy

Governance not only challenges the traditional and established authority of the state that takes binding decisions but also the democratic embedding of this state, in which the state is the manifestation of the 'demos'. In most western countries, state power and democracy are reconciled in the notion of representative or parliamentary democracy.

The observed shifts of collective decision-making to arenas outside the scope of direct parliamentary control seem to pose the potential of a democratic deficit. At the same time, however, governance practices also seem to offer certain opportunities for democratization strategies that can enrich and broaden 'liberal democracy'. Sörensen (2002) mentions four major challenges and opportunities.

First, public governance challenges the idea of an institutional separation of state and society. With the involvement of market actors and civil society actors in public decision-making and with the emergence of various hybrid organizations that combine public and private features, 'grey zones' of societal governance emerge. But within these grey zones, numerous new 'political spaces' exist that offer opportunities for democratization outside the realm of representative democracy. Second, and following from this, the concept of 'the political' has to be expanded outside the context of institutional parliamentary politics. Sörensen points here to the active role of civil servants in public governance. This active role has hardly been given due recognition as yet in democratic theory. She proposes that a rethinking of democracy on this issue has to start with abandoning the idea that it would make sense 'to identify specific elements in the decision-making process as either political or non-political'. On the contrary, the relationship between the political and non-political has to be regarded as dynamic and the drawing of the line between these two is in itself political (Sörensen 2002, 710–11). Third, democratic representation can no longer be seen as restricted to parliaments. 'The right to perform democratic representation' has to be obtained in an ongoing competition between various political intermediaries. For instance, the advent of new ICTs has further added to a proliferation of options for political activism (Van de Donk et al. 2004). This competition may open up a plurality of access points for citizens in collective decision-making. Fourth, the variety of governance practices challenges the notion of the *demos* that can be identified with the inhabitants within a specific nation-state. As we argued above, governance arrangements have to be seen as emerging political orders. The nation-state is only one of a multitude of political orders within which collective decision-making takes place. If we maintain the notion of democracy to be tied to the existence of a *demos,* in terms of certain ties of identity and communality between its members (Mouffe 2001/2002), then the idea of democracy in the context of governance has to be rethought as based on the existence of a multitude of collective identities. We agree with Sörensen (2002, 705) that a plurality of territorially and functionally demarcated communities can be regarded as potential gains instead of threats for democracy.

It is unclear whether the practice of governance has already yielded additional arrangements for democratic representation and accountability via parliaments. This is one of the main empirical questions addressed in this volume.

The Normative Assumptions Behind Governance

Some governance theorists, for instance Frederickson (2005), criticize the 'ideological emptiness' of the governance paradigm. The following definition of governance, used by O'Toole (2000, 105), can be seen as the expression of this emptiness. According to O'Toole, the concept of governance is designed 'to incorporate a more complex understanding of the multiple levels of action and kinds of variables that can be expected to influence the performance of government'. These multiple levels of actions lead to specific shifts of governance in the practice of public administration and become manifest in specific governance practices that can be described as governance modes. However, one can question the ideological emptiness of these shifts and modes, for several reasons. The first reason is that the transfer of problem solving capacity to other bodies of government or societal organizations is not a technocratic and neutral exercise. In most cases, this transfer is also legitimized by referring to specific political values about the role and position of government in relation to society (Bekkers 1998). Ideas about the 'civil society' and 'communitarianism' (like Blair's' and Giddens' ideas of the 'Third Way') are often used to legitimize a shift of governance, and they refer to the importance of the personal responsibility of citizens to engage themselves in the public domain. The shift of governance that relates to the empowerment of citizens as consumers of public services is legitimized by referring to all kinds of neo-liberal ideas that favor the introduction of (quasi-) market mechanism in the public sector. The second reason is that in these governance practices, political decision-making takes place in which binding decisions will be made in order to allocate public goods and values among citizens, societal groups, companies and other government organizations. In this decision-making process, different, and often conflicting, interests and political values have to be taken into consideration and have to be weighted. The third reason is that many governance practices in themselves, especially if they resemble New Public Management approaches, stress the importance of efficiency and individual freedom as important political values. Efficiency and individualism are implicit values, which are embedded in many governance practices. One can even speak of a 'hidden' ideology.

If the emergence of governance implies that shifts occur in how governments and society deal with each other, how are these shifts legitimized and what political values play a role in the process of legitimating governance practices? In order to answer this question, we have to explore the notion of legitimacy. Up until now, legitimacy has been presented as 'the invisible hand' in a political system (Stone 2002). The specification of legitimacy can help us to assess how political decisions can be justified in governance practices. But legitimacy itself is to some extent a black box. One can look at the legitimacy of the input, throughput, output and outcomes of the political decision-making process. We have to identify the relevant issues that tell us something of the democratic quality of these input, throughput and output processes. For instance, who has access to the decision-making processes in a governance arrangement? Who is accountable for its output and outcomes? Or, what is the role of power in these processes? Is there a system of 'checks and balances'? However, an assessment of the quality of the decision-making processes in governance arrangements is a normative assessment, which is based, among other factors, on a normative idea of democracy. This implies that we have to explore the idea of democracy and the traditions of democracy, from which various political values can be inferred in order to assess the legitimacy of governance practices. In the next chapter, we elaborate this line of reasoning by looking at the relationship between legitimacy and democracy.

References

Bache, I. and Flinders, M. (2004), *Multi-level Governance* (Oxford: Oxford University Press).

Barber, B. (1984), *Strong Democracy, Participatory Politics for a New Age* (Berkeley: University of California Press).

Beetham, D. (1991), *The Legitimation of Power* (London: Macmillan).

Bekkers, V. (1998), 'New forms of steering and the ambivalency of transparency', in Snellen and van de Donk (eds), pp. 341–58.

Castells, M. (1997), *The Power of Identity* (Cambridge, Blackwell Publishers).

Donk, W. van de, Loader, B., Nixon, P., Rucht, D.(eds), *Cyber Protest. New Media, Citizen Mobilization and Social Movements* (London/New York: Routledge).

Dryzek (1990), *Deliberative Democracy and Beyond* (Oxford: Oxford University Press).

Easton, D. (1965), *A System Analysis of Political Life* (New York, Wiley).

Etzioni, A. (2000), *The Third Way to a Good Society* (London: Demos).

Fenger, M. and Henman, P. (2006), 'Administering Welfare Reform: Introduction', in: P. Henman and M. Fenger (eds).

Ferlie, E. et al. (eds) *The Oxford Handbook of Public Management* (Oxford: Oxford University Press).

Frederickson, H.G. (2005), 'Whatever happened to public administration? Governance, governance everywhere', in Ferlie et al. (eds) *The Oxford Handbook of Public Management* (Oxford: Oxford University Press).

Fukuyama, F. (1999), *The Great Disruption: Human Nature and the Reconstitution of Social Order* (New York: Free Press).

Henman, P. and Fenger, M. (eds) (2006), *Administering Welfare Reform: International Transformations in Welfare Governance* (Bristol: Polity Press).

Hood, C. (1986), *The Tools of Government* (Chatham, NJ. Chatham House).

Hooghe, L. and Marks, G. (2002), 'Types of multi-level governance', Working Paper, Department of Political Science, University of North Carolina.

Kersbergen, K. van, and Waarden, F. van (2001), *Shifts in Governance: Problems of Legitimacy and Accountability* (The Hague: Social Science Reseach Council).

Kersbergen, K. van, and Waarden, F. van (2004), '"Governance" as a bridge between disciplines: Cross-disciplinary inspiration regarding shifts in governance and problems of governability, accountability and legitimacy', *European Journal of Political Research* 43, 143–71.

Klijn, E.H. and Skelcher, C. (forthcoming), 'Democracy and governance networks: compatible or not? Four Conjectures and their Implications for Theory and Practice'. *Public Administration.*

Kooiman, J. (1993), 'Governance and governability: using complexitiy, dynamics and diversity', in: Kooiman, J. (ed.), *Modern Governance* (London: Sage), pp. 9–20.

Koppenjan, J.F.M. and Klijn, E.H. (2004), *Managing Uncertainties in Networks: A Network Approach to Problem Solving and Decision Making* (London: Routledge).

Lipsky, M. (1980), *Street-Level Bureaucracy: The Dilemmas of Individuals in Public Services* (Cambridge, MA: MIT Press).

Lynn, L.E., Heinrich, C.J. and Hill, C.J. (1999), 'Studying governance and public management: challenges and prospects', Working Paper, Harris School.

Mayntz, R. (1993), 'Governing failures and the problem of governability', in Kooiman (ed.), *Modern Governance* (London: Sage) pp. 35–50.

Morris, C.W. (1998), *An Essay on the Modern State* (Cambridge: Cambridge University Press).

Mouffe, C. (2001/2002), 'Democracy: Radical and Plural', *CSD-Bulletin* 9, 10–4.

Newman, J. (2001), *Modernising Governance. New Labour, Policy and Society,* (London: Sage).

O'Toole, L.J. (2000), 'Research on policy implementation: assessment and prospects', *Journal of Administration Research and Theory* 10:2, 263–88.

Papadopoulos, Y. (2003), 'Cooperative Forms of Governance: Problems of Democratic Accountability in Complex Environments', *European Journal of Political Research* 42, 473–501.

Peters, G.B. (1996), *The Future of Governing,* (Lawrence: University Press of Kansas)

Pierre, J. and Peters, B.G. (2000), *Governance, Politics and the State* (Houndmills: Macmillan).

Pressman, J.L. and Wildavsky, A. (1973), *Implementation: How Great Expectations in Washington are Dashed in Oakland* (Berkeley: University of California Press).

Prottas, J. (1979), *People-Processing: The Street-Level Bureaucrat in Public Services* (Lexington: Lexington books).

Putnam, R. (2000), *Bowling Alone: The Collapse and Revival of American Community* (New York: Simon & Schuster).

Rhodes, R.A.W. (1997), *Understanding Governance* (Buckingham: Open University Press).

Snellen, I.Th.M. and Donk, W.B.J.H. van de (eds), *Public Administration in the Information Age* (Amsterdam, Oxford, Berlin, Tokio, and Washington D.C.: IOS Press).

Sörensen, E. (2002), 'Democratic Theory and Network Governance', *Administrative Theory and Praxis*, 24:4, 693–720.

Stone, D. (2002), *The Policy Paradox: The Art of Political Decision-Making* (New York and London: Norton and Company).

Valadas, C. (2006), 'The fight against unemployment as a main concern of European social policy: implications of a new, local level approach', in Henman and Fenger (eds).

Van Gunsteren, H.R. (1976), *The Quest for Control* (London, Wiley).

Chapter 3

Legitimacy and Democracy: A Conceptual Framework for Assessing Governance Practices

Victor Bekkers and Arthur Edwards

We have argued that the emergence of 'governance' can be regarded as the establishment of new political orders in which binding decisions are made. What is the legitimacy of these new political orders? Do they create a democratic deficit, because 'governing' seems to be unleashed from the traditional institutions of representative democracy? On what basis of authority are these governance practices exercised? How are the political decisions in these practices justified? Political values play an important role in justifying the legitimacy of political decisions. These values can be derived from various traditions in the history of Western democracy. One of the essences of democratic theory is legitimate governing authority (Scharpf 1998, 6). If we want to answer whether governance practices result in a democratic deficit, we have to consider this democratic deficit primarily in terms of legitimacy. Furthermore, in order to assess this democratic deficit, we have to refer to more than just the dominant representative democracy model. Other models of democracy should also be considered.

In section one, we explore the notion of legitimacy, and we relate it to other important notions, such as politics, authority and legality. Moreover, we distinguish several sources of legitimacy that can be used to justify political decision-making in governance practices. We formulate some preliminary conclusions. One conclusion is that normative democratic theories play an important role in the process of legitimating governance practices. These theories refer to relevant political values, beliefs and norms used to justify decisions, and this is why it is important to pay attention to the concept of democracy and the different traditions underlying it. In section two, we consider the concept of democracy and how democracy legitimizes the way that a political community governs itself.

Up to this point, we have used the concepts of legitimacy and democracy seen as a black box. The next step will be to open these boxes. In section three, we break down the general notion of legitimacy by distinguishing input, throughput and output legitimacy. This enables us to formulate a number of norms for assessing the democratic legitimacy of governance practices. For instance, one criterion of input-legitimacy is the availability of opportunities for citizen participation. But how should we assess the importance of participation and the opportunities for participation provided in political systems? This is why we open the other black box, democracy. In section four we describe several models of democracy. We show, for instance, that participation is valued and institutionalized in each model in different ways. We assess these models of democracy in terms of their strengths and weaknesses related to input, throughput and output legitimacy. In section five we draw some conclusions and give a short overview of our theoretical framework.

1. Exploring the Concept of Legitimacy

An exploration of the concept of legitimacy should begin by acknowledging its complexity and the full range of factors that influences the content of the concept (Beetham and Lord 1998, 3). In the rhetoric of politics and public administration, the concept of legitimacy is rather popular. However, a closer look at the concept reveals Babel-like confusion of definitions, perspectives and interpretations.

The Quest for Legitimate Politics

We start our odyssey by looking at the close relationship between legitimacy and politics. Lasswell (1936/1958) has described the nature of politics in terms of 'who gets what, when, how'. In this definition, politics refers to the allocation of public goods, resources and public values for a community. Politics and public policy are about communities trying to achieve collective goals that contribute to economic growth, like the creation of safe neighborhoods, a sustainable environment or a transport infrastructure (Stone 2002).

However, allocations within a community of people are always controversial because the amount of resources that can be distributed is, in essence, scarce. In the fight against crime in large cities, the responsible authorities have to allocate the limited amount of police capacity that can be mobilized for additional surveillance in those neighborhoods that have come under pressure. Some neighborhoods will get more attention than others. Moreover, there is controversy in the specific trade-offs between political values that compete with each other in how policy problems and solutions are defined. For instance, in the creation of a more market driven public health sector, a recurring issue is the controversy between efficiency and liberty on the one hand and equity and security on the other hand. The introduction of a free market system implies a greater freedom for patients to choose their own medical insurance company and the kind of contract they want to have. However, if these companies are forced to compete with each other, leading perhaps to a more efficient health sector, they will likely favor people in good health instead of those whose health care costs will cut into profits. This could lead to the exclusion of people with specific illnesses or disabilities, and it will prevent them from fair and equal access to, mostly, expensive and intensive medical treatment. Thus, the controversial nature of how a political community allocates public goods and values leads us to ask why the members of a community accept the decisions that are made and the outcomes that are produced. How are these decisions justified?

One critique of Lasswell's definition of politics is that he does not pay attention to the 'why' question. In Easton's (1965, 278) description of politics, he pays attention not only to the allocation of values for society as a whole, but also to the issue of why it is right that people accept and obey the authorities and abide by the requirements of the regime. This is why Easton has described politics as the '*binding* allocation of values for society as a whole'. No political system could endure, at least for very long, without support. For instance, the rejection of the new European constitution in May 2005 in France and the Netherlands – by referenda – can be understood, among other reasons, as a legitimacy crisis of the European Union. This crisis is one in which the European integration project has been perceived as a threat for the national identity of France and the Netherlands. Hence, a necessary condition for the existence of a political system is the presence of some moderate belief in its legitimacy, which is based on the validity of the authority used to make decisions.

The Nature of Legitimacy

Legitimacy is a rather fuzzy concept. In some sense, legitimacy is the political scientist's equivalent of the economist's invisible hand: we know that it exists as a force that holds communities together, but we cannot give satisfactory explanations of how to create it or why it is sometimes strong and why it sometimes seems to disappear (Stone 2002, 285). A good starting point for the discussion about the nature of legitimacy is to relate it to authority because the two concepts are rather intertwined concepts. Legitimacy presupposes authority. A legitimate authority is one that is recognized as valid or justified by those to whom it applies. If this is the case, the decisions that have been made will be perceived as binding, as authoritative (Easton 1965, 107). A striking example of the opposite, i.e. of illegitimacy, was the domino effect of the fall of the former communist regimes in Eastern Europe in the summer and autumn of 1989 that ended in the collapse of the Berlin Wall. The installation of a civil regime in Iraq, based on a constitution and free elections thereby replacing the military regime of the United States and its allies, in 2005, can also be seen a way of trying to legitimize the exercise of power in this country.

Legitimating political decisions, which are laid down in a policy program, can be based on either the lawfulness of the decisions that have been made and/or the recognition of a decision as a 'good' decision, i.e. a decision that is just. Both elements can be found in Morris' definition of legitimacy: to be recognized as lawful, just or rightful (Morris 1998, 102).

In the first case, legitimacy is closely related to legality. Legitimacy is derived from the Latin word *lex*, which refers to law. One interpretation of legitimacy is that a political decision is in accordance with the law. From this perspective, legitimacy refers to the general notion of accordance with established norms, rules and procedures that are relevant to the matter at issue (Morris 1998, 103). Legitimacy can be based on the content of norms that have been applied. For instance, in the drafting of specific anti-terror legislation, governments have to consider fundamental constitutional values and norms like the protection of individual privacy if they want to increase the coupling of all kind of personal data for detecting possible terrorists. A decision can also be perceived as legitimate if the proper procedures and rules have been followed in order to arrive at a decision. In this case, it is the decision's process, not the decision's content, which is the basis for legitimacy. In many Dutch municipalities, citizens and citizen groups have been asked to participate in various types of interactive policy making processes, for instance to improve the quality of their neighborhoods. However, one question, which influences the legitimacy of the interactive policy making arrangements is whether all of the relevant stakeholders in the neighborhood actually had the opportunity to participate. Were 'weak' interests properly heard and represented? According to Luhmann (1969, 28), the quality of the procedures and the proper application of these rules and procedures also influences the legitimacy of the decisions made. This is called procedural legitimacy, or '*Legitimation durch Verfahren*'.

In the second case, legitimacy is defined as the expression of recognition by a community. Legitimacy here is something to be conferred by others. Kim (1966, 225) adds that is it important that the conferral by others takes place on the basis of one's own free will. Legitimacy as the expression of recognition is different from more procedural accounts, since recognition may be independent from legality. Legitimacy, then, refers to shared beliefs regarding rights, duties, and liabilities as well as to a certain status (Morris 1998, 104; Beetham, 1991, 20). A constitution as the expression of the will of the people can be seen as the codification of shared beliefs in how a country as a political community should be governed, what are the rights of a citizen (for instance the right to speak) and what are the rights and duties of the people who are called in office to govern as members of parliament, cabinet ministers or mayors.

However, these shared beliefs have been reproduced over time, for instance through the introduction of all kinds of procedures. This is why legitimacy also refers to the, closely related, notion of justification. A political system is legitimate in so far as it is justified. For instance, elections play an important role in the justification of the change of power in a democracy. Legitimacy refers to the ability of a political system to show that the powers it has and powers it uses are just, right or reasonable (Morris 1998, 106).

Legitimacy problems are made most visible in the acceptance of tensions between general interest and particular interests. If the people in a political system share the same beliefs, values and norms, it is easier for them to accept binding collective decisions than it would be in a situation where this consensus did not prevail (Beetham 1991, 142-143). These shared beliefs can refer to more substantial political values, but also to more procedural values. To some extent, the trustworthiness of a political system, which guarantees fairness and non-arbitrary and non-corrupt behavior, can also be seen as an indication of the legitimacy of a political order (Beetham 1991, 141).

Many of the examples used above refer to the functioning of a political system. Can the notion of legitimacy also be applied to a policy program? Potman (1989) reserves the notion of legitimacy as the expression of an institutional characteristic of the political system, referring to general ideas and principles of how to exercise power, while acceptance refers to an individual judgment of a person, a group or an organization of a specific policy program or a specific law. He or she cannot accept the outcomes of a specific law, while continuing to believe in the justness of the political system that was responsible for drafting and executing this law.

In the discussion about the nature of legitimacy, it has been suggested that attention should also be given to the *process* of legitimating instead of only to the content of the legitimacy concept. Legitimacy is established through the process in which a political system tries to justify the decisions that have made been. Friedrich (1963) stresses the importance of 'legitimation' of a ruler instead of the 'legitimacy' of the ruler. 'The political authority of a ruler can be described as the capacity to elaborate what he prefers by reasoning which would make sense to those who follow him. Such reasoning usually involves the values and beliefs, as well as the interests of the group, within which the power is exercised' (Friedrich 1963, 223). Legitimation is therefore the capacity to convince (Daudt 1975, 12), or to engender and maintain the belief that the existing political institutions are the most appropriate ones for a society (Schaar 1981, 20). In this process, one can refer to several sources, sources that generate arguments and are able to convince.

Sources of Legitimacy

In the literature on legitimacy, several sources have been described that enable political systems to legitimize the exercise of power and the decisions that will be made.

Max Weber (1922/1972) has described three 'ideal types' of authority structures, which enable a political system to legitimize its exercise of power. He distinguishes between legitimacy based on charisma, tradition and rational-legality. Charismatic legitimacy is based on the independent belief in the personal qualities of the authorities (Easton 1965, 287). In Weber's account, this could be a king or a religious leader. The legitimacy of authority can also be based on tradition. The authority of a king is perceived as legitimate because he is a member of a royal family that has held the power for a long time and in which the power to rule is handed down from one generation to another. Authority can also be legitimized because it refers to the rational and legal exercise of power. According to Weber, rational-legality can be seen as the third source of legitimacy, which according to Easton can be seen as ideological legitimacy (Easton 1965, 287). Ideological legitimacy refers to the shared moral convictions about the validity of a political regime or of certain authority roles. Rational-legality is rooted in a liberal, thus moral, idea of the *Rechtsstaat* (constitutional state) in which the arbitrary acts, which are typical for the capriciousness of personal and traditional regimes, are abandoned and replaced by general rules that offer security, fairness and predictability. Moreover, the idea of rational-legality not only refers to the 'rule of the law', but it also refers to a strong belief in rationality, in the 'rule of knowledge' that can also be seen as an expression of an ideological belief of the Enlightenment in which the growth of knowledge implies progress. Thus, it is not surprising that in the policy sciences, the reference to knowledge is seen as an important source of legitimacy for a policy program (Brecht 1959; Dror 1989).

Another distinction has been made by Easton (1965, 287). In addition to personal and ideological legitimacy, he distinguishes structural legitimacy as sources of legitimacy. Structural legitimacy refers to an independent belief in the validity of the structure and norms of a political system and the roles that are fulfilled in this system. Structural legitimacy refers to the institutional embeddedness of authority. In the embedding of this authority, however, it is not only the institutions of the *Rechtsstaat* but also all kinds of governing traditions that play a role (Kielmansegg 1971). An example of such a governing tradition is the Dutch polder model, which has historical, cultural and political roots that go back for centuries, in which political decision-making is based on intensive bargaining between stakeholders (Hendriks and Toonen 2000).

Personal legitimacy refers to Weber's idea of charisma, while ideological legitimacy refers to shared moral convictions, norms and values, or to belief systems that legitimize the exercise of authority. In this case, legitimacy is value-driven (Daudt 1975, 7).

According to Easton, a distinction can be made between belief systems that refer to partisan ideologies (like a market liberalism, anti-globalism or communitarianism), which serve to mobilize support for political point of views, policy differences, or for political leadership; and belief systems that refer to the heart of the political system, and which he calls legitimizing ideologies that form the basis of the functioning and internal logic of the political system and which are translated and embedded in the structure of a political system (Easton 1965: 291). Such a belief system is the *Rechtsstaat* as the expression of a normative political and legal theory. At the same time, other political values could be seen as important sources of legitimacy in order to justify decisions, for instance, the importance of the empowerment of the citizen as a consumer of public services.

A Preliminary Conclusion

If we sum up the explorations from this section and in the previous section, legitimacy refers to:

- The judgment of the exercise of power on the basis of authority in terms of:
  - lawfulness (or legality): authority that is based on established or well defined and non-arbitrary rules and procedures
  - Rightness: the authority to make decisions that are based on specific norms and values, expressed through ideology, knowledge, rules and procedures, tradition or personal charisma. They can be seen as shared

    substantial and procedural beliefs (normative justifiability)
- The process of legitimizing in which consent or recognition is achieved on the basis of which political decisions are perceived as socially and politically accepted (Beetham and Lord 1998, 4).

What does this imply for the goal of this book? Legitimating governance practices, in which binding decisions are made, can be based on a) how these decisions have been made in accordance with the law, b) the sharing of substantive political norms and values among those who are addressed by these decisions and c) the sharing of specific political norms and values regarding the quality of the process in which these decisions are made. A discussion about a possible democratic deficit of governance, or, alternatively, about the introduction of governance practices to overcome legitimacy problems in the established methods of (representative democratic) decision-making, refers especially to the last point: to what political values, beliefs and norms do governance practices refer in order to justify decisions? These values can differ if we look at the different traditions of democratic thought that have emerged in the western world. Democratic traditions, and the values and norms that are articulated in them, are an important source of inspiration in the process of value-driven legitimization of political orders (Scharpf 1998, 6). In the next section, we turn to the notions of democracy as they have developed in the Western world and the values that underlie them.

2. The Concept of Democracy

The aim of this section is to develop a normative framework that can help us identify the legitimacy problems and democratic deficits in governance practices. We first propose a general definition of democracy in terms of some basic values. We then elaborate this definition by looking at different democratic traditions in Western political thought. In section four, we explore how these democratic values can be embodied in various institutions. In this way, we avoid those definitions that conceptualize democracy in terms of specific institutions as, for instance, electoral competition. We thereby create more conceptual space for democratization strategies other than the innovation of representative democracy.[1]

    We understand democracy as a political system in which political freedom is guaranteed and in which the members of the democracies have equal, effective input into the making of binding collective decisions. The requirement of effective input holds that inputs must determine outcomes.[2] In sum, our definition includes

---

1   This two-step approach is suggested by Saward (1998) and Engelen and Sie Dhian Ho (2004).

2   Or, at least, outputs, understood as the acts of governance that are the result of the policy process.

three basic values, namely political freedom, political equality and responsiveness.[3] It thereby combines the democratic notions of 'government by the people' and 'government for the people'.

A further elaboration of basic values underlying democracy can be found in different traditions in Western political thought (Held 1996). Modern democracy, as it came into being during the course of the 19th century as a system of representative democracy, can be seen as a compromise between different democratic traditions. In the American context, they are referred to as the populist and pluralist (or 'Madisonian') traditions (Dahl 1956; Birch 2001), and in the European context as the collectivist and liberal traditions (Sabine 1952; Thomassen 1991; Birch 2001).

The central values in the collectivist tradition of democracy are popular sovereignty (or more accurately *'the will of the nation'*; Birch, 2001), *political equality* and *majority rule*. In this tradition, representative institutions are regarded as a mechanism whereby the will of the people can be translated into public policies. Direct democracy is the ideal model for assessing the quality of representative democracy. An essential element is the identity between the voters and the elected, which means that the elected representatives make the decisions that the people would have made if they were able to make the final decisions (Thomassen 1991). The liberal view focuses on the balance between maintaining the state as an arrangement guaranteeing the functioning of the market and civil society on the one hand, and protecting individual freedom against encroachments by the state on the other. In the liberal view, representative institutions function as protective devices, forcing the political leaders to pursue policies that are not contrary to the interests of their subjects, while at the same time safeguarding the making of laws and policies against sectional interests (Held 1996). Central values in this tradition are *individual freedom*, popular sovereignty (but vested in the parliament: *'parliamentary sovereignty'*) and *checks and balances*. The collectivist and liberal traditions are a modern offspring of the republican tradition that can be traced back to the Roman republic and was taken up again by Renaissance thinking in the Northern Italian republics (Held 1996). In the recent literature, this tradition has made a revival in the neo-republican view on democracy (De Haan 1993). Central values that can be attributed to this tradition are *active citizenship*, *self-government* and *free deliberation*.

The values underlying these democratic traditions provide us with a normative framework for assessing the democratic quality of governance practices. Table 3.1 summarizes these values under the provisional headings of conditions for citizenship, notion of democratic rule, and primary decision-making mechanism.

---

3   The notion of 'equal effective inputs' (as a condition for responsiveness) is derived from Saward (1998). He proposes a responsive rule definition of democracy in terms of the 'necessary correspondence between acts of governance and the equally weighted felt interests of citizens with respect of those acts' (p. 51).

Table 3.1   A framework of democratic values

	Conditions for citizenship	*Notion of democratic rule*	*Primary mechanism*
Collectivism	political equality	will of the nation	majority rule
Liberalism	individual freedom	parliamentary sovereignty	checks and balances
Neo-republicanism	active citizenship	self-government	free deliberation

Our next step is to disaggregate collective decision-making into different stages and then to explore, in light of its basic values, what democracy demands at each stage in terms of specific institutions (Saward 1998). Saward follows the stages of the policy cycle by distinguishing agenda-setting, discussion about policy alternatives, decision-making, and implementation. We follow this approach by distinguishing input legitimacy, throughput legitimacy and output/outcome legitimacy. In the next section, we fine-tune these notions against the backdrop of the normative framework developed above. In section five, we proceed with the presentation of various models of democracy, each specifying specific institutions for collective democratic decision-making.

3. Norms for Assessing the Democratic Legitimacy of Governance Practices

Up until now, legitimacy has been explored as a general notion, a general quality that tells us something about how authority is recognized as valid or justified. It has been seen as a general qualification of a political system or a political regime. In this section, we decompose the concept by making a distinction between input-, throughput and output-oriented legitimacy as relevant aspects, in line with a well know distinction in political science (Easton 1965; Scharpf, 1998; Engelen and Sie Dhian Ho, 2004). In this section we specify these notions in terms of norms or criteria for assessing the democratic legitimacy of governance practices.

Input Legitimacy

Input-oriented democratic thought emphasizes 'government by the people' (Scharpf 1998, 6–7; De Jonghe and Bursens 2003, 8; Engelen and Sie Dhian Ho 2004, 20). This democratic idea refers to a number of norms that can be related to the values of political equality, active citizenship and popular sovereignty. Relevant norms include:

- The *opportunities for citizen participation*. The minimal opportunity for participation in a democratic polity is the right to vote in elections. In the context of governance, however, input legitimacy should be enhanced by other means as well. Are citizens actually enabled to express their wishes and interests in political decision-making, and do they have the possibility to engage themselves in public debate and policy-making? And if so, are these possibilities distributed in such a way that they provide equal opportunities for citizens to exert influence on political decision-making?

- If citizen involvement is only indirect or when citizens do not participate, we should assess the *quality of the representation* of interests and preferences by political intermediaries. Do elected representatives and interest groups actually stand for the interests of their constituency? Are all of the relevant interests being included?
- The *openness of the agenda setting* process for demands and concerns of citizens. How easy is it to get issues on the political agenda if someone is not a politician or a powerful stakeholder? This norm refers to the openness of governance practices to respond to specific needs in society.

Throughput Legitimacy

We define throughput legitimacy in terms of certain qualities of the rules and procedures by which binding decisions are made. Solving the problems that confront a community requires collective action. Societal problems could not be solved through individual action, through market exchange or through voluntary cooperation in the civil society (Stone 2002; Scharpf 1998, 11).[4] Relevant norms can be particularly related to the values of majority rule, checks and balances and free deliberation. The following norms tell us something about the throughput legitimacy of governance practices (Engelen and Sie Dhian Ho 2004, 20; see also Scharpf 1998, 13–22):

- How *collective decision-making* is realized. A distinction can be made between decision-making on the basis of the aggregation of individual preferences through voting, or on the basis of integrating mechanisms such as deliberation and debate (March and Olsen 1995). Democracy presupposes that interests and preferences are weighed on an equal footing. As a general norm we stipulate that a political system should provide a combination of aggregative and integrative mechanisms.
- The *quality of participation* in the decision-making process. From the perspective of representative democracy, the legitimacy of the decision-making process is based on the participation of politicians and their election

---

4　The definition we give of throughput legitimacy seems to be incorporated by Scharpf (1998, 11) in his notion of input legitimacy. He makes no distinction between input and throughput legitimacy, with which we disagree. It is especially important to look at how collective decision-making is organized because the procedures and rules that are used tell us something about the quality of authority of these binding decisions, which has to be understood in relation to the notion of procedural legitimacy (see Luhmann, 1969).

by the voters. In the other more participative models of democracy to be discussed later in this chapter, legitimacy also depends on identity and interest-based citizen participation, or on the participation of independent experts. First, incorporating this variety of perspectives can help improve the collective learning process because competing perspectives are brought into the decision-making process. Moreover, it is important to pay attention to so-called 'weak interests': people with specific interests who do not have the resources to organize themselves as a group. The quality of participation is also dependent on information provision on the content and procedures of the decision-making process. We take these aspects of *transparency* as another criterion.

- The quality of the *checks and balances* that are embedded in the decision-making process. Checks and balances include any institutional devices that constrain the use of power by politicians, bureaucracies and private stakeholders. These are important for preventing the specific interests of minority groups or weak interests from being pushed aside by majority rule or by powerful public and private stakeholders.

Output (outcome/feedback) Legitimacy

The output-oriented perspective on democratic legitimacy focuses on the notion of 'government for the people' (Scharpf 1998, 11). This aspect of legitimacy concerns the capacity of government to produce certain output or outcomes that actually contribute toward remedying collective problems. It is not the capacity itself which is judged, but the intended and unintended effects which have been realized. The following norms can be distinguished (Engelen and Sie Dhian Ho 2004, 23–26; see also Beetham 1991, 145), Scharpf 1998, 13–22; Scharpf 1997, 153–154; De Jonghe and Bursens 2003):

- The performance of government, in terms of (1) the *effectiveness and efficiency* of the outputs, produced as the result of the political decisions made and (2) the *responsiveness* of these decisions to the expressed wishes of the people. Governments have to handle collective problems, like the fight against crime or the reduction of traffic-jams. Have the policy goals that were originally formulated been realized? What are the effects of the measures that were taken to accomplish these goals and what kinds of costs were incurred to accomplish them? A distinction can be made between the output of government programs and the actual outcomes, while at the same time the actual performance of government is also influenced by the relationship between output and outcome. For instance, the increasing number of traffic fines (as the output of government actions) does not necessarily imply that the traffic safety (as outcome of government actions) has been improved
- How *accountability* is organized. Accountability refers to a communicative process between an actor and a forum about the actor's performance in

decision-making and implementation (Meijer and Bovens 2005). The authority to make decisions also implies that one is accountable for these decisions and for the results that have been produced. This in turn implies that information should be provided on the decisions and their effects (*transparency*). In terms of the institutional nature of the forum (for instance, electorate and courts), a distinction can be made between political, legal and public accountability. At the same time it is important to examine how the feedback mechanisms are organized and how relevant stakeholders can participate in these mechanisms.

Direct and Indirect Legitimacy

In the literature on legitimacy, we see that attention is also paid to the notion of indirect legitimacy as opposed to direct legitimacy (De Jonghe and Bursens 2003). This distinction is especially important in multi-level governance arrangements, like the European Union or regional public bodies. As a result of the co-operation between autonomous public organizations, binding decisions are made; the legitimacy question of these decisions is not raised at the level of co-operation itself but at the level of specific organizations that were involved in the co-operation. For instance, the legitimacy of the decisions made is derived from the way political accountability is organized at the level of the participating organizations. In such cases, we talk about indirect legitimacy.

4. A Preliminary Appraisal of Modes of Governance in Terms of Legitimacy

In Chapter 2 we distinguished several modes of governance. What expectations do we have concerning the democratic nature of these modes of governance in terms of input, throughput and output legitimacy? What 'educated guesses' can be made?

Governance at a distance emphasizes the importance of deregulation, decentralization, performance management and accountability. Deregulation and decentralization can be seen as ways of improving the decision-making process within (semi-public) organizations since the discretion of these organizations increases. The reduction of detailed rules and regulations makes it easier to develop tailor-made decisions and plans, thereby enhancing the effectiveness and responsiveness of public administration. At the same time, the existence of a general policy framework that still has to be followed, could also improve the accountability for the results that have been accomplished. Governance at a distance stimulates public organizations to make output and outcomes more explicit and thus transparent, which are necessary conditions for the assessment of the efficacy, efficiency and responsiveness of decisions. In sum, governance at a distance may improve the throughput and output legitimacy of public administration. However, at least two weaknesses can be expected. First, governance at a distance relies on a system of delegated legitimacy. This affects the throughput and output legitimacy of the organizations that have acquired more discretion. Citizens or companies have to rely on the quality of the decision-making process of these organizations. In some cases this would not have to be a problem. For instance, a municipality is embedded in a system of democratic participation and control. In other cases, for instance in relation to the gained discretion of (semi-) public agencies, these democratic mechanisms do not prevail. Second, a strong emphasis on performance management and strict auditing and accountability rules could generate a situation in which the results that have been achieved, although they have been in accordance with the defined policy goals and criteria, do not meet the actual wishes and needs of society (in terms of outcomes). More police officers on the street (as a relevant output criterion) does not necessarily imply a safer neighborhood (as a relevant outcome criterion). If outputs and outcomes do not correspond to each other, this may endanger the output legitimacy of government, despite all of the efforts to make government more responsible for the results that have to be achieved.

Another mode of governance is *market governance*. The market mechanism is used to produce outcomes that reflect the desires and wishes of the consumers of public services, like citizens or companies. One could expect that the output legitimacy of this mode of governance is rather high. Providers that do not produce services that reflect the wishes and needs of the consumers (in terms of price and quality) would not survive in a market. In order to produce responsive services, providers have to create possibilities for participation, for instance of consumers, in the design or redesign of services. This could contribute to input legitimacy as well. If we look at the throughput legitimacy of these market governance practices, some problems can be expected. The actual decision-making process regarding what services should be provided, and under what price/quality conditions, is not subject to public control. However, rules of play can be given by a regulatory or supervisory body, which should be taken into account.

Multi-level governance focuses on the co-operation between several layers of government. Examples are regional development bodies in which local and regional governments work together, the European Union and the World Bank. We may expect some problems with regard to input and throughput legitimacy. In many cases, multi-level governance is based on borrowing the legitimacy of other democratic institutions, like a parliament or a municipal council. One could speak about indirect representation and participation of interests. Moreover, problems can be expected in relation to the output norm of accountability. In many cases, citizens are not able to hold the governors of these multi-level governance bodies accountable. Accountability is organized on the level of the participating public organizations. It also depends on the kind of mandate given to the representatives of, for instance, a municipality, which participates in a regional development body. At the same time, co-operation between several layers of government, could contribute to output legitimacy, because many societal problems cross the jurisdictions of the traditional layers of government and their representative bodies. Cooperation is perceived as a strategy to develop and implement effective plans which deal with these boundary problems.

The emergence of *network governance* can be understood as a way of improving the input and throughput legitimacy of political decision-making. Stakeholder participation (issue and interest groups, citizens, companies, societal organizations, other governments) has been seen as a way of improving the quality of the input of the decision-making process. Stakeholders have the possibility of suggesting other, complementary or competing, views on the nature of problems or on possible solutions. If we look at the throughput legitimacy, we see that in many cases of network governance, the production of public policy is viewed as a process of co-production in which the stakeholders have a say in drafting and implementing the policy program. The emphasis lies on mutual learning through dialogue, which might go beyond sheer 'interest representation'. This will enhance the quality of the participation and decision-making, provided that 'weak interests' are also sitting at the table. From the perspective of representative democracy, the co-production of public policies in a network of stakeholders, can be seen as a threat to the primacy of politics. Network governance challenges the monopoly of politicians to make binding decisions. Moreover, network governance challenges the output norm of accountability. Who is accountable for the results that have been accomplished, when actors other than (only) politicians have been involved in the policy formulation process?

The last mode of governance that we have distinguished is *societal self-governance*. In this mode of governance the emphasis is on self-government within a community. Based on the existent social capital, the community itself deals with a number of problems in the public domain, like crime prevention or childcare. Government intervention is not needed. If we look at these forms of self-government, which are created outside the realm of representative democracy, it is interesting to see how the legitimacy of self-government is organized. One issue of concern is the question of who participates in this local community, who sets the agenda and what interests are represented; issues that influence the input legitimacy of societal self governance. Also the quality of the decision-making process in these local and functional communities is an issue of concern. How does this decision-making process actually take place? How are 'weak interests' taken into consideration? And, in relation to output legitimacy, who is made responsible for the results of, for instance, a neighborhood watch program? Did the community adapt the rules of the game of representative democracy, or has it developed other rules?

5. Models of Democracy

We argued above that the nature of democracy is to legitimize the decisions made in a political system and to provide the institutions and organizations that play a role in it. In section three, we specified the legitimacy aspects, but each of these aspects can be institutionalized in different ways. In this context, one can refer to several models of democracy. We use the concept of a model of democracy to denote a configuration of institutional and organizational elements situated around a specific decision-making mechanism (Eder 1995). Furthermore, each model can be related to a certain conception of the appropriate *demos*. Each model provides certain ideal-type institutional devices for meeting the norms of legitimacy. For instance, each model embodies certain notions about opportunities for citizens to participate (input norm), how procedures for political decision-making should be designed (throughput norm) and how accountability should be organized (output norm). However, the different sorts of democracy differ in their power to meet these legitimacy norms. Therefore, we include an overview of their strengths and weaknesses, which can be used in the assessment of governance practices. We give an example. Chapter 9 investigates deliberative environmental forums. In this analysis, the throughput norm *quality of participation* is operationalized in terms of Habermas's concept of the ideal speech situation, which can be seen as a cornerstone of the model of deliberative democracy. Furthermore, the overview of strengths and weaknesses can assist us in suggesting ways for democratization by pointing to those models that are particularly strong in providing the institutional devices that may correct the proven legitimacy deficits.

Representative Democracy

Representative democracy involves the delegation of political decision-making to a small number of professional politicians elected by the people. In modern democracies, the competition between political parties and their candidates is the core mechanism by which the interests and wishes of the people are taken into account (Miller 1983). The conception of the *demos* is a stably defined people exercising sovereignty within a territorially delimitated political community.

A primary contribution of representative democracy to the legitimacy of political systems lies on the input side. With regard to opportunities of participation, 'it center-stages the principle of formal and universal equality and cashes it out as formal voting equality' (Saward 2001, 367). At the same time, the opportunities for active citizenship are limited to the opportunities that political parties provide to their members. Representative democracy delegates the task of making complex political decisions to elected politicians, who supposedly have the qualifications and time to do this job. Insofar this notion of a political 'division of labor' is shared among the citizenry, this is a potential source for the legitimacy of representative political systems. These aspects have to be considered in connection with the quality of representation on the input side and the responsiveness of political decisions and the quality of the practices of holding the politicians accountable on the output side.

With regard to the quality of the representation, one can point to the assumption that voters confer a clear mandate on their representatives in terms of certain policies. This hardly seems to be realistic. Although citizens are to some extent able to select politicians in accordance with their policy preferences, they do not have enough possibilities and information to instruct or judge governments (Przeworski, Stones and Manin 1999). Besides, because of the complexity and dynamics of modern societies, there is an increasing distance between the issues that are anticipated and discussed during election campaigns and the issues that actually appear on the agenda of political decision-makers during tenure (Offe and Preuss 1991). There also seems to be an increasing social distance between the ordinary voters and professional politicians, giving rise to distrust and voter alienation. In terms of openness of the agenda, we can question whether the modern party system, in particular the emergence of 'cartel parties' as described by Katz and Mair (1994), is responsive enough to the citizens' concerns, apart from those broadly accepted themes that are conducive for mounting a successful electoral campaign.

On the throughput side, representative democracy relies on a combination of aggregation (elections) and integration (drafting party platforms and deliberation within parliaments), but both functions are only partly realized. Aggregation suffers from declining voter turnouts, in particular when nonvoting is prominent within specific social strata. The integration function seems to suffer from the emergence of 'cartel parties' and the increasing orientation of professional politicians towards political marketing strategies. The quality of participation (voting) is limited. In traditional liberal theory, representative institutions are seen as protective devices against oppressive popular rule and powerful collectivities (Held 1996). In the context of modern governance practices, this notion of representative democracy providing for checks and balances is very important. This is set out by Habermas (1992/1996, 327–328), who mentions majority rule, representative bodies, checks and balances and oversight and review powers as 'complexity-preserving countersteering mechanisms' against 'illegitimate' power complexes and the 'unofficial' circulation of administrative and social power.

On the output side, the performance of representative democracy, in terms of both its effectiveness and responsiveness, is under dispute. Accountability is one of the cornerstones of liberal representative democracy. The electoral mechanism of accountability is in itself quite strong ('throwing the rascals out'), but rather crude. It works for salient issues that are considered priorities by the voters. For instance, top priorities for the many Dutch voters who voted for the List Pim Fortuyn, a newcomer in the 2002 parliamentary election, were contesting crime and a stricter policy towards asylum seekers (Van Praag 2003). In the relationship between government and parliament, accountability in parliamentary systems is structurally hampered by the executive's dominance over the legislature.

Direct Democracy

In the radical version of the collectivist view on democracy, the popular will is directly translated into legislation. The people assemble together and decide on the laws to be made. Devices of direct democracy are advocated in various forms, ranging from self-government in small territorially or functionally delimitated units to the inclusion of popular initiatives, referendums or recall procedures in representative arrangements. It is important to note here that some direct democratic devices can also be used as protective devices. The 'corrective referendum', in particular, provides the citizens with an instrument to challenge specific decisions made by the elected representatives. Some advocates regard the advent of ICTs as an opportunity to establish a 'push button democracy' in which traditional limits of time and place are overcome. What these visions share is the belief that there are no necessary discrepancies in knowledge or motivation between the political elite and the population that would keep the latter from participation in actual political decision-making (Budge 1996). The conception of the *demos* in this model is variable. It can coincide with the demos conception of the representative model, but also refer to functionally delineated communities of people.

The primary contribution of direct democracy to the legitimacy of democratic political systems is on the input side. It combines the values of direct citizen participation and political equality in the making of specific political decisions. In terms of openness of the agenda, direct democratic arrangements are also strong, provided that they include the citizens' initiative. Because, in theory, there is no intermediation between inputs and political decisions, throughput legitimacy is guaranteed by the right of every member of the *demos* to vote (Engelen and Si Dhian Ho 2004). However, because of the aggregation of only 'yes' and 'no' votes, the quality of the participation is limited. On the output side, responsiveness can be seen as the result of the direct involvement of citizens in decision-making. Furthermore, citizen-initiated referendums challenging prior decisions made by politicians add to the accountability of political decision-making.

The main vulnerabilities of the direct democracy model are, first of all, on the input side. They include the alleged lack of motivation and cognitive abilities of voters to inform themselves about complex issues.[5] Other vulnerabilities refer to the hardly realistic assumption that referendum processes are 'unmediated'. There is a real 'throughput' side, the quality of which is regularly under discussion in view of the role of financially powerful interest groups in the campaigns.

Pluralist Democracy

In the classical version of the pluralist model, political power is seen as dispersed over numerous interest groups. Political decisions are explained by competition, negotiation, and coalition building between interest groups. Institutional politics functions as a neutral mediator or arbiter. Public policies can be expected to be responsive to the wishes of the people provided that the internal functions of interest groups are democratic, interest groups have free access to various power resources and relevant arenas, and there is open competition between interest groups. Moreover, interest groups can be seen as a protective mechanism against encroachments by the state. Within the conditions specified above, pluralist democracy provides essential 'checks and balances' and safeguards for protecting minorities (Dahl 1989).

The emergence of new social movements since the seventies has introduced new avenues for interest mediation. This has contributed to a diversification of public participation in terms of repertoires of action, organizational forms and mobilization

---

5   However, see Budge (1996) for a critical discussion of this argument.

targets, which include non-state actors such as international corporations and supra-national organizations (Norris 2002).

The conception of the *demos* within the classical version of pluralist democracy coincides with a 'weak' version of the demos conception within representative democracy. At the level of the nation state, citizens share a common orientation towards certain basic democratic values and 'rules of the game'. In a post-traditional version of pluralism, various *demoi* could be indicated at different levels, including the global level. The advent of ICTs facilitates the mobilization and possibly also the shaping of identities among geographically dispersed individuals and groups (Van de Donk, Loader, Nixon and Rucht 2004).

The main contributions of the pluralist model to democratic legitimacy lie on the input and throughput side. Interest groups offer opportunities for participation and civic activism. Moreover, since they are the primary instruments for interest articulation they play an essential role in agenda setting. Within a favorable 'political opportunity structure' (Kriesi 1996), the pluralist model can contribute significantly to the openness of the agenda of political decision-making. On the throughput side, democracy is seen as an institutional arena and set of procedural rules for negotiations that, within the conditions specified above, will lead to legitimate outcomes (Lehning 1991). Pluralist negotiations rely on a combination of aggregation and integration. By involving different stakeholders in the design of policies, different desires can be linked together and integrated in a concept that may offer a 'win-win' situation. Moreover, the diversity of interests involved in such practices of co-governance has some potential in terms of quality of participation. Above, we mentioned the functions of pluralism for checks and balances and the protection of minorities. On the output side, interest groups will not only be contributory to responsiveness, but also to the accountability of political power-holders.

The vulnerabilities of the pluralist model refer to the ideal type conditions mentioned above: the internal functioning of interest groups and their relation with the constituency (quality of representation), free access to relevant power resources and arenas, equality of bargaining power and open competition. There is an extensive literature on the biases of existing power structures and interest group constellations, which, for instance, successfully block certain issues from reaching the institutional agenda that is considered by authoritative decision makers (Bachrach and Baratz 1962; Birkland 2001).

Deliberative Democracy

Deliberative democracy is based on the notion of 'government by discussion'. It rejects the idea that the preferences of the citizens can be taken as given and merely have to be aggregated. Instead, the model relies on the integrative mechanism of deliberation: citizens' preferences have to be critically examined and weighted against each other by the exchange of information and arguments. In ideal-type formulations of the deliberative model, deliberation aims to arrive at a rationally motivated consensus, but some authors, including Habermas (1994), also include negotiations as an element into deliberative politics, provided that they are fairly regulated. The deliberative model is one of the most influential models in the literature nowadays, and it inspires various experiments in democratic practices such as citizen juries, round-table conferences and online policy exercises (Chambers 2003; Coleman and Gøtze 2001).

The primary contribution of the deliberative model to democratic legitimacy lies in the throughput side. The central principle governing deliberative arrangements is Habermas's notion of the ideal speech situation. It stipulates that all citizens should have equal opportunities to start or enter a public discussion, and that the participants are required to defend their proposals by arguments and to refrain from using power. Or, as Cohen (1989) has formulated it, the existing distribution of power should not shape citizens' opportunities to participate in a discussion, nor should it play an authoritative role in settling the dispute. Because of the ideal speech situation and the possibility of involving a diversity of stakeholders and experts in the deliberation, the model has high potential on the throughput norm of quality of the participation. Furthermore, Habermas (1992) has indicated that deliberative procedures can function as a 'counter-steering mechanism' by which the communicative power of citizens can be channeled in societal and administrative decision-making ('checks and balances'). On the input side, deliberative arrangements provide avenues for the exercise of active citizenship. According to Chambers (2003: 308), 'accountability replaces consent as the conceptual core of legitimacy' in deliberative democracy. Accountability should then be understood as 'publicly articulating, explaining, and most importantly justifying policy'. In this sense, the deliberative model has a great potential also on the output side.

However, some important weaknesses and vulnerabilities of the deliberative model appear on the input, throughput and output side. On the input side, the deliberative model stands in a somewhat uneasy relationship with the value of political equality. First, if deliberative theorists insist on the idea that preferences have to be subjected to a critical examination in argumentative discourse, 'what is to be done with the participation rights of those who persist in having non-deliberative preferences?' In this respect, the deliberative model might have some exclusive implications (Saward 2000; Saward 2001). Moreover, deliberative arrangements tend to attract participants who already have the motivation, skills and resources to participate (Wille 2001). This may harm the quality of representation. Furthermore, while the ideal speech situation includes the norm that all participants have the right to propose topics or 'to question the assigned topics of the discussion' (Benhabib 1994), deliberative arrangements might be vulnerable on the agenda-setting function. According to Saward (2001, 369), 'deliberative devices are not good at *initiating* issues'. Special efforts have to be made to counter these tendencies. For instance, at least a qualitative representation of all affected interests should be present in order to prevent the agenda and deliberations from being biased to specific interests. On the throughput side, the ideal-speech situation is extremely difficult to even approximate. Various provisions, such as discussion rules, process management and moderation, are required. On the output side, the deliberative procedure lacks a mechanism that guarantees a consensual outcome. This means that deliberative arrangements in concrete practices of governance will have to rely on other devices for closure, such as formal voting procedures derived from the direct or representative models of democracy. In practice, deliberative arrangements are commonly embedded as a complementary ingredient within the framework of representative democracy. Experience shows that they are vulnerable to reversion effects at the stage of final political decision-making when bureaucrats and professional politicians tend to enter in their classical roles with regard to the drafting and authorizing of final propositions (Klijn and Koppenjan 2000). This would be at the expense of the value of responsiveness at the output side.

Associative Democracy

Associative democrats extend the scope of democracy to the associations that are involved in public service provision. Opportunities for effective participation are sought in domains such as education, housing, public health and welfare in which people are directly affected in their everyday life and in which they have specific 'local knowledge' that is directly valuable in decision-making (Engelen 2004). Such a strategy of 'democratizing the organizational society' would involve the devolution of many functions of the state to the civil society, while retaining or even strengthening the public funding and supervision functions of the state (Hirst 2000). Associative democracy draws primarily on the neo-republican values of self-government and active citizenship. As suggested by Hirst, associations could function, at the minimum, as representative democracies, but they could also make use of direct-democratic and deliberative devices. Moreover, at the macro-level of the various sectors, client associations can be involved in the supervision (Bekkers and Homburg 2002). The *demos* conception in associative democracy is variable. In this conception, relevant *demoï* are the territorially and functionally delineated publics who exercise self-government.

The main contributions of associative democracy to legitimacy are on the input and output side. On the input side, it provides the citizen a number of options for expressing their desires and interests in their role of patient, parent, service user or employee. It therefore scores potentially high on opportunities for participation and openness of the agenda. On the output side, the combination of devolution of service functions and the direct involvement of clients increases the chances of responsiveness. The same holds true for the value of accountability. Its specific contribution to throughput legitimacy is dependent on the mechanism used: representative democracy, direct democracy or deliberation. It could be potentially high, when deliberative mechanisms are used. Associative democracy shares some vulnerability with these mechanisms, such as on the norm of quality of representation.

Table 3.2   Strengths and weaknesses of models of democracy in terms of input, throughput and output/outcome legitimacy

	Representative Democracy	Direct Democracy	Pluralist Democracy	Deliberative Democracy	Associative Democracy	Client/ Consumer Democracy
Input - Opportunities for Participation	Voting equality, Political division of labor	Voting equality	Active citizenship	Active citizenship	Active citizenship	'Thin' citizenship
- Quality of Representation	Social distance	–	Unclear	Unclear	Unclear	Unclear
- Openness of Agenda	Problematic	Potentially strong	Potentially strong	Unclear	Potentially strong	Weak/ Unclear
Throughput - Way of Decision-Making	Aggregative/ Integrative	Aggregative	Aggregative/ Integrative	Integrative	Aggregative/ Integrative	Aggregative
- Quality of Participation	Limited	Weak	Potentially high	Potentially high	Potentially high	Weak
- Checks and Balances	Potentially strong	Limited	Strong	Potentially strong	Potentially strong	Limited
Output - Performance (Effectiveness, Responsiveness)	Problematic	Limited	Potentially strong	Problematic	Potentially strong	Limited/ Strong
- Accountability	Strong on salient issues	Limited	Potentially strong	Potentially strong	Potentially strong	Limited/ Strong

Client or Consumer Democracy

Associative democracy and client democracy share their focus on a democratic structuring of public service delivery. Client democracy, however, does not seek its solutions in self-governing associations. Instead, it seeks to generate information about the citizens' preferences via marketing-like instruments, such as focus groups, complaint procedures and client research. This model is closely related to the New Public Management approach (Bellamy and Taylor 1998). Therefore, it might be objected that this model of democracy stretches the meaning of 'the political' too far. However, this model might be broadened to include forms of accountability of agencies and individual street-level bureaucrats to their clients (Hill and Hupe 2005).

In terms of democratic legitimacy, this model has something to add on the output side. Within the context of public service delivery, it may enhance the responsiveness of outputs and the accountability of service providers. On the throughput side, the consumer model scores rather low on quality of participation (thin notion of citizenship). However, the active involvement of clients in public service delivery can be seen as contributing somewhat to checks and balances. On the input side, this model has little to add to legitimacy. Its underlying conception of citizenship is rather 'thin'. The quality of representation depends primarily on the instruments used. It can be high if special efforts are carried out to involve 'weak' categories. As to the openness of the agenda, client democracy probably scores weak here as well. This would depend on the opportunities offered to clients to forward their needs and to question existing services. Table 3.2 above summarizes the results of our discussion.

6. Conclusion

The core of the theoretical framework outlined in Chapters 2 and 3 consists of three elements. The distinction between various modes of governance (Chapter 2) is the first element. The second element is the norms of democratic legitimacy. In the empirical chapters we assess governance practices, characterized in terms of different modes of governance, with this framework of norms. However, governance practices are intertwined with institutional arrangements derived from various models of democracy (the third element of the theoretical framework). First, a mode of governance is always embedded, to a greater or lesser degree, in the institutions of representative democracy, even if this embedding is no more than a loose coupling. Furthermore, we may expect that in the slipstream of governance practices other democratic arrangements are also emerging. This implies that the empirical object of our assessments is governance practices that include democratic arrangements of representative democracy and, possibly, other models of democracy. The conjectures of the legitimacy problems in the various modes of governance (section 4) along with the outline of strengths and weaknesses of the models of democracy in terms of democratic legitimacy support us in assessing governance practices. Furthermore, they assist us in proposing democratization strategies. The focus of these democratization strategies is twofold. First, we seek institutional designs in which different models of democracy coexist and work in ways that, in view of the legitimacy aspects, are mutually supportive (see for instance, Saward 2001). Second, we have to look at how to embed governance practices in representative institutions. Representative democracy has a special position in the democratic design of governance practices since it provides the constitutional rules of the game which provide the basis on which the various (other) democratic arrangements can function.

References

Bachrach, P. and Baratz, M. S. (1962), 'Two Faces of Power', *American Political Science Review* 56:4, 947–52.

Beetham, D. (1991), *The Legitimation of Power* (London: Macmillan).

Beetham, D and Lord, C. (1998), *Legitimacy and the European Union* (London, New York: Longman).

Bellamy, Chr. and Taylor, J. A. (1998), *Governing in the Information Age* (Buckingham, Philadelphia: Open University Press).

Birkland, Th. A. (2001), *An Introduction to the Policy Process: Theories, Concepts and Models of Public Policy Making* (Armonk, New York: Sharpe).

Brecht, A. (1959), *Political Theory: the Foundations of Twentieth-Century Political Thought* (Princeton: Princeton University Press).

Bekkers, V. J. J. M. and Homburg, V. F. M. (2002), 'Administrative supervision and information relationships', *Information Polity* 7:2/3, 129–41.

—— (eds) (2005), *The Information Ecology of E-government* (Amsterdam: IOS Press). Benhabib, S. (1994), 'Deliberative rationality and models of democratic legitimacy', *Constellations* 1:1, 26–52.

Birch, A. H. (2001), *Concepts and Theories of Modern Democracy* (London: Routledge).

Budge, I. (1996), *The New Challenge of Direct Democracy* (Cambridge: Polity Press).

Chambers, S. (2003), 'Deliberative democratic theory', *Annual Review of Political Science* 6, 307–26.

Cohen, J. (1989), 'Deliberation and Democratic Legitimacy', in Hamlin and Pettit (eds.).

Coleman, S. and Gøtze, J. (2001), *Bowling Together. Online Public Engagement in Policy Deliberation* (London: Hansard Society).

Dahl, R. A. (1956), *A Preface to Democratic Theory* (Chicago, London: The University of Chicago Press).

—— (1989), *Democracy and its Critics* (New Haven: Yale University Press).

Daudt, H. (1975), 'Legitimiteit en legitimatie', *Beleid and Maatschappij* 2:1, 5–16.

Donk, W. van de, Loader, B., Nixon, P. and Rucht D. (eds) (2004), *Cyber Protest. New Media, Citizen Mobilization and Social Movements* (London, New York: Routledge).

Dror, Y. (1989), *Public Policy-Making, Re-examined* (Scranton: Chandler Publishing Company).

Duncan, G. (ed.) (1983), *Democratic Theory and Practice* (Cambridge: Cambridge University Press).

Easton, D. (1965), *A Systems Analysis of Political Life* (New York: Wiley).

Edelenbos, J. and Monnikhof, R. (eds) (2001), *Lokale Interactieve Beleidsvorming* (Utrecht: Lemma).

Eder, K. (1995), 'Die Dynamik demokratischer Institutionenbildung. Strukturelle Voraussettzungwen deliberativer Demokratie in fortgeschrittenen Industriegesellschaften', in Nedelman (ed.).

Engelen, E. R. and Sie Dhian Ho, M. (eds) (2004), *De Staat van de Democratie. Democratie Voorbij de Staat* (Amsterdam: Amsterdam University Press).

Friedrich, C. J. (1963), *Man and his Government* (New York: McGraw-Hill Book Company).

Haan, I. de (1993), *Zelfbestuur en Staatsbeheer* (Amsterdam: Amsterdam University Press).

Habermas, J. (1992/1996), *Between Facts and Norms. Contributions to a Discourse Theory of Law and Democracy* (Cambridge, Mass.: MIT Press).

—— (1994), 'Three normative models of democracy', *Constellations* 1(1), 1–10.

Hamlin, A. and Pettit, P. (eds) (1989), *The Good Polity; Normative Analysis of the State* (Oxford: Blackwell).

Held, D. (ed.) (1991), *Political Theory Today* (Cambridge: Polity Press).

—— (1996), *Models of Democracy* (Cambridge: Polity Press).

Hendriks, F. and Toonen, T. (2000), *Polder Politics* (Cheltenham: Edgar Elgar).

Hill, M. and Hupe, P. (2005), *Street-level Bureaucracy and Public Accountability* Paper presented at the Ninth International Research Symposium on Public Management, April 6–8, (Milan: Bocconi University Milan).

Hirst, P. (1994), *Associative Democracy* (Cambridge: Polity Press).

—— (2000), 'Democracy and Governance', in Pierre (ed.), pp. 13–35.

Jonghe, K. de and Bursens, P. (2003), *How to increase legitimacy in the European Union? The concept of multi-level governance legitimacy* PSW-paper 2003:4, (Antwerp: University of Antwerp).

Katz, R. and Mair, P. (1994), *How Parties Organise: Change and Adaptation in Party Organisation in Western Democracies* (London: Sage).

Kielmansegg, P. (1971), 'Legitimität als analytische Kategorie', *Politische Vierteljahresschrift* 12:3, 367–401.

Kim, Y.C. (1966), 'Authority: Some conceptual and empirical notes', *Western Political Quarterly* 19:2, 223–34.

Klijn, E. H. and J. F. F. M. Koppenjan (2000). Politicians and interactive decision-making: institutional spoilsports or playmakers. *Public Administration* 78:2, 365–387.

Kriesi, H. (1996), 'The organizational structure of new social movements in a political context', Mc Adam, D. et al. (eds), pp. 152–84.

Lasswell, H. (1936/1958), *Politics: Who Gets What, When and How* (New York: Meridian Books).

Lehning, P. (1991), 'De theorie van het pluralisme', in Thomassen (ed.), pp. 107–128.

Luhmann, N. (1969), *Legitimation durch Verfahren* (Neuwied: Luchterhand).

March, J. G. and Olsen, J. P. (1995), *Democratic Governance* (New York: Free Press).

McAdam, D., McCarthy, D., Zald, M. N. (eds). *Comparative Perspectives on Social Movements* (Cambridge: Cambridge University Press).

Meier, A. J. and Bovens, M.A.P. (2005), 'Public Accountability in the Information Age', in Bekkers and Homburg (eds), pp. 171–82.

Miller, D. (1983), 'The competitive model of democracy', in Duncan (ed.), pp. 133–55.

Morris, C. W. (1998), *An Essay on the Modern State* (Cambridge: Cambridge University Press).

Nedelman, B. (ed.) (1995), 'Politische Institutionen im Wandel', *Kölner Zeitschrift für Sociologie und Sozialpsychologie* Sonderheft 35, 327–45.

Norris, P. (2002), *Democratic Phoenix. Reinventing Political Activism* (Cambridge: Cambridge University Press).

Offe, C. and Preuss U. (1991), 'Democratic Institutions and Moral Resources', in Held (ed.), pp. 143–71.

Pierre, J. (ed.) (2000), *Debating Governance* (Oxford: Oxford University Press).

Potman, H. P. (1989), *Acceptatie van Beleid* (Zeist: Kerckebosch).

Praag, H. van (2003), 'The Winners and Losers in a Turbulent Political Year', *Acta Politica* 38:1, 5–21.

Przeworski, A., S. C. Stokes, Manin, B. (eds), *Democracy, Accountability, and Representation* (Cambridge: Cambridge University Press).

Sabine, G. H. (1952), 'The two democratic traditions', *The Philosophical Review* 61:4, 451–74.

Saward, M. (1998), *The Terms of Democracy* (Cambridge: Polity Press).

—— (ed.) (2000), *Democratic Innovation: Deliberation, Representation and Association* (London: Routledge).

—— (2001), 'Making Democratic Connections: Political Equality, Deliberations and Direct Democracy', *Acta Politica* 36:4, 361–79.

Schaar, J. H. (1981), *Legitimacy in the Modern State* (New Brunswick: Transaction Books).

Scharpf, F. W. (1997), *Games Real Actors Play* (Oxford: Westview Press).

—— (1998), *Governing in Europe: Effective and Democratic* (Oxford: Oxford University Press).

Stone, D. (2002), *The Policy Paradox. The Art of Political Decision-Making* (New York, London: Norton and Company).

Thomassen, J. J. A. (ed.) (1991), *Hedendaagse Democratie* (Alphen aan den Rijn: Samsom H.D. Tjeenk Willink).

Weber, M. (1922/1972), *Wirtschaft und Gesellschaft* (Tübingen: Mohr Siebeck).

Wille, A. (2001), 'Politieke participatie en representativiteit in het interactieve beleidsproces', in Edelenbos and Monnikhof (eds), pp. 87–115.

Chapter 4

The Idea of Democracy and the Eighteenth Century

Koen Stapelbroek

One of the leading questions of this volume is whether the perceived shift from centralised state politics to more intricate structures of power distribution and its management affects the democratic quality of modern societies.[1] This question triggers many other questions, first of all concerning ideas of democracy. Yet, proceeding to answer the initial question by attempting to define democracy (or the democratic quality of a society) – thus confronting the issue head on – would be hopelessly naïve.

Throughout history, the notion has had too many contradictory meanings to allow for any definitive qualifications. With there being so little grounds for understanding democracy in an unequivocal sense, it is remarkable that the term 'democracy' has been the subject of immense attention in (pseudo-) academic literature in the last few decades. The term democracy worked like a magnet, drawing political scientists, philosophers and historians alike to discuss a wide range of aspects associated with it. The immense variety of recent publications that include the word democracy in their titles may be related to the waning of socialism in Eastern Europe and the former Soviet Union, which contributed to the popularity of the term (in a moralising respect, as well as indicating a successful value for serving national interests) among political leaders and commentators in the West. Capitalism, this use of the term democracy suggested, served democracy better than socialism and was a normatively superior political system. Consequently, the term democracy became increasingly used as a 'measure' for the quality of different aspects of the politics of a nation, or any larger or smaller aggregation of individuals. And so the term now reigns in large parts of society, where it pops up in a myriad variety of political discussions that have an evaluative component. Not surprisingly, due to its assumed catch-phrase property, any substantial homogeneity in use of the term democracy went out of the window.[2] The growing popularity of the term democracy in pseudo-political discourse also contrasts with the fact that the most perceptive theorists of the idea recognise major problems with the inner-logic of any notion of democracy as

---

1   See Chapter 1.

2   As every reader of this volume can imagine, internet searches on publications including the word democracy in the title result in a wild variety of uses of the term.

popular self-government in modern society.[3] And yet, I will argue, it is the case that looking at the flood of titles containing the word and the conflation of perspectives in even more works dealing with democracy can provide a lead in clarifying issues about the relation between democracy and governance. What is required is the right type of distance from the range of outbursts of calls for democracy and freedom at any level of national and international society.

Taking this right sort of distance (without pretending to move towards a true vantage point) to be able to consider democracy and governance in relation to each other also involves moving away from the focus of almost all contemporary political philosophy that inquires about procedures of aggregation, deliberation, etcetera, in order to confront the typical heavily morally laden use of the term democracy. Finding a philosophical way out of the complexities when confronted, for example, with issues of human rights and democracy becomes an impossible task. In contrast, a more observing, open-minded style of doing political philosophy is more at ease with the challenges of popularised debates about political ideas. Surveying the different ways in which one might conceive of notions of democracy, Raymond Geuss (2001, 111–19) distinguishes between concepts of democracy that refer to empirical institutional orders and concepts that refer to an ideal. In evaluations of the quality of democracy, he discerns an instrumental approach as well as a normative approach, with the latter claiming that democracy is the morally superior way of ordering a society. A third approach bridges the first two by viewing democracy as an epistemological enterprise that coordinates the 'realisation of human autonomy' and the production of 'exogenous goods, such as social stability, peacefulness and welfare'.[4]

In this chapter, however, history is the source that is adopted for constructing a view of the relation between democracy and governance. Looking at history with an eye on presentday debates, might shed light on issues about the evolution of political paradigms. While tempting, one approach that is avoided here is looking at democracy through the lens of republican political thought throughout the whole of human history.[5] To obtain a clear understanding of the particular characteristics of alleged democratic movements at various moments in time, one should be able to consider their actual contexts and very diverse historical inspirations. Ancient democracy is usually linked to the major reform experiment by Kleisthenes in Athens in 508 BC, which was in fact an opportunistic attempt, inspired by vindictive motives, to save his own interests against defeat by the power of other aristocrats (Farrar 1992; Hornblower 1992); the Italian city states of the late middle ages and the renaissance

---

3   Classic expressions of fundamental problems are Arrow (1963) and Schumpeter (1976). More recent contributions include Dunn (2002; 2005), Geuss (2001), Shapiro (2003), and Shapiro and Hacker-Cordón (1999).

4   On these evaluations of democracy see Geuss (2001), 119–24, also with respect to Dewey, Geuss (2001), 124–6.

5   See the contributions in Van Gelderen and Skinner (2002), which present a myriad of different ideas about republicanism that taken together are prone to the accusation that they create more confusion than clarification in the history of political thought.

established self-government in the face of papal and feudal power structures that had emerged after the fall of Rome (Skinner 1992); English early modern 'republicanism' had its own much contested circumstances and characteristics;[6] and still later, ideas of 'representative democracy', which were arguably first developed in the course of the French Revolution, are said to have passed through Mill, onwards to their subsequent transformation into the technical discourse of political theory as we know it.[7] Any meaningful continuity over time between such a variety of movements can only be imposed and confuses rather than illuminates the issue at hand.

The focus of this piece is only on the eighteenth century and even then it is limited purely to making one specific suggestion about how one might view the relation between governance and democracy. Moreover, in considering eighteenth-century political thought, I merely present a small and sketchy impression of discussions involving ideas of democracy in that age. Yet, these restrictions are justified by the advantages of choosing the eighteenth century as a reference point for treating the issue of governance and democracy.

One obvious reason for postponing directly delving into the matter of the compatibility of governance and democracy should be that confronting the two elements of the issue results in an elusive equation. This is the case not only because democracy and governance are two highly uncertainly moving ideas, but also because they tend to move at different levels of inquiry: governance concerns the organisation of power management, while democracy concerns how personal preferences are absorbed by a political order. Although the two may have strong mutual links, governance and democracy relate to different objects. Thus, it may seem that governance begins where democracy ends (and *vice versa*), which makes assessing the relative impact on developments on one side of the equation on the other a highly elusive matter. Here, as I will explain, the nature of eighteenth-century debate helps to draw the two closer to each other and bring them together into one frame. By adopting an eighteenth-century perspective, one considers the process by which government became governance through the lens of international economic competition and asks whether states ever had and have the opportunities to resist this shift. Also, after the fall of the iron curtain, the liberal-democratic state was hailed as the only remaining political structure that was capable of accommodating the challenges of modern market societies in an international context. Yet, an eighteenth-century point of view would have been ideally suited to temper the enthusiasm and point to deeper problems. In general, an eighteenth-century perspective helps one recognise the limits of what liberal-democratic regimes can be expected to do by showing how political thinkers first responded to the emergence of intensified political and economic competition between states.

---

6   English republicanism is a true publishing industry. For just an example, see Wootton (1992). The wide-ranging analysis by Pocock (2003) has been very influential.

7   Indeed, the history of modern democratic theory might be seen as starting only in the late nineteenth century (Geuss, 2001, 110).

The purpose of this chapter is to find a proper object, by means of eighteenth-century political thought, for measuring the extent to which governance might be said to erode democracy in the early twenty-first century. Apparently joining some perceptive political thinkers who insisted as early as a few decades ago that the collapse of socialism did not imply that liberal-democracies were optimally geared to meeting the demands of global political and economic competition,[8] writers now draw attention to the fact that governance, itself seen as a by product of globalised competition, might erode the democratic quality of such states. After surveying the eighteenth-century background to this issue, I conclude that rather than to see governance as likely to negatively affect democracy, it might be argued with considerable force (as well as historical accuracy) that governance should be expected to enhance democracy.

1. Democracy Left Behind (the status of the idea before 1790)

Transposing the discussion of democracy back to the eighteenth century forces one to recognise that democracy was a curse word until the very end of the century, when a strand of American republicans attempted to distinguish their own views from other republican ideas and adopted the term democracy. These late eighteenth-century American republicans broke with a tradition, dating back to Plato and Aristotle, of being highly critical of democracy as a concept in political thought.[9]

Previously, it was by no means excessive to judge democracy in such negative terms as Charles I did, in December 1648, just before he was beheaded. Charles declared that the 'liberty and freedom' of the people 'consists in having of government, those laws by which their life and their goods may be most their own; it is not for having a share in government'. In fact, he judged, 'nothing can more obstruct the long hoped peace of this Nation, than the illegal proceedings of them that presume from servants to become masters and labour to bring in democracy' (Dunn 1993, 3). Democracy was the mere illusion that conflict between human beings, fuelled by their divisive passions, had been fundamentally resolved. Popular government was only a thin veil that served to hide such natural conflict. This view, a commonplace for centuries, was also put forward when the United Provinces suffered a joint attack from France and England in 1672. A pamphlet that summarised the state of Dutch republican political thought before the turmoil stressed that democracy should not be confused for a possible form of government. The anonymous pamphleteer cited Jean Bodin as his authority and argued that 'the principle of popular government is that each person desires to be the master over his fellows, and no one desires to obey, if not on the condition that he will reign. But this way the people cannot be held under control' (Huybert 1672, 5–6). More than a century later, coining the single term 'democracy' was still sufficient to silence those in England who might see any merit in the constitutional debates in the course of the French Revolution. Whereas

---

8   See Dunn (1993), 121–137 and Ascherton (1992).
9   See Farrar (1992) and Dunn (1992).

regicide and the abolition of property laws could be topics for serious discussion, the revolutionaries' spirit of 'democracy' made them totally laughable.[10]

'Democracy', as discussed so far, stood for the unordered anarchic chaos of antiquity that was to be left behind. The political theories of Bodin and Hobbes served to demarcate the unwieldy forces of the multitude from the orders of the state.[11] In the eighteenth century, however, democracy had gradually come to be dismissed as a possible system for modern states for new reasons. Enlightenment political thought emerged under the condition of increasing international economic competition between states and developed new approaches to principles of order in societies, as well as between nations. Montesquieu's *Spirit of the Laws* revolutionised political thought by associating principles of society with systems of government and by evaluating them in the context of eighteenth-century European politics. Montesquieu too (like earlier critics of seventeenth-century English tumults) observed that 'it was a fine spectacle last century to watch the helpless efforts of the English to establish democracy among themselves.' In the midst of great turmoil 'the astonished people searched for democracy and could find it nowhere. In the end, after many movements, shocks and jolts, they were forced to come to rest in just the same form of government as they had earlier proscribed'.[12] But Montesquieu's ideas were part of a new type of argument.

Montesquieu held that a large commercial state that had to defend its independence by engaging in foreign trade could not be a democracy. In spite of citizens' zest for liberty, there were higher powers, it seemed, that kept a country like England from being ruled as a democracy. Political advisors, lawyers, merchants and a wide range of scholars writing in the eighteenth century tried to come to grips with these powers. They were consciously aware of the rift between antiquity and modern times, which translated into a gap between democracies and commercial states. Montesquieu was at the absolute forefront of those trying to understand the challenges to eighteenth-century governance. He famously argued that since the late seventeenth century, democracy was a suitable form of government only for some unfortunate small nations; people, for instance, who were 'constrained to hide in marshes, on islands, on the shoals, and even among dangerous reefs' (Montesquieu 1989, 341). The survival of these communities traditionally hinged on virtues of frugality, moral discipline, restraint and hard labour. Almost in spite of its founding principles, the United Provinces had become a wealthy merchant republic based on these virtues. But the geographical characteristics and the history of this country set this society (like Venice, Florence and other city republics) apart from Europe's large states, for which it could not serve as a model. On this account, which was among the best worked out arguments of a general commonplace, democracies were an

---

10 As in Sir Mile's *The Author of the Letter to the Duke of Grafton Vindicated from the Charges of Democracy* (London, 1794). I thank Mark Somos for providing me with this reference.

11 Dunn (1992, 247) hammers in the point.

12 Montesquieu 1989, Bk. III, Ch. 3, quoted by Dunn (1993, 8).

anachronism in Europe. Trade republics were exceptional societies, exemplifying ancient forms of ascetic virtue that were alien to the stuff that modern states thrived on. Such modern states, which Montesquieu called 'monarchies', were market societies in which the ruling principles were not virtue and love of country, but honour and pride. Individuals interacted through their self-interest, love of money, and their lust for luxury. Inequality was the driving force that enabled states to cultivate their economy and protect their national interest, also through the finance of defensive wars, in a global struggle for hegemony. Containing the excesses of people's self-interested behaviour required the centralised power of a monarchical system. For this reason, market societies simply could not be democracies.

If Montesquieu seems deeply aware of the harshness of eighteenth-century political reality to us, this was not what his contemporaries felt. Some of them believed that Montesquieu had been too positive about the democratic element in monarchies and felt that he displayed too much of a love of democracy.[13] Yet, on the other side of the debate, even the fiercest critics of commercial competition between states (anti-globalists *avant la lettre*, as they might be seen) agreed that returning power to the people was not the solution. Reform, they argued, ought not to take place (merely) at the level of the state, but at the level of human nature's capacities for understanding their own true happiness. Getting rid of the threat of economic competition between states spiralling off into all-out global warfare, such as happened in the Seven Years' War of 1756–63, required reforming the corrupt selfish manners of individuals in market societies.

Forty years before Montesquieu distinguished between the tyrannical, democratic and monarchical forms of government, the Neapolitan Paolo Mattia Doria put forward a different division, where he echoed the earlier tripartite division by the French archbishop Fénelon, the arch father of anti-commercial enlightened cosmopolitanism. Doria discussed how market interaction contributed to man's virtue and happiness in three types of political societies.[14] He distinguished between 'the purely *military* one, when a people unites itself under a captain, [second] the *civil economic* one, … when one unites under the civil law, but with a frugal and moderate lifestyle, and [third] the *civil pompous*, which is when one lives in a more cultured and pompous manner' (Doria 1710, 116). The second type of society served the public good and functioned in accordance with the essence of human nature. Yet, in the history of humankind, the first type of society had developed into the third. This was due to the invention of money. It was true that money existed in 'all civil and cultured countries' and increased the efficiency of the structures by which people took care

---

13 For instance, Galiani (1780/1963, 342–3), who judged that Montesquieu had made too much of an attempt to represent monarchies as potentially democratic, which made it seem as though democratic monarchy was within reach, whereby Montesquieu himself caused the imminent Revolution. For Montesquieu's alleged democratic sympathies, see also Keohane (1972, 383–96) and Judith Shklar (1990).

14 Paolo Matta Doria (1710, 319–337) discusses the nature of markets; 117–29 give the outlines of Doria's three types of political societies.

of each other's self-preservation. But money had arisen 'by an ingenious artifice' and as a 'sign' of 'imaginary value'. The invention of money marked the beginning of an 'abstract economy', which was altogether different from the earlier 'natural economy' that existed between people until that point in time Doria (1710, 321–22). Money changed people's ideas of their happiness: 'because of the growth of wealth in cities, and by conquests and commerce, people's ideas extend themselves; from simple conveniences they move on to splendour.' Thus injected with fresh divisive energy, reciprocal exchange turned into competition and human history spiralled off into increasing jealousy between individuals and states.

Doria accepted that the clock could not be turned back and argued that monarchies were a better form of government than democracies for containing the consequences of the introduction of money. Democracies required 'virtues that were more true than monarchical states' and were 'more vulnerable to turbulences and revolts when the virtue of the citizens corrupted and degenerated into vicious ambition.' Instead, a wise king would be able to steer the development of those sectors of the economy that were directly related to the satisfaction of people's basic needs, and abstain from engaging in luxury trade and balance of trade politics.[15]

In this way, early eighteenth-century cultural critics did not advocate the return of political power to the people, but instead devised ways of taking their vices away from them. Their reform proposals did not attempt to let the multitude back in, but rather set out to unite a divided mankind.

2. Commerce, Competition and International Governance: Continuities in the Modern World

If the central concern of present-day political debate across the board involves the term democracy (or the democratic quality of society), the connecting themes in

---

15 It is often claimed that Doria's distinction between different types of government by their principles and his discussion of true and false virtue were an influence on Montesquieu's *De l'esprit des lois*, but it should at least be recognised that Doria's message was rather the opposite of Montesquieu's. Montesquieu's concept of the moral foundations of modern commerce was diametrically opposed to Doria's. Whereas Doria saw money and luxury themselves as a danger, Montesquieu believed that they lay at the roots of the increased happiness of modern societies compared with earlier ones. Montesquieu's message was expressed very clearly in the *Persian letters*, through a critique on Fénelon's reform proposals in the form of a parody on Fénelon's Boetica and the reform of Salentum. Doria's critique of the aristocracy was typical and rehearsed the accusations towards the nobility's expensive fashions, spendthrift and obstructions of the interest of the people. It preceded the critical reception of Montesquieu's *De l'esprit des lois* in Naples (see De Mas 1971). In that sense certainly, Doria's analysis of the sources of moral corruption and its political consequences is more accurately seen as a proto-Rousseauian cultural critique of modern society. It is also possible that Rousseau knew Doria's *La vita civile*. Jean LeClerc's review in 1716 commented on Doria's way of turning his rejection of luxury into an argument that demanded its correction through a system of political absolutism.

eighteenth-century political discourse were commerce and morality. From attitudes towards the reform of nations into viable commercial societies to the level of global governance, this theme dominated Enlightenment politics. It might also be argued that Enlightenment ideas about commerce and morality are, in some sense, the equivalent of ideas about 'democracy' now. To see the grounds for comparison, we need to look beyond the fact that democracy was neither on the cards as a possibility, nor as a desire for improving the well-being and quality of people in civil society. In this way, it becomes possible to recognise that early eighteenth-century politics still revolved around much the same issues as early twenty-first century politics.

In the mid eighteenth century, national states faced large economic pressures resulting from international competition for hegemony between states. In order to protect the preservation of power and wealth in this international context, smaller states sought to align their national interest with alternative forms of international governance. The problem was commercial competition. As Giovanni Francesco Pagnini noted in his introduction to the Italian translation of John Locke's writings on money, published in 1751 in Florence, commerce decisively divided humankind, even in times of peace. The importance of trade as an aspect of the political survival of states had created a world in which governments were 'obliged to compete with others for the society of commerce, in order to attain their own conservation, their wealth and power'. Whereas strategy used to be crucial in warfare, Pagnini argued, now 'one watches with the same eyes at those citizens who by means of arts and manufactures, no less than soldiers, contribute to' the conservation of the state.[16]

In his introduction to Locke's monetary writings, Pagnini stressed the ambivalent consequences of the caesura between antiquity and modernity. Pagnini keenly repeated Montesquieu's dictum that 'the Romans never knew jealousy of trade. They attacked Carthage as a rival nation, instead of as a commercial nation' (Locke 1751, 70–110). Pagnini's remarks were made against Pompeo Neri, a prominent lawyer and government official from Tuscany, who became famous for his role in the census reform in Lombardy in the years after 1750. Neri, had published a work on monetary reform, entitled *Osservazioni sopra il prezzo legale delle monete* (1751), in which he argued that in a modern 'commercial nation, everyone who did not live in solitude' had 'his interest linked to foreigners'. The natural 'universal commerce of mankind' united 'the whole society of mankind' into 'one single universal republic' (Neri 1751, 40, 121). Commerce connected people all over the world in a universal society that had precedence over political societies. Thus, according to Neri, commerce always retained its own supra-national character and was immune for any political manipulations.

Neri's *Osservazioni* formed a crucial statement from Milan in the context of a series of negotiations with the court of Turin to form a monetary union with Lombardy and Tuscany (Venturi 1969, 468–77). Pagnini himself was a government minister in the grand duchy of Tuscany, who was responsible for financial administration and thus on the receiving end of Neri's proposals for an Italian monetary union.

---

16 See Locke (1751), 96–8; see also Stapelbroek (2005), 79–110.

Like Neri, Pagnini described 'commercial society' as 'a type of society' that created 'universal' ties between people and which was '*supereminente*' – it transcended all categories of political power. This type of society emerged when, in the course of history, the 'needs and desires of people' expanded, and more people – as well as more complicated organisational structures – were necessary to satisfy them. Yet, Pagnini stressed, this 'new sort of society [that] was formed between people far away from each other' united people who were also, and already, divided 'by the universal of their relations in various different bodies and societies' (Locke 1751, 160–3).

Commerce united people, but states divided them. Thus Pagnini's message to Neri was that commerce did not actually unite humankind into a single republic. Pagnini agreed with Neri that people's interests were linked through trade, but felt that Neri had been mistaken about the moral foundations as well as the political consequences of commercial society and that this affected the realism of his design of a monetary union. When Pagnini – a Florentine government minister responsible for financial affairs – wrote about Locke and antiquity, the message to Neri (who had also used Locke's ideas in support of his monetary union) was that Tuscan officials held different ideas of the nature of commerce and were not going to support Neri's plan for a monetary union.

Pagnini's response to Neri brings to light a confrontation between two of the most influential European perspectives on international governance in the eighteenth century. These rival views were built on alternative conceptualisations of the nature of market exchange relationships and their political correlates and consequences. Was commerce capable of channelling the most violent passions for domination in human nature or would it amplify them and turn trade into a new object of aggressive competition between states? Neri was optimistic and thought that a monetary union that served to regulate international trade was naturally in every state's interest. Pagnini thought this was naïve but still believed that the aggressive excesses of commercial competition between states would check themselves since the economic costs of warfare would be too high to make belligerent powers emerge as winners in the modern world.

The Italian debate on money and its regulation in an international context was only one slice of the European Enlightenment. The general challenge of the latter was to find moral and political standards for making separate national interests correspond to a global order in which trade competition was monitored and threats to peace were neutralised. With these ideals in mind, eighteenth-century political thinkers reflected on a series of institutional reform arrangements and contemplated large-scale financial experiments involving the national debt. Thus progressing, the term democracy used in a positive sense, quite surprisingly, resurfaced near the end of the eighteenth century.

3. The Invention of Modern Democracy in the 1790s

The enduring pressure of international competitive forces on national states and their policy strategies in the eighteenth century triggered a momentous international exchange of ideas about human nature, self-interest and morality, which is usually referred to as the Enlightenment. The formulation of these ideas, as we saw, went along with reflections on projects for aligning domestic policies with character of international governance. Likewise, the imperative logic of commerce and competition forced French thinkers and, under different conditions, the American founding fathers to reconsider principles of government and mechanisms of aggregation of individual interests into state interest. From these contexts of eighteenth-century policy, redevelopment processes ensued what has become our present-day positive use of the term democracy.

It is necessary to consider two interdependent genealogies of the notion of democracy in the modern world. One involves French Enlightenment political thought, from anti-Louis XIV sentiments in the first decades of the century to the constitutional debates in the aftermath of the French Revolution. The expensive wars of the time of Louis XIV that immersed the nation in debt lay at the root of a century of thinking about reforms. Coming to terms with the lasting consequences of Louis XIV's reign for France's place in Europe and laying out a plan for its economic and political future, the heavily polarised debate oscillated between the two ideological poles of neo-Colbertist 'mercantilism' and Fénelonian moralising cosmopolitan agriculturalism. In order to get rid of the burden of public debt and mitigate the effects of dynastic rule, a series of spectacularly daring attempts to revive the French economy and to prevent the Revolution were proposed. Gradually, the opposed positions moved closer to each other in the course of the century, and mutually adopted elements of the other party's solutions.[17] At the end of process stood the political works and constitutional proposals of the *abbé* Emmanuel Sièyes (Sonenscher, ed. 2003).

Sièyes himself did not so much reintroduce the term democracy into political thought as create the preconditions for it to become a label of the type of state structure that he envisaged as the solution for grounding the finances of the French state upon new constitutional principles. Sièyes became known, not undeservedly, as the main inventor of what is now called representative democracy. In the advent of the Terror following the French Revolution, he was one of the main architects of the system in which the new republic, led by a commercial bourgeois class, took over the public debt of the French royal state and put itself at the head of a market society. For Sièyes it was clear that the type of constitution he invented was not a democracy, but rather it's opposite. In the first place, representative government did not give the power to rule back to the people, but responded to a more pressing and altogether different need: 'The common interest, the improvement of the state of society itself

---

17 See Sonenscher (1997), 64–103, 267–325, for the relation between the public debt in France and the French Revolution as an option for reform in the decades before 1789.

cries out for us to make Government a special profession'.[18] Sièyes' structures formed mainly a solution for the problem of cancelling the national debt and created a buffer against political power abuse through dynastic ambitions that were alien to the national interest. The new French state should simply be led by people who could be expected to act more naturally in its economic and political interest. This system of government that arose out of the French Revolution entailed some idea about the moral accommodation of self-interested market behaviour, but did not necessarily aim principally to sort out any problems of inequality, injustices and inefficiencies of commercial society. It certainly did not abandon the idea that commerce was a primarily selfish activity, in local markets, as well as internationally. Sièyes' state was too firmly grounded in a Hobbesian social psychology to be confused for a cosmopolitan theory of universally united free democracies.[19]

In the same period, the American constitutional debate revolved around similar issues. One of its icons, Thomas Paine, suggested that representative democracy was in fact quite close to democracy, only better. The American state was 'representation engrafted upon Democracy'. While direct democracies were 'inconvenient', nothing was lost, and a lot of efficiency was added in representative democracies. Thus, Paine denied what was initially implicit and increasingly explicit in Sieyes' writings, that democracy was a misnomer for representative government. For Paine, representative government was fortified direct democracy.

Moreover, Paine imagined that representative democracies were the most suitable structures for realising the potential of commerce for transforming competing states into a universal republic of humankind. Paine held that commerce was 'a pacific system, operating to cordialise mankind, by rendering Nations, as well as individuals, useful to each other'. Commerce was set to bring about a 'universal civilisation' and representative democracy was the state form that would make this vision come true (Paine 2000).

Unsurprisingly, in 1792 Paine was the first person in modern times to mention the term democracy in a positive way, in the second part of the *Rights of Man*.[20] Edmund Burke responded to Paine by accusing him of not having the faintest idea what democracy was, that democracy was put of place in modern times, and that it was ultimately naïve to believe that some idea of it might be useful in late eighteenth-century politics.[21] In spite of Burke's immediate critique, and of a host of similar complaints expressed in the form of pamphlets, Paine's idea to call representative government democracy caught on in the American republican constitutional debates

---

18 Quoted by Manin (1997, 3). In his introduction, Manin stresses that Sièyes (and Madison) opposed direct democracy.

19 Istvan Hont (1994, 166–231), reprinted in Hont (2005, 125–141).

20 Thanks to Mark Somos who went through a great many sources of the time to establish this significant fact. See Paine 2000, 229–31. The idea was repeated in Paine's *Dissertations on the first principles of Government*, of 1795.

21 For the context of the French and American debates revolving around Paine and Burke see Gregory Claeys (ed.) (1995), esp. vols. I–II, V–VI.

of the time. Andrew Jackson's hired pens popularised the idea further by exploiting its imaginative appeal, and the idea of democracy was given a new lease.

The differences between Sièyes and Paine were played out against each other directly in correspondence with each other (and about each other to other people). Obviously, Sièyes disliked Paine's use of the term democracy, which made representative government look like something it was not. More importantly, he could not agree with Paine's views that made it seem as though what he called democracy was capable of radically changing the face of the earth. Paine's democracy promised far too much.

A mediocre parody on Paine's *Rights of Man, II* exemplifies the standard reaction among contemporaries to his idealistic image of the role of the American style of government in a global trend towards peaceful universal commerce. The anonymous author of *Buff, or a dissertation on nakedness, a parody on Paine's Rights of Man* (London 1792) interpolated a number of phrases, replacing ideas of freedom with ideas of nakedness, thereby transforming 'the grand chorus of the Rights of man' into 'a canzonetta on Nakedness'. The text of *Buff* included Paine's original critique of Sièyes' alleged hesitation to present his democratic sentiments in the form of a democratic theory:

> The preference, which the Abbé has given, is a condemnation of the thing he prefers. Such a mode of reasoning is inadmissible, because it finally amounts to an accusation upon Providence as if she had left to man no other choice than between two evils, the best of which he admits to be an outrage upon society. This sort of superstition may last a few years more, but it cannot long resist the awakened reason and interest of man. (Anonymous 1792, 15)

In the hands of Paine, Sièyes's views had been seriously disfigured. Paine associated Sièyes political vision with his own ideal of a providentially guided evolution of global politics towards cosmopolitan democracy. This allowed the author of *Buff*, for instance, to suggest that both thinkers advocated a return to primitive nature, and to confuse Sièyes's idea of commercial freedom in a state for pre-social nakedness. Whereas Sièyes's constitutional proposals had a clear limited purpose and remained strictly within the boundaries of a particular eighteenth-century political debate, Paine's promises for the future of democracy seemed designed to virtually overturn the whole of human history. Paine's use of democracy not only provoked critics to revert to classical disqualifications of democracy as uncivilised anarchic lack of order, it also inadvertently invited confusion about the focus and limits of modern politics.

4. Conclusion: Expectations from and Limits of Modern Democracy

In present-day western (and global) politics, representative democracy is the dominant system of government. But what can be expected of it? An excursus into the eighteenth-century history of the term democracy has brought up two interpretations of what representative democracy might be taken to stand for and what citizens of a particular state might reasonably understand to be the purpose of this form of government.

It would be most in tune with Sièyes's eighteenth-century perception to see modern democracy (deceptively) simply as the name of a system of representative government that charges politicians with the responsibility of taking care of the interest of the nation. In the words of John Dunn, the strength of such a system of government resides in its fragility. It preserves its integrity as a counteracting force to democracy and smoothes the sharp edges of capitalism, and for these reasons it has proven resilient in the modern world (Dunn 1992, 246–52, 258). In this perspective, the purpose of the state is not seen as understanding and regulating markets and their moral functioning. Insofar as politics interferes with the outcomes of market interaction, this is based on the notion that the security of individuals is to be protected, not necessarily on theoretical principles of social justice. Similarly, the balance between private and public goods is based on continuous negotiation between actors in the public realm, rather than on an externally imagined, or defined, standard of where the responsibility of the state ceases. Representative democracy, thus understood, is an essentially open-ended, and undefined style of government. One of its strengths, it appears, has been its implicit acceptance of the limits of thinking about the relation between commerce and politics (or capitalism and democracy) (Dunn 1992, 252–5, 259–60, 263). Whereas Paine held ambitious ideals in which nations might be united through commerce, Sièyes's mechanisms of representative government were not based on any particularly fixed idea of markets as playing a role in bridging gaps between states. Consequently, Sièyes's views could not lead to anywhere near the wild promises about the power of democracy that Paine made and that seem much closer to the present-day discourse of democratic government in which democracy eventually became 'the name for the good intentions of states or perhaps for the good intentions which their rulers would like us to believe that they possess' (Dunn 1992, 13). As signalled in the first section, in recent decades the use of the term democracy widened, through which it became a label for various reference points by which politicians, commentators in the media and other writers juxtaposed desirable and reprehensible aspects of their own and other societies. Democracy in an international context is often seen as the opposite of tyranny by the state (and lack of a political system in which elections have a place apparently makes such states illegitimate).[22] Similarly, the idea of a democratic deficit in modern western states (liberal democracies) represents a host of similar complaints, though very moderate versions of real struggles against tyranny: people feel their liberties could be better taken care of, the exercise of their activities is curbed, the desires that people see as part of their identities are somehow interfered with. Democracy can mean the absence of imperfections in how individuals in a nation-state feel about the

---

22 The Second World War Allies, according to John Dunn (2005) converted democracy' into a slogan, in a manner not too dissimilar to how Tom Paine's use of the term turned it into a slogan in the American 1790s.

organisation of their societies and the arrangement of political prerogatives. But one also considers, for instance, the future of Islam in the western world as the question whether Shariya law is reconcilable with democracy. The most convincing argument for winning over popular opinion in western nations to justify intervening in the affairs of a sovereign state is that democracy has to be installed. And, interestingly an important perspective on how violence against western societies might be countered led to a book entitled *Terrorism Versus Democracy* (which was first published before 9/11, but unsurprisingly has had a lot of reprints) (Wilkinson 2001).

Such widespread use of the term democracy in evaluating the state of affairs in disparate fields of society stands in shrill contrast to the serious limitations that contemporary political thinkers perceive in theories of democracy (Shapiro 2001). The real problem does not seem to be that representative democracy is incapable of furthering people's well-being. But there appears to be a genuine gap between the way in which it does so, and the manner in which party politics in the western world suggests more ambitious purposes for representative democracy than are feasible. Insofar as democratically elected politicians set out to remove abuses of power and protect the security and facilitate the interested action of individual citizens, they act in accordance with Sièyes's purpose of representative democracy. But when politicians promise and subsequently, after being elected, are expected to create public happiness, the limits of representative democracy are exposed. The confusion about the limits of modern democracy that arose from the Sièyes–Paine controversy has a prominent place at various levels of present-day politics. While politicians simply do their job, but promise to do more than that, people expect ever more from democratic governments.

To conclude, nowadays – in everyday language, news programmes in the media, as well as in academic publications – the term democracy is predominantly used as a shorthand indicating simultaneously a type of political system and its presumed objective. That is to say, since the second half of the twentieth century, the word democracy increasingly represents an imagined touchstone of desirable political organisation, in which the liberties and maximum happiness of the people are guaranteed. As such, it is often associated with the notion of representative government and the constitutional arrangements that were proposed by the *abbé* Emmanuel Joseph Sièyes in the French Revolution. However, as we have seen, representative democracy, understood as the careful transferral of sovereignty to the nation without abandoning the absolute rule of the state, was at the time specifically proposed as a possible antidote to the escalation, at home and abroad, of economic competition between states. This idea of representative democracy is to be seen as the result of eighteenth-century political thought. Yet, in the course of the last centuries, the word democracy has come to bear other connotations. The term democracy, in its current meaning, effectively implies the success of a specific political order in silencing potential disorders arising from natural and artificial characteristics of communities of people. If this use of the term is taken to be the outcome not of a wild semantic drift, but of a proper development of the idea of democracy caused by a particular logic of historical complexity, how might the idea of governance fit in?

What is called lack of democracy is not the failing of but rather the imperfections of representative government. Representative democracy emerged as a way of correcting domestic styles of governance with an eye on international commercial competition, but it is now expected to perfect national politics. One might explain the perceived shift from government to governance through this context. Could it be the case that the rise of governance, as distinct from centralised state government, is a response (in whatever way) to the gap between authentic purposes of representative government and the promises and expectations that go along with present-day meanings of the word democracy? Thus, governance would be seen as supplementing representative government and forcing Hobbesian states to give way, in a controlled manner, to the forces of the multitude. If this is the case, it would seem more reasonable to wonder whether governance has not increased democracy in modern societies, instead of whether it sustains and enhances a democratic deficit in the modern world. Any positive answers would suggest a historical turning point since democracy, really, was never a realistic notion in modern politics. But for any statement on the issues goes that in order to be instructive, it is crucial to first eliminate basic confusions about the term democracy and its history.

References

Ascherton, N. '1989 in Eastern Europe, Constitutional Representative Democracy as a 'Return to Normality'?', *Democracy: The Unfinished Journey, 508 BC to AD 1993*, (ed.) John Dunn (Oxford: Oxford University Press), pp. 221–237.

[Anonymous] (1792), *Buff, or a Dissertation on Nakedness, a Parody on Paine's Rights of Man* (London).

Arrow, K.J. (1963), *Social Choice and Individual Values*, 2nd edition. (New Haven: Yale University Press).

Claeys, G. (ed.) (1995), *Political Writings of the 1790s*, eight volumes (London: Pickering and Chatto).

De Mas, E. (1971), *Montesquieu, Genovesi e la edizione del spirito delle leggi* (Florence: Olschki).

Doria, P.M. (1710), *La Vita Civile,* 2nd edition (Naples).

Dunn, J. (2005), *Setting the People Free: The Story of Democracy* (London: Atlantic Books).

_____ (1993), *Western Political Theory in the Face of the Future,* 2nd edition (Cambridge: Cambridge University Press).

_____ (1992), 'Conclusion', in Dunn (ed.), pp. 239–66.

_____ (ed.) (1992) *Democracy: The Unfinished Journey, 508 BC to AD 1993*, (Oxford: Oxford University Press).

Farrar, C. (1992), 'Ancient Greek Political Theory as a Response to Democracy', in Dunn (ed.), pp. 17–40.

Galiani, F. (1963), *Della moneta,* A. Caracciolo and A. Merola (eds.) (Milan: Feltrinelli). [1780, 2nd edition (Naples: Raimondi)].

Gelderen, M. van, and Skinner Q.R.D. (eds.) (2002), *Republicanism: A Shared European Heritage,* two volumes (Cambridge: Cambridge University Press).

Geuss, R. (2001), *History and Illusion in Politics* (Cambridge: Cambridge University Press).

Hont, I. (2005), *Jealousy of Trade: International Competition and the Nation-State in Historical Perspective* (Cambridge, MA: Belknap Press of Harvard University Press).

_____ (1994), 'The Permanent Crisis of a Divided Mankind: "Contemporary Crisis of the Nation State" in Historical Perspective', *Political Studies*, John Dunn (ed), 66–231.

Hornblower, S. (1992), 'The Creation and Development of Democratic Institutions in Ancient Greece', in Dunn (ed.), pp.1–16.

Huybert, P. de (1672), *Verdediging van de Oude Hollantsche Regeringh, onder een Stadthouder en een Kapiteyn Generael* (Amsterdam: J. v. Someren).

Keohane, N.O. (1972), 'Virtuous Republics and Glorious Monarchies: Two Models in Montesquieu's Political Thought', *Political Studies* 10:4, 383–96.

Locke, J. (1751), *Ragionamenti sopra la moneta, l'interesse del danaro, le finanze e il commercio*, two volumes (Florence).

Manin, B. (1997), *The Principles of Representative Government* (Cambridge: Cambridge University Press).

Mile, S. (1794), *The Author of the Letter to the Duke of Grafton Vindicated from the Charges of Democracy* (London).

Montesquieu (1989), *The Spirit of the Laws* (translated and edited by A.M. Cohler, B.C. Miller and H.S. Stone, Cambridge: Cambridge University Press).

Neri, P. (1751), *Osservazioni sopra il prezzo legale delle monete* (Milan).

Paine, T. (2000), *Political Writings,* B. Kuklick (ed), (Cambridge: Cambridge University Press).

Pocock, J.G.A. (2003), *The Machiavellian Movement: Florentine Political Thought and the Atlantic Republican Tradition* [1975] (Princeton, N.J: Princeton University Press).

Schumpeter, J. A. (1976), *Capitalism, Socialism and Democracy* [1943] (London: Allen and Unwin).

Shapiro, I. (2003), *The State of Democratic Theory* (Princeton, NJ: Princeton University Press).

Shapiro I. and Casiano Hacker-Cordón (eds.) (1999), *Democracy's Value,* (Cambridge: Cambridge University Press).

Shklar, J. (1990), 'Montesquieu and the New Republicanism', in Gisela Bock, Quentin Skinner, Maurizio Viroli (eds.) *Machiavelli and Republicanism* (Cambridge: Cambridge University Press).

Skinner, Q. (1992), 'The Italian City-Republics', in Dunn (ed.), pp. 57–70.

Sonenscher, M. (ed.) (2003), *Sieyès: Political Writings, Including the Debate between Sieyès and Tom Paine in 1791* (Indianapolis, Ind.: Hackett).

____ (1997), 'The Nation's Debt and the Birth of the Modern Republic: The French Fiscal Deficit and the Politics of the Revolution of 1789', *History of Political Thought* 18:1–2, 64–103, 267–325.

Stapelbroek, K. (2005), 'The Devaluation Controversy in Eighteenth-Century Italy', *History of Economic Ideas* 13:2, 79–110.

Venturi, F. (1969), 'Il dibattito sulle monete', *Da Muratori a Beccaria, Settecento riformatore*, volume 1 (Turin: Einaudi).

Wilkinson, P. (2001), *Terrorism Versus Democracy: The Liberal State Response* (London: Cass).

Wootton, D. (1992), 'The Levellers', in Dunn (ed.), pp. 71–90.

PART II
GOVERNANCE AT A DISTANCE
AND MARKET GOVERNANCE

Chapter 5

Governance, Democracy and the European Modernization Agenda: A Comparison of Different Policy Initiatives

Victor Bekkers, Menno Fenger, Evelien Korteland

'Government matters. We all want it to deliver policies, programmes and services that will make us more healthy, more secure and better equipped to tackle the challenges we face. Government should improve the quality of our lives. Modernization is vital if government is to achieve that ambition'. These are the opening phrases of the vision statement in a document that the Prime Minister of the United Kingdom, Tony Blair, presented to Parliament in March 1999 (Ministry of the Cabinet Office 1999). During the last five years several modernization and public innovation programs have been drafted in different European countries. These initiatives emerged in response to new ideas about the organization and management of public sector organizations – like New Public Management (NPM) and the discussion on 'governance' – on the one hand and the major cut back operations due to public finance considerations on the other hand. In these programs, ideas have been developed about the need for change within the public sector. From a governance point of view, these programs could be assumed to develop a perspective on state-society relations in a world that is growing ever more complex, interdependent and therefore hard to govern. Moreover, these programs might provide answers to doubts concerning the efficacy and efficiency of government, which in the end could influence the legitimacy of government. In response, governments are shifting problem-solving capacity towards other layers of government or towards the private sector. This shift from 'government' towards 'governance' can be understood as a modernization strategy.

This chapter analyses strategic policy documents from four countries in which the outlines have been formulated of the most recent modernization strategies of government. While these programmes might provide an indication of the dominant shifts in governance that occur in public administration, we want to go one step further. A closer examination of these programs could reveal the dominant frames of reference that lay behind these programs and the arguments that have been given for this reform agenda. We can suggest three reasons for this exercise. According to Edelman (1967, 1977) the de-construction of policy discourses, the discovery of 'bias' and the demystification of the stories, myths and symbols that are related and deployed by policy-makers is one of the core challenges of the policy sciences and policy analysis (see also Fisher and Forrester 1993; Parsons 1996). How valid are the claims and demands that have been formulated? Rhetoric, 'language' and symbols play an important role in the (re) construction of a narrative of what caused a problem and what actions should be undertaken to address the problem (Edelman 1967; 1977; Stone 2002). The second reason is that language, rhetoric and symbolism can also play an important role in public administration because it can contribute to the creation of a shared frame of reference, or even a common 'grammar' within and outside public administration (Weick 1969; Pfeffer and Salancik 1978; March and Olson 1989). From this point of view, policy documents might be seen as a source of inspiration that contributes to the enactment of desired policy reality because of its persuasive power (Majone 1989). Meyer and Rowan (1977) suggest the third reason. They have shown the importance of 'myths' and 'ceremonies' that legitimize the transformation of organizations to meet changing environmental conditions in order secure success, survival and resources. New public sector management techniques and reforms – such as NPM – as well as the notion of 'governance' can be seen as myths and ceremonies, which, if adopted and performed, add to legitimacy of an organization towards its environment. Conformity implies success; non-conformity implies failure.

In this chapter we focus on the assumptions – or, more specifically, the language and rhetoric that are used to express them – that lay behind a number of shifts and modes of governance as proposed in four European countries' programs to modernize government. These countries are The Netherlands, the United Kingdom, Germany and Denmark. The first question is: What are the basic assumptions behind the shifts in governance that are presented in a number of strategic policy documents on government modernization? As we have seen in the previous chapters, these shifts in governance might be understood as methods to counter the shrinking legitimacy of these countries' public sectors. Simultaneously, these shifts in governance might have unintended consequences for processes of democracy and legitimacy, even if they have been developed to improve citizens' trust in government. For instance, processes of multi-level governance might lead to a democratic deficit, if we apply the principles of representative democracy. Hence, it is important to look how attention has been paid to the strengthening of the governments' legitimacy in various modernization programs and what these attempts imply for the dominant model of representative democracy. Is it presumed that these efforts strengthen the existing model of representative democracy, or it is necessary to look for other democracy models to fill in possible democratic gaps?

Section one describes our research strategy for selecting and comparing relevant modernization programs. In section two, we analyze the modernization programs of four European countries that were drafted between 1999 and 2003. We try to discern the driving factors behind the quest for modernization, the goals that have been formulated and the measures that have been taken. In addition, we analyse the shifts in governance that emerge from these modernization programs. In the final step of our analysis, we focus on the consequences of these programs for democracy and legitimacy. Section three provides a comparison of the 'modernization of government' initiatives in the four countries. In section four we reflect on the implications of our research findings, and in section five, we draw the conclusion that the major shift in governance is focused on the empowerment of citizens as consumers. Complementary to representative democracy, a new democratic model has emerged that has been described as a consumer democracy.

1. Research Strategy

In the previous section, we suggested why it is important to focus on the assumptions behind the public innovation programs that have been formulated in a number of European countries during the last five years. In this section we present the reasons for selecting The Netherlands, the United Kingdom, Denmark and Germany as countries to be studied. Moreover, we present a framework to analyze the different modernization programs.

Case Study Selection

In order to analyze the assumptions behind these modernization programs, we have compared and analyzed strategic policy programs of four OECD countries: The Netherlands, Germany, the United Kingdom, and Denmark. These countries fit in a specific 'ideal type' of state and governance traditions (Louglin and Peters 1997). The first state tradition is the Anglo Saxon tradition in which the relationship between state and society can be described as pluralistic, resulting in a policy style that resembles Lindblom's notion of 'muddling through'. Loughlin and Peters (1997) define this state tradition as limited federalism, in which there is a degree of decentralization towards the states (United States) and local government (United Kingdom). The second state tradition is the Germanic one, in which the relationship between state and society is viewed as organistic. The political organization can be characterized as that of an organic federation in which the emphasis lies on the cooperation between the different territorial layers of government (cooperative federalism between *Bund* and *Länder*). The dominant policy style is legalistic and corporatist, in which policymaking is the outcome of cooperation between employers, employees and the state. In the French state tradition a strong distinction and antagonistic relationship between state and society prevails. There is a Jacobean perspective on the political organization of the state: the state is 'one' and 'indivisible', which also affects the degree of decentralization. In the French tradition we see a unitary but regionalized state. The dominant policy style is technocratic, while it is at the same time based on the 'rule of the law'. The last tradition is the Scandinavian tradition, in which the relationship between state and society can be defined as organistic, which also influences the dominant policy style. Loughlin and Peters (1997) describe it as consensual. In the Scandinavian state tradition, local communities and municipalities play an important role, based on a strong local autonomy. The dominant political organization of the state is decentralized, although it is perceived as a unitary state. The United Kingdom, Denmark and Germany fit in the state traditions that were named after them. The Netherlands can be seen as the combination of German and Anglo-Saxon elements. There are no countries from the French state tradition in our selection of cases due to the lack of written modernization programs in English.

The modernization of government is not a matter of publishing one single strategic policy document. The programs we have studied are all part of a wider set of policy programs, plans and other documents. Most of the programs have been succeeded by a more detailed policy document that focused on implementation issues. However, we have analyzed the most strategic document during the last six or seven years. We did not study progress reports because we are primarily interested in how the need for modernization has been framed.

A Framework for Analysis

In order to compare the four modernization programs, it is important to have a framework that makes the assumptions that we are seeking explicit. The modernization of government can be defined as the ability of government to adapt to developments in different political, socio-economic and cultural environments in which a government organization operates as well as the ability to respond and anticipate on the needs of different stakeholders in these environments. Stakeholders include citizens, companies, societal organizations and other government organizations. The ultimate test of successful modernization is the ability of governments to act as legitimate political organizations. This refers to the binding allocation of public goods, resources and public values for a community as a whole. Politics and public policy are about communities trying to achieve collective goals that contribute to economic growth, like the creation of safe neighborhoods, a sustainable environment or a transport infrastructure. Modernization can be understood in relation to specific changes in the different environments in which government organizations operate. In order to respond to these changes and developments, it is necessary for governments to reflect on their position and role in society. This can also influence how governments want to intervene in society, and it can lead to specific shifts in power from the central state institutions to other layers of government or societal sectors. These reflections can be translated into specific modes of governance, which can be worked out into more detailed programs of actions. However, if we look at the binding decisions that are taking place in these governance practices, these shifts of power have to be legitimized. This line of reasoning has led to a research design in which the assumptions presented below are perceived as relevant.

Assumptions relating to possible forces for modernization   The nature of the societal problems that governments should address is one set of assumptions that should be analyzed because these problems can be seen as possible forces for modernization. The perception of these problems challenges the problem solving capacity of government; and thus the role and position of government vis à vis other public and private actors. Examples are the aging of the population, the empowerment of the citizen, the rise of the information society or the globalization of the economy, and the importance of the European Union.

Assumptions related to goals of modernization and shifts of governance Given the perception of the problems, what shifts and modes in governance (governance at a distance, market-governance, multi-level governance, network governance and societal self-governance) have been proposed as a strategy for handling these problems? Which modernization goals have been formulated in reaction to these problems and in relation to changing views regarding the role and position of government? Are the shifts of governance that are being proposed perceived as possible answers to strengthening the legitimacy of government? And, if we look at the modernization goals, do they refer to specific political values that should be accomplished, like efficiency, accountability or participation?

Assumptions related to specific measures and actions to be taken The next group of assumptions refers to the specific actions that should be implemented in order to establish these new governance arrangements that will meet the desired goals. For instance, the empowerment of citizens as consumers implies that citizens should be given more personal freedom to choose. How is this freedom of choice realized? What instruments should be deployed? One step could be improving the transparency of government in which citizens could compare the prices of government services, through the Internet for example.

Assumptions relating to the democratic nature of governance The last set of assumptions refers to the attention that is explicitly – or even implicitly – paid to the democratic nature of the proposed governance practices. Are the shifts and dominant modes of governance perceived as a way to strengthen the democracy? Or, do these programs recognize that perhaps these new governance arrangements will result in a democratic deficit if we assess them from the perspective of representative democracy? We have tried to reconstruct these assumptions through a qualitative analysis of the content of policy programs. We have looked at language and arguments that have been used to frame the challenges that government is said to be confronted with and the measures they think will be necessary.

2. Modernizing Government

In this section we describe and analyse four modernization initiatives that have been drafted during the last decade in Denmark, The Netherlands, the United Kingdom and Germany.

Denmark

In May 2002 the Danish government launched its public sector modernization program entitled *Citizens at the Wheel*. The program provides a framework for renewal and describes the goals of the public sector for the future as well as examples of measures that are being implemented. The document might be seen as an isolated document, but it fits into a continuous line of modernization projects.

Forces for modernization   The program *Citizens at the Wheel* claims that renewal of the Danish public sector is essential. However, the program itself is vague about the arguments on which this claim is based.

The program states that 'the public sector needs modernization' (p. 1). The document refers to 'major challenges in the coming years', but only pays attention to the rising number of elderly people while the number of people of working age remains unchanged. This will exert considerable pressure on state expenditure since more people will need to have care provided (p. 19). Externally this will lead to a rising demand for existing and new public services. Internally, within public administration a large number of people will retire, which can affect the functioning and organization of the public sector. In order to manage this problem the public sector should become more efficient and more attractive for younger people (p. 19).

Hence, referring to a profound analysis of societal challenges has not legitimized the modernization program of the Danish government; the aging population is the only motive used.

Modernization goals and shifts in governance   The goals of the Danish modernization program reflect a governance paradigm based on freedom and solidarity. In *Citizens at the Wheel*, the emphasis lies on the establishment of a major shift in governance in favor of the citizen. It must insure that the public sector is based on a) the free choice of citizens, b) is open, simple and responsive and c) provides value for money and is thus more efficient (p. 5). This implies that citizens should be at the wheel (p. 31).

The suggested solutions refer to the public sector's ability to adapt to the needs of the citizens. This requires a critical examination of existing structures and responsibilities (p. 5). In order to do so, government has to create simpler and more transparent rules and to eliminate systems that obstruct the expression of individual initiative (p. 5). However, the increased availability of alternatives does not mean that an individual citizen can get whatever he or she likes. Freedom of choice, which implies the availability of alternatives to choose between private and public organizations (as voluntary organizations) – is especially important in social service areas (pp. 6, 8). However, the availability of these alternative service arrangements must exist with an order of priorities and politically determined service levels (p. 7). Politically elected politicians will decide on the services and the quality level that has to be offered (pp. 7, 22), while operations and the organization of the work within individual institutions will be the responsibility of the institution's management

(p. 22). Accordingly, costs and results must be made visible, because political prioritization of public funds requires that expenditures should be made transparent (p. 22). Moreover, government should create a framework that allows different suppliers to offer innovative solutions and that creates diversity in the services that will be provided (p. 8). In order to meet the needs of the Danish citizen, collaboration between different organizations in the public sector is necessary, especially between municipalities but also between the public sector and voluntary organizations. The interplay between the latter could contribute to the development of solutions that are more responsive to the needs of citizens (p. 23).

Hence, the dominant modes of governance, which emerge in the slipstream of the shift in governance in favor of the citizen, are market governance – because of the emphasis on freedom of choice, governance at a distance – because of the emphasis on the accountability for the services which are rendered, and network governance – due to the emphasis on collaboration.

Measures to be taken   The shift from a state-centered to a citizen-centered mode of governance requires actual measures to be implemented. From the analysis of the modernization program, we can identify three clusters of measures the Danish government seeks to implement.

The first cluster of measures deals with the actual freedom of choice. A prerequisite for the freedom of choice is that there are alternatives to choose among. Government should therefore facilitate alternative suppliers. Furthermore, there should be an adequate level of information concerning the various choices and services that are available. Also, the quality of services to be rendered should be satisfactory (p. 8). In addition to these measures, the legal position of citizens should also be improved (p. 10).

The second cluster of measures relates to a more open, simplified and user-friendlier administration. Rule and administrative simplification and the reduction of administrative burdens are important measures to be taken, not only for citizens but also for the business community (pp. 12, 13, 17). In order to realize this, information and communication technology plays an important role. As e-government becomes more widespread, it is the Danish government's aim to allow citizens and businesses to monitor the progress of their own cases via the Internet, and to be able to receive information on case procedures, decisions and case processing times. The responsiveness of government is not only based on the creation of a more open and transparent administration, but also on the active involvement and consultation of citizens and users (p. 17). This will be more far-reaching than the influence that citizens currently enjoy through user boards etc. It is defined as a fundamental matter of every public institution, which also presupposes that citizens will assume a certain degree of responsibility and to make an active contribution towards helping to shape the public sector (p. 17).

In order to stimulate the necessary changes, the Danish government wants to reward institutions for their efforts. In some areas the amount of financing depends on the number of citizens who choose the supplier of particular services. In this way, the supplier of these services will enter into healthy competition to increase quality (p. 23). Moreover, more competition emphasizes the need for each institution to work systematically to improve quality and efficiency and to organize their work in a holistic way (p. 23). The importance of competition also implies that private companies have the opportunity to challenge the efficiency of the public sector. That is why local and central government should be able to explain why a given task should be undertaken by the public sector, if a company makes the case that it can perform better and at a lower price (p. 24).

Assumptions regarding the democratic nature of governance   The final element in our analytical framework concerns the assumptions that refer to the democratic nature of the proposed shifts and modes of governance. One could state that the fact that citizens do not have a choice in the method and type of public service delivery in Denmark suggests that the existing structure had some shortcomings. This could be defined as a democratic deficit of the existing model of representative democracy. The public sector should adapt to suit the needs of citizens – not the other way around (p. 5). In *Citizens at the Wheel*, this deficit is eliminated by enhancing the freedom of choice of citizens within the framework of representative democracy and the primacy of politics. Politicians can be more responsive to the citizens' needs because they have improved the citizens' access to the political system in such a way that citizens can raise their voice and make clear what their needs are. The openness of the agenda has improved. On the output side, politicians have enabled citizens to a better choice of the kind, number and range of services they want, how they should be provided and under what conditions.

The Netherlands

In 2003 the Dutch government presented a perspective on how to modernize government that was defined as 'Other Government'. The main document is an action program. This program was followed by a vision document from the Cabinet, which conceptually tries to legitimize the actions of the action program.

Forces for modernization   The Action Program states that changing societal conditions have been the motive for the Dutch government to reflect on its role (p. 3). Government has been forced into a position in which it is expected to solve all small and major societal problems through rather detailed regulations. However, it appears that government is frequently incapable of solving those problems. According to the Action Program, this should lead to a re-formulation of the role of government and a re-formulation of the role and position of the citizen. The citizen needs to evolve into an empowered citizen, who is (or should be) willing to participate in society and who is (or should be) self-responsible. A new social contract between these fully empowered citizens and government is needed. Such a contract helps government to define its core capabilities in relation to the core problems of society. At the same time, this new contract makes clear that the handling of other societal problems is a joint responsibility of government, the private sector and the civil society (p. 4).

But what are these changing social problems and conditions that require a new social contract? Some have been mentioned in the Cabinet vision. The main argument is that the emancipation of the citizen has not entirely succeeded. On the one hand, citizens have empowered themselves; on the other hand, this empowerment has not led to a situation in which citizens take more responsibility for the way societal problems can be attacked (p. 6). This should lead to a new balance between the duties and rights of the citizen versus government (p. 7). One aspect that should be considered in this new social contract is that that the existing relationships, especially the financial ones, between government and citizens have become too close, especially in the non-profit sector. We observe here that the budgetary motives (efficiency), which forces government to become leaner, are combined with an ideological motive for modernization, i.e. the need that citizens take more responsibility.

In addition to the reasons mentioned above, the Action Program mentions several other reasons for modernizing government, although not so prominently as the previous ones. The relationship between The Netherlands and the European Union, the avalanche of all kinds of restrictive and detailed regulations – which in some cases have European roots – that causes various enforcement problems, administrative burdens and legal procedures are mentioned as additional causes that urge for a modernization of government and governance (p. 7).

Modernization goals and shifts in governance   In the Action Program (p. 4) and in the Cabinet vision (pp. 11–12), the outline of the Dutch modernization and governance strategy has been sketched as follows. Three goals are distinguished. A modern government should, first, be restrictive in things it wants to regulate. The government should take a distant position and focus on the headlines and general frameworks. Second, government should create space for self-regulation by citizens, companies, agencies and the organizations of the civil society. This implies a new distribution of responsibilities between government and other societal sectors. In a civil society of empowered citizens, the responsibility of government ought to be rather limited. Government should guarantee basic public interests and the rule of the law. The last goal is that government should provide a high quality of those services that have been defined as public services and cannot be provided by private or non-profit organizations.

In the Dutch document, the notion of self-regulation is very important because it is used to legitimize the retreat of government (governance at a distance as dominant mode) and the transfer of responsibility towards the civil society, in which citizens should act as truly empowered citizens (societal self-governance) and towards the market (market-governance). The notion of self-regulation is used to legitimize different shifts of governance: towards citizens, societal organizations, the private sector and decentralized layers of government.

Measures to be taken   Four lines of action have been identified in the Action Program. These lines have been developed further into all kinds of sub-lines and projects. The emphasis lies on increasing the efficiency of public administration. The first line of action is improving the quality of public services by increasing efficiency, creating demand-driven and customer-friendlier services. ICTs should play an important role in order to realize these goals (pp. 7–14). The second line is a reduction of the number of regulations (deregulation) and the development of new and other regulatory frameworks that stimulate self-regulation. (pp. 16–22). This should lead to a reduction of the administrative burden for companies and citizens. The third line is a reorganization of government. Attention should be paid to the number of ministries and the core competencies of these departments, the policy advice system, the civil service, the number of executing agencies, the quality and organization of law enforcement, and the internal administrative system and financial management system (pp. 22–33). The last action line is the improvement of the relationship between central government and local and regional government. Not only should these bodies obtain more discretionary power, but the cooperation between these local and regional bodies and central government should also be improved through the use of chain management approaches. At the same time the performances of local and regional authorities should be made transparent and comparable (pp. 35–38).

What one might observe is that there is some distance between the concrete level of the Action Program and the governance strategy that has been developed in the Cabinet vision. For instance, the notion of self-regulation by the civic society has not substantially been incorporated in the Action Program. It has primarily been translated into a plea for deregulation in relation to a reduction of administrative costs.

Assumptions regarding the democratic nature of governance   The Dutch cabinet concludes in its vision statement that the emancipation of the Dutch citizen is not complete. There is a democratic deficit on the side of the citizen in terms of unfulfilled emancipation. Because of the close ties between government and citizens, citizens have become too dependent on government, which becomes manifest in a lack of self-responsibility on the part of the citizen. The shifts in governance that the Dutch cabinet favors in order to strengthen the civil society can be seen as a way to improve the input and output legitimacy of the political system by introducing elements of associative democracy into the existing tradition of representative democracy. Self-regulation opens the door for the active participation of citizens in all kinds of associations – as consumers, parents, inhabitants of a neighborhood – in the way all kinds of societal problems are defined, solutions are pursued and the outcomes are accomplished.

The United Kingdom

On March 30, 1999, the British government launched a major public sector reform initiative by tabling its *White Paper on Modernising Government* (Prime Minister and Minister for the Cabinet Office 1999). The White Paper states the government's vision for the public sector for the years ahead, and incorporates a wide-ranging set of reforms.

Forces for modernization   Modernizing government to achieve a better government and getting government right in order to make life better for the people of Britain have been defined as a vital part of the renewal of Britain (pp. 4, 9). In order to do so, government should face the challenges it meets. The basic line in the document is a loud call for transformation. However, the White Paper fails to clearly identify the challenges that are the causes for the initiative to modernize government. Only two arguments have been put forward. First, the White Paper claims that better government is about much more than whether public spending should go up and down. Past reforms have been too focused on improving value for money. Modernizing government should be about finding new and better ways to govern in order to meet the needs of the people as consumers and citizens (pp. 5, 15). Second, ICT and the rise of the information age is revolutionizing our lives, and offering a new 'scope for organizing government activities in new, innovative and better ways and for making life easier by providing public services in integrated, imaginative and more convenient forms' (p. 9). Moreover, the document notices that the distinction between services delivered by the public and private sector has been breaking down, which opens the way to new ideas, partnerships and opportunities (p. 9).

Modernization goals and shifts in governance   Looking at the full array of observations, intentions and goals in the document, we observe that all the arguments that are brought forward concentrate on the following five goals. First, it is important that policies deliver outcomes that matter, that meet the rising demands of the people and business, and that are not mere reactions to short-term pressures. According to the document, the separation between policy and delivery, in relation to a fragmented organization of public administration and a risk aversion culture, has prevented this. The second challenge is to deliver responsive public services, which will also meet the needs of citizens and not the convenience of service providers (p. 23). This implies that government should listen and be sensitive to the concerns of people or businesses and involve them in the decision-making process on service-delivery. Moreover, services should be provided in a more integrated way that reflects people's real lives. This prevents people from hunting down services by a process of trial and error (p. 25). Another goal is to improve the quality of public services. The White Paper states that efficient, high quality public services will be provided. Mediocrity will not be tolerated. In order to achieve these goals, the development of information age government has been seen as the main driver for modernization. ICT should contribute to the joined-up working between different parts of governments.

It should provide new, efficient, and convenient ways for citizens and businesses to communicate with government and to receive services (p. 45). The last goal is focused on a re-valuation of the civil service. Government should be committed to public services. It is important to establish a culture of improvement, innovation and collaboration that asks for new skills, new talent and new standards (p. 56).

In general, we conclude that the goals of the modernization program do not provide many clues about possible shifts in governance. However, the emphasis on public service delivery points in the direction of a shift towards the citizen as a consumer of public services.

Measures to be taken   The British document on 'Modernising government' is rather ambiguous. Well-developed measures are difficult to find. The document, which is highly rhetorical, consists of all kinds of intentions that tumble over one another. In order to improve the quality of public policy making, attention should be paid to designing policy around shared goals and carefully defined results and not around the organizational structures or existing functions. The goals should focus on the outcomes to be delivered, which should also lead to a better appraisal of costs and benefits (p. 16) Moreover it is important to develop new partnerships between Whitehall, the devolved administrations, local government and the voluntary and private sector. Consulting experts, those who implement policy and those affected by it early in the policy process can contribute to developing policies that are deliverable from the start (p. 16). This implies that government should regard policy-making as a continuous learning process, not as a series of one-off initiatives. More attention should be paid to the organization of the feedback process (p. 17). In order to design more responsive services, government should listen more to the needs of citizens and businesses and try to involve them in the decisions about how these services should be delivered. Therefore government should consult and work with them, especially in relation to specific target groups like the elderly, women, small businesses and ethnic minorities as well as in specific areas (pp. 27–29). Moreover it is important to deliver joined up delivery of services that have measurable outcomes that provide a better value for money.

The quality of the services to be delivered can be improved to focus on the results that matter to people, by developing general standards, the results of which are monitored and audited (p. 35). Competition is also important in order to deliver improvements. This means that government should look at what services government itself can provide, what should be contracted out to the private sector and what should be done in partnership (p. 35).

Information age government that has been defined as a major goal is, at the same time, the main instrument for achieving many of the described goals. ICT is defined as a set of tools that offers new methods of service delivery, communication, and information sharing, which, in turn, enables new forms of collaboration, and improves the access to and organization of information (p. 46).

The improvement of the public service is primarily seen as the development of a different culture, in which innovation and collaboration are important values.

In order to achieve this, a new human resource policy should be developed that especially brings in skills and experience from outside (p. 56).

A closer reading of the measures that have been proposed makes it possible to discern different shifts and modes of governance. The dominant shift is a shift towards the citizen, who has higher expectations of the services to be provided as well as his involvement in the design of those services. Moreover, improving public service delivery also implies a better collaboration between different parts of government (network governance and multi-level governance). Attention should also be paid to the outcomes of the policy programs, which should provide a better value for money in terms of accountability.

Assumptions regarding the democratic nature of governance   The British document pays no attention to a possible democratic deficit that is connected to the emergence of new modes of governance.

Germany

In December 1999 the German Federal Government launched the program *Modern State – Modern Administration* (Federal Ministry of the Interior 1999). It is a political program of the federal government to modernize the state and administration on the basis of the concept of the 'enabling state' Together with an actively participating society, it will be able to successfully steer a course between a leaner state and a state that reduces state intervention and excessive regulation (p. 7) What are the assumptions behind this idea of the enabling state and the shifts in governance which become manifest in this concept?

Forces for modernization   The main reasons for introducing the program are not very clear and concrete. The program only states that 'the state and the administrative system must redefine their tasks and competences taking into account the changed conditions within society' (p. 6). Moreover, the concept of the 'lean state' which was pursued in the past has been defined as too focused on reducing public tasks. It only focused on a set of perceived negative goals, which were seen as a rather isolated approach of modernization with an internal focus (p. 7). This internal focus was not responsive enough to changing societal conditions. However, the document does not reveal what these changing conditions have been.

Modernization goals and shifts in governance   The concept of the 'enabling state' has been grounded on four pillars. The first one is a new distribution of responsibilities between state and society. On the one hand, the state should continue to protect the freedom and security of its citizens as the core tasks for which it remains solely responsible (e.g. internal security, legal protection, and tax collection). On the other hand, there are many tasks that have been deemed to be public tasks but need not be fulfilled by the state itself. Here, however, the state must ensure that they will be fulfilled (p. 8). In such cases, the reform of the state and its administrative system should be based on a model that creates a new balance between the duties of the state, individual initiative and social commitment. 'This will shift the focus in such a way that the state becomes less of a decision taker and producer and more of a mediator and catalyst of social developments which it cannot and must not control on its own. The enabling state means strengthening society's potential for self-regulation and guaranteeing the necessary freedom of action. Above all, it requires the concerted action of public, semi-public and private players to achieve common goals. This interaction needs to be developed and enhanced. In this context, it is the special responsibility of the federal government to create the legal framework for a state geared to the needs of its citizens, acting like a partner for them and endowed with an efficient administrative system' (p. 8).

The second pillar is a responsive public service, which implies that the interests and motives behind government decisions need to be transparent, and that players in society have better information at hand (p. 8). 'Therefore, the federal government wishes to enhance the transparency of public administration and boost participation by the people. To this end, the state and the administrative system will have to prepare themselves for the transition from a society based on industrial production to a knowledge-based society, and use the possibilities offered by information technologies as a basis for keeping citizens informed and for communicating with them' (p. 8).

The third pillar is better co-operation between the different tiers or bodies of public administration because they have to work together more closely as well as respect each other. In order to achieve this, the document presupposes more freedom of decision, based on the principle of subsidiarity. Moreover, it tries to foster diversity within the federation by reducing the number of federal government provisions (p. 9) and to offer the *Länder* a chance to reform their administrative systems if federal government provides them with more room to manoeuvre (p. 9).

The fourth pillar is an efficient administration, based on a better use of the limited financial resources through the development of more performance-oriented and cost-efficient procedures so that superfluous 'red tape' can be eliminated. This can be achieved through competition and benchmarking (p. 9). At the same time, government should modernize its human resource policies through the introduction of more performance related elements into the numeration and career schemes of the public service and to elaborate on human resource development (p. 10).

Hence, we see that the retreat of government, based on self-regulation, initiates a shift in governance in favor of citizens, companies, societal organizations and other layers of government. The emphasis on self-regulation and accountability favors a mode of governance that has earlier been described as governance at a distance. The emphasis that has been placed on the need to collaborate favors multi-level governance and network governance.

Measures to be taken   Given these modernization goals, the measures to be taken concentrated themselves on four areas of reform, which can be defined as a set of sub-goals of the modernization goals. The improvement of the effectiveness and acceptance of legislation is the first area of change. More attention should be paid to the consequences of legal provisions and on the identification and dismantling of obstacles for new services.

Furthermore, the cooperation between the bodies of government, in which the federal government defines itself as a partner, should be based on the removal of barriers that hamper independent actions by the *Länder* and local authorities. The aim is to extend their scope of action and to strengthen local self-government, which should lead to a shift in competences. Also, it is important to improve the cooperation with the private sector. In line with the argument above, 'the federal government will create scope for the development of self-initiative and self-regulation and will promote voluntary work. It will also remove restrictions and create new forms of cooperation between the state, the private sector, the welfare organizations and other non-profit-making institutions' (p. 13).

Third, measures should be implemented that contribute to a competitive, cost-efficient and transparent administrative system with higher performance targets while cutting expenses. In order to achieve this, government has 'to adapt more and more to competitive conditions, making the use of instruments of business administration, such as accrual accounting and controlling, common practice in the federal administration. However, an administration can become more efficient only if it improves how the citizens are involved in administrative decision-making and if it makes administrative actions more transparent (p. 14). It also implies that government will be engaged in a concrete dialogue with the citizens and to reveal red tape. To this end, the federal government will make use of modern information and communication technologies on a broad basis, thus accomplishing the transition towards 'electronic government' (pp. 14–15).

The last area of reform is the creation of a highly motivated workforce in which 'personal responsibility, better career opportunities and flexible, self-determined working structures (collaborative working) ensure that the existing potential for modernization is actually being used' (p. 16).

Assumptions regarding the democratic nature of governance   In this program, no attention has been paid to the democratic nature of the proposed shifts in governance.

3. A Comparison of the Initiatives

In this section we compare the programs that we have studied and search for striking resemblances and differences. Table 5.1 presents a brief outline of the modernization programs, according to the research questions, which have been formulated in section one.

A comparison of the findings results in the following striking observations. (See Table 5.1 below).

Table 5.1   Summaries of contents of modernization programs

Country/ assumptions regarding program	Denmark	Germany	The Netherlands	United Kingdom
Forces for Modernization	Reference to 'major challenges'. Some attention is paid to the growing number of elderly	A need to redefine tasks and competences in relation to 'changed conditions in society'.	Redefinition of the role of government in relation to changing societal conditions and lacking efficacy to solve societal problems.	To face 'challenges' implies transformation. Focus on two challenges: a) meeting the increasing needs of citizens, b) reacting on the possibilities of ICT
Goals	Public sector should be based on a) the free choice of citizens, b) is open, simple and responsive and provides value for money.	Modernization by a) new distribution of responsibilities between state and society, b) responsive public service which is transparent and boosts participation, c) more collaboration between government bodies, d) an efficient administration.	Modernization by a) retreat in regulation, b) a shift of responsibilities towards self-regulation by the civil society, c) a focus on essential public interests and the rule of the law, d) improving high quality public services.	Modernizing government implies a) focusing policy making on outcomes that meet the demands of citizens and businesses, b) responsive public service delivery of a higher quality c) information age government, d) improving quality of civil service.

Measures and Actions	Creation of alternatives to choose and improving information about alternatives. Administrative simplification and reduction administrative burdens. Strengthening role of ICT Improving competition between service providers	Shifts in competences to improve self-government Improving quality of legislation. Improving cost-efficiency through performance management, citizen participation in defining 'red tape' and ICT. Modernizing human resource policy.	Improving quality of public services, deregulation and self-regulation, other way of organization of the central government, and new relationships with local and regional government	Focus on outcomes to be delivered in services and policies, improving feedback mechanisms; improving consultation and participation of users; central role of ICT; a new human resource policy for the public service
Dominant Shift	Towards citizens	Towards society, other decentralized layers of government, towards citizens	Towards the civil society in order to improve self-regulation by citizens	Towards citizens
Dominant Modes	Market-governance, governance at a distance, network governance	Governance at a distance, multi-level governance, network governance	Governance at a distance, market-governance, and societal self-governance	Multi-level governance, network governance
Dominant Political Values	Responsiveness Freedom of choice Efficiency Value for money	Responsiveness. Efficiency Value for money Accountability	Self-responsibility Participation Efficiency.	Responsiveness Efficiency Value for money
Emphasis on Legitimacy	Input and output legitimacy	Output legitimacy	Input and output legitimacy	Output legitimacy
Democratic Nature	Measures contribute to strengthening the existing model of representative democracy	No attention paid	Democratic deficit on the side of the citizen in terms of unfulfilled emancipation. Self-responsibility and participation of citizens should contribute to input and output legitimacy.	No attention paid

Forces for modernization   If we look at the main drivers for modernization, we might observe that in the policy documents references have been made to changing societal conditions, but that a clear and profound analysis of these developments and their consequences for the role and position of government has not been conducted. Conditions that have been mentioned are the rising number of elderly people (Denmark), the increasing needs of empowered citizens (UK), the incomplete emancipation of the citizen (The Netherlands) and the emergence of the information society (UK). This implies that the drivers for modernization have a rather internal orientation. Two explanations can be given for this. The first is that internal efficiency goals are the hidden motives of the modernization programs; the second is that modernization programs can be seen as a ritual in public administration, through which governments periodically make clear – for internal and external reasons – that they are able to meet new emerging normative reforms or socio-political ideologies, like New Public Management (UK and Germany), communitarianism and the civil society (The Netherlands) or neo-liberalism (Denmark). It is also interesting to see that only Denmark and The Netherlands pay some attention to the rising power of the European Union as a relevant layer of government, which is primarily seen as a source of detailed regulation.

Modernization goals   A comparison of the programs shows that the main emphasis lies on the improvement of the quality of public service delivery. Demand-orientation, public participation and improving openness and responsiveness are relevant aspects that return in all documents studied.

The policy programs in Germany and The Netherlands also suggest the need to redefine the responsibilities of the state. In Germany, this has been phrased in terms of self-government – especially in relation to other layers of government – while in The Netherlands the uncompleted emancipation of the citizen should be compensated by giving citizens more responsibility. This has been captured in the notion of self-regulation.

Moreover, most programs also consider improving efficiency and getting more value for money as goals that should be realized. Sometimes they have been formulated explicitly (The Netherlands, Germany), in other instances they are more implicit. However, a close analysis shows that these goals are quite prominent, for instance in relation with administrative simplification, improving competition, improving performance management methods and feedback mechanisms. What one can observe is that New Public Management as a management theory has been an important source of inspiration for designing these concrete measures.

Shifts in governance   The modernization of public administration, as it has been described in the programs of The Netherlands, the UK, Germany and Denmark, can also be described in relation to a number of shifts in governance. What shifts have been proposed in these modernization programs? A shift towards self-government and self-regulation might be observed. This shift takes several forms. The first expression of self-government has been decentralization in favor of other bodies and layers of government. This is particularly clear in the German and Dutch cases and to a lesser degree in the Danish case. In terms of the modes of governance discussed in chapter 2, this can be described as governance at a distance. At the same time, a plea has been made to improve the cooperation between the layers of government in all of the four countries studied. This is very often related to the provision of integrated, holistic services like in Denmark, the UK and The Netherlands. In chapter 2, this mode of governance has been described in terms of multi-level governance.

The second expression of self-government has been the idea that the private sector and the civil society should have more liberty and autonomy to provide (semi)-public services that substitute or compete with the services provided by government. This is especially the case in Denmark, The Netherlands and Germany. Deregulation and privatization are instruments that can be used to realize the goals. This mode of governance has been described in Chapter 2 as market governance.

The third expression refers to the shift to give citizens a greater responsibility. Three options can be discerned. The first one is to address the citizen as consumer of public services and to improve their information in order to facilitate rational choices. This orientation is dominant in the Danish case. The second option is to design more responsive public service delivery that actually meets the needs of citizens and companies, which is present in all the four cases, but especially in the UK. The last option is to stimulate the self-responsibility of the citizens, not only as a consumer but also as co-producer of solutions for societal problems. This is the dominant Dutch perspective on self-regulation.

Shifts in political values   If we look at the different modernization goals in the programs of Denmark, Germany, The Netherlands and the UK, we observe that they refer to specific political values that legitimize the modernization of public administration in these countries.

The first one is liberty, referring to giving more freedom and autonomy to other bodies and layers of government and to citizens in order to act as rational consumers of public services or in order to take more responsibility for the functioning of society. But liberty also presupposes accountability: to account for the outcomes of the autonomy and liberty that have been given to local and regional government bodies and all kinds of functional public bodies, for example agencies. Many of the measures that have been formulated focus on improving accountability, such as the introduction of performance management methods and bench marking.

Liberty is also a necessary condition for another political value, efficiency. A trade-off between liberty and efficiency can be found when looking at the possibilities for private and non-profit organizations to take over formerly public tasks and provide various public services. It can also be found in the idea to increase competition within the public sector itself, between public services agencies. Another trade-off between efficiency and liberty can be found in the idea of deregulation and rule simplification. This will not only contribute to more freedom and more responsible actions, but it might also reduce the administrative burdens for citizens and companies so that they can operate more efficiently. If we look at this change in political value-orientation, we see that they match neo-liberal ideas about how government should modernize.

Legitimacy and the democratic nature of governance   Our comparison shows that according to these programs, the shifts in governance that have been proposed in the modernization programs will not lead to a democratic deficit. This has not been viewed as an important issue. Looking at the different programs, we might state that the proposed governance shifts are perceived as a way of strengthening the existing representative model of democracy, contributing to the input and output legitimacy of the existing political system.

In the Danish and UK models, the representative model of democracy can be improved if citizens can make clear what kind of services they want to receive in relation to their needs. The input legitimacy of the existing political order will improve by the introduction of elements that can be derived from the political theory of a consumer or client democracy. Through the introduction of various marketing and client research instruments, as well as client participation to gather information about the needs and wishes of citizens, politicians can reformulate their public service agenda. The output legitimacy is being improved because the services that are actually being provided have been more responsive to the needs of citizens. In the Danish model the output legitimacy is strengthened if citizens can actually choose among different services and service providers. Good performance is defined as having the freedom to choose.

In the Dutch program, the legitimacy of the existing model of representative democracy can be improved if citizens will act as truly empowered citizens who are able to take some responsibility for how a society should develop itself. The democratic deficit in the Dutch program refers to an input deficit on the part of citizens who are not able to participate in an emancipated way. If citizens are willing and able to act as empowered and emancipated citizens who actively participate in the shaping of society, the legitimacy of the outcomes will also increase. These outcomes, then, might be viewed as the expression of a joint responsibility of government and citizens, in which both parties act as the co-producers of these outcomes. These ideas can be derived from the political theory of the associative democracy, which tries to increase the effective participation of 'local' knowledge and expertise.

In the German document, very little attention has been paid to a possible democratic deficit that might occur as a consequence of the German idea of the 'enabling state'. One could argue that the existing political system could improve its legitimacy by creating more freedom for other bodies and layers of government and societal sectors to act as autonomous actors with the ability to use their own, local, knowledge and expertise. This is an important notion in the theory of the associative democracy. At the same time, questions can be raised about how these organizations might be held accountable for the decisions they have made. How is this to be organized? Looking at the specific measures that have been taken, we notice that the emphasis lies on improving output legitimacy through the introduction of accountability and performance regimes that have been derived from New Public

Management ideas. Moreover, the idea of 'the enabling state' might be perceived as a way of legitimizing a retreat of government by introducing freedom (in terms of self-government) as a necessary condition for improving efficiency. This adds to the output legitimacy of the German political system.

4. Understanding Modernizing Government: In Search of Legitimacy

In the previous section we have looked at a number of shifts of governance that can be derived from the modernization goals and measures in the programs we have studied. In this section we want to reflect on these findings. What do these findings tell us about the nature of the (ongoing) modernization process that takes places in public administration and how is this process being legitimized?

An important issue is that the legitimacy of the modernization process that has been set out in Denmark, the UK, Germany and The Netherlands has not been strongly linked to various societal challenges. An internal orientation prevailed. What does this tell us about the nature of the modernization process that takes place in these countries?

The (ongoing) need to modernize government can be explained by numerous policy challenges that have to be addressed, like the increasing demands of citizens, the growth of the number of elderly people and the evolving claim on existing and new services or the lack of efficiency within public administration. An alternative explanation is that it might also be understood as the outcome of a sociological process of functional rationalization. As a general theoretical concept, the term modernization has its roots in Weber's modernization theory, in which modernization refers to the further rationalization of organizations and social systems in general. According to Weber, the rationalization process of Western society takes shape through a process of bureaucratization, in which power is being exercised on clearly defined and well known – thus formal and standardized – rules. At the same time, the 'modernization of government' in Denmark, Germany, The Netherlands and the UK, calls for deregulation, de-bureaucratization and rule-simplification. Paradoxically, the modernization of government can be understood as an answer to a process of hyper-modernization. Standardization and formalization can no longer be seen as intelligent answers for stabilizing the functioning of markets and societies, but are considered barriers to the smooth functioning of these markets and societies (Harvey 1989).

The drive to enhance the modernization of public administration might be understood more correctly by relating modernization to Mannheim's concept of functional rationality as opposed to substantial rationality. Functional rationality refers to the extent to which a series of actions is organized in such a way as to lead to predetermined goals with maximum efficiency (Scott 1998, 33). Or, in the words of Mannheim, functional rationality refers to the organization of a series of actions in such a way that it leads to a previously defined goal, in which every element in this series of action receives a functional position and role (Mannheim 1980, 53).

The call for a more managerial approach, like NPM, in public administration might be understood as the expression of this functional rationality. Therefore, public management reforms consist of deliberate changes to the structures and processes of public sector organizations with the objective of getting them, in some sense, to run better (Pollitt and Bouckaert 2000, 8). Efficiency and efficacy are important values for judging if these reforms contribute to a public administration that runs better; values which also stress the importance of the output side of public administration. In contrast to the notion of functional rationality, Mannheim has introduced the notion of substantial rationality. Substantial rationality refers to an act of thought that reveals intelligent insight into the interrelations of events in a given situation (Mannheim 1980, 53). In the case of public administration, the notion of substantial rationality refers to the process of goal formulation in which there are trade-offs between different political values, for instance, between liberty and equality, security and liberty. Within public administration, a growing tension can be observed between the values that are related to the functional rationality, like efficiency, and more substantial values that refer to political values like liberty, equity, security, participation and so on (Ringeling 1992). To some extent this tension might also be understood in terms of a confrontation between 'management' and 'politics' (Clarke and Newman 1997) or between the market model and the polis model of policy making (Stone 2002). If we look at the arguments that have been produced in the documents on modernizing government and the shifts of governments that are proposed in the slipstream of this modernization process, the legitimacy of these changes is primarily based on functional rationality arguments. The dominance of the functional rationality in how policy makers and politicians think is to some extent a major source of inspiration and justification of the modernization road that public administration has taken. Notions that refer to the substantial rationality, like alternative democracy models such as 'strong democracy' (see Barber 1984), are absent in the discussion of the modernization of government. Moreover, it might also be an explanation for the absence of external forces for the modernization programs and for the dominance of efficiency as the major incentive for modernization.

Another reason, but closely related to the previous reflections, is that in order to survive as legitimate organizations, government organizations are forced to comply to specific administrative and management concepts, techniques and reform ideologies, like NPM or even the notion of 'governance'. These concepts and ideologies can be seen as the expression of functional rationalization as a specific, yet dominant pattern of meaning. The adoption of these concepts, techniques and ideologies, which Meyer and Rowan (1977) define as myths and ceremonies to be adopted and followed, add to the legitimacy of an organization. The adoption of these new 'modernization' concepts shows the outside world that an organization is willing and able to change. It shows that it is not old fashioned but modern in order to secure its survival and access to external resources. DiMaggio and Powell (1983) refer to the same process, which they label 'institutional isomorphism'. The learning strategy that lay behind this is that of imitation or mimicking. Organizations tend to reduce uncertainty by imitating other organizations. By doing this, organizations will not stand out be noticed as different. Also, organizations copy specific management reforms because they could enhance their status as being progressive and innovative. To some extent this explains why different organizations in public organizations adapt the same management and governance concepts and ideologies. Moreover, it might be an explanation of the convergence of the modernization programs in the countries that we have studied.

5. Conclusion: The Emergence of a New Political Order

In the slipstream of the modernization of public administration, as it can be derived from the programs that we have studied, we perceive a dominant shift of governance towards citizens. What does this shift imply for the democratic nature of this shift of governance, if we relate it to the different democracy models that have been described in chapter 3?

The dominant shift towards citizens has three consequences. First, we see the emergence of a consumer democracy, blended with ideas about New Public Management, complementary to the existing democratic order. Modernization primarily takes place through a shift of governance towards the citizen as consumer, who a) should be empowered so that he is able, more so than before, to act as a *homo economicus* who actually has a choice (Denmark), b) can obtain more client-friendly and more cost efficient services (Denmark, UK, The Netherlands, Germany), c) and can participate as co-designer in the way services should be provided (Denmark, UK) in order to strengthen the responsiveness and need-orientation of the public service delivery process (Denmark, Germany, UK). In a consumer democracy, the power and scope of the administrative system are limited not by restoring a civil society of the *homo publicus* (which is present in the Dutch cabinet vision but not in the Action Program) but by seeking the realm of the *homo economicus* (Bellamy 2000:40). The consumer democracy model shares the assumptions with economic liberalism and rational choice theory that individuals are to be regarded as active, competent, instrumental and rational in the making of choices and the expression of preferences, as least so far as their consumption of public services is concerned. This also implies a strong claim for information about public service entitlements as well as to the means of enforcing those entitlements (Bellamy 2000:41). ICT is either used to improve the information base of citizens to make more rational choices or is used to improve the information base of government in order to deliver more tailor-made, integrated ways of service delivery that recognizes the dynamics of the needs of citizens.

The second implication is that government can only meet the challenges of a more integrated, more responsive way of public service delivery if it functions like an efficient machine, which can be achieved by deregulation and reducing 'red tape'. Moreover, it implies the monitoring of outcomes that are produced by the machinery of government in terms of value for money, focusing on quality and efficiency. Another condition needed to create an integrated service delivery machinery is the further collaboration between the 'cogwheels in the machinery of government' (collaboration between layers of government and agencies). In order to strengthen the functioning of the central control of the machinery of government, it is important to give more autonomy and to focus on specific parameters, thereby introducing a cybernetic perspective on governance. The introduction of 'modern management techniques', like performance management techniques, which come from the private sector, can support this endeavor.

The third consequence is that this shift in governance in favor of the citizen has not been perceived as a democratic deficit. One could even argue that the emphasis on consumer democracy is presumed to strengthen the representative democracy model and to help to overcome a possible democratic deficit in this model. Traditionally, in the representative model the emphasis lies on the input process of democracy, focusing on electoral and parliamentary mechanisms. The political nexus of the representative democracy model is supplemented with a consumer nexus, focusing on the output process of the political system in terms of the public service delivery process (Bellamy 2000, 40). In a consumer democracy (which Denmark is trying to establish) the wishes and preferences are more effectively channeled, so that politicians can be more responsive to these preferences.

References

Barber, B. (1984), *Strong Democracy: Participatory Politics for a New Age* (Berkeley: University of California Press).

Bellamy, C. (2000), 'Modelling electronic democracy: towards democratic discourses for an information age', in: J. Hoff, I. Horrocks and P. Tops (eds.), pp. 33–54.

Clarke, J. and Newman, J. (1997), *The Managerial State* (London: Sage).

DiMaggio, P and Powell, W. (1983), 'The iron cage revisited: institutional isomorphism and collective rationality in organizational fields', in: *American Sociological Review*, volume 48, 147–160.

Edelman, M. (1967), *The Symbolic Use of Politics* (Urbana: University of Illinois Press).

Edelman, M. (1977), *Political Language, Words that Succeed and Policies that Fail* (New York: Academic Press).

Fisher, F. and Forester, J. (eds) (1993), *The Argumentative Turn in Policy Analysis and Planning* (Durham: Duke University Press).

Harvey, D. (1989), *The Condition of Post Modernity* (Oxford: Blackwell).

Hoff, J., Horrocks, I. and Tops, P. (eds) *Democratic Governance and New Technology* (London/New York: Routledge).

Kingdon, J. (1984), *Agendas, Alternatives and Public Policies* (Boston: Little Brown).

Mannheim, K. (1980), *Man and Society in the Age of Reconstruction* (London/New York: Routledge).

Meyer, J.W. and Rowan, B. (1977), 'Institutionalized Organizations: Formal Structure as Myth and Ceremony', *American Journal of Sociology*, Volume 83, 340–363.

Ministry of the Cabinet Office (1999), *Modernising Government* (London).

Parsons, W. (1996), *Public Policy: An Introduction to the Theory and Practice of Policy Analysis* (Aldershot: Edward Elgar).

Pollitt, Ch., and Bouckaert, G. (2000), *Public Management Reform: A Comparative Analysis*, (Oxford: Oxford University Press).

Ringeling, A. (1992), *Het imago van de overheid* (Den Haag: Vuga).

Scott, R.W. (1998), *Organizations: Rational, Natural and Open Systems* (Upper Sadle River, New York: Prentice Hall).

Stone, D. (2002), *The Policy Paradox. The Art of Political Decision-Making* (New York/London: Norton and Company).

Chapter 6

Police, Policing and Governance in The Netherlands and in the United Kingdom

Arie van Sluis and Lex Cachet

In this chapter, we explore, describe and analyze significant shifts that have taken place in steering and control of the police in The Netherlands and in the UK from a comparative perspective. Our focus is on the police system and on police accountability at the local level because recent reforms pose threats to democratic legitimacy at the local level.

We start with a description of the police system and of policing and local public safety policy in The Netherlands, followed by a description of some recent developments and trends in steering and control of the police and of local public safety. In section 2, we describe the British police system and local public safety in the UK. We will analyze our findings by answering three questions:

- What shifts in governance have taken place (section 3)?
- What problems (if any) of democratic legitimacy have been created (section 4)?
- To what extent does the representative democracy model still apply; what democracy models are developing in steering and control of the police and in local public safety; what other models are preferable (section 5)?

1. The Dutch Police System

In recent years the police system in The Netherlands has undergone significant changes. In 1993, forces of municipal and state police merged into 25 regional police forces. This new, regional police system is basically a decentralized system, like the old one. The need for protection *by* the police has always been accompanied by the need for protection *against* the police. Therefore, arrangements for steering and control of the police are traditionally characterized by checks and balances. No single body should have sole authority over the police. The authority should be divided between two ministers (the Minister of Interior Affairs and Kingdom Relations and the Minister of Justice) on the one hand and provincial and municipal authorities and municipal councils on the other (BZK 2000).

The Minister of Interior Affairs and Kingdom Relations is the central administrator of the Dutch police. He is politically accountable to Parliament. The Minister of Justice is politically accountable for the work of the district attorney and the attorney general in this respect. The Minister of Justice is responsible for the police with regard to law enforcement (BZK 2000).

Each police region has its own force administrator, usually the mayor of the largest municipality in the region. He liaises with the Minister of Interior Affairs and Kingdom Relations. The regional executive makes decisions about the principal lines of policy. All the mayors in a region and the chief district attorney are members of the regional executive. Policies are worked out in detail at the regional level in tripartite consultations, which include the force administrator, the chief district attorney and the chief of police. Day-to-day management is in the hands of the regional chief of police (BZK 2000).

Shifts in Steering and Control of the Dutch Police

In the first period of the new police system (the early 1990s), the Minister of Interior Affairs and Kingdom Relations steered from a distance. Police regions had considerable freedom in formulating policy targets. The counterpart of this relative freedom was increased reporting and accounting for performance. The new police system coincided with the emergence of policy planning as an instrument for steering and control of the police and with an increase in management information systems. The scale and complexity of the new police regions created a need for integral policy planning. Internally, planning was used as an instrument for fine-tuning between the region, the district and the local level within a police force. Externally, planning became an instrument for steering and control by the police authorities and for accountability by the police force.

Gradually, the Dutch police system has shifted from a decentralized towards a more centralized system, in which the role of the Ministry of Interior Affairs and Kingdom Relations has become more dominant (Van Sluis and Van Thiel 2003). At present, the Minister has an important say in the priorities of the regional police forces.

The first shift   In 2000, a national policy cycle for the police was introduced for the first time. Regional priorities had to be compatible with national priorities in the *Beleidsplan Nederlandse Politie* ('Policy Plan for the Dutch Police'). This interference with regional police policy was a significant break with former policy. Previously, police targets were set at the local and regional levels. Now in 2000 all police regions became subject to intensified control by the Minister of Interior Affairs and Kingdom Relations, within the framework of the Policy Plan for the Dutch Police. The initially distant role in administering the police was replaced by intensified steering by the Minister of the Interior. This shift towards centralization in steering and control on a national scale also created a need for standardized information for comparing police performance.

The second shift   The next important shift took place in 2003 when the Dutch Police National Framework 2003–2006 was formulated. This national framework was created in response to the findings of research of the General Auditor and other researchers into the functioning and the effects of the national police policy plan (Algemene Rekenkamer 2003; Berenschot 2001). Their conclusions were similar: national policy planning did not work. There was no connection between local, regional and national planning cycles. The national policy cycle was seen as a ritual rain dance, 'nobody bothered'. There were no criteria to measure police performance. Due to shortcomings in police information systems, performance of the police forces could not be aggregated and compared. In addition, there were too many indicators. Finally, policy planning laid a heavy administrative burden on the regional police forces.

The Dutch Police National Framework 2003–2006 contains the policy targets for the police in the period 2003–2006. This framework is based on a national results-based agreement between the Minister of Interior Affairs and Kingdom Relations and the 25 force administrators. The policy targets are set out in a national covenant and in regional covenants with the individual forces. The sum total of the agreements in the individual covenants constitutes the national agreement. The results are monitored and recorded at the central level for each force. Where necessary, efforts are intensified to achieve the agreed results. A system of performance-related budgeting for the forces is linked to the agreements (BZK 2000).

The aim of the Dutch Police National Framework 2003–2006 is to control and monitor how the police perform their core tasks. The results to be realized by the police are concrete and measurable. They are measured with output indicators (fines and number of cases submitted to the District Attorney's Office), subjective indicators (such as customer and citizen's satisfaction with police work) and indicators for internal performance (such as processing times, efficiency, sick leave and the quality of rendering police services by telephone). Each results-based agreement is linked to one of the targets in the National Safety Program: law enforcement, supervision maintaining public order and efficiency. A small part of the annual budget is dependent upon performance; an improvement of at least 5 per cent in performance as compared to the previous year and in comparison with police forces in the same cluster results in bonuses (LKNP 2003).

Shifts in policy instruments   The results-based agreements are a response to failing national policy planning that had too many pretensions and too few effects. They mark a shift from more traditional types of policy planning towards performance steering, with only a few specific and measurable targets, with fewer pretensions, fewer administrative burdens and less bureaucracy. The results based agreements were intended to obtain a tighter grip on the performance of the police, to improve police performance and to contribute to public safety in The Netherlands in a transparent way.

Shifts in policy content   The agreements also mark a shift in the content of police policy. Only the repressive tasks of the police (maintaining public order and fighting crime) are taken into consideration. Crime-prevention and offering assistance to people in distress are excluded, although these are part of the broad role of the police, as set out in section two of the Police Act 1993: 'The police have the task, subordinate to the competent authority and in accordance with the applicable rules of law, of ensuring effective law enforcement and rendering assistance to those who need it'. Other aspects of police work are the enforcement of legal order through the criminal law and the performance of policing duties for the justice authorities. This shift in policy content represents a shift in thinking about the basic idea of police work among policymakers.

Local Public Safety Policy in The Netherlands

In 2003, the government published the *Towards a Safer Society Program*, which set out the government's goals for 2006 and how they were to be achieved. The overall objective was to reduce crime, tackle anti-social behavior in public places and properly enforce and implement anti-crime measures.

Local public safety policy in The Netherlands is characterized by a broad approach in which repression and prevention are integrated. This is an approach that is the prime responsibility of local government and in which police and criminal justice are important actors, but certainly not the only actors and not by definition the most important actors.

Dutch policy has been influenced strongly by the awareness that the capacity – and especially the effectiveness – of policing and criminal justice are limited. Solving wicked problems – drugs abuse, youth problems, trouble with homeless or mentally ill individuals – is not and should not be the main concern of the police. Solving these types of problems requires skills that the police do not have. Other professionals and professional organizations are needed to cope with these types of problems. In many ways, the effectiveness of the police is dependent on their cooperation with others: social workers, local social service departments, mental health agencies, youth workers, probation officers and many departments within the local government.

One of the main characteristics of the Dutch approach to public safety policy is grounded in the awareness of these interdependencies. Public safety policy at the local level is increasingly a policy of an integral kind – the so-called local Integrated Public Safety Policy (*Integraal Veiligheidsbeleid*). During the past ten years the national government has facilitated local governments to develop their own local Integrated Public Safety Policy. The local policy is characterized by (a) close cooperation among local government agencies, police, criminal justice and many other organizations (b) a broad approach to safety: repression as well as prevention, short term measures as well as long term measures (c) attention to social public safety problems as well as physical safety and (d) public safety policy as linked to policies in other domains such as local economy, housing, infrastructure and recreational facilities (Cachet and Ringeling 2004).

2. The British Police System

In the UK there are 43 police forces, including the City of London Police and the Metropolitan Police. There is no national police force. All police forces have the same structure, consisting of the Headquarters (chief constable, deputy management team and support staff) and Basic Command Units (BCUs) that perform the daily police work (Mawby and Wright 2003).

The British police are a 24 hours emergency service with many different task such as reassuring the public, crime prevention, crime investigation, maintaining the peace, maintaining law and order and ensuring public safety in the streets. According to Mawby and Wright (2003, 183): 'variety is the spice of police work and there exists a widespread feeling that British policing does – and should – have a broad mandate'. BCUs have a legal obligation to cooperate with local agencies to prevent crime.

The police system is decentralized. Steering and control of the police take place in a tripartite structure, with the Home Office, the police authority and the chief constable as the most important actors. Police authorities are independent bodies made up of local citizens who oversee the work of their local police force. Together with the Home Secretary and chief police officers, they are responsible for the management of policing in England and Wales. Traditionally, steering of the police has been guided by the idea of constabulary independence. Policy decisions about the police should be insulated from political interference and left to the professional judgment of senior police officers.

Shifts

From the 1970s on, this principle of freedom for the police from political interference has gradually eroded (Reiner 2000). In recent years the principle of constabulary independence has come under attack. Police chiefs are no longer seen as 'operationally independent', but as 'operationally responsible'. Police activities are influenced by local police plans, made up by the police authority, that also include decisions about priorities. Police activities are also influenced by national priorities.

Since November 2002, the national government formulated national strategic priorities based on three-year periods. Based on the Police Reform Act 2002, a National Policing Plan was introduced, the second for the period 2003–2007. This plan contained the national strategic priorities from the Home Office that guide local police work. These priorities serve as a framework for monitoring the performance of the police forces. The Reform Act also introduced the dissemination and implementation of best practices through statutory codes of practice. Finally, the Reform Act obliges Police Authorities to produce a 3-year strategic plan that reflects the national priorities.

Centralization According to Newburn there has been a long-term tendency towards centralization. This centralization becomes clear in: 'The progressive neutering of local authorities, the emergence of a form of managerialism that involves ever-closer scrutiny of police performance, the growing authority and influence of police representative bodies and, arguably most important of all, the ever-increasing power and influence of central government in policing' (Newburn 2003, 101). Mawby says that: 'It is widely accepted that local government influence on policing has been muted and recent developments have further strengthened the role of central government' (Mawby 2003, 18).

McLaughlin (2005) distinguishes two waves in the modernization of the police system. New Labour introduced first a form of managerialism of policing, as part of a broader effort to modernize the public sector, culminating in the Police Reform Act 2002. The first reform was a managerial reform, accompanying the post-Scarman focus on law and order. New kinds of steering instruments were introduced, like the National Police Plan, the obligation for Police Authorities to ensure Best Values by continuous quality improvement and the creation of a Police Standard Unit at the Home Office with explicit operation remits, in combination with inspections by Her Majesty's Inspectorate of Constabulary (HMIC).

Localization   In the second wave the strengthening of local accountability became important, as a countervailing power against centralization and a correction to intensified planning and control by 'London'. McLaughlin describes this shift as one from New Managerialism toward New Localism, in which the state, civil society and citizenry are connected. This shift evolved between 2000 and 2002. Public services should be delivered locally and should be directly connected to the communities they serve. Home Office Ministers acknowledged that police modernization had become too closely directed by Whitehall and that produced audit overload. The grip of the center closed off the policymaking process to locally expressed policing priorities. Research showed that the public desire was for the return of the local Bobby, patrol officers on foot and the reopening of police stations, keeping the streets and neighborhoods free of pretty crime and antisocial behavior (McLaughlin 2005, 479).

Local Public Safety in the UK

The second National Policing Plan coincides with a strategic policy plan from the Home Secretary called 'Policing: Building Safer Communities'. This plan marked a shift in thinking about local public safety. The motto of this plan is 'working for and with communities, supported by high national standards'.

This strategic plan parallels changes in other parts of the public sector and programs for citizen's renewal. Public safety is of crucial importance for cohesive communities, and local ownership of policing arrangements has to be strengthened. Renewal of the police system is linked with citizens' renewal and the revitalization of communities, as part of wider local government reform that would enable the transfer of services from the town hall to self-governing communities (McLaughlin 2005, 478).

Tony Blair stated in his foreword to the National Policing Plan: 'I want the police to be seriously engaged with the people they serve and to be identifying key priorities with them that are focused on those issues that really matter. But I also want communities to be able to hold the police to account for delivery against those priorities' (Foreword National Policing Plan 2003–2007).

Democratic policing is seen as 'policing by active cooperation'. Starting in 2008, every community will be policed by multi-functional Neighborhood Policing Teams (NPTs), composed of police officers, community support officers, special constables, police support volunteers, neighborhood wardens and security personnel. These teams will work closely with communities and other agencies

Local councilors are a focal point for the community in dealing with agencies responsible for policing. In this way democratic representation of people's concerns is guaranteed. These councilors will also articulate local people's view on the quality of service provided by the police. The powers of the Police Authority (PA) and of Crime and Disorder Reduction Partnerships (CDRPs) were not enlarged.[1] The PAs have to be more actively involved with local councils and local communities. PAs are also responsible for including the priorities of CDRPs in police plan and for providing information about policing performance to local communities (McLaughlin 2005, 484).

3. Analysis

In our description of the developments and changes that took place in the police system and in local public safety in both The Netherlands and the UK, we observed multiple shifts. In this section we analyze these shifts with the help of the typology of governance practices presented in chapter 2.

From Government to Hierarchical Governance at a Distance

Despite institutional and organizational differences, differences in policy, and differences in starting points, policing in the UK and The Netherlands seem to converge. In both countries the police system tends to be more centralized with greater influence of the Home Office and the Ministry of the Interior and Kingdom Relations on police policy. This seems to be the most striking parallel. Both police systems have undergone more than one reorganization. In both countries police reforms follow reforms in other public sectors. The results-based agreements in The Netherlands can be seen as yet another step in a gradual process in which the police system tends to become more centralized, with greater influence of the Minister of the Interior and Kingdom Relations on police policy. A Dutch Home Office is coming into existence. This tendency undermines the traditional decentralized nature of the Dutch police system.

---

1   Crime and Disorder Reduction Partnerships are forms of cooperation aimed at the reduction of crime and disorder in an area.

New public management and the police   In both countries centralization coincided with a growing popularity of steering concepts borrowed from New Public Management (see Van Sluis and Van Thiel 2003). In both countries there is a strong emphasis on the need for transparency in police performance, accountability of the police and 'value for money'. In the UK police performance is measured with the Policing Performance Assessment Framework. Actual and past performances are compared and a comparison is made with the performance of police forces in the same cluster. The differences between comparable police forces have to be within a ten per cent range. The PPAF is also used to monitor the progress in the realization of the national priorities in the National Policing Plan. Her Majesty's Inspectorate of Constabulary (HMIC) also measures performance. These measurements are of a more qualitative nature, while measurement with the PPAF is of a quantitative nature. Police performance in The Netherlands is measured with the indicators from the national policy framework.

Centralization in steering is nowadays a hallmark of both police systems, not in the classical way of command and control but in a more sophisticated way, on a contractual base. In performance steering a variety of performance indicators is used to remedy the problems with traditional policy planning, leaving room for discretion at the regional and local levels.

Centralization in the political and administrative steering and control of the police has been accompanied by a shift within police management towards top-down steering.

Police chiefs in The Netherlands are in favor of running police forces in a more businesslike manner. Recently, a new generation of young police chiefs appeared on the stage, who were open to the idea of 'running the police like a business', whereas the majority of their predecessors were supporters of the community police model (see Boin et al. 2004). These new police managers are heavily influenced by 'new public management approaches'. They put a strong emphasis on the need for transparency in police performance, accountability of the police and 'value for money' (Osborne and Gaebler 1992). They generally favor top-down steering, in a 'quest for control'. They prefer quantitative information instead of qualitative information for monitoring performance. Intensifying top-down steering and control has been the most important objective of this new generation of police chiefs in the last years. These police managers consider rank-and-file officers as implementers of top-down formulated policies that can be controlled with standard operation procedures. Performance targets such as promoting public order, stricter supervision and law enforcement and greater policing efficiency are greatly appreciated by this new generation of police chiefs.

Vertical Downwards Shifts in Governance

Multi-level governance   While there are striking parallels in steering of the police at a national level in The Netherlands and the UK, there are also significant differences. In the UK police reform is part of a broader reform of the public sector and it parallels programs for citizen's renewal. In the UK the reform of the police took place in two waves. The first was a managerial reform, with strong centralistic tendencies.

But in the second wave the '*law abiding citizen*' was rediscovered, due to New Labour. The centralization of powers over the police was an important issue for successive conservative governments. This agenda was taken over by New Labour but adjusted for citizen's renewal. In this regard the New Labour government distinguishes itself from the former Conservative government.

Despite strong centralizing tendencies in modern policing in the UK, there have also been pressures towards more localization and more local accountability of the police and to a strengthening of relations between citizens and police. This development is accompanied by a revival of community policing. Intensified local steering parallels intensified steering of the police at a national level. Local accountability is an important countervailing power against centralization and a correction to intensified planning and control by 'London'.

In The Netherlands there has not been a similarly strong parallel between police reform and citizen's reform. Neither has there been a revival of community policing. On the contrary, community policing is seen by many as a thing of the past (Boin et al. 2004).

In The Netherlands there has been a long-term development towards intensified interaction between the police and citizens, preceding the recent reforms. Two models of policing can be distinguished: the community policing model and the reform model. (Van der Vijver 2004) In the first model police officers are seen as professional problem solvers. Basically, the community must police itself. The police can assist in this task and act as facilitators. This model presupposes intensive interactions between the police and the community and a variety of police tasks to be performed. The community-policing model originated in the report 'A Changing Police' that was published in 1977. Since then, community policing has been a dominant feature of Dutch policing.

The reform model on the other hand, presupposes a limitation of the police tasks to law enforcement and maintaining order; it does not include services to the public and crime prevention. This model also presupposes that other organizations take over the work the police are no longer doing. This work should be the responsibility of social workers, the mental health care system and schools. The police have to concentrate on their core tasks.

Nowadays, the reform model is the favorite model for policing amongst policymakers. The recent police reforms in The Netherlands are characterized by a one-sided centralization of police policy. The local dimension of policing is left out of the reform. The balance between central steering and decentralist steering is shifting, although the starting point was of course a different one, compared to the UK.

Horizontal Shifts in Governance

Market governance; gray policing   One of the most fundamental changes in policing since the mid-1960s is the process of pluralization, or, in other words, the end of the monopoly of the regular police on policing (Bayley and Shearing 2001). There has been a significant proliferation of 'policing beyond the police' (Crawford 2003) or 'gray policing' (Hoogenboom 1994).

This development includes the expansion of the commercial security sector, new forms of public sector policing provision such as local authority patrol forces and municipal police forces, the hiring of commercial security by local authorities, the increase in reported examples of informal policing such as vigilantism and the emergence of new transnational policing forms above the state level (Jones 2003). Policing roles are also performed by a host of regulatory agencies or inspectorates attached to national and local government. These processes of pluralization, fragmentation and expansion of policing have taken place in all western countries.

In terms of modes of governance, a shift towards market governance has taken place. Gray policing challenges existing arrangements for democratic steering and control and poses threats to the quality, democratic legitimacy and accountability of the police.

A shift has also taken place toward network governance and societal governance.

Network governance and societal governance   Both in The Netherlands and the UK, a strong belief in the importance of a strong civil society that produces public safety exists. The commitment of citizens and organizations is indispensable. The police are considered a last resort. In both countries policing has increasingly become co-production, in partnerships between public and private actors and between agencies and citizens, in security networks, as governance.

Newburn (2003) sees the increasing emphasis on partnership and citizen 'responsibilization'. Policing bodies are stretched locally. Some authors emphasize the necessity of a new approach of policing as security governance, in which there is no longer conceptual priority given to public police (Johnston and Shearing 2003; Hoogenboom 1994, 1999).

In The Netherlands societal and network governance are manifest in local integral public safety programs, in which public and private police, together with other agencies and citizens, tackle crime and safety, in loosely coupled networks and alliances. Typical for integral public safety policy on a local level is network steering. Networks are created to solve problems like disturbances of the peace, troubles around pubs or juvenile delinquency. Participants are the police, the justice department and municipal and private agencies.

Recently, policing in The Netherlands has become more oriented towards repression than in the past. Community policing is still important, but in contemporary Dutch policing, maintaining public order and fighting crime are becoming more dominant, as a result of the recent focus on the core business of the police and of the results based agreements between the police forces and the Minister of the Interior and Kingdom Relations. In the UK by contrast, community policing has witnessed a revival, as a steering conception in police practice as well as in the organization of the police.

Ironically, the British 're-assurance policing' was inspired by the Dutch approach according to Ian Blair (Chief of London's Metropolitan Police; Hoogenboom and Punch, 2006). But this model of policing was already on the way out back in The Netherlands.

The police in both countries put a lot of effort in the development of Intelligence Led Policing to improve their performance. The Dutch police follow the British police in this respect.

In sum, multiple and seemingly contradictory shifts have occurred. The first shift is one from (traditional) government towards a modernized hierarchical version of steering at the level of the police system, accompanied by scale extensions and centralization. At the same time a tendency towards localization occurred in an attempt to improve the responsiveness of the police. In The Netherlands this shift preceded the one in the UK, as a consequence of the community-policing model, while localization in the UK is a more recent trend, within the frame of national police policy. In both countries, horizontal shifts from public to private and gray policing and from the public sector to the civil society have taken place. The state withdrew and stimulated self-organizing capacity of citizens. Accountability of the police has been improved, vertically but also horizontally, as has public accountability. Societal governance and network governance can be seen as attempts to enlarge the responsiveness of the police.

Shifts in governance diverge. Partly they go upward (national crime investigation in The Netherlands, performance steering at a national level), partly downward. These shifts resemble the complexity and diversity of police tasks.

4. Police Governance and Legitimacy

To what extent have successive police reforms and shifts in governance had consequences for democratic legitimacy?

Input Legitimacy; Agenda Setting and Citizen's Participation

Too much centralization in steering the police poses a potential threat to the input legitimacy of the police. In the UK countervailing powers against centralization and against a resulting loss of input legitimacy have been created by reviving and strengthening the Police Authorities and by giving more authority to Crime and Disorder Reduction Partnerships. Based on the Crime and Disorder Act from 1998, these partnerships provide a potential framework for reinvigorating local influences over community public safety and policing policy because the police and other local agencies are required to produce regular audit and strategy documents (Loveday and

Reid 2003). Jones (2003) reaches the same conclusions. Citizens are encouraged to participate and to influence police policy and measures are being taken to enlarge the local accountability of the police.

Another countervailing power according to Mawby is the formation of police consultative committees (Mawby 2003). Police Authorities are legally obliged to consult citizens. Some authors however doubt the effectiveness of these arrangements (Jones 2003, Newburn 2003). Empirical research conducted by the Home Office Research department shows various problems in citizens' consultation. The main barriers for more public engagement in the Police Authority are 'consultation overload' and apathy. Especially hard to reach groups pose input legitimacy problems (Myhill et al. 2003). However, the researchers found some evidence for influence of the public on police policy.

In contrast with the UK, where the participation of citizens in police policy has a legal base in the Police Authority with significant legal powers, in The Netherlands there are only informal channels for citizen's to influence police policy. For many years, agenda setting and decision-making on police policy took place in closed and stable networks of civil and administrative actors, out of the public eye and without much public interest. For a long time, police policy and setting police priorities were 'low politics'. Starting from the 1980s and 1990s in the last century, the police have become more visible and more politicized (Cachet and Van Sluis 2003). Gradually new actors have entered this closed police arena, i.e. police complaints commissions, the national ombudsman, commissions of municipal councils that deal with local police policy and organizations that offer aid to victims of crime. The media has also developed an interest in the police.

In more recent years the police started interacting more directly with citizens as a consequence of community policing. For example, the police discuss policy and priorities with stakeholders and citizens advisory bodies in neighborhoods. In setting the priorities, regional police forces incorporate the results of the biannual *Politie Monitor Bevolking* (a bi-annual population wide survey to measure citizen's grievances and desires). So, despite a weak legal base, there are opportunities for citizens to give voice in The Netherlands.

Throughput Legitimacy; Checks and Balances

The political and democratic legitimacy at the local level show shortcomings in both countries. A democratic deficit exists in both countries caused by a lack of powers over the police of democratically elected local councils. Local councils in The Netherlands have only a limited say about the police, and the same applies to the UK. These are stubborn problems, not really affected by successive police reforms.

The shortcomings in the local political and democratic legitimacy of the police in The Netherlands are partly due to the structure of the regional police system. In The Netherlands there are no democratically elected representative bodies at the regional level. For another part, these shortcomings are due to the limited legal power of the local councils over the police. The mayor is in charge of the local police, and as a rule, local councils don't make use of their (limited) power over the police to exercise influence. They are dependent upon the mayor for giving instructions to the police and for police policy. However, local councils do have full authority with respect to local public safety policy. Local public safety programs can be used by local councils to set targets and priorities, also for the local police, but not every municipality uses this instrument.

In the UK as well, the weak local democratic legitimacy of the police has yet to be solved despite strong pressures towards increased localization and local accountability of the police. Although these changes give local people a say in police matters, the actual shifts strengthen citizen's influence as consumers, but not as citizens (Mawby 2003; McLaughlin 2005). A democratic gap at the local level still seems to exist that cannot be bridged by intensified local consultation and local accountability alone. According to McLaughlin local councils should have a stronger mandate to provide for 'democratic localism' (2005, 486).

These problems of throughput legitimacy have not been adequately solved yet, however, in both countries there are recent trends to reinforce the position of local councils. The Dutch government recently proposed strengthening the authority of local councils by legally obliging the regional force administrator to consult the local councils before decreeing the regional policy plan for the police. In recent government proposals in the UK, the position of local councilors, as representatives of the people, is strengthened in dealing with Police Authorities and Crime and Disorder Reduction Partnerships.

Weak local government power   In The Netherlands a variety of actors is supposed to work together in local integrated public safety programs. Public and private police, together with other agencies and citizens, should tackle crime and safety issues in loosely coupled networks and alliances. Typical for integral public safety policy on a local level is network steering.

In practice, the broad approach of public safety in The Netherlands is not yet fully developed. Physical safety drew attention only after the firework disaster in Enschede and the café fire in Volendam. Integral local public safety policy is expensive (because of the many actors involved) and not always effective. Because there is no hierarchy between the parties, decisions are sometimes not taken; sometimes organizations don't want to participate (Ringeling and Cachet 2004). Local government for example has no say about housing corporations, social work and mental health organizations. This situation represents the weak aspects of the Dutch polder model.

A possible solution for these types of problems is enlarging the perseverance capacity of local government. Not the police but local government needs more power to direct local public safety policy. Its only policy instrument now is to follow a facilitating strategy, whereas in the UK, the Crime and Disorder Reduction Partnerships do have some real power.

Output Legitimacy: Police Performance

Many changes at the level of the police system both in The Netherlands and in the UK originate from a common background of public dissatisfaction with police performance – and with unacceptable differences between police forces – and from declining public confidence. Policing in both countries was in need of performance improvement. In both countries the loss of public support has been an important trigger for changing the police. The growing awareness of the lack of public safety, both objective and perceived, and the inability of the police to cope with these problems caused a 'creeping' legitimacy crisis of the police, in combination with still faster rising expectations and new demands on police performance by the public. This crisis was primarily a crisis of output legitimacy.

In The Netherlands law enforcement did not keep up with crime rates. Research conducted by the *Wetenschappelijke Raad voor het Regeringsbeleid* (The Netherlands Scientific Council for Government Policy) showed that each year an average of 80,000 criminal cases was not pursued by the police. These cases were shelved. These shelved cases included serious offences like burglary, street robbery, and physical abuse. A lot of these cases might have had a good chance of being solved, according to case screening. The police could have done a far better job, just like the criminal justice system.

Improving quality and effectiveness　　The police in both countries have put a lot of effort into improving the output in policing for example by introducing systems of quality assessment, by the development and dissemination of best practices and by reinforcing the role of various inspection agencies. An important difference between the Dutch and the British reform of the police system at the national level is the emphasis on innovation. In the UK, a lot of attention is given to the development, dissemination and implementation of best practices, as well as on supervising the results by auditing committees. There seems to be an inbuilt drive for improving performance in the UK. The Dutch system for quality assessment within the police (TQM) is far less obligatory. Besides, due to the introduction of performance steering, the attention for quality assessment in The Netherlands is disappearing. The role of inspectorates in The Netherlands has always been less predominant compared to the UK, where HMIC and Audit Commissions are important in spreading best practices with 'best practices guidelines' and statutory codes of conduct.

Improved public accountability and responsiveness　　Shifts like localization and the involvement of other organizations and citizens with public safety create opportunities for increased public accountability of the police. As we stated before, societal governance and network governance can be seen as attempts to enlarge the responsiveness of the police. These shifts occurred in both countries.

Output and outcomes　　The introduction of performance steering can be explained as a response to serious problems with police output in both countries. Citizens and administrators want more value for money. The two countries differ in one respect. In The Netherlands performance based financing has been introduced in an attempt to improve performance. In The UK this is considered to be a bridge too far.

Recently, we conducted research into the effects and side effects of the national system of result-based agreements with the police (Van Sluis, Cachet, Ringeling e.a. 2006). Many stakeholders don't see a plausible relation between police output and outcomes. Almost all our stakeholders are convinced that success or failure of police performance ultimately has to do with the effects on public safety and the citizens' feelings about public safety, not with increasing numbers of fines and charges. For many stakeholders the presuppositions behind the system of results-based agreements and the supposed effects on public safety are not plausible. The poor validity of the policy theory contains a risk for the police. Negative effects for the public confidence in the police are inevitable if the targets are met and at the same time public safety and citizens' feeling about public safety decrease. In this scenario, results-based agreement will have a boomerang effect.

5. Conclusion: Models of Democracy

In our view the political and democratic steering and control of the police – the representative democracy model – show serious shortcomings at the local level. In this model democratically elected bodies ultimately control the police and the work of the police. We agree with Jones' statement that policing is inescapably political. 'It concerns the expression of fundamental values and, ultimately, the exercise of raw power by intervening authoritatively (and, if necessary, forcefully) in social conflict. It also involves choices, given limited resources, between policing priorities and policing styles. Such questions cannot be left to policing agents alone, but should be located within the realm of political debate. In a democracy such questions are ultimately the responsibility of representative bodies'. (Jones 2003, 606)

Other democracy models are becoming relevant, with regard to steering and control of the police. In local public safety networks, both in the UK and in The Netherlands, deliberative democracy models come into being. Citizens and public, private and semiprivate organizations are considered co-producers of public safety, and a successful fight against crime and danger requires their active participation. In community policing, model types of associative democracy have evolved. The police discuss police policy and priorities with stakeholders and advisory bodies of citizens in neighborhoods.

More recently, types of client democracy are developing as a consequence of the reform model of policing and inspired by New Public Management. Citizens are perceived as clients, as consumers of police services, who have to be served properly. Marketing-like instruments like the *Politiemonitor Bevolking* are used to measure citizen's satisfaction with the police. The adherence of the Dutch and British police to Intelligence Led Policing reinforces the approach of citizens as respondents in surveys instead as co-producers of public safety.

These evolving democracy models undoubtedly serve a purpose in increasing the legitimacy, the responsiveness and the public accountability of the police. They support the representative democracy model in organizing, embedding and steering of the police. But they are added extras, not substitutes for the representative democracy model. They are hardly formalized and are not obligatory. They are unstable and can disappear rather quickly. Problems should not be solved by changing over to other democracy models, but by reinforcing the representative democracy model. Moreover, we would argue that the strength of the deliberative, the associative and the client democracy model is ultimately dependent upon the strength of the representative democracy model.

Both The Netherlands and the UK face the same difficulties in reforming the police and increasing the legitimacy of the democratic policing. Within a more centralized system of steering and control, policing in both countries tends to be co-production in (local) networks, facing not yet solved questions how to deal with external accountability, how to give citizens influence on police policy, how to ensure sufficient local political influence and how to cooperate with other parties in an broad approach of crime and public safety. In both countries there is a need of strengthening the role of local government in directing local public safety and the authority of local council with regard to the police and police policy.

Both countries are in search of arrangements for steering and control that are appropriate in a relatively new context and that fit both local and national demands.

A variety of steering arrangements and checks and balances between steering at both the local and the national level seem to be in place. There seems to be no simple solution. Even divergent solutions for comparable problems can be imaginable, as the comparison between the two countries in this chapter shows.

References

Algemene Rekenkamer (2003), *Zicht op taakuitvoering door de politie* (Den Haag).

Bayley, D. H. and Shearing, C.D. (2001), *The New Structure of Policing, Description, Conceptualization and Research Agenda* (U.S. Department of Justice, Research Report).

Bekkers, V.J.J.M. and Ringeling, A.B. (eds) (2003), *Vragen over beleid, perspectieven op waardering* (Utrecht: Lemma).

Berenschot (2001), *Vooruitgang of regendans* Evaluatie Beleids- en Beheerscyclus Politie (Bestad/Berenschot Procesmanagement).

Boin, A.R., Torre, E.J. van der, and 't Hart, P. (2004), *Blauwe bazen. Het leiderschap van korpschefs* (Apeldoorn: Politie en Wetenschap).

BZK, Ministerie van Binnenlandse Zaken en Koninkrijksrelaties (2000), *Policing in The Netherlands.*

Cachet, A. and Sluis, A. van (2003), 'Perspectieven op veiligheid', in Bekkers and Ringeling (eds.).

Cachet, A. and Ringeling, A.B. (2004), 'Integraal veiligheidsbeleid: goede bedoelingen en wat ervan terecht kwam', in Muller (ed.).

Crawford, A. (2003), 'The pattern of policing in the UK: policing beyond the police', in Newburn (ed.).

Fynhaut, C.J.C.F. et al. (eds) (1999), *Politie, studies over haar werking en organisatie.* (Alphen aan den Rhijn: Samson).

Hoogenboom, A.B. (1994), *Het Politiecomplex: over de samenwerking tussen politie, bijzondere opsporingsdiensten en particuliere recherche* (Gouda: Quint/ Kluwer, Arnhem/Antwerpen: Rechtswetenschappen).

Hoogenboom, A.B. (1999), 'Privatisering van de politiefunctie', in Fynhaut et al. (eds).

Hoogenboomm, A.B. and Punch, M. (2006), 'Tien redenen om niet te nationaliseren', *Tijdschrift voor de Politie, 68*, 13–15.

Jones, T. (2003), 'The governance and accountability of policing', in Newburn (ed.).

Johnston, L. and Shearing, C. (2003), *Governing Security* (London: Routledge).

Keating, M. and Loughlin, J. (eds), T*he Political Economy of Regionalism* (London: Frank Cass).

LKNP (Landelijk Kader Nederlandse Politie) (2003), Staatscourant 72:11, 11 April.

Loughlin, J. and Peter, B.G. (1997), 'State traditions, administrative reform and regionalization', in: M. Keating and J. Loughlin (eds), pp. 41–61.

Loveday, B. and Reid, A. (2003), Going Local. Who Should Run Britain's Police? (London: Policy Exchange).

Majone, G. (1989), *Evidence, Arguments and Persuasion in the Policy Process* (New Haven/London: Yale University Press).

March, J.G. and Olsen, J.P. (1989), *Rediscovering Institutions* (New York: The Free Press).

Mawby, R.C. (2003), 'Models of policing', in Newburn (ed.).

Mawby, R.C. and Wright, A. (2003), 'The police organization', in Newburn (ed.).

McLaughlin, E. (2005), 'Forcing the Issue: New Labour, New Localism and the Democratic Renewal of Police Accountability', *Howard Journal of Criminal Justice* 44:5, 473–89.

Muller, E.R. (ed.) (2004) *Veiligheid, studies over inhoud, organisatie en maatregelen* (Alphen aan den Rijn: Kluwer).

Myhill, A. et al. (2003), 'The role of police authorities in public engagement', Home Office Online Report 37:03 (Home Office).

Newburn, T. (2003), 'Policing since 1945', in T. Newburn (ed.).

Newburn, T. (ed.) (2003), *Handbook of Policing* (Devon: Willan Publishing).

Osborne, D.E., and Gaebler, T.A. (1992), *Reinventing government: How the Entrepreneurial Spirit is Transforming the Public Sector* (New York: Plume).

Pfeffer, J.G. and Salancik, G.R.(1979), *The External Control of Organizations* (New York: Harper & Row).

Reiner, R. (2000), *The Politics of the Police* (Oxford: Oxford University Press).

Sluis, A. and Thiel, S. van (2003), 'Mogelijkheden en onmogelijkheden van prestatiesturing bij de Nederlandse politie', *Het Tijdschrift voor Veiligheid en Veiligheidszorg* 2:4, December, 18–31

Sluis, A. van, Cachet, A., Nieuwenhuyzen, C.N., Jong, E.T. de, and Ringeling, A.B. (2006), 'Cijfers en stakeholders. Prestatiesturing en de gevolgen voor de maatschappelijke en politiekbestuurlijke relaties van de politie', *Politie en Wetenschap* 32a (Den Haag: Elsevier).

Stokkum, B. van and Gunther Moor, L. (eds) (2004), *Onoprechte handhaving? Prestatiecontracten, beleidsvrijheid en politie–ethiek.* (Dordrecht: Stichting Maatschappij, Veiligheid en Politie).

Vijver, K. van der (2004), 'Kerntaken, sturing en professionaliteit', in Stokkum and. Gunther Moor (eds).

Weick, K. (1969), *The Social Psychology of Organizing* (Reading, Mass.: Addison-Wesley Publications.

Chapter 7

The Accountability of Professionals in Social Policy: Or Why Governance is Multi-Focal and Democracy is Multi-Local

Peter Hupe and Michael Hill

How does the governance of social policy take place and what are the consequences for democracy in that sector? That is the leading question in this chapter.[1] Related questions are who are the governing actors and on what grounds do they govern. Third Way rhetoric has drawn attention to the complexity of accountability for public policies. Writers such as Janet Newman (*Modernising Governance* 2001) have highlighted the contradictions in initiatives that seem to aim at combining greater central accountability and local empowerment. There has also been increased attention on issues about the accountability of professional staff.

The conventional approach to dealing with these issues is to turn to the traditional stages model of the policy process to argue that implementation issues should be seen as embedded within prior policy decisions with elements of discretion at the local level set in a hierarchical context. This approach is linked with a normatively anchored general view on the relationship between representative democracy and government. In terms of the political system, democracy provides legitimacy on both the input-side and output-side. Politics provides the translation of demands into policy actions, while administration takes care of turning these actions into policy outputs. As the bearers of democracy, citizens appear in the beginning, particularly as voters, and in the end, largely as consumers of public services. What happens in the throughput part of the cycle, from the perspective of representative democracy is less relevant, as long as the outputs – and, in fact, the outcomes – correspond with the agreed upon policy intentions.

---

1 Some of the material was also used in 'Analysing Policy Processes as Multiple Governance: Accountability in Social Policy' written by the authors and published in the July 2006 edition of *Policy and Politics*. A few theoretical notions were introduced in the paper 'Powers behind Control: An Essay on Democracy' presented by Peter Hupe at the Annual Work Conference of the Netherlands Institute of Government held at Erasmus University Rotterdam, 29 October 2004.

This generally accepted view on the relation between democracy and government and the approach to issues of accountability stemming from it have consequences for both practice and research. They seem to imply an underestimation of the complexity of many policy issues and of the organizational arrangements for modern governance, as well as a view of democracy that neglects the potential of seemingly illegitimate but in fact co-producing actors in policy processes. To avoid this underestimation it is necessary to look at issues of accountability as an operationalization of democracy in an empirical rather than normative way. While it cannot provide answers to what are essentially normative questions about competing legitimacies, an alternative to the stages model of the policy process can help to increase clarity about the strategic choices to be made. By highlighting the interrelationships between decisions, this alternative analytical framework can guide research on social policy and assist those who want to exercise greater control over policy processes, whether from the top or from the bottom.

Instead of the conventional preoccupations of policy analysis with successive policy 'stages', in this chapter we use an empirically open approach to determine how policy decisions are inter-related. Specifically, we use the Multiple Governance Framework. Built upon Elinor Ostrom's 'institutional analysis and development' framework (1999) this framework enables us to look at the public policy process as a multidimensional as well as a nested phenomenon. It is suggested as a conceptual device to assist with framing empirical studies. In particular the framework is used here to cast light on issues of accountability in social policy.

In the next section, we further explore the relationship between democracy and governance. In the second and third sections, we apply the framework to two cases: health care and the management of schooling in England.

1. Democracy and Governance

The generally accepted view on the relation between democracy as representative democracy on the one hand and government on the other pictured above and normatively anchored as it is, in fact implies a very narrow view. The essence of this is a triple hierarchy – one that may collide with complex reality. Sketching the nature of both this hierarchy and the possible collision as meant provides a key to understanding issues of accountability in policy processes.

A Threefold Hierarchy

The first element in the triple hierarchy is the relationship between state and society at the macro-level. In the widespread view on liberal democracy, legitimate power stems from the people (Held 1996). What politicians come up with is rooted in the problems as seen by the members of the *polis*. Politics is the designation of the process through which agendas are translated into action intentions. Within this process, on the input-side of government, one could speak of the primacy of society.

What has been agreed upon between the people's representatives and the Executive as ways of dealing with matters of society is laid down in laws and public policies. It is up to the institutions of the Executive to produce societally desired results. As a follow up of a logically preceding agenda setting in the relationship between society and government ('democracy'), *within* government the stage of policy making ('government') then occurs. This second relationship, traditionally labeled as the one between politics and administration, also has a hierarchical character (Wilson 1941; see also Frederickson and Smith, 2003). The hierarchy within this relationship – on the throughput-side of government – has traditionally been characterized as the 'primacy of politics'.

There is a third relationship as well. In what can, in fact, be seen as a stages model at the macro-level, there is a final hierarchical relationship, namely between government and performance. On the output-side of government, the latter is supposed to produce the desired action, implicitly the outcomes as agreed upon with society through the democratic process on the input-side of government. One may speak here of the primacy of the governing center.

The general assumption in this model is that (representative) democracy on the input-side plus government in the throughput leads to legitimate government performance on the output-side, as a dependent variable in a linear equation. In this traditional view on democracy as representative democracy, the relationship between society and performance in the general interest in fact has been a vertical, stagist and threefold hierarchical one. Society is supposed to have the primacy over government, and politics over administration, while government controls the production of desired results. This being a normative view, its empirical explanatory power can be questioned. Given the complexities of modern-, post-modern-, or even post-post-modern society the linear, chain-like connections implied here seem to have been cut through at two spots. First, between society and government: lower voter turn outs and diminishing involvement in party politics are seen as a major expression of a smaller basis of legitimacy for what politicians are doing. This legitimacy problem on the input-side of the political system is the essence of the so-called democratic deficit in a narrow sense. Second, the connections between government and performance have been cut through or in any case been loosened; that is the essence of what has been called the relocation of politics (Bovens et al. 1995). What can be observed now is that government performance has become public performance. Because 'government' has become 'governance', it is often unclear in policy processes who the deciding actors are and how they take various interests into account. This is the nature of the legitimacy problem on the throughput- and output-side of government.

Thus the problem is one of legitimacy, and it has a dual character. In terms of government, particularly concerning the throughput-side, there is a shortage of visibility. If (central) government can no longer *a priori* be supposed to be the central and leading actor in policy processes, who then *de facto* are the governing actors and on what grounds do they make their decisions? In terms of democracy, there is a problem of accountability: Who is held accountable to whom?

If the replacement of government by governance forms an important aspect of this problem definition, the analysis of the meaning of the latter term may provide ways to deal with empirically observed situations. Furthermore, if the relationship between democracy and government is no longer a hierarchical one, the relation between the former and governance, instead, –multiple horizontal and vertical as the concept of governance is – may supply ways for identifying new forms of democracy in the situations observed. Therefore an appropriate analytical framework is needed in order to avoid the normative biases mentioned above. Such a framework is set out in the next section.

Multiple Governance

According to O'Toole (2000, 276) the concept of governance is designed 'to incorporate a more complete understanding of the multiple levels of action and kinds of variables that can be expected to influence performance'. Conceptualizing this performance in the public domain as governance has consequences. First, the focus is on action, rather than government as formal institution. 'Who is the governing actor?' becomes an empirical question; it may be a public or a private one; it may be an official policy maker or an actual one. Second, where the various actions take place is also empirically open; differentiating between administrative layers and action levels is important. Third, in the concept of governance, the separation of policy from management has been abolished. Governance implies both, while the act of managing can be observed in all loci of political-societal relationships (Hill and Hupe 2002).

Table 7.1   The multiple governance framework

	Action levels of governance (=Focus)		
	Designing Institutions	Giving direction	Getting things done
Scale of Action Situations (=Locus)			
System			
Organization			
Individual			

Adaptation of Hill and Hupe (2002), p. 183.

Taking our lead from Kiser and Ostrom's (1982) 'three worlds of action', we distinguish a structure-, content-, and process dimension of the concept of governance as a focus. Each of these refers to a broad set of related activities: those concerning institutional design, giving direction, and getting things done. Respectively, we speak of constitutive, directive and operational governance (2002). Different from the traditional so called 'stages model' of the policy process, each of these activity clusters can be observed at any administrative layer. Both the number of acting actors and of potential action situations can logically be thought of as infinite. Categorizing the scale of action situations, we speak in a summarizing way of three loci in political-societal relations: the locus of the system, of the organization, and of the individual. In fact, the vertical stages view on the policy process can thus be replaced by a multi-dimensional framework for the conceptualization of the policy process as multiple governance (see Table 7.1 above).

In this conceptualization, governance is essentially both 'mixed-focus' and 'multi–local'. Not only does it involve giving direction (cf. the stage of policy formation), but also managing activities (cf. the stage of implementation) and even designing institutions. On any layer, formal-administrative or not, each of these activity sets can take various forms according to the specific action situations in which they take place. The distinction between administrative layers, levels of action and loci as action situations is important since in practice, what should be the appropriate layer for the location of particular decisions may be an issue while analytically our concern is to explicate that these layers may vary and be the subject of dispute. Thus in the education example discussed below, we find strongly held views about appropriate divisions of responsibility between central and local government.

The nested character of the framework implies that, conceptually, one action level is not necessarily confined to one administrative layer. Whether, for instance, in a given policy process a layer of government practices just 'implementation' or rather 'policy co-formation' is an empirical question, resting upon an interpretation of the extent of observed change. Any judgment about whether the observed action is desirable is a normative matter.

By using a matrix form, the aim is to avoid a vertical bias. In the analytical framework the various activities in a policy process are seen as taking place at different moments, at different spots, by different actors. An activity cluster ('stage'), identified here as one specific level of action and usually associated with one particular layer, is supposed to go on all along the line of vertical administration, as, legitimately or not, practiced by actors at other layers but in a variety of action situations as well. There will be great variation in the extent to which these activities do occur as result of certain action level/action situation combinations while there may be controversy about the extent to which policy outputs are affected by these activities. Reality in these systems will, we hypothesize, be a combination of an explicitly and not easily amended system, conveying certain expectations of the system as a whole together with locally determined management arrangements and rules affecting discretion at the street-level. But not only is there likely to be great variation around these themes, there will also be controversy about the appropriateness or inappropriateness of the structuring involved. Such arguments will not be merely about discretion at the street-level but also about the appropriateness of 'prior' structuring decisions.

Implied in the notion of 'government' has been one prevalent 'mechanism of social control', that of hierarchy (Lindblom 1977). Differently, 'governance' arrangements may take various forms. They have in common that binding collective decisions are made and public power is exercised.

Multi-Local Democracy

Our concern then is with situations in which the normative principles of the *Rechtsstaat* and democracy remain valid but power, with more or less legitimacy, is exercised by various actors and at many places in the public domain. These situations have consequences for the institutional position of democracy. If (central) government cannot be supposed to be the only policy determining actor in policy processes and visibility has become a problem, but, nevertheless, public performance is at a high level, it becomes relevant to observe on what grounds the *de facto* governing actors in their decisions contribute to that public performance. In addition to vertical relationships accountability may be practiced in more horizontal settings. Now the notions of associative and client democracy elaborated elsewhere in this book can be linked with the terms used in the framework presented above. For instance, national associations of professionals in a specific vocation can be seen as a direct countervailing power in the system-locus. An essential institutional feature of liberal democracy, such countervailing power may give structure to random behavior of single practitioners, sometimes even opposing that behavior. The formulation of codes of conduct, certification procedures, citizen's charters, et cetera can be addressed as structure-oriented activities of governance taking place with consequences for systems (of police, social work, and so on) as a whole. The same goes for appeal procedures. Forms of (self-)organizing of users, customers, clients, patients, or other stakeholders can be seen as institutions functioning as checks on the exercise of power as well; though in a different locus, that is the one of single organizations. There organization-bound complaint procedures can also be localized. In the locus of inter-individual relations, phenomena like peer review function as mechanisms limiting the uncontrolled exercise of power. Addressing institutional 'democratic devices' like the ones mentioned can lead to answers to the 'on what grounds and for whom' question of accountability as formulated above. Referring to the relation between democracy and governance, these answers complement the 'who is the governing actor' question of visibility.

In the next sections we apply our framework using English data relating to two policy areas: health care and the provision of education in schools. The discussion of each is divided into three parts. In the first part, the basic framework is used to look at the policy-making roles of the various actors involved. Setting out the dimensions of multiple governance, the leading question here is: Who are the actual 'governing actors'? In the second part of the two case studies, we explore the implications and reach of the formal arrangements for representation, identifying the characteristics of multi-local democracy in that field. The guiding question here is: What is the character of the checks on the actions of the governing actors as identified? In a third and concluding part per case, we draw out some of the implications of what has been discussed to analyze the extent to which it is possible to speak about a democratic deficit in the policy area concerned.

2. Case A. The Policy Framework for Health Care in England

Multiple Governance in Health Policy

The National Health Service (NHS) operates throughout the United Kingdom, but the governance arrangements differ between the constituent countries of England, Scotland, Wales and Northern Ireland; only the system in England is discussed here. Since its inception, the NHS has a) embodied tax funded, generally free hospital services with controlled access (largely through primary care gate-keepers), b) provided through central government designed local organizations, c) included practitioners with high levels of decision-making freedom. The first of these features has been a common theme running through since 1948, despite intermittent political threats of something different. The second feature has been the subject of wave after wave of changes in institutional design. The third feature, has, particularly in recent years, been substantially challenged from above and below, provoking a range of innovations. We can observe a continued reinforcement of the basic system, within which extensive institutional changes can be seen as nested, in the behavior of central government.

The system operating at the time of writing is comparatively simple and has the following features:

- A national network of Strategic Health Authorities.
- Below them a network of Primary Care Trusts with responsibility for the organization of primary care and the commissioning of services for the patients under their primary care from hospitals and other secondary care services.
- Trusts that organize hospitals and other secondary care services in their areas.

All of these bodies are appointed by the Secretary of State but in doing so he or she has regard to the need to include representatives of the professions and, in the case of the Primary Care Trusts, the providers of overlapping services (primarily here the local authorities responsible for social care).

What differentiates health policy from education policy in England is that the formal arrangements seem to imply a very simple hierarchical relationship. The politician responsible for the establishment of the National Health Service, Aneurin Bevan, fought off suggestions from one of his Cabinet colleagues, Herbert Morrison, that local government should have a mainstream role in the control of the health service (Foot 1975, 132–3). Only a limited range of preventative community health measures were left with local government and even these largely disappeared when structural changes were made in 1971.

But three considerations meant that in reality the NHS was not set up as a simple hierarchy. One was the practical need for local managerial arrangements for so large a policy delivery system. A second was that voluntary (charitable) hospitals were being nationalized, and a conciliatory gesture to the local elites who had been serving on management boards required their incorporation into the new administrative arrangements. The third, and most important one, was that to secure the acquiescence of doctors, the Minister had to devise ways of involving them in local management.

NHS at system scale Self evidently, the main ingredients of structure have been set on the scale of the NHS 'system' as a whole. However, over the years there have been various occasions on which structural changes have been possible through the operation of choice in the locus of the organization. The original experiments of the last Conservative Governments with General Practitioner Fund holding involved relatively localized choices that produced incremental structural change. The trial and error aspects of this development have been analyzed by Glennerster and his colleagues (1994). The shift from that system to Primary Care Teams was also initially a piecemeal one. The contemporary development of Foundation Trusts (see discussion below) has some similar features, application to secure this status has to come from the Trust and be supported by indications of the managerial arrangements to be set up.

Hospitals: professional autonomy Looking at directive governance it is very clear that professional participation in policy making has a significant impact on both the scale of single organizations and of individual practitioners. But professional autonomy has some impact on the 'system' scale, too. We refer here not so much to how professionals are embedded into the policy making process at all levels within the NHS, but to how doctors (particularly general practitioners) still have a great deal of latitude in how they organize their services. The intended effect of the professional norms indicated here is multiple: binding oneself, colleagues, and third parties, via codes of conduct, professional standards and associations. It should be noted that the dual meaning of the term 'institution' becomes visible then: sets of values materialized (curdled) into practical rules. While the term 'organization' singularly refers to structural features of the division of labour and the like, the concept of 'institution' implies those features, but also sense making. In fact referring both to aspects of 'structure' and 'content' therefore 'institution' has a double meaning.

Issues about the re-organization of hospital services tend to involve an interaction between the central ministry and the local Trust. Overall pressure for rationalization will come from the former, the nature of the local response will be a matter for the latter. But then there will be processes of public consultation at the local level and lobbying at the center. For example local Members of Parliament will often intervene with the minister to try to influence events. At the same time there will be forms of local participation taking forms like this:

The proposals we have described in this document have been developed following a process of extensive discussion with the public, local interest groups, voluntary organizations and other health and social care partner organizations. Many of our stakeholders have taken part in a series of local meetings and four large events, launched as part of the Best care, best place initiative. Findings from this 'discussion phase' have been presented to the various Trust boards… (Consultation document issued for residents of Central Sussex, about changes proposed by a group of Trusts in their area, November 2004, 25).

Of course it remains an empirical question about how far beyond 'informing' that this exercise in participation moved up Arnstein's often quoted 'ladder of participation' (1969).

Issues about the complex loci of content decisions can best be illustrated by a crucial issue in the determination of the content of health policy: budgeting. It is an inherent characteristic of budgeting in a system like the NHS that it has a nested character with detailed allocations being determined within the context of a general gross amount of money. In an account of the financing of healthcare, Glennerster supplies a complex flow diagram (2003 62 Table 4.3) illustrating the various interactions between both organizations and specifically localized decision makers. The politics of budgeting is such that efforts to prescribe from the top are open to a shifting discourse about underspending and overspending, 'virement' between spending categories and so on. A particular feature of health service politics has long been a debate about the extent to which spending can be needs led, in that developments at the scale of the individual (the incidence of disease and practitioners choices about how to treat it) may drive ultimate expenditure outcomes.

Practitioners: 'clinical governance'   The issues about process are particularly interesting given the conflict between system locus political aspirations and traditional claims of professional autonomy. In this complex and controversial area the behavior of the UK Government at present is very interesting. The issues that arise here involve not merely questions about system, organization and individual locus decisions but also ones about the extent to which structure and content influence process. It has only been since 1997 with the arrival of ideas about the use of performance indicators, so called clinical governance and a more interventionist stance through the National Institute for Clinical Excellence (NICE) and the Health Commission that the center has sought to have a strong impact on operational governance. A crucial element in the contemporary development of the management of doctors is the notion of 'clinical governance' or 'clinical audit'. The British Government sees this as 'a partnership between the Government and the clinical professions. In this partnership, the Government does what only the Government can do and the professions do what only they can do' (Department of Health 1998a, para 1.13). The same document goes on to argue (para 3.9):

Clinical governance requires partnerships within health care teams, between health professionals (including academic staff) and managers, between individuals and the organizations in which they work and between the NHS, patients and the public.

We see here recognition of issues about mixed management, as well as a highlighting of issues about choices of forms of management and about ways of combining different forms in the same system. Clearly, there is much controversy around the Government's view of clinical governance. There seem to be some boundaries that might be used in determining prerogatives in this matter. A view may be taken on one side in the argument about medical autonomy that there is still a need to impose much stronger standards upon doctors; on the other side, it is argued that medical discretion is already seriously constrained. Examinations of the Blair Government's view of its objectives have highlighted the continuing tension between their views about delegation of responsibilities and their desires to enforce standards from the top (Newman 2001). A typical illustration of this in the health field lies in statements like the following in the NHS Plan:

> Because we trust people on the frontline, the center will do only what it needs to do; then there will be maximum devolution of power to local doctors and other health professionals. The principle of subsidiarity will apply. So the center will: set standards, monitor performance, put in place a proper system of inspection, provide back up to assist modernization of the service and, where necessary, correct failure, Intervention will be in inverse proportion to success; a system of earned autonomy. The centre will not try and take every last decision. There will be progressively less central control and progressively more devolution as standards improve and modernization takes hold (NHS Plan, para 6.6, 2000).

In sum: We trust you, and will give you more autonomy when we are sure you are doing what we want! Even stronger examples of this phenomenon can be found in the second of our case studies. But our object here is not to criticize, it is to point out the complexity of a policy system with delegated operational management.

One of us has taken a more detailed look at issues of process in the field of obstetrics. This is an interesting area in which there is some effort to impose guidelines from the top, strong deference to the profession but a recognition that there is a patient at the 'street-level' who is increasing likely to want to influence the way she is treated. The sources of guidelines are almost entirely the profession itself, with a strong emphasis upon research evidence. While lip service is paid to issues of choice by women, there is no indication that maternity service users have been explicitly consulted or surveyed during the guidelines formulation process. It seems generally to be the case that the patient is absent from the clinical governance process.

The following statement seems a typical view on guidelines from a practitioner who describes himself as sympathetic to them:

> Guidelines guide those in need of guidance along the line drawn by the guideline maker. This definition may seem facile but it exposes the limitations of guidelines. They are only useful to those who need guidance. They bring the outdated physician back into line, as recommended by the expert and they can be used to herd the weak and less focused down a politically expedient path. However, sophisticated medicine is an art (Johnson 2002, 495).

Studies not surprisingly therefore indicate that adoption of guidelines depend very much upon local practice, as well as individual disposition (Berrow et al. 1997; Dye et al. 2000; Foy et al. 2001; Templeton et al. 2001). Similarly McDonald and Harrison show how the formulation of local guidelines involves a negotiation process in which doctors 'hoped to pursue their existing options, either through imposing them on others, or by creating a framework of legitimation for themselves' (2004, 223).

Clinical governance and clinical audit put these issues on local agendas but leave much to local decision. Given their growing official status, National Service Frameworks and the work of NICE become of increasing importance. The extent to which these developing guidelines change practices particularly will depend upon the expectations by the Department of Health about the effective use of Clinical Audit by hospitals.

Multi-Local Democracy in Health Care

The consequence of the arrangements for the health service has been that, in practice, there is what may reasonably be described as a 'democratic deficit'. The structure is too complex for the operation of a simple top-down hierarchical control model. Yet there are only very limited representational arrangements at the local level. Over the years since 1948, various governments have shown an awareness of the problem, but they have not been prepared to resolve it by bringing local government properly into the business. In fact between 1948 and the present day, three approaches to this issue have been attempted. In the early period the local authorities were required to nominate members of the various local governing bodies. They generally did this by nominating elected councilors, most of whom played minimal roles since they were too heavily occupied with roles within their own local authorities. The next approach was to set up 'community health councils' whom health bodies were required to take into account and consult. These bodies were composed of local government representatives, representatives of a wide range of local voluntary organizations and health service nominees. From the very beginning, the arbitrary manner in which these bodies were constituted came under attack. In addition they were poorly resourced. In 2002 these were replaced by more complex arrangements for public consultation – the word representation would be too strong here. There is a central Commission for Patient and Public Involvement in Health and a requirement that every Trust should set up a Patients' Forum. There are separate arrangements to assist people with complaints about services, a Patients Advocacy and Liaison Service. While the note on the Primary Care Trusts above mentions local government representation, this is designed to deal with service overlaps and implies the presence of local government managers, not elected representatives. However a new place has now been found for local government. 'Scrutiny' committees of elected members may examine health policy matters with implications for the citizens of the areas they represent. These committees are purely investigatory but have the potential to ensure that local views are clearly conveyed to Trusts.

There is one other system complexity that requires a brief mention. Since 2004, some hospital trusts have been allowed to take on the status of Foundation Trusts with a greater degree of autonomy. If they do this, they are required to include representatives of their patients (in practice their past or potential future patient population), elected by way of a complex procedure, in their managements:

> ... residents in areas covered by these hospitals get the chance to register as 'members' of the trust, allowing them to vote for a board of 'governors' to whom the directors of the trust are nominally responsible. Out of more than two million people served by the first ten such hospitals, 34,000 registered as members and (including hospital staff) only 20,000 voted in elections for governors (Runciman, 2005, 6).

This does not, however, represent a new injection of representational democracy in any realistic sense. While democratization efforts directed at input or throughput efforts have been weak at the output end, consumerism has been seen as the route towards greater patient involvement. Efforts are being made to increase the scope for choice – for example over where secondary care should be provided – informing this through the provision of performance data. The significant feature of health policy is that while we are all health service recipients at some time, fewer of us are health service recipients all the time (and very few are recipients of institutional care and other very intensive forms of care all the while). In that sense there is logic in addressing democratic deficit problems not through the design of universal representative devices but through attention to time and place limited issues about participation. On the other hand in the absence of the right structural and organizational arrangements (and particularly resources) these participatory forms may be beside the point.

Health Care: Conclusion

The NHS has been described as a system in which there has been a continuing tendency for the government to see the general public as represented through centralized democracy, and to be reluctant to countenance local democratic arrangements. On the other hand, in relation to health service staff, and above all the doctors, the recognition of professional power has led to efforts to incorporate ways for them to participate at all levels. However, there has been a continuing ambivalence about this, inasmuch as participation seems to involve the risk that central control will be given away. In a context where expert decision-making is important, this risk is perceived particularly as far as directive governance is concerned, but even in some respects with regard to operational governance.

There is a paradox here; it is the centripetal impact of the efforts of the doctors to protect their autonomy that is seen as providing an important part of the case for central control. The impact of scandals arising from medical malpractice has been an intensification of central control efforts (for example the introduction and strengthening of the Health Commission). However, while the traditional arguments about democratic deficit have typically been about the refusal to allow local government to be a serious participant, attention has also been given to other ways of enhancing citizen participation in directive governance.

Perhaps, after all, in terms of models of democracy the picture in English health care overall can be called a mixed one. Observed can be elements of representative democracy: elected councilors and 'scrutiny' committees of elected members. Pluralist devices have been visible as well, like the Community Health Councils including representatives of local voluntary organizations. The extent to which these Councils and their successors the Health Forums fulfill token functions to influence policy throughput in this way is an empirical question.

Perhaps more significant is the attention given to direct patient participation in operational governance through attention to issues about choice. The new institutions in which patients are involved may be identified as forms of client democracy, with the hospital trusts including representatives of patients as elements of associative democracy.

3. Case B. The Policy Framework for the Management of Schooling in England

Multiple Governance in Education

Between 1944 and the mid-1980s, 'the post-war settlement' operated in which central government provided the broad policies that were then 'administered and interpreted by the local education authorities which in turn entrusted curriculum decision-making and pedagogy largely to the professionals on the ground' (Hudson and Lidström 2002, 32–3, citing Whitty, 1990). We see here then again an apparently simple division of policy–making labour. The important difference from health policy here is that the 'middle' party in this process, local education authorities are elected local governments, whereas the equivalent bodies in the health service were and are appointed ones. Distinct issues about the prerogatives of layers of government therefore enter more clearly into arguments about relative responsibilities.

The education system   Since the mid 1980s the system has experienced dramatic change. Change in the system has consisted of a great deal of centralization but also some decentralization. Centralization has involved a great increase in government control over the school curriculum, and the development of a testing system and a strong inspection system to go along with it. Decentralization has involved the weakening of local authority control over the schools. There has been a sort of 'hollowing out process' in which power has gone down to schools and parents have been given more scope to choose schools for their children and to participate in the government of schools.

Bache (2002) highlights two features of this 'hollowing out'. First, the complex formulae governing the funding of education which central government modified in ways that force increasing proportions of the money going to local government to be passed on in pre-determined ways to the schools. Second, the scrutiny of the performance of local authorities as managers of the school system that include powers – that have been used – to take functions away from them.

On the whole, centralization has limited the extent to which local authorities can influence the constitutions of their local system. There remain a very few authorities that have clung to selective secondary education systems. Where new local governments have come to power, they often want to get rid of these: the result of a shift to the Left at the local level. This means that (at the time of writing) central government is not a constraint upon change, but the law now requires ballots of parents before change can take place. In that sense, action taken by individuals may be significant.

Schools: towards more autonomy   What is also apparent is that inasmuch as there is a quasi-market in the education system, something that comes very close to constitutive governance occurs as a result of processes that are outside conventional forms of government control. In the very thickly populated areas (in particular in inner London), parental choice may govern the evolution of schools in ways that neither central nor local government can easily bring under control. In effect, unpopular schools are being driven out of business. In some areas, the presence of choice between co-educational and single sex schools add complications. Most significantly of all processes of ethnic segregation are emerging or being enhanced. Where once local authorities could zone schools in creative ways to try to influence social or ethnic mixes, the law relating to parental choice now prevents this. Currently under discussion is complex legislation trying to promote school autonomy while at the same time ensuring social mixes. The document is likely to lead to more legislation.

In the contemporary English education system we find, as with hospitals, a substantial concern at the central government layer with issues about content and process. At the same time we have noted a tendency to marginalize, even in relation to operational governance, the role of local government. To some extent, this implies moving the direction level to the top of the national school system, in other respects it involves moving it to the schools themselves, who make choices in a quasi-market system on how to organize and orientate themselves. We noted in the last section how this may even generate structural changes. Again, the issues about structure and the funding aspect of content are subject to contributions at all three loci. However, those who wish to control education from the top have found it rather easier to be prescriptive about the kinds of school arrangements that can be allowed and about funding than have their colleagues in health policy. Clearly, the political weakness of teachers as a profession may be relevant here.

Teachers' and managers' concern: the curriculum   Interesting issues about operational governance in education concern the curriculum and how it is taught. Here it is difficult to draw a clear distinction between directive and operational governance (or content and process). Issues about what is taught and how it is taught come together in the debate about control over the curriculum. The national curriculum and the associated testing shifts control over activities away from managers at the street-level. These are replaced by both stronger central directives and by the imposition of another organization, the inspectorate (OFSTED) as a party to operational governance. But as Bowe and his colleagues have argued, the resultant policy-making partnership is complex given the complexity of curricula (1992). Curriculum design is a complex process, likely to leave matters for decision at both middle management levels and at the classroom level.

One of us has made a more detailed study of one aspect of curriculum control, efforts at the scale of the system as a whole to control the teaching of literacy. Critics of the strong curriculum control associated with this area of teaching have attacked it as a form of Taylorism, changing teachers from professionals into technicians (Hilton 1998; Fisher et al., 2000). However, the assessment of its impact is difficult because of the extent to which prescriptions about teaching take their place in the context of other measures – parental choice, the publication of results, and the inspection system – that clearly limit teacher's autonomy and may increase parental participation. The key concern in relation to the measurement of performance is not what is done, but an outcome (performance in a test) that depends upon the contribution of the child as well as the teacher. Research evidence suggests therefore that centrally determined guidelines are at their strongest when the organizations required to apply them are least secure, i.e. likely to achieve poor test results (Lofty 2003). Of course the latter is determined to a considerable extent by the social class composition of the pupil intake. Though efforts are being made to use a 'value added' approach to the evaluation of these, taking into account pupil improvement from a measured baseline, this is complicated and is not easily reflected in publicity about schools. There is then a second level effect that organizational controls over individual practice are most likely to occur when head teachers have least confidence in individual teachers. In that sense, those most constrained are those with least experience. Again then we see directive governance (rule setting) replacing operational governance (managing trajectories).

Multi-Local Democracy in Education

In terms of representative democracy the pattern established in education after the 1944 Act involved an explicit partnership between central and local government. This was most cogently illustrated by the system changes that occurred gradually after 1944 with the piecemeal adoption of comprehensive as opposed to selective education at the secondary level. This process started with a limited number of local innovations, driven as much by circumstances as by ideology. Then increasingly Labour controlled local authorities shifted all or most of their secondary education system in the comprehensive development. Across the late 1950s and early 1960s, Conservative ministers were quite content to let them do this (Chitty 2004, chapter 2).

But the story of the development of comprehensive education is interesting inasmuch as the roots of the shift towards centralization lie in how comprehensive education became an issue that divided the political parties at the national level. When Labour won national power in 1964, it issued a circular urging local authorities to develop schemes to shift towards comprehensive education. While this was a 'permissive' approach, local authorities were expected to take note; failure to do so might affect their negotiations with the center on other matters. The next turn of the wheel, however, was much more decisive. In 1976 a later Labour government passed an Act requiring local authorities to submit proposals for comprehensive education.

While Labour governments made the early running towards the increased centralization of the education system, developments under Conservative governments after 1979 were crucial for the 'hollowing out' process described above: a combination of increased central control and increased autonomy for schools. A significant feature of the weakening of local government in respect of the latter has been what may be called 'quasi-marketization'. Funding depends on pupil numbers. Inasmuch as this interacts with parental choice (and how much this really applies depends upon geography), it has an impact on school success or failure. The publication of test results for individual schools can then further influence this process. To some extent, then, competition between schools drives the development of the system. In fact the Conservative governments did very little to directly reverse the trend towards comprehensivization but they allowed schools a greater range of choices in terms of how they should be organized and to what extent they should specialize, accompanied by measures to allow some selection of pupils. In a context of socially diverse catchment areas and parental choice, this generated school diversity. Since 1997 the new Labour government has actually reinforced rather than reversed this process.

The centralization measures are attacked using arguments in favor of local democracy. The central response to this tends to involve raising questions about the effective accountability of local government in respect of education, with its lower electoral turnout levels and frequent one-party domination. Since 1997, central government has imposed strong performance targets for local government, and has been prepared to take power away from underperforming authorities.

The democracy of the (quasi) market, with the increased scope for parental choice (at least in the most populous areas) is posed as a preferable alternative to simple local democracy. However, the other important development is increased parental involvement in the management of schools. There are now requirements to have parent governors elected by the parents of current children in the school. However, the impact of this is blunted by the fact that this element in the governing body is outnumbered by other ones (governors from the ranks of the teachers, local education nominees and co-opted governors).

Education: Conclusion

The paradox here is that centralization has been used to some extent to increase local control but cut out local government. This makes this case rather different to the health one. Where a strong profession has had an important limiting influence upon efforts to delegate power down to patients in health care, governments have been much readier to over-ride objections from teachers to these processes in education. Elements of client- and associative democracy can be observed here, as introduced versus enhancing local representative democracy.

Despite this, the formal shift in power seems to have been minimal. To what extent the election of parent governors functions as a symbolic measure is an open question. A complication here is the fact that continuity of contact with a clearly identifiable body of people, the parents of existing pupils, will be hard to establish. Perhaps in education this is even more so than in the case of health care (and particularly hospital care). In the consultative document mentioned above, ways are sought to increase parental 'ownership' of local schools, but there seem to be problems about the extent to which people with an essentially temporary interest in any particular school – that is: as long as their children are pupils there – may assume such a role.

Despite the introduction of elements of what may be conceived as client democracy, in Hirschman's (1970) terminology the question seems to be to what extent it is 'choice' that is the crucial source of a form of democratization in education. It has been noted that issues about school choice can have an effect not simply at the middle action level but also upon both constitutive governance – the determination of the structure of the local system as a whole – and operational governance, the determination of test results and therefore indirectly how subjects are taught.

Since the use of the 'exit' option is limited by the parental desire not to disrupt their children's education unduly (in other words, choice is mainly crucial at initial school entry and then at the primary/ secondary transition points), for parental influence over education 'voice' seems important. The contemporary high emphasis upon school autonomy coupled with head–teachers' inevitable sensitivity to the factors that influence school choice, appear to facilitate the exercise of voice.

4. Conclusions

How does governance in social policy takes place and what are the consequences for democracy in that sector? Reporting on two English cases we have explored who *de facto* are the governing actors in health policy and education, making governance visible. We have also looked at how, and in what kinds of accountability relationships, decisions are made that together make up for public performance. We have done so using an analytical framework that has been developed as an alternative to the so called 'stages model' of the policy process. A function of this framework is the empirically open observation of action of 'real' rather than normatively presupposed actors in governance. Another function of the analytical framework is to aid the identification of action choices.

A great deal of the literature on implementation has been preoccupied with a normative argument between 'top-down' and 'bottom-up' perspectives. Both stem from deeply held views about democratic accountability. Faced with what they regard as defects in implementation, both perspectives concern themselves with efforts to increase the capacity to control the public policy process, either from the top or the bottom. By contrast, a model that recognizes that influencing the policy process can involve adjustments to a complex nested system of levels, loci and layers may help actors to identify alternatives for action. Those with a strong top-down perspective may be assisted by an analysis of this kind, recognizing that they have choices between fundamental restructuring, adjusting specific substantive arrangements, or curbing street-level discretion. Conversely, from a bottom-up perspective, there will be questions about whether what is crucial is devising new ways of making street-level decisions or whether there are institutional and/or structural modifications that need to be made before these would be feasible. In both the examples explored here the crucial opposed positions are between those who see it as necessary to curb professionalism (probably from the top) and those who defend professional autonomy. A second theme most evident in the education example concerns the respective prerogatives of central and local government. The hollowing out phenomenon in the latter also suggests that attention needs to be given to how top-down measures may enhance rather than inhibit bottom-up opportunities.

Between these strong ideological positions, we follow Day and Klein (1987; see also Pollitt 2003, chapter 4), arguing that both governance in practice and governance research imply dealing with 'multiple accountabilities'. In this respect, it may be important to try to develop policies so that they follow complex pathways across the items in table 7.1. Design issues about how, and by whom, the overall structure and content should be determined may differ from issues about arrangements to determine the detailed policy process, while each again may differ from the concerns about the discretionary behavior of practitioners. All are connected, but there are many options about how these connections may be made.

As an implication of the traditional normative theories on representative democracy, what has been called the 'democratic deficit' in the public debate thus far has been perceived primarily in terms of deficiencies on the input-side of the political system: the loss of function of political parties, and so on. On the basis of the principles of the *Rechtsstaat* and democracy, however, it seems essential to acknowledge that developments around legitimacy on the throughput- and output-side of government deserve attention as well. The concept of governance as used here provides a way of identifying what actually happens, particularly on the throughput-side of government. Guiding decisions are made not only on the input-side of the formal relationships between society and government, but by various actors in often-long policy trajectories.

The consequence of the replacement of government by governance is that democracy is conceptualized in a corresponding manner: away from only looking at the formal organs of representation. If governance is viewed as multi-focal, comprising different sets of activities, than it appears to be possible to reflect on democracy as being multi-local. This then means, first, acknowledging that the empirical fact of the involvement of more participants in certain sets of activities of governance does not say much yet about the legitimacy of their involvement. Nevertheless, other than would be expected on normative grounds regarding the traditional democracy/

government relationship as institutionalized in representative democracy, often the actual participation of many of those actors in practice is accepted or even enhanced. Other models of democracy like the ones of direct-, pluralist-, deliberative-, associative- and client-democracy seem actor-based and horizontally oriented, rather than system-based and vertically oriented like representative democracy is. These alternative models of democracy have in common that they provide a degree of legitimacy to the participation of societal actors – individuals or organizations – in governance as well as in the public control of governance, other than to the citizen in his or her role as just a voter. What has been proclaimed as a 'deficit' then in fact proves to be a political claim, expressed from a specific perspective, which is the model of representative democracy.

Second, making the variety of these actors, action levels, action situations and administrative layers visible in specified contexts, can be seen as a precondition for governance research. Third, action situations for holding public actors accountable may be identified, reflected upon and institutionalized further. As far as accountability is concerned, inasmuch as relevant action situations are no longer to be sought exclusively in the traditional centers of representative democracy, the analytical framework used here contributes to making them detectable and distinguishable. Though obviously in mixed forms, the two case studies presented above show that characteristics of the various models of democracy already could be observed in reality.

The tri-focal character of the concept of multiple governance also implies that the direct and all-encompassing participation of citizens is not always the only requisite that can be thought of. Co-direction in policy processes (cf. 'policy co-formation') going vertically along various layers of government may provide checks on top-down rule setting exclusively from the political center. Besides, it appears that there are other alternatives as well, particularly on the action level of constitutive governance. As Van der Meer and Ham (2001) state, it is the possibility of intervention that becomes important, maybe even more than the intervention itself.

References

Arnstein, S.R. (1969), 'A ladder of citizen participation', *AIP Journal* July, 216–24.

Bache, I. (2003), 'Governing through Governance: Education Policy Control under New Labour', *Political Studies* 51:2, 300–14.

Berrow, D., Humphrey, C., and Hayward, J. (1997), 'Understanding the relation between research and clinical policy: a study of clinicians' views' *Quality in Health Care* 6, 181–6.

Bovens, M.A.P., Derksen, W., Witteveen, W., Becker, F. and Kalma, P.(1995), *De verplaatsing van de politiek: Een agenda voor democratische vernieuwing* (Amsterdam: Wiardi Beckman Stichting).

Bowe, R., Ball, S.J. and Gold, A. (1992), *Reforming Education and Changing Schools* (London: Routledge).

Chitty, C. (2004), *Education Policy in Britain* (Basingstoke: Palgrave Macmillan).

Day, P. and Klein, R. (1987), *Accountabilities* (London: Tavistock).

Department of Health (1998), A First Class Service: Quality in the NHS, Consultation Document (London: HMSO).

Department of Health (2000), *The NHS Plan* (London: HMSO).

Dunleavy, P., Gamble, A. and Peele, G. (eds.) (1990), *Developments in British Politics 3* (London: Macmillan).

Dye, T.D., Alderdice, F., Roberge, E. and Jamison, J.Q. (2000), 'Attitudes toward clinical guidelines among obstetricians in Northern Ireland', *British Journal of Obstetrics and Gynaecology* 107, 101–7.

Fisher, R., Lewis, M. and Davis, B. (2000), 'Implementation of the National Literacy Strategy in England: Indications of Change', *Childhood Education* 76:6, 342–9.

Foot, M. (1982), *Aneurin Bevan* vol 2. (London: Granada).

Foy, R., Penney, G. and Greer, I. (2001), 'The impact of national clinical guidelines on obstetricians in Scotland', *Health Bulletin* 59:6, 364–72.

Frederickson, H.G. and Smith K.B. (2003), *The Public Administration Theory Primer* (Boulder: Westview Press).

Glennerster, H. (2003), *Understanding the Finance of Welfare* (Bristol: Policy Press).

Glennerster, H., Matsaganis, M., Owens, P. and Hancock, S. (1994), *Implementing GP Fund holding: Wild Card or Winning Hand?* (Buckingham: Open University Press).

Held, D. (1996), *Models of Democracy,* 2nd Edition (Cambridge: Polity Press).

Hill, M.J. and Hupe, P.L. (2002), *Implementing Public Policy: Governance in Theory and Practice* (London: Sage).

Hilton, M. (1998), 'Raising Literacy Standards: The True Story', *English in Education* 32:3, 4–16.

Hirschman, A.O. (1970), *Exit, Voice and Loyalty* (Cambridge Mass.: Harvard University Press).

Hudson, C. and Lidström, A. (eds.), *Local Education Policies: Comparing Sweden and Britain* (Basingstoke: Palgrave).

Johnson, N. (2002), 'Guidelines on using guidelines', *British Journal of Obstetrics and Gynaecology* 109, 1495–97.

Kiser, L.L. and Ostrom, E. (1982), 'The three worlds of action: A metatheoretical synthesis of institutional approaches', in Ostrom (ed.), 179–222.

Lindblom, C.E. (1977), *Politics and Markets: The World's Political-Economic Systems* (New York: Basic Books).

Lofty, J.S. (2003), 'Standards and the Politics of Time and Teacher Professionalism', *English Education* 35:3, 195–221.

McDonald, R. and Harrison, S. (2004), 'The micro-politics of clinical guidelines: An empirical study', *Policy and Politics* 32:2, 223–39.

Meer, J. van der, and Ham, M. (2001), *De verplaatsing van de democratie* (Amsterdam: De Balie).

Newman, J. (2001), *Modernising Governance* (London: Sage).

O'Toole, L.J. jr (2000), 'Research on Policy Implementation: Assessment and Prospects', *Journal of Public Administration Research and Theory* 10:2, 263–88.

Ostrom, E. (ed.) (1982), *Strategies of Political Inquiry* (Beverly Hills: Sage)

Ostrom, E. (1999), 'Institutional Rational Choice: An Assessment of the Institutional Analysis and Development Framework', in Sabatier (ed.), 35–71.

Pollitt, C. (2003), *The Essential Public Manager* (Maidenhead: Open University Press).

Runciman, D. (2005), 'Institutional Hypocrisy', *London Review of Books* 27:8, 3 –7.

Sabatier, P.A. (ed.) (1999), *Theories of the Policy Process* (Boulder: Westview Press).

Templeton, A., Charny, M., Thomas, J. and Dhillon, C. (2001), 'The implementation and uptake of clinical guidelines in obstetrics and gynaecology', *The Obstetrician and Gynaecologist* 3:2, 93–5.

Whitty, G. (1990), 'The Politics of the 1988 Education Reform Act', in Dunleavy et al. (eds.).

Wilson, W. (1941), *The Study of Public Administration* in: Political Science Quarterly 56 (December), 197–222 (originally published in 1887).

PART III
NETWORK GOVERNANCE AND SOCIETAL SELF-GOVERNANCE

Chapter 8

The Legitimacy of the Rotterdam Integrated Public Safety Program

Peter Marks[1]

In the last couple of years, public attention has shifted toward fighting crime and ensuring safety. A reason for this shift is an increasing feeling and/or awareness among citizens that they are not safe, especially in the larger cities of the Netherlands. Public safety policies have been on both the national and local political agendas for quite some time. In the mid-1980s, the Dutch government began thinking about a more integrated public safety policy; this resulted in the first integrated public safety policy with its main focus on public safety in the mid-1990s (Ministerie van Binnenlandse Zaken 1999). During the government formation of 1994, the four largest cities in The Netherlands (Amsterdam, Rotterdam, The Hague and Utrecht) requested more attention for problems specific to large cities. Consequently, they were asked to set up workable plans that addressed employment, safety and livability. Together with the remaining fifteen largest cities, certain action programs were formulated (Haan 1997, 8–16). The action program contained three goals: 'reduction of long-term unemployment in deprived areas, change the objective (measurable) and subjective (experienced) degree of safety on the street, and increase the livability of deprived areas and improve care for the most vulnerable.' (Haan 1997, 15–16) This thinking about integrated public safety policy resulted in the first integrated safety program in 1999 (Ministerie van Binnenlandse Zaken 1999).

In 1994, evaluations of the Rotterdam public safety policy showed that organizations involved in public safety had failed to make the citizens of Rotterdam feel safer (Gemeente Rotterdam 2001a, 11). The launch of the national integrated public safety program in 1999 triggered the Rotterdam government to develop a local version. In comparison with the 1994 public safety policy, the 1999 policy shifted focus from more or less contingency oriented action to programmatic oriented action. The integrated public safety policy, launched mid-2001, was formatted into a five-year program that states that local public safety policy not only concerns local police and the Justice Department, but also local government agencies, societal organizations, civilians and corporations (Gemeente Rotterdam 2001a, 5). The main goal of the program is increasing public safety in the city as a whole and in each of its thirteen municipal districts and sixty-two district quarters (Gemeente Rotterdam

1   A special thanks goes to Arthur Edwards for comments and feedback.

2004, 7). In addition to its focus on safety improvements, the integrated program focuses on the structural improvement of public safety and livability. A key focus in the local public safety program is execution at the lowest level (Gemeente Rotterdam 2001a, 5–11)

Since the old public safety policy failed to produce the required results, the Rotterdam government attempted to create a safer and more livable city by formulating, implementing and executing the Rotterdam integrated public safety program. First, the national program was reformulated to a local equivalent by the Steering Committee on Safety (SCS). The local integrated public safety program was then implemented by the Safety Program Office (SPO) and used as a guideline to formulate the action programs at the municipal district execution level. After acquiring enough experience and information, the Rotterdam integrated public safety program was further strengthened by the SCS, the SPO and the municipal districts (MD) by means of continuous evaluations, fine-tuning and program updates (Figure 8.1).

Figure 8.1   Local public safety policy

The change in governance from contingency oriented action to programmatic oriented action is based on a couple of steps through which the change has been organized. Governance has changed by means of a downward vertical shift from the national to the (sub) local level as well as through a horizontal shift from public to private organizations and civil society (Chapter 2, this volume). Because of the changes in how governments and society deal with each other, these shifts in governance have to be legitimized. That is, the governance practice can no longer be seen solely in the perspective of the representative democracy background: a democratic deficit has arisen. In the formulation, implementation, execution and strengthening of the Rotterdam integrated public safety program, different (forms of) underlying democracy models can be distinguished. Different democracy models are reflected in the particular forms of governance in the respective situations of the policy process. In this chapter, we map the different relevant underlying democracy models in order to analyze the Rotterdam integrated public safety program and to determine the basis for its legitimacy.

In the next section, we briefly review some arguments of legitimacy that are applicable in the analysis of the Rotterdam integrated public safety policy process. A short description of the policy process is presented in section 2. Based on the different aspects of legitimacy, we analyze the shifts in the city program in section 3 by applying the underlying democracy models. We present our conclusions in section 4.

1. Governance and Legitimacy

According to Bekkers and Edwards, the emergence of 'governance' seems to be unleashing 'governing' from the traditional institutions of representative democracy.' (Chapter 3, this volume) This influences the democratic legitimacy of the binding decisions made in governance practices. Several decompositions are possible given the legitimacy problem of binding decisions in governance practices; different shifts in governance, aspects of legitimacy, and the type of underlying democracy model (for more thorough and complete descriptions: see Chapter 3).

First of all, many governance practices can be described as a shift of power from the central, state-level to other territorial layers of government, functional layers of government, or to other societal spheres. Shifts in governance imply new authority structures and arrangements that go beyond the jurisdiction of the state (international and supranational cooperation) as well as cross-traditional jurisdictions of the intra-state public organizations. The new governance arrangements also make binding collective decisions and exercise power. In these arrangements, two elements are distinguishable: setting the agenda and deciding the outcome. Second, legitimacy in general says something about the qualification of a political system or regime, but this qualification can be more specific. Is the governance practice legitimate in its articulation of citizen interests (input), in its rules and procedures for solving collective problems (throughput), or in its capacity to produce outcomes that contribute to attack collective problems (output)? Last of all, various models of democracy are reflected in governance practices. These democracy models conceptualize how, when and where citizens should be involved in public decision-making, how political conflicts should be resolved and how accountability should be constituted. These three elements of examining legitimacy will be the basis for our analysis of the Rotterdam integrated public safety policy process.

2. The Rotterdam Integrated Public Safety Policy Process

Following the development of the national integrated public safety program in 1999, the Rotterdam government began developing the local equivalent. The idea of the national program has set an example of how integrality may improve conditions for fighting crime and reducing public fears about safety. Rotterdam's recent political history has influenced local integrated public safety policy. The sharper edged program of the late Pim Fortuyn, and the local political party Livable Rotterdam (LR), founded in 2001, attracted a lot of attention to the city of Rotterdam in 2001 and 2002. At the end of 2001, the policy issue voters considered most important was *fighting crime and ensuring safety* (named by 43 per cent of a large sample of voters) (Van Praag 2003, 14–15). All political parties, but especially LR (Fortuyn's local political party) and the subsequently founded national party List Pim Fortuyn (LPF), made public safety policy issues the spearhead of the party programs during the Rotterdam city council election. Livable Rotterdam became the largest party in the Rotterdam City Council after the March 2002 election garnering 17 out of 45 seats, giving them a vote in the new municipal executive board. The new municipal executive board fine-tuned, intensified and extended the Rotterdam integrated public safety program (Gemeente Rotterdam 2002a, 8–16).

Steering Committee on Safety

The municipal executive board consists of aldermen appointed by the city council coalition parties and the mayor who is appointed by the Dutch Crown (through the Minister of Internal Affairs). The City Council supervises the municipal executive ex ante by producing outline policies and ex post by holding the executive accountable. Aldermen are responsible for particular policy fields and head the respective staffs. The mayor, chairman of the municipal executive board and the City Council have specific (constitution based) tasks for maintaining civil order and managing the police corps (Local government law, art. 174 'Gemeentewet, 1993'). The mayor together with the Police Commissioner and the Chief Prosecutor are responsible for public order. These three officials form the Steering Committee on Safety, which is an important institution in Rotterdam public safety policy. The SCS monitors and supervises the progress of implementation and execution of the Rotterdam public safety program. Also the SCS primarily deals with bottlenecks in policy at both the national and local levels, as well as bottlenecks in implementation, finance and organization (Gemeente Rotterdam 2002b, 2–4). Other permanent members of the Committee are the aldermen responsible for Public Safety and Districts, the chief and a communication advisor of the Safety Program Office, an external advisor, and a planning and control staff. Depending on the agenda of the SCS, other aldermen, chairmen of municipal districts, chief executives of local departments and experts in specific topics can join the SCS meetings at their discretion (Gemeente Rotterdam 2002b, 3).

The goal of the SCS is to make the city of Rotterdam safer by structurally improving public safety and livability. If they reach this goal, the aldermen in the SCS have a higher probability of being re-elected because the issue of public safety is high on the public agenda.[2] To create a safer and more livable city, a five-year program was formulated based on a programmatic and integrated approach to public safety issues (Gemeente Rotterdam 2001a, 11). 'The five-year program is characterized as 'work-in-progress'. This creates the flexibility necessary to be able to adjust and fine-tune the program based on practical experiences learned during execution. The measures are developed in the first two years (2001–2002), and redefined in later years on the basis of practical experiences.' (Gemeente Rotterdam 2001a, 5, translation by PM) As mentioned before, a key element of the program is implementing and executing it at the lowest performable level, i.e. in the sixty-two district levels. The SCS decentralized the direct governance over the implementation and execution of the five-year program to the Safety Program Office (SPO).

The Safety Program Office

The SPO ensures that execution at the (municipal) district level does not contradict city policy. Furthermore, the Safety Program Office boosts the process of implementing and executing the five-year program by the partners, and assists the partners in ad hoc situations[3]. In order to assist partners in executing the public safety program, in both ad hoc and more structural situations, knowledge and information are collected, processed, distributed and used (Gemeente Rotterdam 2001a, 35–37; 2002b, 6). 'The Safety Program Office is the administrative linchpin in the Rotterdam public safety policy.' (Programmabureau Veilig 2005, translation by PM)

Besides examining and increasing the pace in implementation and execution, the SPO also gathers a substantial amount of information. The SPO produces three different measurement instruments:

- The Safety Index provides a (updated) grade every six months on how safe or unsafe a district is or has become. The Safety Index was developed to give information about (the development of) public safety in the city of Rotterdam as a whole and each of the districts separately. The Safety Index reports the status quo of the public safety program, but also maps out the possible results of changes in program. The Safety Index is an instrument in which various resources are combined into one index. A multitude of resources, and not just

---

2   In the future, this will probably hold true for the mayor as well since there are currently plans to change the mayor from an appointed to an elected position.

3   An example of assisting in ad hoc situations are the activities undertaken by SPO to prevent the closing of a supermarket at the Crooswijkseweg on the 28th of November 2002, caused by youngsters hanging about, stealing, causing nuisance and threatening personnel (Rotterdams Dagblad (2003). The SPO activated municipal district, police, social workers, community workers and youth workers to develop joint approaches and interventions.

police declarations, are used to fill the gap between the real number of crimes committed and the willingness to declare and report these and thus the index gives a more realistic image of the status quo. Several police monitors and a 'livability research' on 13,000 inhabitants are used (Gemeente Rotterdam 2006, 3). The livability research focuses on experiences and victimizations of vandalism, theft, burglary, nuisance, drug abuse, violence, et cetera. That is, both the objective and subjective elements of safety and livability are taken into consideration. The quantitative and qualitative part of this Index are weighed and graded resulting in a grade on the Safety Index for the district quarters, municipal districts and the city of Rotterdam as a whole (Gemeente Rotterdam 2006). Context variables such as average income of the population, average time of stay and other physical, economic and social variables are also added to these subjective and objective data (Gemeente Rotterdam 2004, 8). These grades show how safe a district is in various respects and how it has evolved (into a less or more safe district).

- 'Maraps' (Management Reports) give specific quarterly updates on all related local specific policy issues, such as district safety status quo, drugs, youth, et cetera. Maraps state the agreements made in the district safety plans and the monitoring of these plans. These quarterly 'evaluations' are presented in standardized formats that provide information about the targets set in district safety plans and the implementation to reach these targets. In Maraps, updates are provided on which targets are met, what results are achieved, and what bottlenecks have occurred (Andersson Elffers Felix 2002, 4).
- The Annual Reports combine the aforementioned two. This report gives an overview of the development of the safety index and its influencing variables as well as the progress of all safety issues related to district safety, drugs, youth and violence. Based on the Annual Report, further completion and possible adjustments can be made to the goals and activities for the rest of the period of the five-year program (Gemeente Rotterdam 2002b, 36–37).

The SCS lacks the capacity and time to monitor the execution and implementation of the five-year program closely and to gather all the information. Thus the interventions of the SCS are based on the information provided by the SPO (Gemeente Rotterdam 2001a, 36).

The five-year program is a guideline for the SPO in the implementation of public safety policy and the formulation of district safety plans together with the municipal districts (in Dutch, 'Wijkveiligheidsactieplannen') (Andersson Elffers Felix 2002, 3). District safety plans contain analyses of problems in a district, and approaches to solving these problems. 'The tasks of the SPO are to report on the developments of district safety, support municipal districts in their analyses for the district safety plans, design networks for sharing knowledge and disperse best practices.' (Gemeente Rotterdam 2001a, 36, translation by PM) 'The SCS has put a lot of emphasis on the formulation of the district safety plans. The actual steering is done by the SPO.' (Rekenkamer Rotterdam 2005, 38, translation by PM)

Municipal Districts

An approach to increasing public safety at the district level was developed in the five-year program, and issues of public safety in individual districts are examined and dealt with in a seven-step analysis approach. The first step is the analysis of size and sort of problem in a specific district; this analysis is followed by focusing on the cause(s) of the problem(s). The third analysis shows what is already being done to solve problems or potential problems. A list of targets is set on what level (fourth analysis) and how (fifth analysis) the priorities are to be reached. The sixth analysis defines the projects including, for instance, costs, causal relations and evaluation criteria. In the seventh and last part of the analysis, the organization and evaluation of the approach to the issues are established (Andersson Elffers Felix 2002, 6–8; Gemeente Rotterdam 2002c) In analyzing the problems, formulating measurements and executing the program in districts, it is evident that inhabitants, entrepreneurs and societal organizations in the district should be involved. Their knowledge of the district should be utilized when defining the arrangements (Gemeente Rotterdam 2002c, 9).

'Within the Dutch constitutional system, the Rotterdam local government has a special form of government. [...] Even though municipal districts are not independent, they have their own tasks, powers and budgets. [...] Municipal districts (should be able to) pursue their own policy as much as possible' (Molenaar 2001, 55, translation by PM). The local government of Rotterdam consists of eleven municipal districts, and two corresponding administrative bodies. A bylaw delegates the tasks and powers of specific policy fields to the municipal districts and their executive board. Municipal districts are charged with implementing and executing large parts of the city program. The program is to be implemented not only at the level of municipal districts but also at a lower level. Districts are the central unit of implementation and execution. 'District safety plans' are used to execute the Rotterdam integrated public safety program at the district level. The Safety Program Office and the Steering Committee on Safety assess the district safety plans after they have been approved by the municipal district councils and have been geared to the police and local Justice Department. 'An assessed and approved district safety plan is a prerequisite for granting city funding' (Gemeente Rotterdam 2001a, 35, translation by PM). However, municipal districts still have a certain freedom of action in creating district safety plans, and where and how they spend their funds. This leeway creates the possibility for the districts to pay more attention to their specific major problems in the respective district safety plans. Because municipal districts have their own elected councils and executives, solving public safety problems in the districts and the municipal district as a whole increases the chances of getting re-elected. Many issues dealt with in the Rotterdam public safety program can migrate from one area to another. 'One of the risks of the district safety approach is occurrence of the water bed effect' (Gemeente Rotterdam 2001a, 6, translation by PM). For example, if nuisance drug abusers are strongly repressed in one area or (municipal) district, it is likely that they will move to another district, as occurred, for instance, during the

Victor-approach of drugs abusers in Rotterdam-West after the closing of Perron Nul (Torre 1999, 185). If the problems are volatile, every municipal district benefits from a city wide integrated approach; that is, every (municipal) district has to do its part of the integrated approach to public safety issues.

3. Analyzing the Rotterdam Integrated Public Safety Program

Shifts in the Public Safety Program

Several steps have to be taken before the idea of a local integrated safety program can be fully developed into a sustainable program. The Steering Committee on Safety supervises the city program and can be held accountable by the city council. The goal of the SCS is to formulate a local public safety program based on the national integrated public safety program. The Safety Program Office, founded by the SCS, gathers the necessary and relevant information and (helps) formulate the Rotterdam integrated public safety program. After formulating the five-year program, the SPO uses it as a guideline in their meeting with the municipal districts who are the main executors of the integrated program. They meet to see how specific public safety issues of the municipal districts fit into the five-year program, which is the basis for dividing the city funds available for public safety over the municipal districts. Municipal districts are responsible for their district safety. Municipal districts prioritize public safety goals and issues, and the measures necessary to reach these goals, based on analyses and input from various partners (Gemeente Rotterdam 2001a, 5–6, 17–22). The various partners that are requested to provide input while formulating the district safety plans vary from citizens to entrepreneurs, from district fire department to the housing agency. In the last step of the Rotterdam integrated public safety policy process, the five-year program is strengthened, i.e. it is intensified and fine-tuned to make it sustainable and executable. In this last situation, all three actors interact: the SCS, the SPO and the municipal districts. The municipal districts maintain their position as director towards the sub-local partners, the SPO remains the administrative linchpin and the main gatherer and provider of information, and the SCS develops and supervises the policy outlines. Other partners[4] are relevant in this third phase, but they gain entrance through one or more of the three actors – the SCS, the SPO or the municipal districts (Gemeente Rotterdam 2001a, 6, 20, 35; Baaij 2004, 34).

The Rotterdam government has attempted to create a safer and more livable city by formulating, implementing and executing the Rotterdam integrated public safety program. First, the national integrated public safety program is handed down to the Rotterdam government. The Steering Committee on Safety translates the national program into a local one; i.e. a vertical shift from national to local level. The Safety

---

4   Again the various partners are similar to the ones in the input phase in the second situation. However, now it is the information collected by the SPO that carries more weight than the partners in having a real say in the matter.

Program Office uses this outline to create district safety plans together with the municipal districts that can be implemented; i.e. another vertical decentralization shift from local government to sub-local government as well as a horizontal shift from public to semi-public and private organizations and civil society. Finally, the SCS, the SPO, the municipal districts (and other partners) strengthen and execute the continuously updated Rotterdam integrated public safety program. The shifts in governance, both vertical and horizontal, are depicted in the aforementioned Figure 8.1.

Legitimacy of the Public Safety Program

The work in progress version of the Rotterdam integrated public safety program is formulated by the SCS and the SPO. The translation of this program to workable district safety plans that can be implemented is done by the SPO and the municipal districts, and finally results in a strengthened Rotterdam integrated public safety program (all three functional partners). This program is continuously monitored, updated, adapted and executed. The decisions made by the different partners of the government should result in a safer and more livable city. That is, the performance of the government, or their effectiveness and efficiency, depends on the decisions they make to tackle the safety problems that exist in the districts (and in the city as a whole). The Rotterdam government is held accountable by the public as well as the municipal council if the city is not becoming safer or more livable.

> Citizens protest increasingly louder against the unsafe and unlivable conditions of their district. They don't expect words from the government, but deeds to create a safer city. People ultimately want to see results. Is there a chance to achieve this with the new five-year program? A straightforward 'yes' according to the city authorities. This program means a total turnaround in handling public safety. A change that must deliver results that will be quickly visible to the citizens. Livability should increase and degeneration decline. On this, the Rotterdam citizens should hold their city government accountable. (Gemeente Rotterdam 2001b, 2, translation by PM)

The Rotterdam municipal executive even has its own fate connected to making the city safer. So far, however, the municipal executive has nothing to fear because the Rotterdam integrated public safety program is working (Trouw 2005a). Citizens of Rotterdam want the city to be safer and more livable. It is not the citizens who have a direct input in formulating the local program (government by the people), but it is the local government that formulates the program in congruence with the preferences of the citizens (government for the people). Even though the Rotterdam government seeks legitimacy in its throughput by defining qualitative rules and procedures to solve its problems, the main emphasis (at least from the perspective of the citizens, but probably from the government as well) is to achieve a safer and a more livable city, that is the legitimacy of the Rotterdam integrated public safety program is based on its output:

- The Rotterdam integrated public safety program has been effective because the goals in the 2001–2003 period have been reached and the government is on its way to reaching the ultimate goal which is 'no unsafe district in 2006' (Rekenkamer Rotterdam 2005, 11). The Rotterdam city safety index has risen from 5.6 in 2001 to 6.9 in 2005 and the amount of unsafe districts has declined from 10 to 1 in that same period (Gemeente Rotterdam 2006, 3)
- The political decisions and outputs are in congruence with the (expressed) desires of the Rotterdam citizens
- The municipal executives are held accountable to the public by, for instance, publishing the safety index and safety reports and by providing information through debates and contacts with the media. They are accountable to the council by providing the Maraps and the safety index. And they are legally accountable because their laws and regulations have to be geared to the respective justice and police departments.

What are the underlying democratic bases for the governance structure of the Rotterdam integrated public safety program that might be able to produce the required output? In the next section, we describe the underlying democracy models that are present in the formulation of the Rotterdam integrated public safety program, the district safety plans, and the strengthening of the program.

Underlying Models of Democracy

We analyze the shifts in the Rotterdam integrated public safety policy process by looking at the underlying democracy models from the moment it was handed down as a national program that required translation into a local one, through the process of formulating the district safety plans based on this local program to, finally, the continuously updated and strengthened Rotterdam integrated public safety program (also see the aforementioned Figure 8.1).

Shift 1: National Program → Local Program (SCS and SPO)   In the first shift, the national public safety program has to be translated and (re)formulated into a local version. This is done by the municipal executive within the bylaws of the Rotterdam city council. This task is delegated to the Steering Committee on Safety, which partly consists of the members of the municipal executive. The (political) decision-making is mainly done by professional politicians elected into office by the Rotterdam citizens. There are limited possibilities for citizens to directly participate in the political system. Elected politicians are held accountable by the public as well as certain (non-) governmental organizations and have to respond to questions from the people when the goals formulated are not reached or are reached but in manners that is incongruent with the desires of the people. As mentioned before, it is not only the citizens that can change their vote during elections; the municipal executive is connected to its own fate and will leave office if the city is not 'measurably' safer in 2006 (Rekenkamer Rotterdam, 2005, 20; Trouw, 2005a, 2005b). The underlying democracy model in this first shift is one of a representative nature where a number of professionals represent (or at least consider) the interests and wishes of the people. This means that with the shift from the national to the local level, the same underlying model still exists, but at a lower level.

Shift 2: Rotterdam Safety Program → District Safety Plans (SPO and MD)   In the second shift, the Rotterdam integrated public safety program is used as a guideline by the Safety Program Office to create executable district safety plans together with the municipal districts, based on analyses of the particular problems in the respective (municipal) districts (the aforementioned seven step approach). The SPO is the administrative linchpin in the Rotterdam integrated public safety program. It assists partners, collects and shares knowledge and information, and produces the information needed by the SCS. The emphasis of the five-year program is the implementation and execution at the lowest possible level; hence district safety plans are formulated. However, the five-year program not only states that analyses and information are relevant for a 'good, executable district safety plan' (Gemeente Rotterdam 2002c) but,

> [...] the district safety approach must be of and for its citizens. Not only should they recognize themselves in the approach, they should also contribute to the improvement of safety in their district. In all stages of the district safety approach, the inhabitants and entrepreneurs must be involved in the process: during the analysis of the problems and current approach, in the choice of measurements and in the evaluation of the progress in the execution. (Gemeente Rotterdam 2002c, 4, translation PM)

The citizens' preferences are critically examined and weighed against each other by the exchange of information and arguments. The district safety plans are not just formulated based on 'merely given and aggregated' preferences, but they are formulated based on the notion of free and reasoned agreement of people. That is, the primary source of legitimacy in this case is deliberative procedures. Of course, the municipal districts will still be held accountable and need to respond to questions from their district inhabitants if they fail to produce the output they promised. The second shift can be characterized as building on the models of both representative and deliberative democracy.[5]

---

5   In the formulation, implementation and execution of the district safety plans, it is not only the citizens that need to be involved in the process but also interest groups, (non) governmental organizations as well as the so-called *stadsmarinier* (city mariner). These partners are all mostly geared and activated in the process of execution, but they are also involved in the formulation (Rekenkamer Rotterdam, 2005). The negotiations, competitions and coalition building between these partners can be interpreted as a form of pluralistic democracy because through these partners, the desires of the people can also be expressed as well as the protective mechanism through the functioning of the interest groups. However, the focus is more on the output side of the Rotterdam integrated public safety policy and not so much on the throughput side.

Shift 3: Strengthened Public Safety Program (SCS, SPO, MD) After adaptation and implementation, the Rotterdam integrated public safety program is constantly evaluated. For the program to be strengthened, it needs to be assessed on its performance, and in cases of sub-optimal performance, updates and improvements of the program are called for. The continuous stream of feedback helps assess and evaluate all aspects of the integrated public safety program. In this situation, the SCS, the SPO, and the municipal districts have the same goal; to make the city safer by having a continuously assessed, updated and improved integrated public safety program. In this strengthening process, the SPO, in cooperation with other partners, collects, processes and distributes a lot of information; i.e. the Safety Index, the Maraps and the annual report. The Safety Index is probably the most important of these (at least for the citizens) because the index is published on the internet (<www.rotterdamveilig.nl) and (parts of it) distributed throughout the media. The public holds the Rotterdam government, both at the municipal and district level, accountable based on the Safety Index. If the Safety Index shows that the targets set by the partners of the integrated public safety program have not been reached, they have to show what went wrong and what they are going to do about it in response.

A highly relevant element underlying this strengthening of the Rotterdam integrated public safety program is the fact that it is not just objective criteria that are used – because that would show only half the picture. Since the safety program is not only for but also of the people, it must also take into account many aspects related to the livability of the districts. For this reason, the safety index includes both objective and subjective criteria. The objective data are separated into factual (police) data and context variables. The factual data are the total amount of reports from the police, fire department, et cetera, in the context of physical, social and economical variables of the specific districts. In the collection of the subjective data, over 12,000 citizens have filled out population inquiries; that is a minimum of 175 per district, which is a significant amount in sociological research (Gemeente Rotterdam 2004).

> The subjective data are collected from population inquiries. The questions concern the citizens' safety perceptions and whether one has been a victim. It is important that the opinion of both autochthons and immigrants are taken into consideration in the research. Two independent research offices have done the research. Office Intomart particularly questions the autochthonic part of the population. Research office Mediad exclusively addresses the five largest minority groups in the city, namely Turks, Moroccans, Surinamers, Antilleans/Arubans and Cape Verdians. This way the composition of the group examined is representative to ethnic grouping for the total population of Rotterdam. (Gemeente Rotterdam 2004, 8)

The local knowledge of the citizens (and local entrepreneurs) is of direct value for the delivery of a safer city (through the Rotterdam integrated public safety program). A substantial amount of information is gathered on the preferences of the citizens. Both the representative and client democracy underlie the strengthening part (shift) of the Rotterdam integrated public safety program.

The shifts in governance for the Rotterdam integrated public safety program and the underlying democracy models are depicted in Figure 8.2.

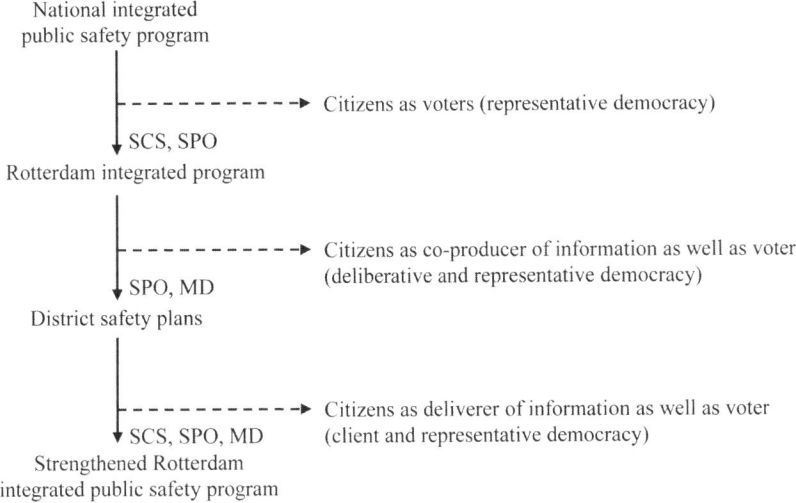

National integrated
public safety program

– – – – – – – – – –➤ Citizens as voters (representative democracy)

↓ SCS, SPO

Rotterdam integrated program

– – – – – – – – – –➤ Citizens as co-producer of information as well as voter
(deliberative and representative democracy)

↓ SPO, MD

District safety plans

– – – – – – – – – –➤ Citizens as deliverer of information as well as voter
↓ SCS, SPO, MD   (client and representative democracy)

Strengthened Rotterdam
integrated public safety program

Figure 8.2   Underlying democracy models in the shift in governance for the Rotterdam Integrated Public Safety Policy

4. Conclusion

After having failed in making the city of Rotterdam safer and more livable in the past, the Rotterdam government formulated a new policy, effectuated in the Rotterdam integrated public safety program to produce the required output (a safer and more livable city). This resulted in a change from contingency oriented action to programmatic oriented action. In and after the formulation of the local integrated public safety program, how government and society deal with each other has changed. A democratic deficit had arisen because the Rotterdam government and society were in a different relation to each other and the legitimacy of the Rotterdam public safety policy no longer had its basis in the representative democracy.

We have shown in this chapter that in formulating the Rotterdam integrated public safety policy, the local government has tried to increase its democratic legitimacy by incorporating the Rotterdam citizens in the safety process. The focus of governance shifts from national to (sub)local level in the formulation of the integrated program. An essential part of the program is the implementation and execution at the lowest (district) level. The citizens and local entrepreneurs of the respective districts know best the specific problems of their districts. Instead of using the citizens only as voters the district safety plans are formulated by explicitly going into rational debates with them. The program should comply with the wishes of the (municipal) district citizens and attack the 'correct' collective problems, thus creating safer and more livable districts and hence a safer and more livable city as a whole. The government requires the public to hold them accountable when they fail to make the city safer and more livable, and they respond to questions raised when citizens do not think that their desires are in (total) congruence with policy. After the formulation of the district safety plans (the most important part of the Rotterdam integrated public safety program), a continuous feedback of information, collected and processed by the Safety Program Office, is used to strengthen the program. By generating substantial information through population inquiries, the citizens as clients help strengthen the local integrated public safety policy.

The City of Rotterdam government needed a different form of governance after formulation of the Rotterdam integrated public safety program. This new form of governance no longer fit into the old democratic legitimacy of solely the representative democracy. By involving citizens, local entrepreneurs and local stakeholders, the Rotterdam government based its new policy on different underlying democracy models to legitimize it. The representative democracy model is handed down from the national to the lowest level when the local level translates the national public safety model to the local level. A deliberative democracy model is present in formulating and implementing the district safety plans. And finally, the underlying democracy model takes on a client nature in the strengthening of the integrated public safety program throughout the course of implementation.

References

Andersson, E.F. (2002), *Handleiding Wijkveiligheidsplannen Rotterdam* (Rotterdam: Programmabureau Veilig).
Baaij, N. (2004), 'Prestatie-afspraken op niveau? Een onderzoek naar de ervaringen met het wijkveiligheidsactieprogramma in het Oude Noorden', (Rotterdam: Erasmus Universiteit, Faculteit Sociale Wetenschappen Rotterdam).
Gemeente Rotterdam (2001a), 'Versterking veiligheid Rotterdam: vijf jarenprogramma in samenwerking tussen stadsbestuur, deelgemeenten, stedelijke diensten, politie, justitie, bewoners, maatschappelijke organisaties en bedrijven', behorende bij raadsstuk 2001–723 (Rotterdam).
Gemeente Rotterdam (2001b), 'Werken aan een veiliger Rotterdam: geen woorden maar daden', (Rotterdam: Programmabureau Veilig).
Gemeente Rotterdam (2002a), 'Het nieuwe elan van Rotterdam.en zo gaan we dat doen: collegeprogramma 2002–2006', (Rotterdam: College van Burgemeester en Wethouders).
Gemeente Rotterdam (2002b), 'Sturingsmodel Stuurgroep Veilig', (Rotterdam: Stuurgroep Veilig).
Gemeente Rotterdam (2002c), 'Het Wijkveiligheids–actieprogramma', (Rotterdam: Programmabureau Veilig).

Gemeente Rotterdam (2004), 'Veiligheidsindex 2004, meting van de veiligheid in Rotterdam: rapportage bevolkingsenquête januari–februari 2004 en feitelijke criminaliteitsgegevens en stadsgegevens over 2003', (Rotterdam: Programmabureau Veilig).

Gemeente Rotterdam (2006), 'Blik op de veiligheidsindex 2006, meting van de veiligheid in Rotterdam: verkorte rapportage bevolkingsenquête januari 2006 en feitelijke criminaliteitsgegevens en contextgegevens over 2005', (Rotterdam: Programmabureau Veilig).

Gemeentewet (1993), *Tekstuitgave gemeentewet 1993* (Allphen aan den Rijn: H.D. Samsom and Tjeenk Willink).

Haan, W.J.M. de (1997), 'Evaluatie integraal veiligheidsbeleid: een verkennende studie in Amsterdam en Rotterdam', (Rijswijk: Sociaal en Cultureel Planbureau).

Ministerie van Binnenlandse Zaken (1999), *Integraal Veiligheidsprogramma. Bureau Integraal Veiligheidsprogramma en Coördinatie Onderraden* ('s-Gravenhage: Ministerie van Binnenlandse Zaken en Koninkrijksrelaties, Bureau Integraal Veiligheidsprogramma en Coördinatie Onderraden; Zoetermeer: Centrum Zoetermeer district).

Molenaar, G. (2001), 'Subsidiëring door Rotterdamse Deelgemeenten', *Bestuurswetenschappen* 55:1, 49–66.

Programmabureau Veilig (2005), *Wie zijn wij? Programmabureau Veilig* <http://rotterdamveilig.nl/do.php?fct=pages&op=showPage&pageId=291, accessed 31 July 2005.

Rekenkamer Rotterdam (2005), *Veilig zijn, veilig voelen* (Rotterdam: Rekenkamer Rotterdam).

Rotterdams Dagblad (2003), 'Politie naar ouders foute jeugd; gemeente denkt uitwassen als in Crooswijk te kunnen voorkomen', *Rotterdams Dagblad*,12 February.

Torre, E.J. van der (1999), *Politiewerk: politiestijlen, community policing, professionalisme*. (Alphen aan den Rijn: Samsom).

Trouw (2005a), 'Ook Rotterdamse 'hotspot' wordt minder onveilig', *Trouw*, 20 April.

Trouw (2005b), 'Gemeenten op de goede weg met aanpak criminaliteit', *Trouw*, 20 April.

Van Praag, Philip (2003), 'The Winners and Losers in a Turbulent Political Year', *Acta Politica: Tijdschrift voor Politicologie* 38:1, 5–22.

Chapter 9

Embedding Deliberative Democracy: Local Environmental Forums in The Netherlands and the United States

Arthur Edwards

Environmental public policies are pursued within a tense field of divergent interests and concerns. This has led to responses in governmental policy styles that tend to emphasize cooperative arrangements involving governments, the business sector and environmental organizations. Industries may find competitive advantages in developing new practices of managing the environment, thereby avoiding confrontations with environmental groups and preserving their attraction for consumers, (future) employees and the wider public. Civil society and governmental actors are attracted to possibilities of acquiring the cooperation of companies by other means than regulations.

Since the 1990s, there has also been a growing recognition that local governments and communities have a significant role to play in environmental protection. Again, various agendas and discourses come together here. Companies are discovering the role of 'good neighbor relations' for obtaining local goodwill. Regulatory agencies are acknowledging the importance of the involvement of empowered citizens for ensuring more voluntary compliance of companies. Governments and civil society organizations have come to endorse the notion of the community as a necessary social basis for the pursuit of sustainability (Portney 2005). From a normative point of view, the involvement of local communities in environmental decision-making can be based on the principle of 'affected interests', according to which all those potentially affected by environmental risks should have a meaningful opportunity to participate or otherwise be represented in the decision-making that generate such risks (Eckersley 2000,19). In the United States, the neighborhood level is a central element in the Environmental Justice philosophy, which began as a grass-roots movement and was established by the Clinton administration as a priority for the administration's environmental policy (Schlosberg 1999). Environmental justice refers to the unequal burden of environmental pollution and health hazards suffered by low income and minority communities. It demands that public policy be based on 'procedural equity', namely open and inclusive participation between equal partners at all levels of environmental decision-making (Bullard 1999). All these developments have given an impetus to the emergence of various deliberative arrangements at the local level.

This chapter aims to provide an assessment of these deliberative arrangements in terms of the legitimacy criteria outlined in Chapter 3. We argue that local environmental forums have important signaling and monitoring functions within the system of environmental governance, but that the leverage that local communities can exert through these functions is, to a large extent, dependent on appropriate linkages with other models of democracy, particularly pluralist and representative democracy. Acknowledging the importance of embedding deliberative arrangements in a system context that includes deliberative as well as representative and pluralist devices concurs with discussions in the literature on democratic innovations, in which new designs are sought and different models of democracy work together in ways that can be mutually supportive (Saward 2001; Budge 2000).

We examine deliberative arrangements that have emerged at the local level in the greater Rotterdam (or Rijnmond) region in The Netherlands and in the city of Cleveland in the United States. Two environmental forums, in which companies, regulatory agencies, residents and local authorities discuss environmental issues, will be examined in detail. We establish the extent to which the ideal of procedural equity is reached, and which conditions can account for this. We then focus on how the observed strengths and weaknesses can be explained by the presence (or absence) of linkages with pluralist and representative democracy.

In the next section, we look at the deliberative model of democracy and present the evaluative framework. In section 2, a Residential Advisory Board in the Rijnmond region will be analyzed. In section 3, we look at the Environmental Committee of a neighborhood-based organization in Cleveland. In section 4, we give a comparative assessment of the two forums, followed in section 5 by an examination of how linkages with pluralist and representative democracy may affect the functioning of these forums and the leverage of local communities in environmental decision-making. In section 6, we draw some conclusions.

1. Environmental Governance and Deliberative Democracy

Since the 1990s, the deliberative model of democracy has inspired various experiments in democratic practices, such as citizen juries, round-table conferences and online policy exercises: 'it has moved beyond the theoretical statement stage into the working theory stage'. (Chambers 2003, 307) In the academic literature on environmental decision-making, new forms and styles of policymaking have been discussed, which bring together the different stakeholders, experts and lay people around the table (Fischer 1990; Eckersley 2000). Eckersley has argued that the central features of deliberative democracy make it especially suited to dealing with the complex environmental and ecological problems:

> It invites reflexivity, self-correction and the continual public testing of claims (…). [This] also makes it possible to expose and subject to scrutiny the assumptions, interests and

world-views of technocratic policy professionals, politicians and corporate leaders. (Eckersley, 2000 123)

In real-world situations, deliberative democracy should be understood as a counterfactual regulative ideal that provides a vantage point for critically assessing particular deliberative arrangements. The notion of unconstrained dialogue, for instance, implies that no relevant information is withheld and no misinformation is spread (Eckersley 2000). In the analysis of strengths and weaknesses of the deliberative model that we conducted in Chapter 3, we noted that unconstrained dialogue (in the 'ideal-speech situation') is extremely difficult to even approximate. The model also suffers from other vulnerabilities and weaknesses. We pointed to the exclusive tendencies of the deliberative model that conflict with the value of political equality. We also referred to the criterion of openness of the agenda, quoting Saward's critique that 'deliberative devices are not good at *initiating* issues' (Saward 2001). Our contention is that an important strategy for coping with these vulnerabilities and weaknesses consists of seeking appropriate linkages between deliberative devices and devices derived from other models of democracy.

Based on the analytical framework outlined in Chapter 3, the following criteria are used for assessing deliberative forums: (1) quality of the representation, (2) openness of the agenda, (3) quality of the participation, (4) checks and balances, (5) effectiveness of the participation, (6) responsiveness and (7) accountability.

On the input side, deliberation has to be governed by the criteria of inclusion (corresponding with the notion of quality of representation, mentioned in Chapter 3) and openness of the agenda. With regard to the criterion of *inclusion*, Eckersley (2000) emphasizes that representation in deliberative arrangements should be as diverse as possible. Here, we take the inclusion criterion to mean that the deliberative arrangement is broadly representative of the wider population (see also Saward 2000, 71). From an environmental justice perspective, ensuring the presence of minority or disadvantaged groups is particularly important. The second input criterion we use is the *openness of the agenda*. The definition of a deliberative procedure includes the principle that all participants have the right to propose topics or to question the assigned topics of the conversation (Benhabib 1994).

The throughput criterion of quality of the participation can be translated in terms of Habermas's notion of the *ideal speech situation* (Habermas 1971), which constitutes the core of the deliberative model of democracy. It stipulates that all citizens should have equal opportunities to start or enter a public discussion, as well as to advance positions or proposals and to oppose the positions and proposals of others. Participants are required to defend their proposals by arguments and to refrain from using power. On a meta-level, the ideal speech situation also includes the principle that 'all have the right to initiate reflexive arguments about the very rules of the discourse procedure and the way in which they are applied or carried out' (Benhabib 1994). Following Smith (2000) and Eckersley (2000), we look at the following conditions that facilitate unconstrained dialogues within an ideal speech situation:

- The participants are exposed to a wide range of information, no relevant information is withheld by the participants and no misinformation is spread.
- The participants have the opportunity to question witnesses, or to consult independent experts.
- The discussions are facilitated by an independent moderator, who ensures that all points of view are heard and the discussion is not dominated by any of the participants (see also Edwards 2002).

The second throughput criterion we use is *checks and balances*. This criterion has a special place in our investigation, as we use it to assess the position of local environmental forums within the whole system of environmental governance. In our discussion of the deliberative model of democracy in Chapter 3, we referred to Habermas's suggestion that deliberative procedures can function as a 'counter-steering mechanism' by which the communicative power of citizens can be channeled in societal and administrative decision-making (Habermas 1992). By looking at environmental forums in a system context we can examine whether they have the institutional position and resources to function as a check on corporate decision-making, and how regulatory agencies, local administrations and non-governmental organizations are involved in this relationship.

The first legitimacy criterion on the output side is effectiveness of participation, which can be understood in terms of the requirement of effective input in Saward's definition of democracy that we adopted in Chapter 3. We understand effectiveness in terms of *the weight of the results of the deliberation* on final decision-making by regulatory agencies and businesses. Following on Arnstein's (1969) well-known ladder of citizen participation, five degrees of influence on decision-making can be distinguished (see also Konisky and Beierle 2001):

1. Information exchange: The decision-makers solely inform citizens about pending decisions. Citizens are invited to ask questions. The citizens' reactions are treated as information or suggestions, without any commitment to consider them in the final decision-making.
2. Consultation: The decision-makers put their proposals before the citizens for comments. Citizens are invited to react. The decision-makers commit themselves to take the comments seriously in the final decision-making.
3. Advising: The decision-makers are willing to share some agenda-setting power. Citizens are given the opportunity to comment on the problem-definitions in the proposals, and to bring forward their own problems and proposals. The decision-makers commit themselves to consider these recommendations and to give feedback on how they have used them in their final decision-making.
4. Co-production: Citizens, private and public stakeholders, and politicians develop joint solutions on the basis of a commonly agreed agenda. The decision-makers commit themselves to these solutions, but they may amend them or make specific selections or combinations. These have to be

communicated to the citizens before the final decision-making.

5. Co-decision-making: The decision-makers give a mandate to the stakeholders to reach joint solutions for commonly agreed problem definitions. The decision-makers adopt these solutions, unless they do not conform to the basic limiting conditions that were set in advance of the deliberative process.

In view of the requirement of effective input and because deliberative procedures have to conform to the criterion of openness of the agenda, methods of citizen involvement can only be considered as forms of deliberative democracy if they reach at least the level of advising (level 3). We include the *responsiveness* of the final decisions in relation to the concerns of citizens as a separate point for attention. The last output norm we use is *accountability*. Table 9.1 gives an overview of the legitimacy norms.

Table 9.1   Conceptual Framework for assessing legitimacy in deliberative arrangements

Input	Throughput	Output
• Quality of the representation (inclusiveness) • Openness of the agenda	• Quality of the participation (ideal-speech situation) • Checks and balances	• Weight of the results • Responsiveness of final decisions • Accountability

2. Residential Advisory Boards in the Rijnmond Region

Introduction

In The Netherlands, there is a long-standing tradition of a consensus-oriented style of governing. So-called covenants negotiated between the central government and policy target groups are a mainstay of Dutch environmental policy. Various forms of cooperation between governments, companies and civil society actors have also emerged at the regional level (for example: Klijn 2003).

The Greater Rotterdam or 'Rijnmond' region covers an area in the southwest of Holland. With one of the largest ports in the world, it fulfills a main port function for Europe. This main port function, with its concomitant industrial activities (chemical industry, oil refineries and storage firms), exerts a greater environmental pressure than elsewhere in The Netherlands. In the 1990s, several Residential Advisory Boards (RABs) were set up in the region as organized forms of consultation in local communities. In these platforms, the residents, businesses, local authorities and the regional Environmental Protection Agency Rijnmond (DCMR) are represented. The first RAB was set up in the municipality of Rozenburg in September 1996 (*Klankbordgroep Rozenburg*). There are now five RABs in the region. At the regional level, a Regional Platform on Nuisance and Safety exists, in which local councilors, government agencies, businesses and local citizens meet regularly to discuss how to improve the quality of the environment in the Rijnmond region. The provincial alderman for the environment chairs this regional platform.

The official aims of the Residential Advisory Boards include:

- A free exchange of information and an open discussion about current environmental issues.
- Developing trust between residents and businesses.
- Providing a forum for residents' desires and complaints.
- Finding joint solutions.

With these ambitions, the RABs can appropriately be assessed as a deliberative arrangement within 'network governance' that is characteristic for environmental policy in The Netherlands. To a certain extent, they could also be seen as forms of 'societal self-governance', in so far they provide a platform for problem solving by residents and businesses within communities.[1] The set up of the RABs was stimulated by the DCMR, the regional environmental protection agency in the Rijnmond region. The DCMR is based on a formal cooperation between the 18 municipalities in the region and the province of South-Holland. This means that the democratic legitimation of the DCMR in terms of representative democracy is only indirect. There is, therefore, also a multi-level aspect to be considered in the analysis. Attempts to establish a separate regional government or 'city province' in the area failed in the early 1990s (Schaap 2003). The case-study will be focused on the Rozenburg RAB.[2]

The Residential Advisory Board of Rozenburg

The municipality of Rozenburg has about 13,000 inhabitants. In surveys conducted among the Rozenburg population in the beginning of the 1990s, it came out that the residents felt a great need for information and a more open attitude of the industry on issues of safety, environment and health. In 1996, a public manifestation was organized in which eight companies presented themselves to the public. About 2,000 residents visited this manifestation. As a result of this success, the Environmental Protection Agency Rijnmond (DCMR) and the municipality took the initiative to set up a consultation platform. Civic organizations and institutes were invited to delegate representatives. In 2003, a Declaration of Intention was signed by 16 companies, the municipality of Rozenburg and the DCMR. In this declaration, the participants expressed their commitment to 'an open, honest and active dialogue' between the industry and the residents. The participating companies referred to the

---

1   Somewhat closer to this model is the Shell Pernis Advisory Board.

2   Interviews were conducted with the secretary of the RAB, a representative of the citizens and the representatives of the DCMR.

notion of Responsible Care, a worldwide initiative of the petrochemical industry 'to improve its performance in the field of environment, safety and health, and to communicate with the society'. It encourages the companies to establish community advisory panels.

The Rozenburg RAB is a platform of citizens, businesses and the municipality of Rozenburg. The platform meets four times a year. During three of these meetings, a visit is organized to one of the participating companies. One meeting is devoted to a special theme, for instance, air quality or transport of hazardous substances. During the company visits, residents have the opportunity to ask questions. The meetings end with a so-called 'company round', a discussion of incidents that occurred during the previous period. For this discussion, representatives of the involved companies are invited to give an explanation. The mayor of Rozenburg is the chairman of the RAB. A municipal civil servant fills the secretariat. The DCMR fulfils an advisory role. The RAB Rozenburg has an own website on which the minutes of the meetings are published.

Quality of representation   Participants are representatives of the 16 companies who signed the Declaration of Intention, the municipality and residents. There are no permanent representatives of the residents. All meetings can be freely attended. On average, about 30 to 50 residents attend the meetings, 20 to 30 of them are regularly attending. From the beginning, one resident is the informal leader and spokesman. She was active within a local environmental group that has dissolved in the meantime, but she still has a wide network within the community. Residents have various motives attending a meeting. Some residents have specific questions, for instance when incidents have occurred. Others may want to have some influence on the policies of the companies. Curiosity can be a motive too. For this last category, the company visits seem to be particularly attractive.

Openness of the agenda   The agenda of the meetings is prepared in a working group, which includes representatives of the companies, the municipality and one citizen (the informal leader). This working-group decides on the annual program of company visits, the specific topics to be discussed during the theme-evenings and also on the incidents to be discussed during the 'company round'. According to the citizen, the municipality and the companies have a predominant influence on the agenda, in particular on the special theme-evenings. With regard to the company rounds, the agenda-setting process is more open. The DCMR draws up a list of all incidents that occurred during the previous period. The working-group decides on which incidents are relevant enough to be discussed in the meeting. According to the citizen, she has a decisive voice in this.

Ideal speech-situation   According to the interviewed citizen, the openness of the companies in terms of information provision is 'disappointing'. A distinction has to be made between 'reactive openness' and 'proactive openness'. The interviewed citizen always prepares the meetings for which a company visit is programmed with a personal visit in advance. At that occasion, the company provides her all information she wishes, including safety reports and the DCMR inspection reports. However, during the public meetings, the companies tell their own stories, the provision of information on potential problems being dependent on the questions posed by citizens. According to the DCMR advisors, the companies tend to use the company visits as a public relations instrument. There is always a certain bias in the presentations, because matters that are going well get more emphasis than matters that are going less well. Additional sources of information for the citizens are former employees and environmental organizations in the region. The former employees fulfill an expert function by drawing their fellow citizens' attention to hazardous situations and by commenting on the explanations given by the companies. Environmental organizations provide background information on residents' request.

According to one of the advisors, the citizens are fairly assertive, but they are often not competent enough to obtain adequate answers. Often, questions are answered in a language that is not understandable for ordinary citizens. According to both advisors, the communication rarely reaches the level of a real discussion. One of the advisors observes that this can be partly attributed to the fact that the chairman of the Board (the mayor of Rozenburg) is not supportive enough in this. This also implies that a consensus in terms of commonly agreed solutions is seldom reached.

Checks and balances   The architecture of the RAB in which companies have committed themselves to sit at the same table with residents, is a non-negligible institutional resource for residents' influence. However, several factors tend to offset this circumstance. Among these are the absence of a permanent representation of residents and the weak support of neighborhood-based organizations and environmental advocacy groups. These factors are conducive to maintaining the knowledge advantage of the companies. An interesting aspect in this assessment is the roles played by the municipality and the regional environmental protection agency (DCMR). We saw above that the role of the mayor as chairman of the RAB has been criticized as being too passive. On the other hand, the interviewed citizen praised the mayor's role in stirring companies to render explanations about incidents. The DCMR has to perform a 'balancing act' between the companies, the residents and the municipality (one of their administrative bosses).

Weight of the results   According to the citizen and the advisors, the interaction is mainly 'informative' and 'consultative' (levels 1 and 2). On the one hand, companies tend to give more attention to the opinions of citizens. On the other hand, however, the municipality and, particularly, the companies do not provide the citizens an opportunity to give inputs that have a real influence on policies. According to the citizen, companies occasionally make promises, but there is almost never a feedback on concrete measures. She has repeatedly called upon the participating companies to agree on an annual evaluation of the meetings of the boards, in terms of the issues that have been discussed and subsequent actions undertaken by the companies. Until the time of writing this chapter, she has received no response on this.

Responsiveness of decisions   None of the interviewees was able to mention concrete results. This does not mean that there are no improvements. On the contrary, citizens who have taken the opportunity to visit the same companies for the second time (after 4–5 years), say that a lot has changed for the better, in particular with regard to energy saving and recycling. However, it is not possible to relate these improvements to previous discussions in the Board. According to the citizen, the safety practices in the companies have deteriorated: 'All involved companies emphasize that they comply with the safety requirements, but nevertheless things often go wrong, in particular in the context of maintenance' (translation, AE). The citizen wants a more active role of the DCMR, which by its licensing, inspection and enforcement tasks could exert more influence on the companies. Nevertheless, she thinks it important to continue the communication with the companies, hoping that they will become more aware of the advantages of taking the wishes of the citizens into account. Some companies do take an open attitude, admit their mistakes, and do their best to implement improvements. They might be an example to other companies that still withhold information.

All interviewees indicate that the communication in the Board has no direct bearing on the policies of the DCMR. According to the advisors, there might be some indirect influence, in that the DCMR takes account of the opinions of citizens and companies when drafting new policies.

Accountability   The minutes of the Board meetings are published on the RAB's website. The local newspapers publish regularly about the RAB meetings. Because of her expertise, the journalists often invite the active citizen to draft the articles. These two elements constitute the public accountability. We could not establish that RAB meetings were discussed in the municipal council, although individual councilors sometimes visit the meetings. It has to be noted that the municipal council has the 'constitutional' position to monitor the RAB and, in particular, to render the mayor accountable for her role as chairman of the Board (political accountability).

3. Collaborative Environmental Problem Solving in Cleveland (Ohio)

Introduction

Environmental policies in the United States have been shaped by various normative discourses in society and policy programs of national administrations. In the 1980s, the Right-to-Know movement promoted the right of employees and local communities to have access to information about the health hazards of industrial production processes (Williams and Matheny 1995, 189–190). An underlying premise of legislation based on Right-to-Know principles is that expanding and improving upon the information provided to the public will improve the quality of public input into regulatory processes. Another aspect is that public information can be used as a tool to encourage voluntary improvements in environmental performance by the regulated facilities. This agenda was taken up during the Bush Sr. administration. In the Pollution Prevention Act (1990) the use of voluntary programs was made a national priority. In the 1980s and 1990s, the Environmental Justice debate also developed as a grass-roots movement (Illsley 2002). In 1994, President Clinton issued an Executive Order to establish environmental justice as a priority for the administration's environmental policy. Public participation and information are key elements in this strategy. Currently, the Environmental Protection Agency (EPA) follows an innovation strategy that is marked by stakeholder collaboration, a preference for voluntary compliance and market-based incentives (Edwards 2006).

Cleveland is situated on the southern shore of Lake Erie in northeastern Ohio. The city has about 500,000 inhabitants. The total population of the area, including the suburbs, is about 2.9 million. Heavy industry is basic to the city's economy. Similar to many metropolitan areas, Cleveland has experienced a decline in heavy manufacturing and population since the 1960s. Suburban living has become more popular for those who could afford the lifestyle, and downtown neighborhoods deteriorated. Today, Cleveland is gaining much recognition as a city experiencing a turnaround. Because of its environmental problems and the presence of an active civil society sector, Cleveland is often chosen as a model city for several new initiatives in environmental governance, in particular for partnerships between the federal, state, local and neighborhood level (multi-level governance).

The Environmental Committee of St. Clair Superior[3]

St. Clair Superior is a neighborhood of about 30,000 residents. Originally, the neighborhood was one of the most important centers of heavy manufacturing in the city. In the 1960s and 1970s, many businesses disappeared. White residents (of predominantly East-European origin) moved to the suburbs; African Americans (from the southern states) came in and found jobs in service industries outside the neighborhood. In 1976, the St. Clair Superior Coalition was formed. In 1999 the Coalition merged with the St. Clair Business Association to form the St. Clair Superior Neighborhood Development Association (SCSNDA).

The two major environmental concerns within the neighborhood are air quality and hazardous waste. In 1996, the Environmental Committee was formed in response to resident concerns and to help residents organize around environment issues. Initially, the committee was educational in nature. Residents and leaders in the St. Clair-Superior neighborhood were among the first graduates of the Sustainable Cleveland Partnership. The committee became more action oriented with the pending review of the air permits for the Cleveland Electric Illuminating Company's Lakeshore Plant (1999) and Day Glo. The committee advocated for knowledge and

---

3   Interviews were conducted with representatives of the St. Clair Superior Neighborhood Development Association, officials of the United States Environmental Protection Agency and Ohio Environmental Protection Agency and a representative from Earth Day Coalition, a non-governmental organization in Cleveland.

experts sitting at the same table, and submitted an environmental justice petition to the Ohio EPA. With the assistance of local NGOs, including the Earth Day Coalition and the Sierra Club, a collaborative meeting process developed between the Environmental Committee and representatives from the Ohio EPA. The U.S. EPA and the Cleveland Department of Air Quality were requested to participate in monthly meetings designed to address neighborhood concerns. The Environmental Committee chaired this Working Group, and Ohio EPA acted as facilitator and secretary. This may have been the first initiative in the United States to bring the state, federal and city environmental agencies into a monthly neighborhood working group setting to address environmental justice concerns. In 2003, the Environmental Committee and the Working Group were consolidated.

Quality of representation   The Environmental Committee is one of the active issue committees within the SCSNDA. The membership is well embedded in the organization. The SCSNDA coordinates 15–30 street and block clubs in the neighborhood to ensure citizen involvement and action. Several community leaders are active in the committee.

Openness of the Agenda   Through the collaboration in the Working Group, the opportunity for more community input was secured, including an informal review and comment period. Furthermore, the Environmental Committee composed a list of 'companies of concern', based on community concerns, toxic release inventory data, visual behavior indicators and type of business. The state and city agencies used the community input to conduct several unannounced inspections in addition to the standard inspections within the neighborhood.

Ideal-speech situation   Initially, there was a great mistrust and a lot of tension between the regulatory agencies and the communities. The regulatory agencies had to learn in terms of how neighborhoods experience and perceive problems. Building individual relationships with community leaders and creating room for communication in informal settings have been essential. A process followed, in which the regulatory agencies provided information on permits and inspections. The committee received, when possible, copies of permits and the most recent inspection reports.

The merger of the Environmental Committee and the Working Group marked a new phase in environmental problem solving in St. Clair Superior, a transition from a confrontational style to a more collaborative style toward the companies in the neighborhood. A turning point was the Phillips Electric case. This company was found to be in violation of hazardous waste regulations. When a fine was imposed that would absorb its complete annual profit, the company approached the committee for consultation. The two parties found a solution that would not put the business in financial peril but still address the desired health and safety concerns of the community. The committee decided to support Phillips Electric in its dealings with the Ohio EPA. The company's director even joined the Environmental Committee.

The neighborhood's new policy line was the outcome of intense discussions within the SCNDA. Some community leaders in the committee only reluctantly agreed with the arrangement with Phillips Electric. The committee embarked on an ongoing dialogue with Day-Glo Color Corporation (and other businesses) to create an informal 'Good Neighbor' relationship. This involved establishing meetings with the corporation that involve discussion of their environmental safety procedures.

Checks and balances   Because of the absence of businesses, the architecture of the Environmental Committee/Working Group differs substantially from the Residential Advisory Board Rozenburg. The set up of the Working Group was, first of all, conducive to the emergence of trust between the residents and the regulatory agencies. Together, they developed some leverage towards the corporations. Non-governmental organizations played an important empowerment role. While the list of 'companies of concern' and the unannounced inspections by the EPA initially caused negative reactions from the businesses, it ultimately contributed to increasing the power of the Environmental Committee, which in turn might have contributed to the emergence of more collaborative relations with businesses later on.

Weight of the results   In the first, more confrontational period, the Environmental Committee played an advisory role. With its list of 'companies of concern', it had some effective input on the inspection agenda of the regulatory agencies. After the consolidation of the Committee and the Working Group, a collaborative process developed among residents, (some) businesses, and regulatory agencies that, at least in some cases, reached the level of co-production.

Responsiveness of decisions   Because of the relationship that developed between the committee and the Ohio EPA, the agency considered the committee's recommendations in its permit and penalty decisions.

The goal of the SCNDA is to build a community for all stakeholders. Efforts have to be directed at 'mending fences, building connections, and producing positive energy' (interview). It is acknowledged that sustainability requires a broader approach than regulatory measures. Furthermore, education efforts are directed to small businesses that do not have the resources to acquire the necessary environmental knowledge themselves.

Accountability   Accountability is primarily embedded in the SCSNDA (associative accountability). Environmental Committee updates are published in a (free) bi-monthly publication of the Association (public accountability).

4. Assessment

In both cases, the quality of the representation is dependent on community leaders. In the Rozenburg case, this basis is very small, and any cohesion between the attending residents on the basis of which a common expertise could develop, is lacking. In the Cleveland case, the representation is embedded in the associative democracy of a neighborhood-based organization and its internal structure of block clubs. With regard to the openness of the agenda, the overall picture is mixed. In the Rozenburg case, openness exists with regard to the signaling function of the Board, but on other aspects of the agenda, the influence of the municipality and the companies is predominant. The Environmental Committee in Cleveland exerted a significant influence on the inspection priorities of the EPA.

Turning to the throughput side, the communication in the Rozenburg RAB generally seems to get bogged down in information provision, and the communication can hardly be regarded as equivalent ('deliberative') even at that level. On this criterion, the Environmental Committee seems to perform better. Because of their different architectures, the two forums are difficult to compare. However, if we only look at the interaction between regulatory agencies and residents, we may conclude that the participants in the Environmental Committee developed a more productive relationship, also in terms of leverage vis-à-vis the businesses. The same holds true for their position in a checks and balances perspective.

On the output side, the Cleveland Environmental Committee also performs better than the Rozenburg Board. In terms of the weight of the results of the deliberation, the Rozenburg RAB cannot even be regarded as a form of deliberative 'democracy' in contrast to the Cleveland case that reaches the levels of advising, and at some occasion even co-production.

We can conclude that the RAB Rozenburg does provide a forum for residents' concerns and complaints but that the knowledge advantage of the companies and their reluctance to share relevant information with residents are impediments to the stated aim of 'free exchange of information and open discussion about current environmental issues'. Furthermore, the interactions suffer from a lack of commitment by the companies to render account of their efforts to solve observed problems. The aim of finding joint solutions is seldom reached.

5. Linkages with Other Models of Democracy

By focusing the assessment on the functioning of local environmental forums, we risk losing the broader view of the system of environmental governance in which these forums function. From the analysis above, two specific functions emerge. The first one is signaling problems. Both forums provide a platform on which citizens can express their complaints, concerns and demands. The second emergent function is monitoring environmental problem-solving. In the Rozenburg case, this function is not uncontested. The refusal to adopt a system for monitoring the results of the meetings of the RAB is an indication of the reluctance on the side of the other parties to upgrade the status of the Board to a forum on which companies can be held accountable.

Our main argument is this chapter is that deliberative arrangements themselves cannot provide the conditions for giving residents the needed leverage in environmental decision-making. The support of environmental organizations and politicians is indispensable. This implies that the forums have to be linked with pluralist and representative institutions. In order to highlight this, we turn to the system level of environmental governance, specifically to the institutional conditions within which the signaling and monitoring functions of the forums are performed.

Empowering Communities in Signaling Environmental Problems: The Role of Non-Governmental Organizations

A first condition for the performance of the signaling function is information provision based on Right-to-Know principles. In this respect, European countries are lagging far behind the United States. On the basis of the Emergency Planning and Community Right-to-Know Act of 1986, a nation-wide infrastructure of online information resources emerged in the USA that facilitates community-based organizations in environmental problem-solving. A second condition is enhancing the capacity of communities to use these information resources effectively. In 1997, the Sustainable Cleveland Partnership (SCP) was founded, in which non-governmental organizations, community-based organizations and regulatory agencies joined forces to improve the capacity of local communities to address environmental problems. The SCP grew out of the common finding that residents participated infrequently in the decision-making processes that had shaped environmental problems, and that inadequate access to environmental information resources and tools was a root cause of this (Kellogg and Mathur 2003). The Earth Day Coalition, a non-profit environmental education and advocacy organization, initiated the SCP. The first goal of the SCP was to enhance the availability and relevance of environmental information to urban neighborhoods. The second and third goals were to improve the capacity of community leaders to use the Internet as an information access tool and to use environmental information effectively to address environmental problems these leaders identified as priorities. The various projects fostered networking and collaboration among divergent groups in Cleveland, thereby facilitating new and enhanced working relations among Cleveland's neighborhood-based organizations, regulatory agencies and environmental advocacy groups (the fourth goal of the partnership) (Kellogg and Mathur 2003). Residents and community leaders in the St. Clair-Superior neighborhood were among the first graduates of the Sustainable Cleveland Partnership. The success of the SCP indicates that a strong and pro-active civil society sector is a major success factor for community empowerment in terms of environmental information and problem solving.

Leverage in Monitoring Environmental Performance: The Role of Representative Institutions

With regard to the monitoring function, we can look at the legal approaches that local communities in the United States have applied to increase industrial accountability. Various types of conditions have been negotiated in Good Neighbor Agreements, including community access to information, the right to inspect the facility, accident preparation and environmental performance (Lewis and Henkel 1997, Illsley 2002). In return for these company commitments, the citizen group may settle ongoing litigation, end protests or negative publicity, or generate positive publicity about the company. In some situations, a Good Neighbor Agreement is linked to an environmental permitting process. In such cases, the permits can be used as tools to give citizen groups some leverage in confronting a company (Lewis and Henkel 1997). Lewis and Henkel (1997) conclude that these agreements can make significant advances in community control over corporate activities, although even a binding agreement does not necessarily mean that a firm will be a 'good neighbor' in reality. Community groups have to muster extensive political and legal power to successfully confront the power yielded by corporations. Therefore, local citizens have to find whatever leverage is available to support local pressure to negotiate. Heiman (1997) observes that firms can be pressured to participate in negotiations, if they are subject to collective bargaining agreements, or at times of license renewal, in particular when permit violations have been revealed or when an accident has occurred leading people to question the operation of the plant. This underscores the importance of the support of federal and state officials. Such support from regulatory agencies was visible in the Cleveland case. However, this is not self-evident because regulatory agencies may serve as a buffer 'that protects corporations more than the communities placed at risk' (Lewis and Henkel 1997). This brings us to the necessary linkages with representative democracy.

In the governance practices we discuss in this chapter, politicians have two roles. First, they are the politically responsible designers of environmental public policies and the political administrators of the regulatory agencies that implement these policies. Second, governments can fulfill a governance role as 'process manager'. This role includes activities as facilitating and coordinating interactions, connecting actors and organizing research and information processes (Kickert, Klijn and Koppenjan 1997). In both roles, governments can affect the leverage of communities in environmental decision-making. In their governance role, they can affect the conditions within which deliberative forums function, by monitoring (and improving the conditions for) inclusiveness, the openness of the agenda-setting process, the quality of participation and interaction, and by helping to establish arrangements by which companies can be hold accountable. These roles are not self-evident, as 'local politics and policy tended to be dominated by, or at least primarily responsive to, local business interests', as indicated by Portney (2005, 579) for the American situation. With regard to these politicians' roles, we can learn some lessons from the Dutch experiences.

As we noted above (section 2), the 'political boss function' of the environmental protection agency in the Rijnmond region, suffers from a democratic deficit, because this responsibility is spread over 18 municipalities and the province. With regard to the governance function, however, the province of South-Holland is the most important player. In the Dutch polity, the province is generally regarded as an intermediary authority with coordinating functions. The provincial alderman for the environment chairs the Regional Platform for Nuisance and Safety. However, an active governance role of the province with regard to the RABs was not visible in our investigation.

6. Conclusion

This chapter elaborates on the analysis of strengths and weaknesses in the deliberative model of democracy that we conducted in chapter 3. In terms of the legitimacy criteria outlined in that chapter, several vulnerabilities and weaknesses were noted. Here, our main contention is that an important strategy for coping with these vulnerabilities and weaknesses consists in seeking appropriate linkages between deliberative devices and devices derived from other models of democracy, in particular pluralist and representative democracy. This concurs with discussions in the literature on democratic innovations, in which new institutional designs are searched for, in which different models of democracy work together in ways that can be mutually supportive.

Since the 1990s, the deliberative model of democracy inspires various experiments in democratic practices. In this chapter, we looked at two environmental forums, one Residential Advisory Board in the Rijnmond region in The Netherlands, and a neighborhood Environmental Committee in the city of Cleveland in the United States. The analysis reveals that both forums fulfill important signaling and monitoring functions within the system of regional environmental governance. With regard to the Dutch case, the knowledge advantage of the companies and their lack of commitment to render accounts of their efforts to solve observed problems came out as two hindrances to fulfill these functions and meeting the legitimacy criteria that were outlined in chapter 3. The design of deliberative arrangements itself is not sufficient for providing the conditions for giving residents the needed leverage. The support of environmental organizations and politicians is indispensable.

With regard to the role of non-governmental organizations, the American case is very instructive. The performance of the signaling function can be enhanced by information provision based on Right-to-Know principles and by empowering communities to use these information resources effectively. In several American cities, non-governmental organizations have initiated collaborative projects to enhance the availability of environmental information to neighborhoods, and to improve the capacity of community leaders to use this information in environmental decision-making processes. In Cleveland, such a partnership had an empowering effect on the community leaders in the Environmental Committee. With regard to the monitoring function we looked at legal ('Good Neighbor') approaches to increase industrial accountability. We conclude that linkages with pluralist democracy, in terms of a strong and pro-active civil society sector are a major success factor for local environmental forums. Linkages with representative democracy are twofold. First, elected officials are the politically responsible designers of environmental public policies and the administrators of the regulatory agencies that implement these policies. Second, governments can fulfill a governance role as process manager. This role includes activities as facilitating and coordinating interactions, connecting actors and organizing research and information processes. In both roles, the backing of representative democracy is essential for providing the conditions within which environmental forums can function as a 'check' on corporate decision-making.

References

Arnstein, S.R. (1969), 'A ladder of citizen participation', *Journal of the Institute of Planners* 35, 216–24.

Bekkers, V.J.J.M., Duivenboden, H. van, and Thaens, M. (eds.) (2006), *ICT and Public Innovation: Assessing the ICT-Driven Modernization of Public Administration* (Amsterdam etc: IOS Press).

Benhabib, S. (1994), 'Deliberative rationality and models of democratic legitimacy', *Constellations* 1:1, 26–52.

Budge, I. (2000), 'Deliberative democracy versus direct democracy – plus political parties', in Saward (ed.), pp. 195–209.

Bullard, R.D. (1999), 'Dismantling environmental racism in the USA', *Local Environment* 4:1, 5–19.

Chambers, S. (2003), 'Deliberative Democratic Theory', *Annual Review of Political Science* 6, 307–26.

Denters, B., Heffen, O. van, Huisman, J. and Klok, P.J. (eds) (2003), *The Rise of Interactive Governance and Quasi Markets* (Den Haag: Kluwer Academic Publishers).

Eckersley, R. (2000), 'Deliberative Democracy: ecological representation and risk', in Saward (ed.), pp. 117–131.

Edwards, A.R. (2002), 'The moderator as an emerging democratic intermediary: The role of the moderator in Internet discussions about public issues', *Information Polity* 7:2002, 3–20.

—— (2006), 'Empowering Communities for Environmental Decision-Making: Innovative Partnerships in Cleveland (USA)', in Bekkers et al. (eds.).

Fischer, F. (1990), *Technocracy and the Politics of Expertise* (Newbury Park: Sage)

Habermas, J. (1971), *Toward a Rational Society* (London: Heineman).

Habermas, J. (1992), *Between Facts and Norms. Contributions to a Discourse Theory of Law and Democracy* (Cambridge, MA: MIT Press).

Heiman, M.K. (1997), 'Community Attempts at Sustainable Development through Corporate Accountability', *Journal of Environmental Planning and Management* 40:5, 631–43.

Illsley, B.M. (2002), 'Good Neighbor Agreements: The First Step to Environmental Justice?', *Local Environment* 7:1, 69–79.

Kellogg, W.AA. and Mathur, A. (2003), 'Environmental Justice and Information Technologies: Overcoming the Information Access Paradox in Urban Communities', *Public Administration Review* 63:5, 573–85.

Kickert, W.J.M., Klijn, E.H. and Koppenjan, J.F.M. (eds) (1997), *Managing Complex Networks* (London: Sage).

Klijn, E.H. (2003), 'Does Interactive Decision Making Work: Expanding Rotterdam Port', in Denters et al. (eds), pp. 15–41.

Konisky, D.M. and Beierle, Th.C. (2001), 'Innovations in Public Participation and Environmental Decision Making: Examples from the Great Lakes Region', *Society and Natural Resources* 14, 815–26.

Lewis, S. and Henkel, D.D. (1997), 'Good Neighbor Agreements: A Tool for Environmental and Social Justice', *Social Justice* 23:4, 134–51.

Magone, J.M. (ed.) (2003), *Regional Institutions and Governance in the European Union* (Westport (Conn.): Praeger).

Portney, K. (2005), 'Civic Engagement and Sustainable Cities in the United States', *Public Administration Review* 65:5, 579–91.

Saward, M. (2000), 'Less than Meets the Eye. Democratic Legitimacy and Deliberative Theory', in Saward (ed.), pp. 66–77.

—— (ed.) (2000), *Democratic Innovation* (London and New York: Routledge).

—— (2001), 'Making Democratic Connections: Political Equality, Deliberation and Direct Democracy', *Acta Politica* 36:4, 361–79.

Schaap, L. (2003), 'Government or Governance in the Rotterdam Region', in Magone (ed.), pp. 153–71.

Schlossberg, D. (1999), *Environmental Justice and the New Pluralism* (Oxford: Oxford University Press).

Smith, G. (2000), 'Toward deliberative institutions', in Saward (ed.), pp. 29–39.

Williams, B.A. and Albert R. Matheny (1995), *Democracy, Dialogue, and Environmental Disputes* (New Haven and London: Yale University Press).

Chapter 10

The Limits of Donor-Induced Participation: An Analysis of a Participatory Development Program in Mozambique

Geske Dijkstra and Lieve Lodewyckx[1]

This chapter analyzes the results of the introduction of citizen participation in a non-western context, namely in Mozambique. It is based on an empirical analysis of the MAMM program[2], a participatory integrated rural development program in Nampula, Northern Mozambique, carried out in 2003. The donor, a Dutch NGO (SNV), made a serious attempt to build effective local ownership and participation in development efforts. The program is seen as an experiment for new decentralized governance structures that the government aims to develop at the national level with support of the UNDP and the World Bank as well as some bilateral donors. Yet, it is already clear that participation as promoted through this program can only have limited success. The chapter analyzes the reasons for these limitations.

Participation is increasingly seen as important for development, both as an instrument of enhancing aid effectiveness and as an end in itself (Brohman 1996). With respect to the first, it is expected to enhance the efficiency, effectiveness and long-term sustainability of projects (Vainio-Mattila 2000, 432). As to the second, the ability to participate in decisions that shape people's lives is an important component of 'human development' as defined by UNDP (UNDP 2002). Similarly, sustainable development is only considered possible if 'basic liberties' exist along with opportunities for individuals (Sand 1994). Participation has to do with transparency, openness, and voice in both public and corporate settings (Stiglitz 2002). Participation also enhances the political sustainability of government policies, and promotes

1 The authors are grateful to the Netherlands Development Organization (SNV, A Dutch NGO) for helping to organize the empirical research for this chapter, and to Januário João Pereira for his participation in this research. Thanks are also due to Harry Daemen, José Hoogervorst and Gerard Prinsen for thoughtful comments.

2 The name MAMM is derived from the initials of the four districts Mogovolas, Angoche, Mogincual and Moma.

'social development': the ability of society to peacefully resolve conflicts (Stiglitz 2002, 171).

All this means that aid donors have at least a stated interest in promoting participation. Yet, donor attempts to improve participation often fail or do not live up to their promises. There are many reasons for this, but basically two types of explanations can be distinguished in the literature so far. These include a lack of serious commitment to participation on the side of the donor and/or a lack of political will on the side of the government in the country concerned.

At the project level, Vainio-Mattila stresses many factors that form obstacles to real participation, such as the fact that aid is often defined for a certain sector, which leaves no choices for the recipient (Vainio-Mattila 2000). In practice, donors often restrict a participatory methodology to only one component of a program or project because it is difficult to work with unforeseeable outcomes of participatory processes. Donors often use a logical framework. This precludes real participation because it predetermines the institutional structure of development interventions. Even if participation leads to a high degree of commitment during project lifespan, this commitment tends to end when donors withdraw support (Vainio-Mattila 2000, 444).

Real participation implies a political process, and this process may lead to outcomes that are not in the interest of the government in power. Governments may stop participatory processes when participation threatens to challenge the position of elites, as happened in Costa Rican health care policies (Morgan 1990) and many other documented instances.

This chapter brings to the fore a *third* and so far neglected obstacle to donor-induced participation, namely the absence of *effective* democratic structures and institutions. In fact, too often the presence of institutions such as elections and parliament creates an appearance of democracy, but does not guarantee real democratic participation and accountability. Finer (1970, 442–45) introduced the idea of a 'façade democracy' for such a system. A 'façade' of democratic institutions is built up, but the country remains an oligarchy. Hague, Harrop and Breslin (1998) use the term 'semi-democracy' for a system in which democratic and authoritarian elements coexist.

We begin by giving a brief sketch of the history of Mozambique and of the current political system. Section 2 presents the MAMM program and its aims. In section 3 we describe results of the program. We further analyze those results in section 4, and present our conclusions in section 5.

1. The Context

Mozambique is one of the poorest countries in the world. The Portuguese colonizers exploited the local population and brought very little development in return. The growing resistance against Portuguese rule led to the establishment of the *Frente pela Libertação de Moçambique* (Frelimo) in 1962 that promoted Mozambique's independence. It began its military struggle from its basis in neighboring Tanzania but with limited success. Ultimately, it was the fall of the Salazar dictatorship in Portugal itself, on April 25, 1974 that brought independence to Mozambique (Bossema 1995). Frelimo set up a socialist economy based on the Soviet example. The Politbureau of the party was the highest organ. The same persons usually held high positions in government and party. Economic and social policies were also based on a socialist model. All private businesses were nationalized, and peasants were forced to move in order to live together in community villages where they were supposed to have better access to social services. They had to work in cooperatives or state farms. In the course of the 1980s, it was clear that this strategy not only failed, but that it had created widespread resistance amongst the population against Frelimo itself. During the 1980s, Frelimo began to reform its economic policies and gradually re-established a market economy.

Frelimo's support to liberation movements in South Africa and Zimbabwe provoked the government of those countries to set up a guerrilla movement against the government of Mozambique, Renamo (*Resistencia Nacional de Moçambique*) in 1984. This resulted in a civil war that devastated numerous roads, bridges, railways, schools and hospitals and killed hundreds of teachers and nurses, as well as thousands of other Mozambicans (Bossema 1995; Chabal et al. 2002). The war only ended when, after the fall of the Berlin wall and the beginning of the De Klerk government in South Africa, both parties lost their sources of income. A peace treaty was signed in 1992. A UN peace force enforced this agreement until the first democratic elections were held in 1994.

Since 1994, economic growth rates have been high and aid agencies are lining up to provide assistance. Mozambique has become a donor darling. But the problems are still immense. Economic growth rarely benefits the majority of the population who lives in rural areas. During the war, primary school enrollment declined from 95 per cent in 1981 to 60 per cent in 1992, but since 1995, it has increased and it is now at 92 per cent. Still, seventy per cent of adult women cannot read or write. In addition, rates of infant mortality and maternal mortality are high, and the high incidence of diseases such as malaria, cholera and HIV–AIDS contributes to a life expectancy at birth of only 42 years (World Bank 2003).

In 1994, the country held national presidential and parliamentary elections for the first time. They were repeated in 1999 and 2004. While both Frelimo and Renamo had always participated in the elections thus far, Frelimo always won. This means there has always been a Frelimo president. In 1998, elections for municipal councils were also held in 33 cities, but only 20 per cent of the population lives in these cities. Again, Frelimo won but this time Renamo withdrew at the last moment because of alleged fraud. The extent of abstinence was very high, however (87 per cent to 92 per cent in the three largest cities (Alden 2001)). In 2003, municipal elections were held again. This time Renamo participated but abstinence was again high, at 72 per cent on average.[3]

---

3   J. Hanlon, Mozambique Bulletin No 29, December 2003.

The villages and communities where no elections are held, are ruled by 'village secretaries' who are appointed by the next higher level, usually the chief of the administrative post (an administrative post comprises several villages). The village secretaries and chiefs of the administrative posts are called 'local authorities'. The chief of the administrative post is appointed by the district administrator, the district administrator by the governors of one of Mozambique's eleven provinces, while the governors are appointed by the President.

In practice, the local authorities enjoy minimal legitimacy with the population. During the second half of the 1990s, the government became concerned about this lack of legitimacy and effectiveness of local governance. It began to take measures for enhancing local participation. The decentralization experiment referred to in the first paragraph of this chapter is one of these. But three other measures are worth mentioning in this context.

First, in 2000, the government re-established an important role for traditional local authorities, in particular the *régulo*.[4] After independence in 1975, Frelimo considered all *régulos* as persons who had worked for the colonizer, despite the fact that many *régulos* had cooperated with Frelimo against Portuguese oppression. Frelimo began to prosecute the *régulos* and jailed many of them. It then appointed its own party members as new 'village secretaries'. Since these appointees often came from other regions, they were not trusted by the population, thus they contributed to resistance against Frelimo and support of Renamo (Harrison 2000). Even after 1992, Frelimo maintained the village secretaries and was unable to successfully execute governance in local communities. The rural population continued to consider the *régulos* as their leaders, and consulted them secretly in cases of problems or disputes.

The so-called Decree 15/2000 aimed to regain the confidence of the rural population by legitimizing the informal power of the *régulos*. They are now supposed to be intermediaries between the local state authorities and the population. The *régulo* forms a council in which other traditional and religious leaders of the community participate. In practice, these community authorities help execute tasks that were earlier carried out by the local state authorities, and *régulos* are supposed to encourage participation of the population in the solution of practical problems. On the other hand, *régulos* are now responsible for tax collection at the local level. They are entitled to 5 or 10 per cent (depending on kind of tax) of tax revenues. Although communities are generally happy with their newly recognized representatives, the exact division of power between community authorities and local state authorities is not very clear. For example, village secretaries still exist and often have substantial

---

4   *Régulos* have a complicated history in Mozambique. Originally, local power and legitimate authority was with the *Mwene*. During colonial rule, the Portuguese tried to dominate the local population by convincing the *Mwenes* to rule on their behalf. *Mwenes* who did so were called *régulos*, but most of them refused and in that case *Mwenes* and newly appointed *régulos* existed side by side. *Mwenes* were considered legitimate leaders, but *régulos* had most powers as they were backed by colonial rule. *Régulos* indeed worked for the Portuguese: they organized forced labor if that was required, and they collected taxes for the colonial rulers (Harrison 2000).

(hindrance) power because of their close connection to Frelimo, especially when traditional authorities sympathize with Renamo (Andrade and Quinamine 2002).

Second, two laws were approved at the end of the 1990s that could play a role in increasing the rights of rural populations, the Land Law and the Forest and Wildlife Law. All land is state owned, but local state authorities can issue licenses for land use if it is below certain acreage thresholds. The 1997 Land Law obliges state authorities to consult the population before issuing licenses to third parties. If peasants can prove that they are cultivating the land, they can veto such licensing to other parties. The Law also stipulates that communities and individuals, including women, can apply for licenses themselves in order to further secure their land use. Similarly, the 1999 Forest and Wildlife Law protect peasant communities and society as a whole against exploitation of forests by third parties. Peasant communities must be consulted before licenses for large-scale lumbering or hunting are given. Peasants also have a first right to obtain such licenses, and they are always allowed to enter forests for which licenses to third parties have been issued. It remains to be seen to what extent these laws will be implemented.

2. The MAMM Program

In 1998, the SNV (Netherlands Development Organization, a Dutch NGO) started a program in the districts of Mogovolas, Angoche, Mogincual and Moma in Nampula province to strengthen the position of local communities in their interactions with local authorities. The program was explicitly set up as part of a national decentralization experiment, established by the Mozambican ministries of Planning and Finance and of State Administration. This national program, the *Projecto de Planificação e Financimento Distrital* aims at the drafting of regional socio-economic plans by means of consulting the most important stakeholders. Stakeholders not only include NGOs, the private sector, political parties and religious organizations but also local communities. This national program is supposed to be executed in different regions with the support of different development NGOs. In 1998, SNV has taken up the challenge to do this in the MAMM region. By 2003, plans were developed to apply the methodology of the MAMM program in five other provinces, financed by other donors. If the donors accept these plans, the program will be executed in six of the eleven Mozambican provinces.

In order to organize participation of local communities in the MAMM region, the SNV-MAMM hires Mozambican professionals to act as ADL (*Agente de Desenvolvimento Local*) (Agents of Local Development). These ADLs support the communities by teaching people the skills they need to act together and to strengthen their position with respect to the local authorities. They help communities install local development commissions, the CDL (*Commissão de Desenvolvimento Local*). CDL are meant to be the local community's instrument for becoming aware of and formulating the most urgent needs of the community. They are also expected to advocate for these needs with local authorities and to help resolving them. Between 1998 and 2003, 63 CDLs have been established (SNV Year Plan 2003).

The designers of the MAMM program believe that consultation and participation of the local communities must be embedded in a formal/legal framework. It is expected that future laws will allow for local elections in the countryside so that CDL can be formally elected and can become municipal councils with formal capacities. In the absence of these elections, it is expected that Decree 15/2000, as well as the Land Law and the Forest and Wildlife Law provide a legal basis for participation of local communities. These laws and the decree have in common that participation of local citizens is a prerequisite for their execution. It is expected that the MAMM program will enhance the skills of CDLs to represent the population in general and to advocate for their rights vis-à-vis the state authorities, but in particular for the execution of these two laws.

In order to examine the results of the MAMM program in terms of effective participation and improved living conditions of local communities, field work was conducted in March and April 2003 in the four MAMM districts. The aim of this research was to find out:

- The experiences of CDL in participation and in resolution of urgent community problems.
- The nature of the interaction of CDL with local state authorities and with the régulo.
- The knowledge (awareness) of, and opinions on the contents of the Decree and the two Laws among all relevant groups: CDL, local authorities and régulo.
- The experiences with applications of the Decree and the Laws.

In each district, interviews were held with the administrator, and with a selection of the chiefs of administrative posts, *régulos* and CDL. In total, 34 interviews were conducted (see Table 10.1). A questionnaire with structured answers was developed, and this same questionnaire was used for all interviewed individuals and groups. Interviews lasted for about an hour. In addition to these indirect observations, direct and subjective observations of the environment, living circumstances, and body language of respondents were also used to interpret results and reach conclusions.

Since the rainy season had just ended and certain roads and bridges were destroyed, access to certain regions was hampered. The selection of villages and respondents was therefore partly determined by their accessibility. Nevertheless, the fieldwork took place in distant villages in the interior of the country where inhabitants were unaccustomed to meeting white people. As a result, visits always started with extensive ice breaking before the actual interviews could begin.

Table 10.1   Interviews per category and per district, in absolute numbers and in per cent of the total per category in the respective districts

District	District Administrator		Chief of Administrative Post		Régulo		CDL	
Mogovolas	1	100%	2	50%	2	7%	3	21%
Angoche	1	100%	2	67%	3	6%	3	16%
Mogincual	1	100%	2	67%	3	6%	3	21%
Moma	1	100%	2	67%	3	8%	2	13%
Total	4	100%	8	61%	11	6%	11	17%

3. Results

The CDL and their Achievements

The CDL seem to have brought about positive changes in the attitude of the rural population. In the past, most farmers believed that remaining passive was their only option for resisting the obtrusiveness of the state authorities, and to maintain grip of their situation. Whenever they dared to take initiatives themselves, the authorities punished them severely. In the context of the MAMM program, the community workers have talked a lot with the people and with the *régulos*. After extensive explanation and persuasion, the villagers have abandoned their resistance and have begun to discuss the problems of their villages. People have come to understand that passivity does not resolve their problems and that they can do something to improve their situation. The *régulos'* support played an important role: it is practically impossible to start a CDL without the consent of the *régulo*.

Most CDL have succeeded in improving the living conditions of their communities. At the instigation of CDL, community members began working together to carry out many small projects, such as cleaning access roads to the village and laying trunks across the rivers when bridges fell down. They opened and maintain old wells, or let some youngsters take the daily care of the aged people. Men decided to clean a field in order to have a soccer playground. They set up a small savings system for purchasing the ball.[5]

In view of the distance to the hospital, villagers built their own maternity home, and they sent women to a special course to become midwives. Latrines have been built and garbage has been removed, burned or buried. Girls are encouraged to attend school and parents are discouraged from marrying off their daughters at a young age. Together, community members have taken measures against illegal fishing in

---

5   According to the principles of the MAMM program, local communities should be self-supporting and no money is provided by SNV to finance these items.

the lakes and against forest-fires. Villagers have saved money to buy bicycles to carry sick people to the hospital or for the use by midwives so that they can attend deliveries in a timely manner. The persons and groups interviewed unanimously agreed that CDL not only led to material improvements, but also to more involvement and greater solidarity in communities.

In the MAMM program, contacts between different CDL are encouraged and organized so that they can exchange experiences and remain motivated. CDL members expressed the opinion that they learned a lot from the MAMM program. Other research also shows that there are fewer tensions and conflicts in regions where CDL are active than in other regions (Grobbelaar and Lala 2002). A contributing factor is probably that CDL members are not politically active. The villagers share the experience that party membership leads to conflict, disintegration, and ultimately to war.

The Relations Between CDL and Local Authorities

While local state authorities have regular meetings with the *régulos*, their contacts with CDL are sporadic and irregular. In practice, *régulos* are the intermediaries between CDL and state authorities. They often undertake long journeys to the offices of the authorities to bring local problems to their attention. Meetings between local state authorities and CDL members are informal and no reports are written. This means that what has exactly happened or what has been agreed upon cannot be verified.

Some chiefs and administrators perceive CDL members as a threat to their position. They do not want their position in the ranks of their political party to be put in danger, and therefore they prefer to keep the people from local communities at a distance. Many of them came to work in Nampula province but are originally from the South of the country. They believe that this northern region needs severe and tight leadership in order to prevent uprisings and to maintain the unity of the country. Others favor participation, in principle, but doubt whether CDL have enough skills to deal with complicated matters, or they question their legitimacy. They refer to the absence of a legal basis for CDL, arguing that only the state has the power to make decisions.

There were two positive exceptions to these overall negative attitudes toward CDL, namely one district administrator and one chief of an administrative post. Both have regular and formal contacts with the CDL in their area. The district administrator tries to involve the community in policy making in several ways. He visits the villages on a regular basis and has many informal contacts with the villagers. He walks around and invites the people to get in contact with him and to talk about their problems. He knows all CDL members in his district personally.

The chief of an administrative post who proved to be the exception to the rule decided to give the CDL more formal power and created a local consultative council to this end. In this council, some members of the CDL meet with him monthly. There is a formal agenda, and they discuss all the important matters of the region.

Agreements are made, and detailed meeting reports are available. In this way a commitment for decisions made is created.

Some communities were lucky and obtained money from the district administrator to build a school, which the villagers then built themselves. One of the district administrators pointed out that he was always willing to support villagers financially if they were doing their best, for example, by building a school. Although he meant it kindly, this statement shows that providing resources does not depend on formal rules, but on the administrator's good will and therefore, resource allocation is arbitrary. On the other hand, district administrators reported having only limited competencies and resources at their disposal. They basically carry out orders of the province governor. Likewise, the governor is not empowered to make important decisions because he is dependent on higher authorities. Regional and local authorities spend most of their time reporting to and asking permission from higher levels in the state hierarchy.

The Land Law and the Forest and Wildlife Law

The district administrators and the chiefs of the local administrative posts overall possessed of a good knowledge of the Land Law and the Forest and Wildlife Law, and of how these laws must be executed in practice. They derived their knowledge from meetings for government officials. All district administrators and chiefs of local administrative posts found the Land law and the Forest and Wildlife law very important because of the fact that they help to prevent and resolve conflicts. In the past, conflicts tended to occur when they issued licenses for pieces of land where no one seemed to live or work. The owner would show up too late, when the license had already been issued. Now they are obliged to consult the farmers first and they expect that these problems will no longer occur.

For the traditional authorities these laws, in principle, offer the opportunity to distinguish themselves as community leaders thanks to the fact that they play an important part in the process of consultation and information of the people. When the process turns out to have good results, it can strengthen their position. However, the investigation showed that the knowledge of the *régulos* fell short. From all people interviewed, the *régulos* were least aware of the contents of the laws.

The knowledge of CDL about these laws was generally limited. They had many confused ideas about these laws. However, some had been informed by the Rural Mutual Support Association, an NGO aimed at defending peasants' land rights and they were distinctly more familiar with their rights.

The majority of CDL were located in regions where no one had a license for the use of the land. Two CDL found themselves in an area where some communities jointly had applied for a license for the whole territory where they lived and worked. Because of the questions asked during the interview, CDL members sometimes realized that companies had confiscated pieces of land without consulting the community. Other CDL remembered that they had been asked something while they had not understood the reason why. In another case, a license had been given out to a firm while villagers had clearly refused its presence. Afterwards they found out that the chief of the administrative post had issued the license in spite of the community's refusal. The villagers supposed that the fact that they sympathize with Renamo was the reason why the chief gave the license without their consent. Another possible reason the villagers mentioned was corruption. Local administrators may have accepted money from the firm in exchange for the license. CDL members pointed out that these practices frequently occur.

The people in the villages do not have the slightest idea where to go to appeal to the authorities' decisions. Peoples Tribunals are only entitled to give judgment on conflicts between villagers and villages. There is a court in the city but that is far away and people do not know how the court functions.

The CDL and the *régulos* were happy with the new information from the interviews because *it opened their eyes* – as they told the researchers. They decided to look for more information themselves, showing that they understood that the subject was of great importance for them.

Decree 15/2000

All respondents believed that Decree 15/2000 was important because it ended a situation that no one desired anymore. The already recognized *régulos* declared themselves to be very proud of their new position. It was striking that all *régulos* pointed out that they considered the collection of taxes as their most important task. This is not surprising, as taxes prove to be an important topic for all concerned. Local state authorities had not succeeded in collecting taxes due to the resistance of the population, so they depend on the work of the *régulos*. For the communities, taxes imply a great pressure on their living standards due to the extreme poverty under which they live.

Asked about the difference between state and traditional authorities, almost every one responded that traditional authorities are the true representatives of the people. They are the entrance to the community for the state authorities. The *régulos* are considered neutral because in general they are not openly members of one of the two rival political parties. This allows them to bridge the party differences within their communities. However, since the (Frelimo) government now officially recognizes *régulos*, there is some confusion in regions with majority support for Renamo. In Angoche, in particular, some CDL members suggested that the *régulo* had now become a Frelimo member. This was not illogical in view of the tasks the *régulo* obtained since his recognition.

4. Analysis of Achievements and Limitations

The Idea of Participation

The notion of citizenship in general is connected with the feeling of being a member of a state (Belinfante and De Reede 1997). However, villagers in the MAMM districts perceive the state as an unfamiliar entity. The boundaries of Mozambique are the product of 'dinner table discussions' in Europe and not the organically grown result of decisions of its own people (Chabal 1992 and Chabal et al. 2002). The current ruling party, Frelimo, considers itself first and foremost as the guardian of the state, and in particular of the 'unity of the state' – since this unity is not self-evident. To some extent, citizen participation and the decentralization of the public administration have been sacrificed in name of the 'unity of the state'.

State authorities in the MAMM region usually come from other regions, and generally from the south. Many of them do not speak any of the local languages. In the perception of the local population, these authorities set rules that interfere with the people's lives, even though the villagers themselves never asked for these rules. For this reason, the villagers do not experience the state as a guarantor for the maintenance of law and order, but rather as a threat to their existing order. Interventions of state authorities may lead to the collapse of the rules made by their ancestors and respected through consecutive generations. Something like this happened in the years after independence when the villagers were forced to live in communes.

Against this background, a big achievement of the MAMM program is that it has brought an end to the apathy of the villagers towards improving their collective situation. It has also enhanced a sense of solidarity. The villagers are now collaborating to improve their living environment and they support each other. CDL are working in close cooperation with the traditional local leader, the *régulo*, and his local council. *Régulos*, in turn, seek help from formal state authorities for the resolution of problems that the villagers cannot deal with themselves.

The Limits to Participation

However, it is clear that the MAMM program can only bring improvements up to a certain point, and then it faces limitations. As shown above, when villagers want to build a school they need financial support from the local authorities, in particular from the district administrator. However, whether they receive such support is dependent on his discretion. There are no rules involved, nor is there any possibility to appeal his decision. The villagers are subject to the mercy of this particular administrator.

In addition, state authorities may also still damage the interests of the local population. This occurs when the authorities sell land or forest to third parties, or give licenses for the exploitation of the forest. According to the Land law and the Forest and Wildlife Law, state authorities must consult the population before making decisions on allocating land or issuing licenses. However, the population does not know the laws nor does it have legal assistance at its disposal. Therefore, villagers may still be presented with a *fait accompli*, forcing them to leave the land of their ancestors.

These findings point to fundamental weaknesses of the Mozambican political system. First, and as reminiscent of the socialist period, state and party are still largely one and the same. The President of the country is leader of Frelimo, and the national flag is Frelimo's flag. Party membership or at least loyalty with Frelimo is condition for recruitment in government positions from the lowest to the highest ranks, and from the capital Maputo to the most distant interior of the country. So far, the electoral system is characterized by 'the winner takes all', and policies in general do not take the views of the political minority into account. District administrators and the chiefs of administrative posts in the MAMM districts usually obtained their position by being active Frelimo members and their term of office is not restricted to a certain period. In practice, they combine political and administrative responsibilities. This means that there is no separation between legislative and executive power. As there are no local elections in the MAMM districts,[6] no independent legislative force is available to support the people in case of power abuse by these authorities.

An independent judiciary power is also absent. Formal Courts of Justice are only available in the larger cities, and they are weak in terms of skills and can hardly be called independent, since all judges are appointed by the President. In the countryside, traditional People's Tribunals are still operating. Although there are a few People's Tribunals in the MAMM region, they only deal with disputes between citizens, and are not allowed to deal with disputes between citizens and state officials. In fact, local authorities are therefore their own judges.

We can speak of a democratic constitutional state when the execution of power is bound by the law and not by the arbitrariness of a particular official. In addition, actions of authorities have to be predictable, made on the base of laws and susceptible to the interventions of a controlling body. When a district administrator in a MAMM district, in answer to a request from villagers to build or finance a school, makes a decision, that decision should be put on paper and should be justified by reasons. These reasons must be grounded in the law. Practice in the MAMM districts shows that this is usually not the case. One person makes decisions on the basis of his personal considerations, and they are transmitted by verbal message without providing any justification. The actions of the state authorities in the MAMM region are thus unpredictable and arbitrary. This means that the significance of the 'rule of law' is limited in Mozambique's countryside.

The only more or less representative 'body' in the communities in the MAMM region that could provide a check on the state authorities is the *régulo*. However, because of his insufficient knowledge of the laws, and the fact that there is no independent legislative power to support him, his power is limited. Moreover, after

---

6   The 33 cities where local elections are held only represent 20 per cent of the population, see above.

his formal recognition based on Decree 15/2000 and his new tax collection capacity, his interests may be harmed by being critical to the state authorities.

A separation of powers between different layers of the administration is also important. This fulfills the democratic demand of allocating government tasks across different state organs. It also means that central state agencies are less burdened with local issues, and that citizens can be more involved. In the MAMM region, there is a certain extent of deconcentration and delegation of power, but no real decentralization.[7] The state apparatus looks like a pyramid with the President of the Republic at the top. The local state authorities are only accountable to a higher layer in this apparatus. The President exercises all power and mandates his subordinates to exercise some of these competences under his responsibility. Indirectly the President decides on all local matters.

The fact that *régulo*s have been recognized as local representatives by Decree 15/2000 has probably enhanced the establishment of CDL and the material improvements they have brought about, as explained above. On the other hand, Decree 15/2000 has not led to an increased separation of powers. To the contrary, it has eroded an existing separation of powers by making the *régulo* part of the state apparatus. This threatens to affect his neutrality. He collects taxes for the local government, and in front of his house flies the flag of Mozambique – which is also the flag of Frelimo.

Policy Making as an Interactive Process

In established democratic countries, interactive policymaking is usually an initiative of local authorities. They involve citizens, non-governmental organizations and the private sector by means of, among other possibilities, community planning, citizen participation and co-production of public tasks. Interactive processes are supposed to reduce the distance between local administrations and the population, to improve the quality of public policies and to enhance their legitimacy (Edelenbos and Monnikhof 2001). Ultimately, this may strengthen the representative democracy. However, there may also be a tension between interactive policymaking, or forms of deliberative democracy, and the existing representative democracy. What is the role of elected bodies if several groups of citizens already participate directly in public decision-making?

Following up on Milbrath (1965), Pröpper and Steenbeek (1999) develop a *participation ladder*, showing that there are different styles of steering in interactive policymaking: a facilitating, a cooperative, a delegating, a participatory, a consulting and an open or closed authoritarian governing style. The first four of these are instrumental to interactive policy making, while the consulting and the authoritarian governing styles are not. On the other hand, they argue that a participatory governance style is the only one that corresponds with a representative democracy because the

---

7   Or devolution, in terms of the distinction of Rondinelli (1981) between deconcentration, delegation of some specific tasks and devolution.

role of the participants is restricted to join the conversation and not to decide. In their view, elected bodies should have final decision-making power.

In contrast to most northern experiences, the CDL in the MAMM districts originate from outside (donor) initiatives, and not from decisions of local state authorities. In particular, they are the consequence of a decentralization experiment of the Mozambican government aimed at promoting consultations of local communities. This means that it is likely that not all parties at the beginning of the initiative accept participation of the population. We observed that the local authorities in the MAMM districts often withdraw from this interactive role, communicating as little as possible with the local communities.

Looking at the governance styles in which the local authorities manifest themselves in the MAMM region, and in particular, in relation to the Land Law and the Forest and Wildlife Law, we concluded that they do not involve the population in decision-making. The governance style of these authorities can be seen as consulting at best, but more often, it is open or closed authoritarian, depending on the situation. In their views, the population has to be persuaded to co-operate in the aims of the state.

One district administrator and one chief of an administrative post were the exceptions in displaying a participatory government style. They created the opportunity for CDL to define their own problems and to propose solutions for them. These two authorities invited CDL for advice and they allowed them opportunities for a real contribution. The existence of this intensive cooperation between CDL and these two local authorities with a participatory governance style came as a surprise. Further research should be undertaken in order to find out the factors conducive to this participatory style, as well as its results.

5. Conclusions

We cannot expect participation in political programs if people experience the state as a threat. At the beginning of the MAMM program, it was difficult for community members to accept the idea of participation. Nevertheless, the MAMM program succeeded in bringing villagers together to discuss their collective problems and to seek solutions for them. This is a major achievement in the context of Mozambique.

Still, community members are confronted with state authorities that, for their own sake, or on order of the President, interfere with all aspects of their life and are able to manipulate, mislead and seriously harm them. Local state authorities are only accountable to a higher hierarchical layer in the state apparatus. Because they report themselves, it is clear that they can interpret everything in their own interest. The population is at the mercy of the goodwill of these officers. Decisions of these authorities are not made in public, so they cannot be checked. The actions of the state authorities in the MAMM region are unpredictable, arbitrary and legally ungrounded. Communities do not have access to resources or expertise for legal assistance.

The research in the four districts of the MAMM program shows the limits of participation in this 'façade democracy'. The lack of separation of powers at the local level in Mozambique and the lack of accountability structures severely limits the chances of success of the MAMM program. It not only reduces the possibilities for effective participation and citizenship, but also for improving the material well being of the rural population.

The results of this study also shed new light on the issue of a possible tension between deliberative democracy and representative democracy as it is often posed in the context of established democracies. In fact, our study suggests that the existence of a legitimately elected and representative legislative body is a *necessary condition* for the success of interactive policymaking, rather than a complication or a redundancy. The presence of a representative democracy enforces accountability in the delivery of public services and offers bottom-up initiatives a fair chance, instead of being at the mercy of local party-'dictators'.

When designing their participatory development programs, donors appear to be assuming either that these conditions are not necessary, or that they are automatically in place once a country has regular 'elections'. Instead, this chapter suggests that donors should study the actual political and governance structures more carefully when setting up participatory projects.

Finally, one can ask the question whether, in the Mozambican context, participation may play a role in *bringing about* a representative democracy. The MAMM program may help creating the conditions for local elections. This would imply encouraging CDL members to test the boundaries of their participation and to defend their rights vis-à-vis the state authorities. The extent of participation and power of current CDL will then depend on the response of local state authorities. Because actual government styles are mainly authoritarian and at best consulting, there is still a long way to go. The attitude of traditional authorities is also important. With an ongoing democratization process, they must be prepared to gradually loosen their authority. In addition, effective local democracy requires real devolution of power and resources from the central government to local bodies.

References

Alden, C. (2001), *Mozambique and the Construction of the New African State* (New York: Palgrave).

Andrade, G.M. and Quinamine, F. (2002), *O Impacto do Decreto 15/2000 e a sustenabilidade juridica das CDL's no projecto MAMM–SNV* (Nampula: SNV).

Belinfante, A.D. and De Reede, J.L. (1997), *Beginselen van het Nederlands Staatsrecht* 13th Edition (Alphen aan den Rijn: H.D. Samsom and Tjeenk Willink).

Bossema, W. (1995), *Mozambique* (Amsterdam and The Hague: KIT/NOVIB/NCOS).

Brohman, J. (1996), Popular Development: Rethinking the Theory and Practice of Development (Cambridge Ma: Blackwell).

Chabal, P. (1992), *Power in Africa: An Essay in Political Interpretation,* 2nd Edition. (New York: St. Martin's Press).

Chabal, P. and Daloz, J.P. (1999), *Africa Works: Disorder as Political Instrument,* 1st Edition. (Oxford and Indiana: The International Africa Institute in association with James Currey and the Indiana University Press).

Chabal, P., Birmingham, D., Forrest, J., Newitt, M., Seibert, G. and Silva Andrade, E. (2002), *A History of Lusophone Africa* (London: Hurst and Company).

Chambule, A. (2000), Organização Administrativa de Mozambique, Maputo, Mimeo.

Edelenbos, J. and Monnikhof, R. (eds) (2001), *Lokale interactieve beleidsvorming* (Utrecht: Lemma).

Finer, S. (1970), *Comparative Government.* (Kingdon: Allen Lane, The Penguin Press).

Government of Mozambique (1997), *Constitução de Mozambique* (Maputo: AWEPA).

Grobbelaar, N. and Lala, A. (2002), *Conflict Assessment Report Mozambique,* Managing group grievances and internal conflict project (The Hague: Clingendael, Conflict Research Unit).

Hague, R., Harrop, M. and Breslin, S. (1998), *Comparative Government and Politics: An Introduction* 4th Edition. (London: Macmillan).

Harrison, G. (2000), *The politics of Democratisation in Rural Mozambique: Grassroots Governance in Macufi* (UK: The Edwin Mellen Press).

Lederman, D., Loayza, N. and Soares, R. (2001), *Accountability and Corruption: Political Institutions Matter* Policy Research Working Paper 2708 (Washington: The World Bank, Latin American and Caribbean Region).

Milbrath, L.W. (1965), *Political Participation: How and Why Do People Get Involved in Politics?* (Skokie, Il: Rand McNally).

Molenaers, N. and Renard, R. (2002), *Strengthening Civil Society From the Outside? Donor-Driven Consultation and Participation Processes in PRSP: the Bolivian Case* IDPM–UA Discussion Paper 2002–5 (Antwerp: Institute of Development Policy and Management, University of Antwerp).

Morgan, L. M. (1990), 'International politics and primary health care in Costa Rica', *Social Science and Medicine* 30:2, 211–19.

Pröpper, I., and Steenbeek, D. (1999), *De aanpak van interactief beleid: elke situatie is anders* (Bussum: Uitgeverij Coutinho).

Rondinelli, D. (1981), 'Government decentralization in comparative perspective: Theory and practice in developing countries', International Review of Administrative Sciences 2, 133–45.

Sand, K. van de (1994), 'Human rights as a precondition for development', *Development* 2, 27–8.

SNV–Moçambique (2003), *Plano Annual* (Programa MAMM, Unidade de Desenvolvimento Comunitário).

Stiglitz, J. E. (2002), 'Participation and development: Perspectives from the comprehensive development paradigm', *Review of Development Economics*, 6:2, 163–82.

Tendler, J. (2000), 'Why are social funds so popular?', in S. Yusuf, W. Wu and S. Evenett (eds), *Local Dynamics in the Era of Globalization* (Oxford: Oxford University Press for the World Bank), pp. 114–29.

UNDP (2002), *Human Development Report 2002* (New York: UNDP).

Vainio-Mattila, A. (2000), 'The seduction and significance of participation for development interventions', *Canadian Journal of Development Studies* 21, 431–46.

PART IV
MULTI-LEVEL GOVERNANCE

Chapter 11

Democratic Legitimacy of Inter-Municipal and Regional Governance

José Manuel Ruano de la Fuente and Linze Schaap

Throughout Europe, local authorities are facing problems of scale. Municipalities have a variety of tasks, including service delivery and local policymaking. Furthermore, they represent the local society at other levels of government. The physical scale of local authorities is inadequate for many of these tasks; some are too small, and others are too large. Although this is a problem of all time, the downward vertical shift of governance (as discussed in Chapter 2 of this volume) is increasing the scale problem in sub-national tiers of government.

European countries apply a range of strategies for solving problems of scale. This chapter focuses on those strategies in which scale enlargement is the main element. In other words, it addresses strategies in which regional governance serves as a solution to the problem of limited local governmental scale. Some countries have decided to create new layers of government at the regional level, and others have improved inter-municipal cooperation. Responsibilities may be vested exclusively within a regional tier of government, or they may be shared by a number of cooperating authorities.

Little is known, however, about the practice of regional governance (either by a regional tier of government or through inter-municipal cooperation) in different systems. Although a worthy goal in and of itself, filling a gap in empirical knowledge is not the sole aim of this chapter; knowledge is lacking at the theoretical level as well. Many academic scholars have published works that propose governance, network management, and other models as alternatives to 'governmental' models (Rhodes 1997; Kickert, Klijn and Koppenjan 1997; John 2001). Others have published volumes on urban or metropolitan governance (Heinelt and Kübler 2005). Many of these books are of an international comparative character; more precisely, they involve country-by-country comparisons. Although they provide relevant information and insight into developments in individual countries, they are less useful for analyzing the effects of specific policies, such as the creation of regional tiers of government. Comparative evaluations from a thematic point of view may fill that gap. This is the topic of this chapter, which provides a comparison of various kinds of regional governance arrangements in a number of western European countries on legitimacy. The evaluation criteria were derived from the theoretical chapters of this volume (Chapter 3).

In this chapter, we aim to answer the following questions:

- In what way does the creation of a regional tier of government affect the democratic legitimacy of local and regional governance?
- In what way does inter-municipal cooperation affect the democratic legitimacy of local and regional governance?

To answer these central questions, we present an exploratory comparison of four cases of regional governance. The exploration started with the selection of two cases of regional tiers in government (Copenhagen and London) and two cases of inter-municipal cooperation (Hanover and Madrid). In the course of this exploratory study, however, it became obvious that these cases were not as 'pure' as we had expected. With the possible exception of Madrid, all cases contain elements of both regional government and inter-municipal cooperation. Most of the regional governance that is considered in this exploratory study involves regional policymaking, whereas the inter-municipal cooperation in the Madrid area primarily involves service-delivery.

In the next section, we discuss the concept of regional governance. A distinction between two strategies of regional governance will be introduced, 'consolidation' and 'new regionalism.' In Section 2, we link these two approaches to the issue of democratic legitimacy and develop a number of tentative lines of reasoning. In Section 3, we outline the selection of the four cases. Sections 4 and 5 contain descriptions and analyses of the cases with regard to various aspects of legitimacy. In Section 6, we present several tentative conclusions.

1. Regional Governance

As mentioned in the introduction, the concept of regional governance has multiple meanings. The literature contains a variety of modes and strategies for governance at the regional level (cf. Heinelt and Kübler 2005). In this chapter, we discuss two models: 'consolidation' and 'new regionalism.' The consolidation model is equivalent to what we understand as 'regional government.' New regionalism resembles inter-municipal cooperation.

The consolidation strategy specifies that regional policymaking must be accomplished by a single regional governmental body; institutional boundaries are considered obstacles for effective policymaking. Within this strategy, the creation of a new tier of regional government or the strengthening of an existing one is the answer to problems of scale. Regional governments are expected to function as the authority at the regional level by developing and executing regional policies. For these purposes, regional governments must have exclusive capacities and sufficient financial means.

This strategy can easily be linked to a general approach to the study of public administration, the 'government approach' (John 2001, 17; Schaap 2005). This approach considers public administration as a single entity, as if it were governed according to the principles of Weberian bureaucracy. Problems in the functioning of systems of sub-national government are primarily due to overlapping authorities, unclear distinctions of responsibilities, excessive centralization, and a lack of autonomy for local governments. This strategy therefore emphasizes the necessity of clear distinctions between the various levels of government, in a hierarchical and consolidated structure, combined with direct central-governmental control. These distinctions are preferably constitutional, or at least legally based. In addition, a clear division of tasks between governmental levels is considered essential; capacities and authorities should be as exclusive as possible, the division fixed, networks closed, and policies routinized. Inter-municipal cooperation is rejected as a solution, as such cooperation is assumed to obscure the separate responsibilities of each autonomous municipality. If the geographic scale of a local authority is too small relative to the scale of the societal problems at stake, amalgamation – or even the creation of a new layer of government – is preferable.

The new-regionalism strategy supports the idea that cooperation between authorities and other actors will stabilize policymaking, thus ensuring effective policy. Existing bodies of local or functional governments continue to exist, although the way they function may be subject to discussion and change. Safeguarding cooperation and preventing free-rider behavior are important issues in this strategy. Whereas consolidation is based on the government approach, new regionalism has strong theoretical ties to the 'governance' approach[1] (John 2001, 17; Schaap 2005) and to policy-network management (Kickert, Klijn and Koppenjan 1997; Rhodes 1997) and similar concepts.[2] These approaches also focus on cooperation between governmental actors and between governmental and non-governmental actors. This approach is derived from insights gathered from policy-network studies (Kickert, Klijn and Koppenjan 1997) and governance studies (Rhodes 1997).

In addition to network governance, multi-level governance is another mode of governance that can be found in this strategy. In the consolidation model, regional governments are expected to function as *the* authority at the regional level, having exclusive capacities. In contrast, new regionalism endorses the 'pooling of problem-solving capacity' among governments at different levels (Chapter 2 of this volume). When this approach is applied, the focus shifts from creating new layers of government to making things work. It emphasizes the relevance of checks and balances as necessary

---

1   We use the term 'governance' in two ways. First, it is a generic term that refers to the act of governing. The second use of the term is specific, with governance referring to a specific kind of governing.

2   According to John (2001: p.17), however, there may be a number of differences between the two approaches. Whereas many network approaches focus on intergovernmental relations, governance approaches deal primarily with flexible relations between governmental and non-governmental actors.

features of a pluralistic society (normative statement). The strategy assumes that decisions are made within a context of interdependencies in extensive networks (empirical observation). Many actors, governmental and non-governmental, are involved. Although governmental responsibilities may be specific, government agencies do not escape interdependencies; they often require the cooperation of non-governmental actors. In other words, governmental actors are not in control simply by virtue of the fact that they are governments. Policy processes are characterized by trial and error; experimentation is common. Structures are decentralized and fragmented; they are intended to ensure flexibility and innovation in governmental performance, and control is decentralized.

The governance approach recognizes that problems are centered on the difficulty that municipalities experience in cooperating with each other, the possible inflexibility of the present division of tasks, and the existence of veto power for some actors, as well as the existence of somewhat closed frames of reference (Schaap and Van Twist 1997). The solution is to facilitate cooperation by creating overlapping authorities and making the system more efficient. According to this approach, structures that appear efficient at face value are often pennywise and pound-foolish. Inter-municipal cooperation is considered essential for all governmental entities, as it may prevent the concentration of power. Autonomy is both impossible and unwise.

2. Regional Governance and Democratic Legitimacy

The two approaches to regional governance that are discussed in the preceding section, consolidation and new regionalism, can be linked to concepts of both democracy and legitimacy.

The type of democracy that is associated with the government approach and consolidation is representation. The assumption of the paradigm of representative democracy is that government by the people itself (as was the case in the ancient Greek city-states) is impossible. Citizens are too numerous; they are considered unwilling to act as self-governors, and large-scale participation is assumed to have negative effects on the stability of governmental systems (Luhmann 1981; Almond and Verba 1963; Daemen 1983). From this perspective, representation is the most suitable means of citizen participation. Policies aimed at enhancing such participation are therefore targeted at strengthening representation in order to perfect the representative system. This strategy aims to improve the effectiveness of government and the functioning of democracy within the existing system of representative democracy, in which citizens appear mainly as subjects, voters, and clients (Tops and Depla 1993).

The type of democracy that is linked to governance and new regionalism is not only representative; it is experimental and participatory as well, and it proceeds from a different angle. In addition to acting as clients or voters, citizens participate in 'the processes of formulation, passage and implementation of public policies' (Lowndes 1995), both as individuals and in organizational contexts. Within this concept, improving citizen participation refers to enhancing the participatory dimension of democracy. Its main characteristic is a fundamental change in the role of the citizen. In this strategy, citizens are addressed as creative contributors to the policy-making process. They are assumed to act as 'co-producers of policy.' The entire configuration of policymakers and their roles must therefore be reconsidered; the government is no longer the key actor in the policy-making process; instead, it is the facilitator of self-governing, self-steering citizens and associations of citizens. Social capital, self-steering and self-government, decentralization of responsibilities, interdependencies between societal actors, and civil society are key concepts in this participatory strategy. In The Netherlands, several strategies have been conceived and several experiments with 'interactive policymaking' have been conducted (Edelenbos and Monnikhof 2001).

Despite the theoretical linkage between new regionalism and participatory democracy, several problems might be expected to occur in terms of democratic legitimacy. First, with regard to new regionalism as multi-level governance, problems of input and throughput legitimacy are likely. Multi-level arrangements are based on the notion of 'borrowing' legitimacy from municipalities; one could speak of indirect representation and participation of interests. Second, it remains to be seen whether the participative arrangements in network governance are limited to organizations in their role as stakeholders, or whether they also provide opportunities for the participation of (individual) citizens and 'weak interests.' Any empirical exploration of concrete regional arrangements that focuses on input and throughput legitimacy must highlight these issues.

3. About the Exploration

The remainder of this chapter contains an analysis of the input and throughput legitimacy of two cases of consolidated regional governments and two cases of inter-municipal cooperation (new regionalism). All four cases are described according to the following questions:

1. What does the case involve, and what type of governance arrangement does it illustrate? (Is it an inter-municipal structure, or is it a regional level of government?) What is the basic issue? Which actors cooperate and in what sense? Which actors are otherwise involved and in what roles? Which actors make the final decisions?
2. What is the extent of input legitimacy, with regard to:
   a. opportunities for participation;
   b. quality of representation;
   c. openness of agenda?
3. What is the extent of throughput legitimacy with regard to:
   a. manner of decision-making;
   b. quality of participation;
   c. checks and balances?

The discussion begins with an analysis of the following two cases of consolidated regional government:

- England: spatial planning in Greater London. The Greater London Authority bears responsibility for several regional policy fields, which related primarily to spatial development, transport, planning, and the environment.
- Denmark: spatial planning in the Greater Copenhagen region. The Greater Copenhagen Authority is responsible for regional spatial planning and transport in this region.

The chapter continues with a discussion of the following two cases of inter-municipal cooperation:

- Spain, Madrid. Several small cities in the region of Madrid collaborate in order to design and implement social policies by creating municipal associations.
- Germany, Hanover. The neighbor cities of Hanover have implemented a policy of cooperation that has generated in-depth changes in the organizational and functional structure of regional and local governments within a section of the Land of Lower Saxony.

As noted in the introduction, these cases were not as 'pure' as we had initially expected. In particular, the regional arrangements in Copenhagen constitute a regional tier of government (with its own jurisdiction) that is nonetheless organized as an intergovernmental authority. Although the Madrid case of cooperating municipalities is possibly the most pure case, we must note that a regional tier of government (the Autonomous Community Madrid) does exist in the Madrid area.

Differences in state traditions were taken into account in the selection of cases. Loughlin and Peters (1997) suggest that four state traditions (Anglo-Saxon, Germanic, French/Napoleonic, and Scandinavian) can be distinguished in Europe. Norton (1997) describes the following three European state traditions (in addition to a North American and a Japanese tradition): South European, North European, and the British tradition. Individual countries belong primarily to one tradition, but may share features with others. Among other characteristics, different state traditions are associated with different kinds of decentralization and sub-national governments. For this study, we selected a Scandinavian case (Copenhagen), an Anglo-Saxon case (Greater-London), a Germanic case (Hanover), and a Southern-European case (Madrid region).

Data were collected using several methods. First, we analyzed written sources. Second, we conducted interviews with civil servants in the authorities involved, civil servants in the national government, members of representative and executive bodies, and societal actors (for example, regional business and civil society leaders). The exact selection of respondents obviously depended on the specific characteristics and operations of the various arrangements.

4. Practices of Consolidated Regional Government

This section presents a description and analysis of the two cases of regional policies made by a consolidated structure (by a type of regional government).

England: Spatial Planning in Greater London

The first case involves Greater London. The Greater London Authority was established in 2000 (for example, see Pimlott and Rao 2002; Goldsmith 2005). This metropolitan authority consists of a directly elected Mayor and an Assembly that is elected by proportional voting. The mayor prepares and executes policies, whereas the Assembly's main function is scrutiny. Within the London area, the boroughs kept their jurisdictions as well. The primary policy fields relate to spatial development, transport, planning, and the environment.

In the Greater London region, the Mayor of London determines the 'Strategic Development Strategy' (SDS). The Mayor must consult with the national government through the Secretary of State (Secretary of State for the Environment, Transport and the Regions 2000). The Secretary of State may prevent the publication of the SDS in order to avoid 'any inconsistency with current national policies or relevant regional planning guidance' or 'any detriment to the interests of an area outside Greater London' (Secretary of State for the Environment, Transport and the Regions 2000).

The Mayor has supervisory powers and may demand changes in local plans. These powers, however, extend even further: 'The boroughs are required to consult the Mayor on planning applications of 'potential strategic importance'. He is able to command on and support these applications or, if he considers it necessary on strategic planning grounds, direct the borough to refuse planning permission' (GLA 2002). The boroughs are currently bound to formulate spatial policies within a 'Local Development Framework' (LDF). Substantial community involvement is one of the aims of these frameworks.

With regard to the implementation of spatial policies, cooperation appears to be the keyword. The Mayor is not the executing body, but must first collaborate with the local authorities in the London area (public–public cooperation). Public–private partnerships have received considerable attention in the London plans. The plans expect the private sector to play a major role, largely because of their financial resources (Thornley 2003).

Input legitimacy   The input legitimacy of the government of London is apparently safeguarded rather well. The quality of representation is particularly visible. At the regional or metropolitan level, the Greater London Authority consists of a directly elected Assembly and a directly elected Mayor. The GLA has considerable statutory powers regarding spatial planning. The Mayor is responsible for developing and deciding on a Spatial Development Strategy, and the Assembly scrutinizes the activities of the Mayor. Directly elected councils exist at the local borough level as well. In some cases, these councils are accompanied by directly elected mayors.

When the other criteria of input legitimacy are taken into consideration, however, the positive score seems to diminish. Opportunities for participation do exist. Everyone is entitled to make proposals for the Spatial Development Strategy, albeit within frames, which are set by politicians, thus restricting the openness of the agenda. Consultation procedures and cooperation with public and private actors are additional expressions of opportunities for participation. It is important to note, however, that the present kind of cooperation is less the result of statutory requirements than it is of decisions and demands made by the present Mayor of London. Opportunities for participation do exist; in practice, however, they seem to lead to a lack of openness. The Mayor is rather selective in inviting actors to participate.

Throughput legitimacy   Remarkably, the actual planning process strongly resembles a pure governance arrangement. Although governmental actors, particularly the Mayor of Greater London, play the leading roles, other actors are important as well. Boroughs have their say, direct citizen participation is encouraged, and cooperation with private actors and civil society is created. All of these activities take place relatively early in the planning process. Reaching consensus and agreements seem to be among the primary goals of this process. It can be assumed that such planning processes are characterized by checks and balances. On the other hand, such situations are somewhat vulnerable, as they tend to be the result of mayoral decisions rather than statutory provisions.

The quality of the participation in such situations is questionable. As previously observed, the planning process lacks openness. Citizen involvement in the priority-setting process is rather limited (Thornley 2003). In 2002, the Planning Advisory Committee of the Greater London Assembly published a report entitled 'Behind Closed Doors' (GLA 2002). This report severely criticized the planning practices of the Mayor of London, placing particular emphasis on the habit of acting behind closed doors. It states that there is a lack of information for the London citizenry. If that is the case, actual participation may not be as straightforward as expected.

The London case also barely meets the third criterion of throughput legitimacy: checks and balances. The previously mentioned report, 'Behind Closed Doors' (GLA 2002), states that the Mayor apparently disregarded feedback from the boroughs. Despite its statutory duty to scrutinize the Mayor's policies, the Assembly similarly lacks information and influence. If this is the case, checks and balances can hardly exist. On the other hand, because the central government is influential in this situation, there are checks and balances in the central–regional relations.

Denmark: Spatial Planning in the Greater Copenhagen Region

The second case is Denmark, in particular, spatial planning in the metropolitan area of the capital city of Copenhagen.

Spatial planning in Denmark is highly decentralized. The planning system is based on the 'principle of framework control' (Enemark 2002, 2). This principle specifies that sub-national authorities are free to make their own spatial policies, as long as these policies are not contrary to national plans. National spatial plans provide frameworks and advisory guidelines to regional and local authorities. The national government, however, has a binding instrument as well. It can issue 'national planning directives' that are legally binding for sub-national authorities. The regional authorities, in their turn, make regional plans every four years, and they are legally binding for local spatial plans. One important function of regional plans is to conduct Environmental Impact Assessments of large spatial projects. Finally, authorities make two kinds of plans. First, they formulate municipal plans (*kommuneplaner*) for the entire municipality every four years. These plans contain policies, maps, and land-use regulations. These guidelines are elaborated and specified at the neighborhood level in local plans (*lokalplaner*), which are legally binding for landowners (Enemark 2002, 2–3; European Union 1997).

This spatial-planning structure is completely coupled to the structure of sub-national government and intergovernmental relations. Whether physical boundaries are the same as administrative boundaries is debatable, as is the question of whether spatial developments occur within administrative boundaries. It is likely that they do not, particularly in such metropolitan areas as Copenhagen. With regard to economic development (e.g., labor market, transport, housing), administrative boundaries tend to become obsolete. Whether this will be solved by the installation of new counties is difficult to predict.

This issue has been recognized in the Copenhagen region. The Greater Copenhagen Authority (GCA) was created in 2000 for this reason. The GCA consists of three counties (regional governments): Copenhagen, Frederiksborg, and Roskilde. Their formal tasks and capacities regarding spatial planning and transport have been transferred to the Greater Copenhagen Authority. The GCA consists of a council and a board. The members of the county and municipal councils in the Greater Copenhagen area elect the members of the GCA Council from among their own members. The GCA Council, in turn, elects the board according to a proportional system. The primary tasks of the GCA are to coordinate regional spatial policies, to coordinate and develop policies for industry and tourism, and to coordinate and manage regional public transport.

The GCA is characterized as a 'weak metropolitan authority' (Anderson 2002, 44–51). A number of factors are apparently at stake. In Denmark, local authorities are strong, while counties tend to be weak. The GCA has taken over regional rather than local tasks. The statutory powers of the GCA are therefore no match for local authorities. Second, both councilors and board members have double duties, as they fulfill tasks in both the GCA and the municipalities or counties at the same time. This situation is likely to generate split loyalties. Because the constituencies are at the municipal and county level, fierce decision-making contrary to local and county interest is unlikely. This issue obviously calls for further study.

Two competing preferences exist in spatial policymaking in the Copenhagen area (Anderson and Hovaard 2003, 6). On the one hand, there is a need for economic growth and for an integral authority that is able to attract private enterprise and reach agreements with economic actors. This policy-making preference is typical of a city or metropolitan area that must compete with other 'global cities' by being entrepreneurial. This concept requires cooperation between the governmental and private sectors, particularly private companies. In the Copenhagen area, this has been tested in the 'Oerestad project,' for which Urban Development Plans have been made. Features of that project included public–private partnerships, the involvement of quangos and, participation by private business. A special 'Vision Group,' which is 'a group of high-level politicians and bureaucrats' (Desfor and Jørgensen 2004, 487) played a role. This group functioned outside the usual planning processes and had an alleged lack of concern for democratic practice (ib., 492)

On the other hand, bottom-up policymaking and the participation of citizens and civil society are strongly advocated. This preference is derived from such concepts as participatory democracy, bottom-up policymaking, and decentralization. The central issue here is '(t)he (re-)instatement of participatory planning and policy instruments, which stimulate local participation/community empowerment and foster the transparency of good practice and learning' (Andersen 2001, 143). As stated previously, participation is a feature of local planning processes.

Input legitimacy   With regard to the first type of legitimacy (the extent of input legitimacy in the GCA), the answers are rather negative. Few opportunities for participation exist at the regional level. The primary focus of spatial planning in Denmark is at the local level. Citizens are consulted in local, but not regional, spatial-planning procedures. At best, input legitimacy is of a 'borrowed' kind, with local representatives playing a role at the regional level.

Throughput legitimacy   The picture changes little in light of information on throughput legitimacy. Decision-making is apparently closed, and citizens are not consulted; indirectly elected councilors and the even more indirectly elected members of the board make the decisions. The quality of participation is non-existent, as citizen participation regarding local spatial plans is possible only at the local level. Consultation is apparently somewhat reactive, as people can express their wishes once a draft plan has been made public. The third criterion in the analysis of throughput legitimacy, the existence of checks and balances, is difficult to assess. The national government does have considerable say, thus rendering a 'going-alone' strategy unlikely for the GCA. At the same time, the position of local authorities in spatial planning remains strong.

5. Practices of Inter-Municipal Cooperation

Spain: Municipal Associations in Madrid

An initial analysis of the Spanish territorial structure reveals the weakness of local authorities. Most are too small in terms of spatial size and population to deliver the main public services of the welfare state efficiently. Most (60.4 per cent) Spanish municipalities have fewer than 1,000 inhabitants, and 85.8 per cent have fewer than 5,000. This structural condition has resulted in the concentration of the capacity for delivering public services within the regions (*comunidades autónomas*), through a long process of devolution of decentralization from the State. Nevertheless, municipalities have retained the power to intervene in any matter that is considered of interest to the local community. In this sense, it is customary for medium and small authorities to collaborate with other authorities to deliver compulsory services or participate complementarily in services for which they are not formally in charge (for example education, health care, economic development). The associations of municipalities (*mancomunidades de municipios*) are voluntarily created to manage services that local authorities could not efficiently manage on their own. The inter-municipal association 'the ILEX' is an example of this type of community. The ILEX consists of four municipalities that are located in the west of the Madrid region; these municipalities have a combined population of nearly 36,000.

The fundamental norm that regulates this association, the Statute, was published on December 28, 2000. This statute specifies the association's name, territory, objectives, and way of functioning, as well as economic and budgetary conditions, and the governmental and representative organs that are intended to represent all of the associated municipalities. The ILEX was created to allow the joint delivery of social services. The statute, which was passed by the councils of the associated entities, establishes the following governmental organs: the board (*junta*), which consists of the councilors in charge of social services in every municipality, and the president and vice-president, who are elected by the members of the board. These organs receive legal support from the municipal secretary.

The general aims of the association are to be responsive to residents' collective and individual social problems, to develop comprehensive programs of prevention and intervention, and to have information concerning the needs and social resources of the municipalities in this domain. The inter-municipal association must therefore strive to complement and perfect the social assistance that is provided by the regional Government (which is formally in charge of social services in general), and which is focused particularly on immigrants and the elderly, according to the social composition and the specific circumstances of each municipality. The annual community reports provide a precise description of the policies that are derived from these general objectives: programs for under-age youth (for example, nutrition, truancy, and risky behavior), immigrants with special needs, and the elderly (domestic help, maintenance of the quality of living accommodations).

The center of social services is located in the largest town (Villanueva de la Canada), although the services are delivered in all of the municipalities by personnel consisting primarily of social workers and clerical staff. The contribution of municipalities to the budget is proportional to the number of inhabitants. It is important to note that this formula of inter-municipal cooperation creates a small organization based on the political representation of the associated municipalities.

This organization strives to decrease the costs of service delivery while increasing their social impact.

The regional government fosters such associative models, and it contributes 85 per cent of the budget. We must note that the creation of such an association requires a previous political decision concerning the joint delivery of services for which local authorities are not always in charge. This fact illustrates the increased sensitivity of local politicians to the problems of the citizens due to their physical proximity.

The type of collaboration that is undertaken depends on a number of structural elements. The character of the cooperation is based on the number of inhabitants. Although the smaller municipalities lack the capacity to manage some services autonomously, they do have the capacity (in terms of human and material resources) to be connected. Cooperation offers the opportunity to participate in collaborative projects. Physical proximity between settlements to deliver territory-based services and the existence of similar problems and realities are factors that facilitate cooperation. Although the establishment of collaboration demands prior political will, personal contacts between politicians or civil servants are of equal importance. These contacts create informal relations that can give rise to additional, more formal, forms of cooperation.

On the other hand, a number of factors pose obstacles to cooperation. Such factors include bargaining about the location of the infrastructure and cost sharing, the different functional and political divisions in each municipality, and the lack of coincidence of the territorial networks belonging to the various governments (areas of the state and the region), which require populations of different sizes if they are to manage public policies and programs efficiently.

Finally, we should note that one indirect and positive effect of the inter-municipal collaboration is the establishment of new foundations for citizen participation, especially among the focused social sectors (e.g., youth, the elderly, and immigrants).

Input legitimacy   The legitimacy of origin is indirect, as the members of the cooperative organs are directly elected within their municipalities. In other words, the members of the collegial body of the association represent the municipalities in which they were directly elected. Citizens thus do not elect their representatives in the inter-municipal council.

Opportunities for participation do exist, however, especially for focus groups. These groups provide additional openness for the agenda.

Throughput legitimacy   Although participation is not one of the stated objectives, inter-municipal cooperation in the domain of social services facilitates interaction between policy-makers and the focused sectors. The needs and demands that are expressed by some of these sectors (primarily immigrants and the elderly) are taken into account in the program-design phase because of this interaction. With regard to checks and balances, it is important to note that decisions that are made by the cooperative organs must be passed by the councils of each municipality. All of the decisions that are made in the inter-municipal council are also subject to the approval of each municipal council. The cooperative council therefore does not have the autonomy to make any kind of decision, as democratic legitimacy remains with each municipal council.

Germany: Inter-Municipal Cooperation in Lower Saxony

On June 5, 2001, a unique structure of inter-municipal cooperation was formally created in Lower Saxony. On November 1, an extensive collaboration went into effect around the city of Hanover to manage some supra-municipal matters. Competition between a large urban area (Hanover) and its neighboring towns (20 local authorities) was replaced by a cooperative organization charged with the management of common policies. Its territorial area comprises 3,000 square kilometers and nearly 1.2 million inhabitants in the city of Hanover (46 per cent) and its area of influence (54 per cent).

Roughly following the model of the former district of the state (*Land*), the new supra-municipal government was organized in a directly elected assembly, a committee, and a president of the executive, who was also directly elected. The cooperative area of Hanover became the largest territorial corporation (*Gebietskörperschaft*) in Germany, only distantly comparable to the cooperative structures of Saarbrücken, Frankfurt, and Stuttgart, considering the differences in the populations involved and the fact that these cases did not change the institutions of the state in the way Hanover did. Indeed, the creation of the Hanover area carried with it a partial and functional reform through the transference of powers from the district and the department of Hanover (*Bezirksregierung/Kreisebene*) and from the former municipal association. The result was the creation of a new inter-municipal cooperative structure that has the typical features of a district (*Landkreis*). In other words, this structure has an autonomous organization that assumes powers in economic development, employment, schools, housing, environment, refuse collection and water supply, and which is responsible for matters (e.g., suburban trains, regional planning) that had previously been managed by the municipal association (which ceased to exist) and the local authorities.

Although the strengthening process at the local level is an important feature of the reform, the role of the municipalities is conditioned by their size. Although the city of Hanover has a special status as a district city (*Kreisstadt*), social policy, youth, and similar matters belong to the responsibilities of only those settlements that have more than 30,000 inhabitants (9 out of 20). The principle of subsidiarity is thus compatible with this asymmetric system of task distribution, in which responsibilities are unequally distributed over layers of government.

The new governmental design faced a number of challenges. Examples include the existence of several political and cultural experiences, the common management of personnel belonging to various entities (1,800 workers initially, excluding hospitals and some enterprises), the necessity of developing skills in regional planning to design a new corporate identity, the tensions between the city of Hanover and the

Table 11.1   Legitimacy in four European regions

	ILEX, Madrid	Greater Copenhagen Authority	Hanover	Greater London Authority
Type of Regional Governance	Voluntary inter-municipal cooperation	Obligatory inter governmental cooperation	Inter-municipal cooperation, directly elected	Consolidated, directly elected regional government
Input Legitimacy: Opportunities for Participation	New foundations for participation, especially by focus groups	Barely exists at the regional level	Low, but representative democracy strengthened	These exist: consultation, cooperation
Input Legitimacy: Quality of Representation	Indirect representation	Indirect representation	Direct elections for council and president of executive board	Direct elections of both Assembly and Mayor
Input Legitimacy: Openness of Agenda	Partially open to focus groups	?	Closed. Different levels of agenda-setting	Frames are set by political actors
Throughput Legitimacy: Way of Decision-Making	Support by all municipal councils required, thus consensual	Closed and consensual	Vague distribution of responsibilities	Public-public cooperation; consensual
Throughput Legitimacy: Quality of Participation	Potentially high	Non-existent	Low	Little quality, due to closed nature of networks
Throughput Legitimacy: Checks and Balances	Necessity of consensus between municipalities may guarantee checks and balances, but may also lead to veto power.	Influence of central government	Guaranteed by unclear distribution of responsibilities?	If any, then through influence of the central government

rest of the associated municipalities; and the fusion of operative systems to manage common services.

Without any doubt, the creation of the cooperative area of Hanover has brought many advantages. It has improved the external representation of the whole region and built a service-delivery system based on an autonomous and single administration through a mechanism of charges and benefits sharing. It has improved the effectiveness policy management in several areas (e.g., territorial management and environmental protection), deepened democracy with the direct election of the representative and executive organs, and enhanced the transparency and accountability and budgetary processes.

The association of Hanover nonetheless raises a number of issues with regard to its operations and performance. The cooperative experience was the fruit of an engagement between somewhat divergent interests. The aspiration of the city of Hanover to incorporate the neighbor cities into the financing, charges linked to centrality dysfunctions, and the interest of these cities in gaining additional powers to preserve their self-governing status are examples of such divergent interests.

The expanded geographic space and number of citizens involved in the cooperative project could pose a threat to democratic accountability, which should be balanced through the direct election of the politicians in charge and through the strengthening of the local governments. Nevertheless, most of the new tasks were transferred to municipalities that have greater management capacity. At the same time, the supra-municipal government maintained responsibilities in other domains, thus impeding the transparency of global public action.

We must also note a certain contrast of situations from an internal and external perspective. Internally, the institutional weight of the city of Hanover in relation to the rest of the associated cities was made more acute by the disappearance of the former district of the state, which had played a balancing role between Hanover and its rural area of influence. Externally, the different status of the governments belonging to the cooperative structure and the rest of the municipalities in Lower Saxony will probably increase the demand for change at the municipal level.

Input legitimacy   Perhaps the most innovative element of the Hanover experience is the power of the citizens to elect the members of the representative board and the president of the executive directly, thus clearly enhancing democratic legitimacy. This space of collaboration serves as a substitute for the de-concentrated institutions of the state, and this is reinforced by the maintenance of traditional governmental structures in the municipal domain.

Throughput legitimacy   Considering the democratic legitimacy of the institutions in the policy-making process, it is evident that the management of supra-municipal services by a directly elected board is as positive as it is rare within the field of inter-municipal cooperation. Nonetheless, a number of other variables (for instance, the large size of the territory and the number of inhabitants) may not encourage citizen participation, and the system by which responsibilities are distributed can impede transparency and hinder political accountability in supra-municipal programs.

6. Analysis and Conclusions

Formal political and administrative structures are not always useful as arenas for public action. Other models of inter-institutional networks and new forms of cooperation between the public and private sectors may arise in their place. These organizational models involve ways of steering that are more open and flexible, and they are associated with different forms of relations and a common perception of interests by external parties. The success of these initiatives depends on the establishment of clear and distinctive tasks in relation to other governments, effective leadership, equitable distribution of advantages and charges, and – most importantly – capacity to achieve a sufficient degree of legitimacy.

After conducting the case studies, we must conclude that the cases are not as pure as we had expected them to be. The Greater London Authority is a genuine example of a regional government, and the ILEX (the inter-municipal cooperation of municipalities near Madrid) is exactly what it says. The other two cases, however, are not as easy to characterize. The Greater Copenhagen Council was established by law and has a number of statutory powers. Its structure, however, is one of cooperation. The Hanover case suggests yet another model. Although it is based on inter-municipal cooperation, the council and the president of the executive board are elected directly. We might therefore consider Copenhagen and Hanover hybrid types of regional government.

That having been said, we now provide an overview of the findings regarding democratic legitimacy (Table 11.1).

The exploratory character of the case studies allows us to draw only tentative conclusions. In general, it is obvious that there are no clear relations between the structure of regional governance and legitimacy. We therefore provide a brief discussion of the various aspects of legitimacy:

- Opportunities for participation (input legitimacy) seem to be best safeguarded in the two 'pure cases'. In London, the creation of the GLA was accompanied by increasing opportunities for participation. The same is true of Madrid with regard to inter-municipal cooperation. Copenhagen and Hanover have experienced less progress in this respect.
- On the other hand, the quality of representation (input legitimacy) is highest in London and Hanover. In both of these cities, citizens are entitled to elect representatives as well as the mayor. In Copenhagen and the ILEX near Madrid, representation is indirect, with local councilors electing representative organs at the regional level.
- It is hard to draw conclusions regarding the third element of input legitimacy, the openness of agendas. The insights provided by the case studies suggest

that the agendas are rather closed in these four cities. Only the ILEX near Madrid showed evidence of opportunities for focus groups to exercise some degree of influence on the agenda.

- In most cases, decision-making (throughput legitimacy) is consensual, although the actors who must find consensus differ. In London, public and private actors cooperate, while only governmental actors seek consensus in Copenhagen and the ILEX.
- With regard to the quality of participation (throughput legitimacy), the four cases present a disappointing picture. In Copenhagen, participation in policymaking is nearly non-existent, and in London and Hanover, its quality is rather low. Only in the ILEX is it potentially high, although we found no indication that such participation actually exists.
- Checks and balances (throughput legitimacy) do exist, sometimes due to the influence of central government (London and Copenhagen), and sometimes because of the cooperative nature of the regional governance structure (ILEX).

We now formulate a number of final hypotheses. First, the type of regional governance (a consolidated regional tier of government or inter-municipal cooperation) does not seem to be the only factor determining the legitimacy of regional governance; additional factors are at work. In London, the actions taken by the Mayor and the manner in which he deals with his obligations seem relevant. In Copenhagen, the statutory arrangements regarding citizen participation apparently play a role. In the inter-municipal cooperation in Madrid, legitimacy has been stimulated by the decision to work with focus groups. Finally, the Hanover case shows that the legitimacy of inter-municipal cooperation can be strengthened by the direct election of the regional council and the president of the board.

Second, regardless of the model of regional governance, input legitimacy seems to be better safeguarded than throughput legitimacy is (this may be the case for in government in general). Third, even when potential opportunities for participation exist, they apparently tend to generate participation by private companies, interest groups, and other institutionalized private actors.

References

Almond, G. and Verba, S. (1963), *The Civic Culture: Political Attitudes and Democracy in Five Nations*, (Princeton: Princeton University Press).

Andersen, J. (2001), 'The politics of gambling and ambivalence: struggles over urban policy in Copenhagen', *Geographische Zeitschrift* 89: 2-3, 134–143.

Andersen, H.T (2002) et al, 'The fall and rise of metropolitan government in Copenhagen', *GeoJournal* 58:2002, 43–52.

Andersen, J. and Hovgaard, G. (2003), *Welfare and urban planning in transition; a Copenhagen case study*, Research Paper 8 (Denmark: Roskilde University).

Daemen, H., (1983), *Burgerzin en politieke gematigdheid*, (Enschede: Technische Hogeschool Enschede).

Desfor, G. and Jørgensen, J. (2004), 'Flexible urban governance. The case of Copenhagen's recent waterfront development', *European Planning Studies* 12:4, June..

Edelenbos, J. and Monnikhof, R. (eds) (2001), *Lokale interactieve beleidsvorming*, (Utrecht: Lemma).

Enemark, S. (2002), *Spatial Planning System in Denmark; The Danish way*, The Danish association of chartered surveyors.

European Union (1997), *EU Compendium on Spatial Planning Systems and Policies, – Denmark*, (28C) European Communities Commission. Directorate-General XVI: Regional policies and cohesion (Luxembourg: Office for official publications of the European communities).

GLA (2002), *Behind Closed Doors: Scrutiny of the Mayor's Planning Decisions*, Planning Advisory Committee.

Goldsmith, M., (2005), 'The experience of metropolitan government' in Heinelt and Kübler (eds), pp. 81–100.

John, P. (2001), *Local Governance in Western Europe*, (London: Sage).

Kickert, W.J.M., Klijn, E.H. and Koppenjan, J.F.M. (eds) (1997), *Managing Complex Networks* (London: Sage).

Heinelt, H., and Kübler, D. (eds) (2005), *Metropolitan Governance: Capacity, Democracy and the Dynamics of Place* (London: Routledge).

Judge, D., Stoker, G. and Wolman, H. (eds) (1995), *Theories of Urban Politics* (London: Sage).

Keating, M. and Loughlin, R.J. (eds) (1997) *The Political Economy of Regionalism* (London: Cass).

Loughlin, R. J. and Peters, B.G. (1997), 'State Traditions, Administrative Reform and Regionalization', in Keating and Loughlin (eds), pp. 41–62.

Lowndes, V. (1995), 'Citizenship and Urban Politics', in Judge et al. (eds), pp.160–81.

Luhmann, N. (1981), *Politische Theorie im Wohlfahrtsstaat* (München: Gunter Olzug).

Norton, A., (1994), *International Handbook of Local and Regional Government*, (Cheltenham: Edward Elgar).

Pimlott, B. and Rao, N. (2002), *Governing London* (London: Oxford University Press).

Rhodes, R.A.W. (1997), *Understanding Governance* (Buckingham: Open University Press).

Salet, W., Thornley, A. and Kreukels A. (eds.) (2003), *Metropolitan Governance and Spatial Planning: a comparative study of City-Regions in Europe* (Oxford: Routledge and Spon).

Schaap, L. and Twist, M.J.W. van (1997), 'The Dynamics of Closedness in Networks', in: Kickert et al. (eds.), pp. 62–78.

Schaap, L. (2005), 'Reform and democracy in the Rotterdam region', in Heinelt and Kübler (eds.).

Secretary of State for the Environment, Transport and the Regions (2000), *Strategic Planning in London; Greater London Authority Act 1999*, The Secretary of State for the Environment, Transport and the Regions' guidance on the arrangements for strategic planning in London, GOL CIRCULAR 1/2000.

Thornley, A. (2003), 'London: institutional turbulence but enduring nation-state control', in Salet et al. (eds).

Tops, P.W. and Depla, P. (1993), 'Vernieuwing van de lokale democratie: een ordening van de discussie', *Acta Politica,* 3, 327-361.

Chapter 12

Democratic Legitimacy of Economic Governance: The Case of the European and Monetary Union

Frans van Nispen and Johan Posseth

For many years, democratic legitimacy was not an issue within the European Union (EU). Since there were no major questions about its state of democracy, there was no broad debate either. There are at least two reasons for this popular and academic consent. First, there was a sense of shared problems and the EU seemed to be quite effective in dealing with it. The citizens of the member states benefited from 'Europe' promoting peace and security and economic growth, making them support and legitimatize the EU, i.e. utilitarian support or 'government for the people' (Höreth 1998, 6–7). Second, the logic of legitimacy stemmed from intergovernmental co-operation, based on the principle of unanimity. The legitimate national governments controlled the decision making process, whereas unanimity ensured consensus about the decisions made, 'leaving the democratic legitimacy at the national level intact' (Höreth 1999, 252). Democratic legitimacy is thus vested by the indirect participation of EU's citizens by their legitimate authorities, i.e. 'borrowed legitimacy' or 'government of the people' (Svetlozar 2004, 6).

A number of changes in the scope and depth of the European project, however, alienated many Europeans from the Union's work (European Commission 2001, 7). The ongoing broadening and deepening of European integration heated the debate about EU's policy agenda (the question of subsidiarity) and the level of governance on which these issues should be dealt with (the question of proportionality). Besides, the further transfer of national sovereignty to the supranational level had 'weakened democratic influence and control at the national level without having been compensated by equally strong democratic institutions and processes at the European level' (Höreth 1998, 4). As a result, 'government for and of the people' is no longer a given source of legitimacy. In fact, 'the so-called "democratic deficit" has been identified as the main challenge for legitimate European governance' (Höreth 1999, 253).[1]

---

1   For an elaborate description of EU's democratic deficit, see for instance Höreth, 1998 and Jolly, 2003.

Though Europe's transformation confronts many policy sectors, it can be argued that up to now, its impact has been most profound on economic and monetary affairs, both in terms of policy scope as governance structure. In fact, some even go so far as to argue that '(t)he advancement of European economic and monetary union (…) threatens to dismantle the national welfare state' (Kohler-Koch 2001, 5). The countries in the Eurozone, the member states joining the third stage of the European Monetary Union (EMU), indeed lost a great deal of sovereignty to Europe. The independent European Central Bank (ECB) manages their monetary policy and EMU's fiscal 'do's and don'ts' considerably infringe upon the national budgetary playing field. Besides, it is equally true that the EMU has fuelled policy disputes as the common policy aims at bringing different policy preferences and traditions closer together. Apart from this, the 'democratic deficit' is further unfolded by '... secretive coordinative deliberations of a 'problem-solving' style in ... formal and informal institutions and informal groups' (Wessels and Linsenmann 2004, 66) and by limited accountability.

In this chapter, we further examine the democratic legitimacy of the common monetary policy and the coordination of the fiscal policy of the European member states using the theoretical framework introduced in Chapter 3 and supplemented by some key insights from the academic debate on EU's democratic legitimacy. More specifically, we focus on the following questions:

1. What is the current level of democratic legitimacy?
2. Is this level acceptable?
3. What improvements can be made?

At first glance, there seems to be a democratic deficit concerning economic and monetary affairs since the democratic control of the European Parliament (EP) and the national parliaments on European decisions is limited (Verdun 1999, 110). Democratic legitimacy is, however, not just about democratic decision-making (throughput legitimacy). It is equally important that governing bodies deal with the issues people care about (input legitimacy) and deliver results that meet the public's expectations (output legitimacy). Therefore, we pay attention both to the mere procedural aspects of democratic legitimacy as well as substantive aspects. In addition to distinguishing input, throughput and output legitimacy, we stress the importance of differentiating between parliamentary and non- parliamentary modes of governance. Whereas it is fair to assess parliamentarian systems by how decisions are made, in some instances, this is less appropriate. The technical nature of both the monetary and the fiscal policy explains the limited participation of EU's citizens and their representatives. In such cases, it is a widespread practice to give instrumental autonomy to a group of experts on a specific issue, to guarantee desirable outcomes (Scharpf 1999, 16). When it comes to acceptability, the focus should accordingly (predominantly) be on the substantive aspects: do the objectives of the institution(s) represent the will of the people; and do the results meet the people's expectations? We conclude the chapter with a discussion on the improvement of democratic legitimacy of economic governance.

1. Democratic Legitimacy in the European Union

Democratic Legitimacy

In the opening chapter of this volume, a multi-stage model of democratic legitimacy was introduced. Taking the well-known distinction between input legitimacy ('government *by* the people') and output legitimacy ('government *for* the people') (Scharpf 1999) as a point of departure, the editors of this volume draw our attention to the conversion of inputs into outputs that they have labeled throughput legitimacy ('government *of* the people').[2] We adopt that model even though it is not completely applicable to our subject, which is economic governance in the European context. First, participation, already low in the European context, is almost non-existent in economic governance due to the rather technocratic character of monetary and budgetary issues. However we believe that generic support among the population for the European institutions and their policies may be used as a proxy for input legitimacy. Second, the lack of input legitimacy underscores, once again, the importance of how decisions are made. One may argue that throughput legitimacy of both the common monetary policy as well as the coordination of the budgetary policy suffers from their technocratic character, but it is a widespread practice to remove specific issues from the direct control of electorally accountable office holders and to rely on the judgment of independent expert bodies (Scharpf 1999, 16):

- The mechanisms of electoral accountability are thought to be unsuited, and may be counterproductive, for assuring public-interest oriented policy choices.
- The policy choices are characterized by a high level of technical complexity, whereas there is a broad agreement on the criteria for distinguishing desirable from undesirable outcomes.
- The electorally accountable office holder may override, if necessary, the judgment of independent expert bodies.

However, one may question the 'checks and balances' that are built in to avoid that, for instance, the small European countries are overruled by the big European countries. Third, it is often argued that effectiveness compensates for the lack of participation in the European context, but what can be done if this is not the case? We would like to underscore the importance of (the system of) public, often limited to parliamentary, accountability. However, it should be noted that parliamentary

---

2   In addition, a distinction can be made between outcome legitimacy and feedback legitimacy (Van Schendelen 2002; Engelen and Ho, 2004).

accountability is only one mode of public accountability (Bovens 2005).[3] In addition, we distinguish a non-parliamentary mode of accountability (Figure 12.1).

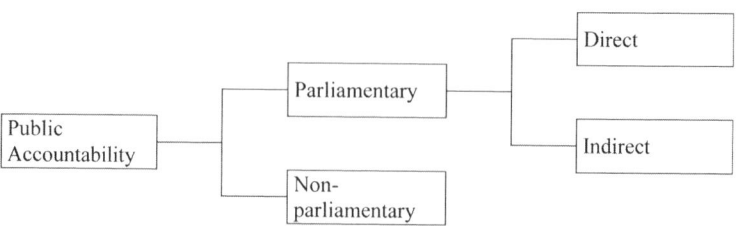

Figure 12.1   A classification of public accountability

As we will see, accountability for, and therefore legitimacy of, the coordination of the fiscal policy of the European member states is at best parliamentary, though indirect. The accountability for the common monetary policy is non-parliamentary since it is deliberately left in the hand of professionals, i.e. bankers. We conclude that this does not mean that there is a legitimacy gap.

The European Debate on Democratic Legitimacy

In chapter three the multi-stage policy model is introduced as a framework for analyzing democratic legitimacy. Before applying this model on the governance of EMU, some additional remarks about its notions and the specific European context have to be made.

First of all, given the social and cultural diversity, it is a priori quite difficult to improve the state of democracy within the European Union. A common indicator for the legitimacy of a political system is the 'thickness' of the collective identity. Lacking a common history, language, culture and ethnicity it can be quite difficult for the people(s) of the EU to understand and trust each other and accept the majority rule of voting (Scharpf 1999, 7–9; Höreth, 1999: 261).

Input legitimacy is just one source of legitimacy, though. The legitimacy gap might well be reduced by other sources of legitimacy. Apart from the 'will of the people', democratic legitimacy also depends on the problem solving capacity of the governing bodies. Dealing with some issues collectively might be more effective, and thus more legitimate, than individual actions of each member state. In addition to choosing the 'right' issues, it is equally important that the 'right' persons (those who know best how to deal with these issues) are in charge. Though inherently weak on (perhaps) the most basic democratic aspect participation, at least some essential

---

3   In addition, he mentions administrative, judicial, professional and social accountability (Bovens 2005).

mechanisms can be built-in on the back-side (for example, peer review and public accountability) for sufficient 'checks and balances'.

A final remark relates to the multi-stage policy model as an assessment tool of legitimacy. It should be stressed that using this model requires clear delimitation of the concepts of input, throughput and output legitimacy since most of its indicators are valid for each policy phase. For example, for each separate phase, it is important to assess the actors involved, the openness of the procedures and the results of that stage. However, following this line of reasoning, it is difficult to make a clear distinction between input, throughput and output legitimacy as introduced in chapter three. Taking the indicators of chapter three as starting point, we suggest the following delimitation. Concerning input legitimacy, popular support is key, which means that we will focus on the (mis)match between citizens' preferences and the policy agenda and the level of support for the institutions in charge. Sources of legitimacy are thus both substantive (what will be done) and procedural (how will it be done: the institutional structure). For throughput legitimacy, we focus on the phase in which the preferences are translated into policy, the decision-making process, as well as the phase in which this policy is implemented. Participation or representation is the central element. On output legitimacy, we reflect on effectiveness, responsiveness and accountability.

2. European Governance

Shifts in Governance

As pointed out in the introduction, the EU embodies a unique political system, evolving from an unprecedented transformational shift in governance. Whereas in the first decades of European integration, the process could be captured relatively easily by the concepts of inter-governmentalism and neo-functionalism, nowadays it seems that even the more comprehensive concept of multi-level governance is no longer sufficient. Multi-level governance (MLG) questioned the state-centric inter-governmentalism in an attempt to better characterize the pooling of sovereignty from the member states to European institutions. The point of departure was the EU as a 'system of continuous negotiation among nested governments at supranational, national and regional territorial tiers' (Hooghe and Marks 2002, 4). Given its focus on the vertical mechanisms between different layers of government (national, supranational and sub-national), it might be best described as multi-level govern*ment*. Later on, MLG was expanded horizontally, including more policy areas and non-governmental actors (Hooghe and Marks 2002, 4). In this way, MLG jumped on the academic bandwagon of governance, to better handle with the perceived shift from 'government to governance'. In general the governance-approach sees the EU as

> (…) an emerging centre of governance that involves a plurality of state and non-state actors on different levels who are concerned to coordinate activities around particular functional problems with a variable territorial geometry (Jessop 2004, 7).

The typical characteristics of the emerging new modes of governance resulted in some authors framing EU-governance in the governance-as-network literature (Kersbergen and Van Waarden 2001, 44), characterized by a changing role for the state, from authoritative allocation 'from above' to the role of an 'activator' (Kohler-Koch and Eising 1999, 5). The European Commission's White Paper on European Governance subscribes to this view, stressing the importance of networks. In addition, the White Paper emphasizes the idea of *good* governance and assigns five principles for good governance.[4] All together, according to the Commission, openness, participation, accountability, effectiveness and coherence are key variables for making more effective policies and for diminishing the democratic deficit (European Commission 2001, 10). Furthermore, they are supposed to be instrumental for the principles of proportionality and subsidiarity.

At first glance, the Commission's initiative for good governance should be welcomed, as it seems to be helpful to reduce the democratic deficit. Besides, who can be against a call for good governance? From closer reading, however, one might wonder if the proposals will actually bring better governance: the White Paper has been broadly criticized as arbitrary, incoherent and vague in its criteria of good governance.[5]

Economic Governance: A Bird's Eye View

To put it simply, economic governance deals with the government of the economy. Given the big share of economic affairs – 'the common market' is *the* core business of the EU – it is surprising that until the EU Convention on the Future of the Union (…), little attention was paid to European economic governance as a concept. Falling short of a clear definition, the actual macro-economic governance has to be deducted from practice, which includes:

- The common monetary policy, which aims at maintaining price-stability (the *internal* value) and exchange rate of the single currency (the *external* value). The main instruments are the interest rate(s) and money supply.
- The coordination of the fiscal policy of the European member states with the convergence of the budgets deficit and public debt as main objective. Main instruments are the Stability and Growth Pact (SGP) and the Excessive Deficit Procedure (EDP).
- The coordination of the structural economic policy, which aims at coordinating

---

4   Briefly, good governance stresses 'political, administrative and economic values of legitimacy and efficiency' (Kersbergen and Van Waarden, 2001: 16), used both in politics ('government governance') as in business ('corporate governance').

5   The White Paper argues 'in favour of redressing the institutional balance (…), is biased in favour of efficiency and effectiveness (…), and reflects an understanding of 'good governance' that neglects basic principles of democratic legitimacy' (Kohler-Koch, 2001: 2). In addition, no attention is paid to the trade-off between efficiency and equity.

structural issues, such as combating unemployment, exploiting the growth potential of the euro area and budgetary implications of aging populations. Main instrument is the Open Method of Co-ordination (OMC).

At least two aspects are important, namely path-dependency and differences in the governance structure.

Path-Dependency

The creation of the EMU can be seen as a logical step or, as some say, a path-dependent process (Dyson 2000, 126–129). First, economic and social changes, such as liberalization, globalization and demographic changes (aging) made European governments to rethink their policies. Second, previous decisions in the 'European project' pressed for closer coordination: since exchange rate volatility hampers smooth functioning of the single market, it seemed profitable to introduce a single currency. Another important factor was the common agreement of key decision makers, initially divided in two 'advocacy' coalitions, about the future direction of European economic and monetary affairs. In place of the two 'advocacy' coalitions, an 'epistemic' community emerged around a shared belief in economic stability with the principle of independence of the central bank as the main variable (Dyson 2000, 103–104).

Besides, it is widely believed that budgetary or fiscal coordination is a necessary, though not sufficient condition for a sound monetary policy (Collignon 2004, 910). As a consequence, budgetary convergence is a prerequisite for the qualification for and participation in the EMU as enforced by the SGP and the EDP. As such, the SGP may be seen as the link between the common monetary policy, as pursued by the ECB, and the budgetary or fiscal policy of the European member states. It is a pivot in the framework of economic governance. Meanwhile, it has become clear that coordination of the fiscal policy of the European member states is a necessary, but not sufficient condition for an effective monetary policy and that some degree of employment policy convergence is required as well (Collignon 2001). This link between fiscal and economic coordination is embodied in the Lisbon strategy and was recently reinforced by the decision to integrate the Broad Economic Policy Guidelines and the Employment Guidelines.

Modes of economic governance   Though there are clear similarities, it should be stressed that the governance structure of the monetary and economic policy, as with other EU policies, is highly differentiated and 'varies over time and across policy areas' (Kohler-Koch and Eising 1999, 32). The key-player of monetary policy is the independent ECB, operating on the principle of simple majority voting – 'one man, one vote' – without veto. It can, therefore, be labeled as supranational governance. The fiscal policy is directed by the principle of proportionality and subsidiarity, with the European member states in the driver's seat. It can thus be best described as multi-level governance (Van Nispen and Ringeling 2006). The member states are not completely free to pursue their own fiscal policy, though, since it is subject to benchmarking, coordinating and monitoring or surveillance, including sanction mechanisms. The third pillar, dealing with structural economic policy, is intergovernmental, as well. Different from the coordination of fiscal policy, however, it doesn't have any form of hard coordination. It consists of a bundle of 'soft' coordination and monitoring mechanisms, 'providing general policy orientations, benchmarking and the publication of 'best practices', lacking legal enforcement or financial sanctions (Wessels and Linsenmann 2004, 58–59 and 69). The main characteristics of the various modes of governance, summarized below (Table 12.1), provide a survey of the key variables.

Table 12.1   Modes of economic governance

Policy Area	Governance Mode	Main Actor	Objective	Instruments	Coordination Mode
Monetary	Supra-national	ECB	Price stability	Interest Rates	Hard
Fiscal	Inter-governmental	ECOFIN	Balanced budgets	SGP	Mixed
Economic	Inter-governmental	ECOFIN	Economic growth	OMC	Soft

We now turn our focus to the democratic legitimacy of the common monetary policy and the coordination of the fiscal policy that is, inter alia, geared to a reduction of the budget deficit below the reference value of 3 per cent of GDP at market prices. The composition of the 'policy mix', i.e. the revenues and expenditures, is left to the various European member states. The fiscal policy itself, i.e. the composition of the 'policy mix' at the national level, is excluded from consideration. Zandstra will deal with the legitimacy of the coordination of the structural economic policy by the Open Method of Coordination (Chapter 13).

4. The Common Monetary Policy

Institutional Framework

The consensus about the importance of sound public finance has cleared the way for an almost unprecedented centralization of monetary policy (Wessels and Linsenmann 2004; Van Nispen and Ringeling 2006). Since the third stage of the EMU, the Euro-countries no longer control their own monetary policy. The establishment of the EMU represents a two-stage shift in responsibility for monetary policy. First, national governments ceded control of monetary policy to their national central banks[6] and second, national banks in turn ceded control to the European System of Central Banks (ESCB), consisting of the independent European Central Bank (ECB) and the national central banks of the European member states (Hodson and Maher 2001, 4). It is directed by a Governing Council composed of the members of the Executive Board plus the governors of the national banks in the Eurozone that serve as 'representatives' of their countries. Though they may try to shape the common monetary policy according to the preferences of their governments, they are supposed to be completely independent in order to avoid a situation where common monetary policy is abused for political reasons, notably at the eve of an election.[7] It should be underscored that they may not take directives from their governments.[8] It is generally agreed that independency of the central bank is a prerequisite for price stability (De Grauwe 2000, 154; Eijffinger and De Haan 2000, 38–43).

The main objective of the ECB is to reduce inflation and to maintain price stability, i.e. to control the *internal* value of the euro.[9] The inflation rate is set at a maximum of 2 per cent. The main instrument is the interest rate. Decisions are made by a simple majority – 'one man, one vote' – which means that the governors of the national central banks have no veto. Contrary to other central banks like the U.S. Federal Reserve (FED), the ECB is not in charge of the *external* value of the euro. It has to share the responsibility for exchange rate policy. The exchange rate of the euro is seen the outcome of both economic developments and economic policy, rather than an independent objective (European Council 1997). In absence of an exchange rate system, the ECOFIN may formulate general orientations that should respect the primary objective of maintaining price stability. In addition, these general orientations may only be initiated by a recommendation of the ECB or the European Commission, after consultation of the ECB (Scheller 2004, 91). The final say about the contents of the orientations lies with the ECOFIN, which makes decisions by a qualified majority (Scheller 2004, 31), reflecting an intergovernmental rather than a supranational mode of 'governance'.

---

6   In most northern European member states, the central bank was already in charge of the monetary policy. The observation applies therefore mainly the southern European member states.

7   Though, for instance, the Dutch president of the national central bank meets with the minister of Finance weekly for lunch, but takes no directives.

8   The concept of independence includes: institutional independence; legal independence; personal independence of the members of its decision-making bodies; functional and operational independence; financial and organizational independence (Scheller 2004, 122).

9   It should be noted that three countries – Denmark, Sweden and the United Kingdom – opted-out the third stage of the EMU for various reason and, therefore, pursue their own monetary policy. However, their monetary policy is basically in line with the strategy followed by the ECB to contain inflation.

Democratic Legitimacy

Lacking a constituency and, therefore, an identity, the input legitimacy of European institutions and, consequently, their policy is inherently weak (Scharpf 1999, 2). In case of the common monetary policy, this is reinforced by the independency of the ECB, the technical expertise that is required and the secrecy of the policy process (Verdun 1999, 113).[10] Trust is, therefore, an important indicator, as there seems to be a relationship between perceptions of performance and trust. Applied to the ECB, when the citizens of Europe tend to trust the ECB to a high degree, there is reason to believe that they appreciate its (past) performance and, consequently, support its policy agenda.[11]

The support for the monetary policy seems to score quite high as well. The average support for the single currency exceeds the 60 per cent mark in the EU-12, with recent peaks of 75 per cent.[12] Though there are no opinion polls about this subject, it seems fair to believe that the ECB's policy on price stability is in line with the preferences of the population. The *internal* value of the single currency has been rather stable since the establishment of the ECB though there have been complaints about the increasing costs of living. The same is true for the *external* value of the single currency. The abolition of exchange rates in the Eurozone is appreciated by the population, though the current dollar/euro ratio is not very profitable for exports and, therefore, for economic growth and employment. When asked about their concern about the euro/dollar ratio, 51 per cent indicated that it doesn't concern them at all and 32 per cent were just a little concerned (Eurobarometer 2004a, 34). The opinion of the population is rather surprising because European citizens repeatedly put economic issues such as combating unemployment and job security on top.

The locus of throughput legitimacy is the decision-making mechanism. As previously mentioned, the Governing Council is the decision-making body of the ECB.[13] It consists of the Executive Council Board plus the governors, i.e. the presidents of the national central banks. Though this national representation might

---

10 In addition, she points at the asymmetrical development of the monetary integration process compared to the political or budgetary and fiscal integration process (Verdun 1999, 113).

11 In general, the level of trust in European institutions, notably the ECB, is relatively high in comparison with, for instance, national institutions: the per centage of people (EU-15) who tend to trust respectively the ECB 46 per cent, with 27 per cent who tend to distrust. The level of awareness among EU citizens of the European institutions is high enough to compare the level of trust in these institutions with national institutions. To give an example, 92 per cent of the EU15 citizens have heard of the European Parliament; for the ECB this level is 74 per cent (Barometer 61, page 12).

12 The support declined recently from 75 to 66 per cent, but that exceeds the level of support in pre-ECB-period 1993–1998 (about 50 per cent).

13 The 'opt-outs' as well as the new European member states have no say in the common monetary policy. They are represented in the General Council that serves as an advisory body.

create some playing field for national preferences, we should keep in mind that they are appointed as experts and are supposed to be independent. Moreover, the president of the Council and a member of the Commission may participate in the meetings of the Governing Council without the right to vote.

The ECB's decisions are made by simple majority on the basis of 'one man, one vote', participants thus lack veto power. Unfortunately, we have to guess what is happening behind closed doors. The minutes of the sessions are confidential to insure the independence of the ECB. Openness and transparency may put the common monetary policy at risk, though they may foster credibility and, therefore, performance (Smaghi and Gros 2000, 5). However, the decision-making mechanism is geared to building consensus rather than casting votes.

In sum, EMU decision-making, is quite technocratic, leaving little room for politics, though politics has been brought back covertly into monetary policy by the upgrading of the Eurogroup under the French presidency (2000).[14] Consisting of the ministers of Finance of the Euro countries and meeting in advance of the ECOFIN session, it provides national governments the opportunity to discuss European monetary policy.[15] The regular participation of both the president of the ECB and the EU's commissioner for Economic and Financial Affairs, in combination with the informal working method, makes the Eurogroup a useful and valuable platform for talks.[16] It is excluded when it comes to the accountability of the ECB and the common monetary policy. The president of the ECB is mainly accountable to European Parliament (Jabko 2003, 712), though its role is restricted to consultation and hearings.

The performance comes, as Dyson has correctly argued, before the accountability for and explanation of that performance (Dyson 2002, 353). The output legitimacy of the common monetary policy may be assessed by the price stability, though it takes about two years before the impact becomes clear (Bini-Smaghi and Gros 2000, 4). The inflation target was first related at the average of the three best performing European member states plus 1.0 per cent, later set at 2.0 per cent. The record of the

---

14 The process of European integration is still a political project. The establishment of the EMU and the statute of the ECB and the rules of the game were a political decision. In this context, the ECB is completely free to operate and to pursue its own policy.

15 The discussions are prepared by the European Commission in consultation with the Economic and Financial Committee, a high-level consultative Community body, consisting of senior officials of *all* member states and the ECB.

16 The commissioner 'acts as a lead speaker and introduces the main developments and prospects for the euro area and the wider global economy'. The ECB's president elaborates on the ECB's analysis of the economic conditions, the reactions of monetary policy, the international monetary developments and the euro exchange rate. Besides, for the former ECB President Duisenberg it was common to discuss countries' individual policies and the possible interventions. The informal working method was characterized by a 'restricted format, the confidentiality of the discussions and the focus on substantial and technical issues' (Puetter 2004, 861–862).

ECB is rather successful. The average inflation rate increased first to stabilize then on the 2 per cent mark.

A closer look at the national level reveals that 7 out of 12 countries top the 2.0 per cent mark, with Greece (3.5) as the front-runner. Even more importantly, inflation has risen in 8 out of 12 countries in the Eurozone in Fiscal Year (FY) 2005 compared to the pre-ECB-period (Figure 12.2). Apart from this, we should consider that, despite the relatively low actual inflation rates, people complain about the consequences of the introduction of the single currency for the cost of living (Scheller 2004, 46).[17]

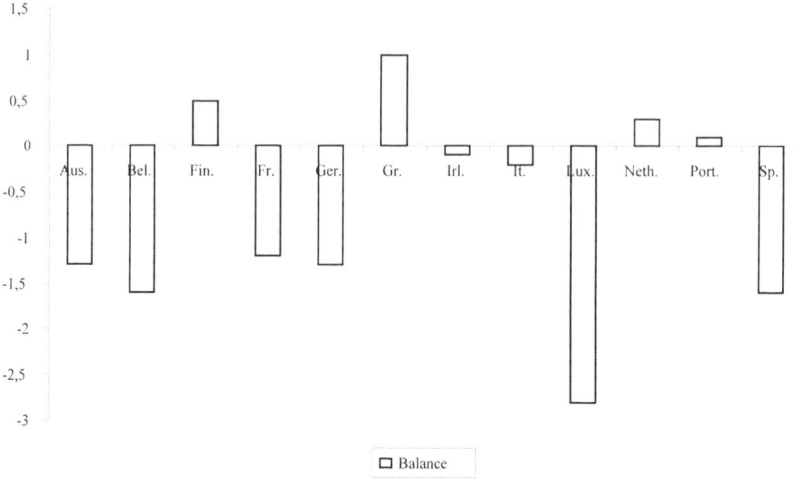

Figure 12.2   The development of the inflation rate per country, for years 1998–2005

Source: ECB, EBI 2006

Explanation: A positive sign indicates a reduction, a negative sign a growth of the inflation rate

The external value of the euro made a slow start losing ground in the early years, but the euro now outweighs the dollar. One may question if this is profitable. A strong Euro does not foster exports and, therefore, economic growth and employment.

In addition, we would like to underscore the importance the accountability of the ECB for the common monetary policy. Accountability refers to 'the act of listening to criticism and responding to questions about the past and future behavior that may be put forward by a democratically elected body' (Bini-Smaghi and Gros 2000, 2).[18]

---

17 The single currency is originally referred to as the 'teuro' in Germany, short for 'teuer euro' ('expensive euro').

18 Accountability should not be confused with democratic control, which refers to responsibility. It consists of accountability ex ante and ex post plus a popular mandate. The

A precondition for accountability ex post is control ex ante. In contrast to other central banks, the ECB is doing relatively well on control ex ante, though the role of the European Parliament is limited. It has a say in the statutes of the ESCB and its mission and the rules of the game (Scheller 2004, 130–131). In addition, the European Parliament is consulted on the appointment of the president, vice-president and other members of the Executive Board, but they cannot be fired. The Committee of the Economic and Monetary Affairs invites the president of the ECB for hearings, but contrary to, for instance, the chairman of the Board of Governors of the U.S. Federal Reserve System, he is not obliged to answer questions or to take directives. The committee has no influence on the common monetary policy. In practice, the executives of the ECB accepted the principle that accountability and independence are two sides of the coin, providing more detailed information to justify monetary decisions, especially inflation projections (Jabko 2003, 711, 726).

Finally, we may question how accountability can be measured[19] and even more importantly, what can be done if performance does not meet expectations of the citizens for this case. It should be underscored that the governors of the national central banks, serving as the main representatives of the European member states, are supposed to be completely independent. The outcome might have disastrous consequences on the economy. The dilemma, following Nicolas Jabko, is how:

> … to reconcile the need for effectiveness, which serves to justify the independence of central bankers as monetary experts, and the principle of democracy, which at the very least entitles politicians to examine the decisions made by these experts (Jabko 2003, 712-713).

The ECB needs political support for its main objectives, but at the same time political involvement should be limited to maintain the credibility of the ECB and the effectiveness of the common monetary policy.

5. The Coordination of Fiscal Policy

The Institutional Framework

The authority to pursue a budgetary or fiscal policy is still very much decentralized, but the governments of the European member states are not completely free to pursue their own fiscal policy. The size of the budget deficit and public debt are subject to benchmarking, coordinating and monitoring or surveillance. Consequently, a distinction should be made between the coordination at the centralized, i.e.

---

latter is not relevant. The central bank is not free to choose its own objective (Bini-Smaghi and Gros 2000, 2–3).

19 A set of 15 criteria is provided by Bini-Smaghi and Gros (2000), categorized in three groups reflecting the multi-stage model of legitimacy.

intergovernmental level and the composition of the 'policy mix' at the decentralized, i.e. the national level.

The budgetary policy of the European member states is more or less directed by the reference value of the budget deficit that serves as a criterion for the qualification for and participation in the Economic and Monetary Union that was agreed upon at the Maastricht Summit (1991)[20]. The rules prohibit a budget deficit exceeding 3 per cent of GDP with the exception of exceptional and temporary circumstances. It was reinforced and strengthened at the Amsterdam Summit in 1997 when the heads of state committed themselves to a balanced budget or a budgetary surplus[21].

The governments of the European member states are free to pursue their own budgetary or fiscal policy as long as the budget deficit and the public debt are kept below their reference value. However, they have to submit a convergence or stability report every year that, inter alia, assesses the state of the economy and the measures that they have taken to keep the budget deficit and public debt below the reference value[22]. An early warning system – the so–called 'yellow card' – comes in operation when the budget deficit comes close to the reference value.

The convergence and stability reports are examined by ECOFIN based on an assessment of the European Commission in consultation with the Economic and Financial Committee. If the reference value is exceeded, the excessive deficit procedure (EDP) might come in operation – the so-called 'red card' – but that requires a decision by the ECOFIN that a European member state is in derogation. A qualified majority is needed for all votes that include the European member state in derogation. It allows the ECOFIN to make recommendations. In the end, the procedure may lead to financial sanctions against those who fail to comply. The decision is made by a two-third majority of the votes, and the European member state in derogation is excluded from voting.

Finally, the budgetary policy is subject to coordination through the Broad Economic Policy Guidelines (BEPGs) that may be seen as a form of open coordination *avant la lettre*. A major difference with the EDP is that these are only political commitments that cannot be legally enforced. The link between budgetary and economic coordination was recently reinforced by the decision to integrate the BEPGs and the Employment Guidelines as the centerpiece of the reintroduction of the Lisbon strategy.

---

20 The budgetary policy is further directed by the reference value for the national debt that is set at 60 per cent of GDP at market prices.

21 The reference values are set out in a protocol and are, therefore, easier to change than the treaty.

22 The main difference is in the monetary policy. The European member states that do not participate in (final stage of) the EMU pursue their own monetary policy and, therefore, should provide information about inflation and interest rates in addition to the state of the budget. The participants in the EMU have to provide information only about the state of the budget since the (common) monetary policy is left in the hand of the European Central Bank (ECB) that is located in Frankfurt, Germany.

Democratic Legitimacy

The membership of European institutions such as the ECOFIN and the Eurogroup gives the government the opportunity to formally participate in the decision making process (Wessels and Linsenmann 2004, 58, 68). The involvement of the representatives of the population is channeled through the government and, therefore, we take public support as an indicator of input legitimacy. The score of the SGP (Stability and Growth Pact) is rather good: about 75 per cent of the population in the Eurozone believes that the SGP is a good thing because it results in the Euro being a stable and strong currency (Eurobarometer 2004a, 57). As for the enforcement of the SGP, there is no such 'unanimity'. A relative majority of the population in the Eurozone is for a more flexible interpretation (49 per cent for, 43 per cent against). The situation per European member state shows a wide variety with Finland as the

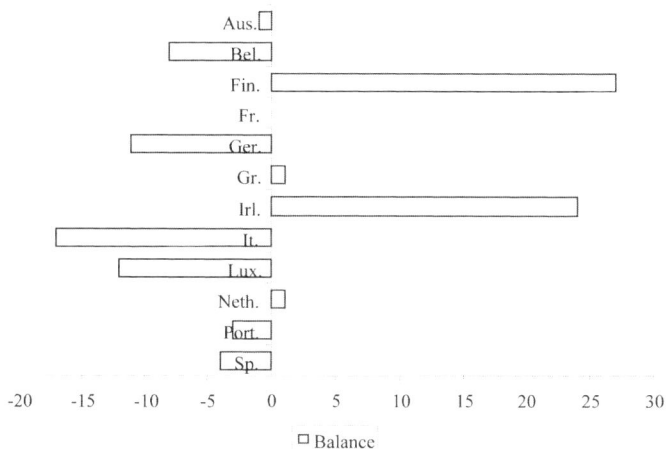

Figure 12.3   Strict enforcement of the SGP in difficult economic periods

Source: Eurobarometer 2004a: 55
Explanation: A positive sign indicates that proponents outnumber opponents of strict interpretation (and reverse).

greatest proponent and Italy as greatest opponent of strict interpretation (Figure 12.3).[23] It should be noted that the SGP already contained some room for interpretation. The

23   A closer inspection of the ECOFIN decision not to issue penalties in the case of France and Germany reveals a mismatch on two cases between the voting behavior of the minister of Finance and the will of the people. The Irish minister of Finance voted for a flexible application of the SGP whereas 58 per cent the population turned out to be in favor of going by the book. The opposite applies for Spain where 42 per cent of the population was in favor of a less rigid

budgetary situation is subject to peer review, and there is a provision for exceptional and temporary circumstances.

However, we should be careful with the interpretation of these figures because about 80 per cent of the respondents admitted that they either never heard of the SGP or were not very familiar with the SGP (Eurobarometer 2004a, 52). Finally, a relative majority (48 per cent for, 38 per cent against) of the people of the Eurozone thinks that the economic sanctions against countries that do not respect the SGP are not applied in the same manner to all Member States' (Eurobarometer 2004a, 59).

The coordination of the budgetary or fiscal policy is conducted by the ECOFIN reflecting the intergovernmental rather than a supranational mode of governance. The ministers of Finance of the European member states participate in the ECOFIN on the basis of equality. In principle, it enables them to shape the policy according to the preferences of their citizens. However, there is no guarantee that the 'will of the people' is reflected in the decisions about the reduction of the budget deficit since they do no longer require unanimity. The relative weight of the European member states is loosely related to the size of their populations. At the moment, a qualified majority is needed of the number of the European member states plus, at least, 232 out of 321 votes. In addition, the number of votes should represent 62 per cent of the total population.[24] On the one hand, the current decision making mechanism may be considered a step backward since the outcome might no longer reflect the whole population. On the other hand, a single state can no longer serve as a roadblock (which is a disadvantage of unanimity). Besides, a qualified majority is still better than a single majority. The big states are unable to outnumber the small states, though it is plausible that the influence of big states is greater than small states.

The involvement of national parliaments in the preparation of the ECOFIN meeting may be used as a proxy for throughput legitimacy of the coordination of the budgetary policy of the European member states. In most of the national parliaments, there is some kind of examination of EU documents. A report by the Conférence des Organnes Spécialisées dans les Affairs Communautaires (COSAC) shows a wide range of arrangements, running from ad hoc arrangements to a more or less comprehensive and systematic examination of EU documents (Maurer and Wessels 2001; Holzhacker 2002; Maurer 2002; COSAC 2005). A distinction can be made between two general scrutiny systems.[25] First, there are *mandatory* systems in which the government representative has very little discretionary power as, for instance, is the case in Austria as well as the Scandinavian countries. Second, there are *document-based* or *supportive* systems leaving the government representative

---

interpretation of the rules, but that did not prevent the Spanish minister of Finance from voting against (Council meeting November 25, 2003).

24 In the future, if the European constitution is accepted, a majority of the European member states, reflecting 55 per cent of the European member states, will be required for a qualified majority. The majority must represent 65 per cent of the population;

25 The scrutiny systems can be refined by making a distinction between the examination of EU documents ex ante and ex post. It is obvious that the examination should take place in advance of the decision to have any impact at all.

room to maneuver such as the Dutch scrutiny system in which the government has to inform parliament by so-called 'fiches' of each new proposal.[26]

In addition, scrutiny systems may be created by the institution in charge of examining the EU documents. In most national parliaments there is an EU-committee, but the examination of EU documents is often carried out by one of the standing committees or even by the plenary committee (Table 12.2).

Table 12.2   A survey of scrutiny systems in national parliaments

System / Platform	*Mandatory*	*Supportive*
EU Committee	Austria, Denmark	Ireland, United Kingdom
Standing Committee	Finland, Sweden	France, Germany, Italy The Netherlands

Source: COSAC, 2005

In most of the European countries where a scrutiny system is lacking – Belgium, Greece, Luxembourg, Portugal and Spain – the examination of EU documents is not proactive but reactive and, therefore, national parliaments have no impact on the decisions about the implementation of the SGP and the EDP regarding countries being in derogation.

A mandatory system is, of course, the best guarantee that the will of (the representatives of) the people is reflected in decisions, but there is no clear demarcation line in practice. On the one hand, in a mandatory system, the level playing field of a minister is primarily bounded in case of fundamental issues and basically used for strategic reasons. Besides, the EU documents and government opinion, if any, are often duly noted without discussion in plenary or a standing committee. Finally, the growing use of qualified majority voting (QMV) has seriously curtailed the effectiveness of mandates. In sum, the involvement of members of national parliaments is limited, which is a fortiori true with more technical issues as the coordination of the fiscal policy of the European member states.

A look at the budgetary situation of the European member states reveals that the average budget position in the Eurozone is close to the 3 per cent mark (2.9 per cent of GDP in FY 2005). A number of countries, notably France, Germany, Greece Italy and Portugal, were in derogation in FY 2005, a few others were close.[27] For the 'opt-outs' it is about the same, though they are all on the positive side of the coin partly due to the economic cycle. The development over time is mixed (Figure

---

26 A document based scrutiny system is often accompanied by a scrutiny reserve, which provides that ministers should not agree to EU proposals in the Council until parliamentary scrutiny has been completed.

27 In addition, the Greek government has provided incorrect statistics of its budget deficit and national debt and, therefore, was accepted as participant in the EMU on dubious grounds.

12.4), though the budgetary position is better than in the past, notably in the southern Eurocountries. A majority of the people, however, thinks more should be done on a

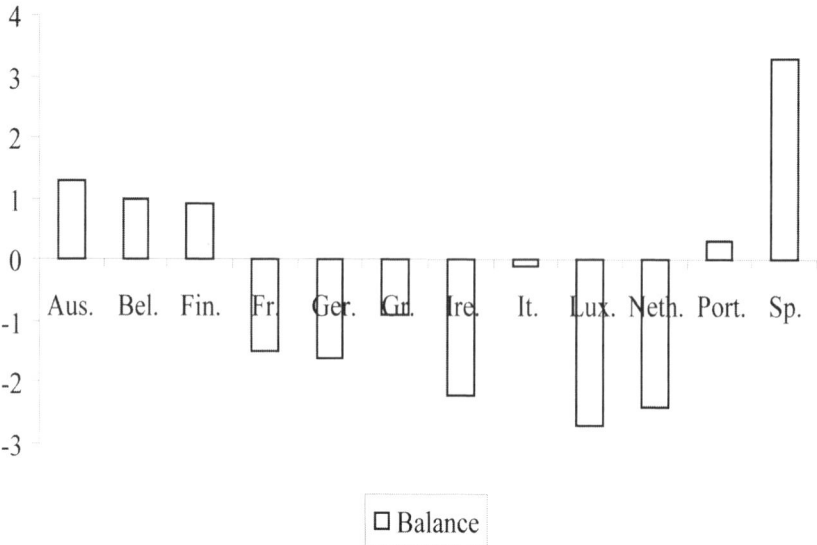

Figure 12.4   Net borrowing/lending in the Eurozone for years 1998–2005
Source: European Commission 2006
Explanation: A positive sign indicates a lower budget deficit; a negative sign a higher budget deficit

European level to deal with it. For 45 per cent of the people (EU12) the economic policies' coordination is not sufficient (Eurobarometer 2004a, 48).

The situation regarding national debt is even worse with only 5 out of 12 countries meeting the reference value of 60 per cent of GDP. The primary balance, leaving out interest payments, illustrates the impact of the national debt. It is obvious that the interest payments constitute a major component of the budget deficit. Not surprisingly, the heads of states have agreed to look at the national debt more carefully, taking into account the local economic situation when making a decision about the existence of derogation concerning the budgetary deficit.

The coordination of the budgetary or fiscal policy is conducted by the ECOFIN reflecting the intergovernmental mode of governance. Consequently, the members of the ECOFIN are primarily accountable to their own governments and parliaments. Strangely enough, almost none of the European member states – irrespectively of their scrutiny system – provides comprehensive and systematic feedback to their parliament about the proceedings and outcome of the ECOFIN meetings (Maurer 2002, 20). At best, decisions and/or press releases are forwarded to the national parliament. The role of European Parliament in fiscal affairs is limited to deliberations about coordination of fiscal policy in the framework of the BEPGs, the EDP and multilateral surveillance (website EP).

6. Conclusion

In this chapter, we have assessed the democratic legitimacy of economic governance. We have addressed the question of whether there is a legitimacy gap and, if so, if that constitutes a problem. In doing so, a distinction should be made between parliamentary and non-parliamentary modes of legitimacy. We have come to the conclusion that the coordination of the budgetary or fiscal policy fits into the first category, though indirect, and the common monetary policy fits into the second category. The outcome can be summarized as follows (see Table 12.3), referring to the multi-stage model of democratic legitimacy.

Table 12.3   The democratic legitimacy of economic governance

Legitimacy Aspect / Policy Area	*Input*		*Throughput*	*Output*	
	Support Institution	Support Policy	Decision-making	Performance	Accountable
Monetary: Price stability	+	+	-	+	-
Fiscal: Balanced budget	+/-	+	+/-	+	-

Monetary Policy

The input legitimacy of the common monetary policy has been assessed in terms of popular support. This is almost completely built on the performance of the ECB in terms of the internal and, to a lesser degree, external value of the single currency. The track record of the ECB is rather good. The exchange rate is a different matter, however, because:

• The level of trust in the ECOFIN is lower than the level of trust in the ECB
• The impact of the exchange rate on people's welfare is less clear and
• People are indifferent about the exchange rate (Eurobarometer 2004a, 34).

On throughput legitimacy, it is the other way round: due to the technocratic character of the monetary policy, the involvement of (the representatives of) the population in the common monetary policy is almost non-existent. The role of the EP and the national parliaments is limited for both policy fields. For output legitimacy, we have introduced two indicators.

Taking performance as a source of legitimacy, monetary policy is doing quite well. The ECB succeeded in achieving its main objectives. However accountability is weak. Especially when performance does not meet expectations, this can be a problem. Though the ex ante control is sufficient, the way in which the accountability is exercised fails to meet many democratic criteria. The role of the EP is restricted to informal hearings for the Committee of Economic and Monetary Affairs, lacking any formal status. The added value of these hearings is up for discussion since:

> ... neither the general public nor even arguably its elected representatives have the necessary expertise and information to monitor central bankers' decisions in a rigorous way (Jabko 2003, 728).

The members of the EP can hardly be blamed for their lack of expertise and information, but it creates a legitimacy gap. The authority to pursue the common monetary policy is deliberately left in the hands of experts, i.e. bankers, in order to avoid the common monetary policy being used for political, notably electoral reasons. One may even question the added value of a bigger role of the EP given the expertise that is required to assess the consequences of the common monetary policy. Besides, it may cause delay and consequently may have a negative impact on the performance of the ECB and the common monetary policy. As such the concept of '*expertocracy*' or '*technocracy*' (Scharpf 1998, 91; Wessels 2000, 104–105) seems to be appropriate to characterize the legitimacy of the common monetary policy.

Finally, we should address what can be done to improve the democratic legitimacy of the common monetary policy. A couple of small adjustments, rather than major changes, seem to be possible to make the ECB more accountable. A first option is to engage the ECB in substantive discussions about its policy where it is pressed to provide the information about the background analyses such as inflation forecast that have led to policy decisions. The confidentiality of the background analyses suggests that the ECB has something to hide (Bini-Smaghi and Gros 2000, 5). In addition, structuring of information in such a way that the general public can understand it may facilitate the accountability of the ECB (Scheller 2004, 126).

Last but not least, we may look at the outcome of the European Convention that above all reconfirms the institutions, rules and procedures under the treaty. The working group on economic governance recognized the need to maintain the Eurogroup as an informal forum for discussion, but was not in favor of a proposal that would place the ECOFIN, in its configuration of the Eurogroup, in charge of the decisions related exclusively to the Eurozone. A minority of the working group on economic governance argued that there is scope for improving the accountability of the ECB, enhancing the ECB's reporting to the European Parliament, giving the EP a greater role in the designation of ECB Board members, and providing for the obligatory publication of ECB minutes (European Convention 2002, 3). However, it is argued that an extension of the power of the European Parliament, as well as the role of national parliaments, are bound to be ineffective since they fail to address the cause of the problem of democratic legitimacy, i.e. the complex and diffuse structure of political authority (Van Staden 2003). It all comes down to the question, *'quis custodiet custodies'* ('who will guard the guards') since the governors of the national banks are supposed to be completely independent. They are neither accountable to their governments nor to their parliaments. One may wonder if this constitutes a problem. We believe it does not as long as the objectives and 'modus vivendi' of the ECB are clearly defined, politically backed by both the ECOFIN and the EP, and as long as the ECB operates within its mandate. In other words, the democratic legitimacy of monetary policy is best guaranteed in a situation of dependence in terms of objectives, but independence when it comes to instruments to attain these objectives (Sousa 2001).

Fiscal Policy

The SGP and EDP constitute the link between the common monetary policy and the fiscal policy of the European member states. The coordination of the fiscal policy is done by the ECOFIN reflecting the intergovernmental mode of governance. As mentioned before, the level of trust in the ECOFIN is relatively low (as compared with other European institutions). The public support for the SGP is rather high.

Concerning throughput legitimacy, one could argue that the possibilities for national involvement are greater since the implementation of the decisions is mainly at the national level. Since we are primarily interested in the *coordination* of the budgetary policies (which predominantly takes place at the European level), we focused solely on the involvement of national parliaments in these European decisions. It became clear that there are big differences between the countries. In most parliaments, there is some kind of scrutiny of EU documents, though not always in a comprehensive, systematic and timely way. Consequently, the ministers of Finance enjoy considerable discretion.

The performance of the ECOFIN, in terms of budgetary convergence, was good until recently when the economy took a downturn. Besides, the authority of the ECOFIN was challenged by the French government, with the support of a majority of the other countries. The decision of the ECOFIN to set the SGP and the EDP aside has been brought to the European Court of Justice, which ruled that the decision was illegal. The reference value of the budget deficit was salvaged, but a more flexible interpretation of the EDP was the outcome or the price that had to be paid for this rescue operation.[28]

The accountability is a matter of concern. First, as a group, the ECOFIN is not accountable for its decisions to any political institution. Second, the accountability at the national level is quite weak as well because very few of the European member states provide comprehensive and systematic feedback to their parliament about the performances and the national parliaments themselves chose a low profile.

---

28 The ministers of Finance should take the local economic situation, notably regarding the national debt, into account. As compensation, the European member state should pursue a more restrictive budgetary or fiscal policy in time of economic growth.

The concept of *borrowed* legitimacy seems to fit the coordination of the budgetary or fiscal policy. It argues that input legitimacy at the intergovernmental or supranational level can be deduced from the input legitimacy at the national level.

We may ask what these changes in the SGP will bring. On the one hand, they may lead to more input legitimacy since the local situation can be taken into account. In addition, the integration of the Broad Economic Policy Guidelines and the Employment Guidelines may be a part of the reinforcement of the Lisbon strategy (Subacchi 2005). On the other hand, they may hollow-out the performance of the budgetary or fiscal policy and, consequently, the rest of the framework of macro-economic governance, notably the common monetary policy.

Finally, one may consider making the ECOFIN accountable to the EP since national parliaments lack the instruments to monitor and safeguard the democratic legitimacy of the coordination of the budgetary or fiscal policy. They may hold their own minister of Finance accountable, but they have very little say in the rest and, therefore, we have to live with a legitimacy gap with regard to the coordination of the fiscal policy of the European member states.

References

Bini-Smaghi, L. and Gros, D. (2000), *Is the ECB Accountable and Transparent?* Paper delivered at the European Institute of Public Administration (EIPA) conference: EMU Halfway through the Transition Period. September (The Netherlands, Maastricht) 18–19.

Bovens, M.A.P. (2005), Public Accountability, in: E. Ferlie, L. Lynn and Chr. Pollitt (eds) *The Oxford Handbook of Public Management* (Oxford: Oxford University Press) 182–209.

Collignon, S. (2001), *Economic Policy Coordination in EMU: Institutional and Political Requirements*, Paper presented at the Center for European Studies.

Collignon, S. (2004), 'Is Europe Going Far Enough? Reflections on the EU's Economic Governance', *Journal on European Public Policy* 11:5, 909–25.

COSAC (2004), *Report on developments in European Union procedures and practices relevant to parliamentary scrutiny*, prepared and presented to XXXI Conference of Community and European Affairs Committees of Parliaments of the European Union, 19 – 20 May (Ireland: Dublin).

COSAC (2005), *Developments in the European Union, Procedures and Practices Relevant to Parliamentary Scrutiny*, Third Bi-annual Report prepared and presented to XXXII Conference of Community and European Affairs Committees of Parliaments of the European Union, 17–18 May (Luxembourg).

De Grauwe, P. (2000), *Economics of the Monetary Union* (Oxford: Oxford University Press).

Dyson, K. (2000). *The Politics of the Euro-Zone. Stability or Breakdown* (Oxford/ New York: Oxford University Press).

Dyson, K. (ed.) (2002), *European States and the Euro. Europeanization, Variation and Convergence* (Oxford/New York: Oxford University Press).

Dyson, K. and Featherstone, K. (1999), *The Road to Maastricht. Negotiating Economic and Monetary Union* (Oxford/New York: Oxford University Press).

Eaton, D. (ed.) (2006), *The End of Sovereignty? A Transatlantic Perspective*, Transatlantic Public Policy Series 2, Lit Verlag (Münster).

Engelen, E.R. and Sie Dhian Ho, M. (eds) (2004), De s*taat van de democratie. Democratie voorbij de staat*, Verkenning Wetenschappelijke Raad voor het Regeringsbeleid, volume 4 (Amsterdam: Amsterdam University Press).

Eijffinger, S.C.W. and de Haan, J. (2000), *European Monetary and Fiscal Policy* (Oxford/New York: Oxford University Press).

European Commission (2001), *European Governance. A White Paper* COM Final (Brussels).

European Commission (2003), *Report from the Commission on European Governance*, Office for Official Publications of the European Communities (Luxembourg).

European Commission (2004), *The Euro, 3 years later*, Flash Eurobarometer 165, 2004a (Brussels).

European Commission (2004), *Eurobarometer* Spring 2004b, volume 61.

European Convention (2002), *Final Report of Working Group VI on Economic Governance*, 21 october, Conv. 357/02 (Brussels).

Holzhacker, R. L. (2002), 'National Parliamentary Scrutiny over EU Issues: The Goals and Methods of Governing and Opposition Parties', *European Union Politics*, vol. 3/4, Dec. 2002.

Hodson, D. and Maher, I. (2001), *EMU: Balancing Credibility and Legitimacy in the Policy Mix*, South Bank European Papers, No. 3 (London).

Hooghe, L. and Marks, G. (2002), *Types of Multi-Level Governance*, Working Paper (University of North Carolina, Department of Political Science).

Höreth, M. (1998), *The Trilemma of Legitimacy. Multi-level Governance in the EU and the Problem of Democracy* Discussion paper Center for European Integration Studies (ZEI), number 11.

Höreth, M. (1999), 'No way out for the beast? The unsolved legitimacy problem of European Governance', *Journal of European Public Policy*, 6:2, June, 249–68.

Jabko, N. (2003), 'Democracy in the Age of the Euro', *Journal of European Public Policy* 10:5, 710–39.

Jessop, B. (2004), *The European Union and Recent Transformations in Statehood*, Lancaster University <http://www.ru.nl/socgeo/colloquium/ EUAndTransformationOfStatehood.pdf, accessed June 19, 2006.

Jolly, M.E. (2003), *Debating Democracy in the European Union. Four Concurrent Paradigms.* Paper delivered at the EUSA Eighth Biennial International Conference 27–29 March (Nashville, Tennessee).

Kersbergen, K. van and, Waarden, F. van (2001), *Shifts in Governance: Problems of Legitimacy and Accountability*, Social Science Research Council (MAGW) (The Hague).

Kohler-Koch, B. (2001), *The Commission White Paper and the Improvement of European Governance*, paper prepared for the symposium Mountain or Molehill? A critical appraisal of the Commission White Paper on Governance, New York, <http://econpapers.repec.org/paper/erpjeanmo, accessed June 19, 2006.

Kohler-Koch, B. and Eising, R. (eds) (1999), *The Transformation of Governance in the European Union*. (London: Routledge).

Lord, C. (2000), *Legitimacy, Democracy and the EU: When Abstract Questions Become Practical Policy Problems*. Policy paper on Europe, August, number 3.

Maurer, A. (2002), *National Parliaments in the European Architecture: Elements for Establishing a Best Practice Mechanism*, paper delivered to the working group on the Role of National Parliaments (working group IV) of the European Convention, July 10 (Brussels).

Maurer, A. and Wessels, W. (eds) (2001), *National Parliaments on Their Ways to Europe, Losers or Latecomers*, Nomos Verlagsgesellschaft, Baden-Baden.

Pijpers, A. (1999), *The mythe van het democratisch tekort, Een discussiestuk over de Europese politiek*, Netherlands Institute of International Relations Clingendael (The Hague).

Puetter, U. (2004), 'Governing informally: the role of the Eurogroup in EMU and the Stability and Growth Pact', *Journal on European Public Policy* 11:5, 854–70.

Scharpf, F.W. (1999), *Governing in Europe: Effective and Democratic?* (Oxford: Oxford University Press).

Scharpf, F.W. (2003), *Problem-Solving Effectiveness and Democratic Accountability in the EU*. Working Paper, Max Planck Institute for the Study of Societies, number 03/1, February.

Scheller, H.K. (2004), *European Central Bank: History, Role and Function* (Frankfurt am Main: European Central Bank) <http://www.bportugal.pt/euro/emudocs/bce/ECBHistoryRoleFunctions2004.pdf, accessed June 19, 2006.

Sousa, P. (2001), 'Independent and Accountable Central Banks and the European Central Bank', *European Integration online Papers* (EIoP) 5:9, <http://econpapers. repec.org/article/erpeiopxx/default2002.htm accessed June 19, 2006.

Subacchi, P. (2005), 'Reforming Economic Governance in Europe: Exploring the Road to Effective Coordination', *International Affairs* 81:4, 741–55.

Svetlozar, A. (2004), *The 'EU Crises of Legitimacy' Revisited: Concepts, Causes and Possible Consequences for the European Politics and Citizens* (working paper), (University of Westminster).

Van Nispen, F.K.M. and Ringeling, A.B. (2006), 'The Concept of Subsidiarity in a European Context: The End of National Sovereignty?' in Eaton (ed.).

Van Schendelen, R. (2002), *Machiavelli in Brussels: the Art of Lobbying the EU.* (Amsterdam: Amsterdam University Press).

Van Staden, A. (2003), *The Right to Govern: The Democratic Legitimacy of the European Union* (The Hague: Clingendael Institute).

Verdun, A. (1999), 'The Institutional Design of EMU: A Democratic Deficit?', *Journal of Public Policy* 18:2, 107–132.

Wessels, W. and Linsenmann, I. (2002), 'EMU's Impact on National Institutions: Fusion towards a "Gouvernance Économique"or Fragmentation?', in Dyson (ed.).

Wincott, D. (2001), *The White Paper, the Commission and the 'Future of Europe'*, *EUSA Review* 14:4, 1, 3–8, <http://aei.pitt.edu/74/01/GovernanceForum.html, accessed June 19, 2006.

Chapter 13

The OMC and the Quest for Democratic Legitimization: The Case of the European Employment Strategy

Patty Zandstra

The search for new forms of governance has not been limited to the local and national levels. After the rapid expansion of both the number of members, and the areas of activities of the European Community during the second half of the twentieth century, European decision-making stagnated considerably. In addition to deregulation and the codification of the principles of subsidiarity and proportionality, attempts were made to strengthen the role of the European Parliament and to reinvigorate the Community Method. However, in spite of it all, the need to improve governance and policy-making persisted. Especially since in addition to the impact of general processes of growing international interdependency, the EU is increasingly confronted with the consequences of its asymmetrical development (Wendler 2003, 4).[1] Tensions arising from the advanced economic cooperation on the one hand, and the limited mutual coordination in policy areas that have hitherto remained more national on the other hand, have led to an impasse.

Some ten years ago, Scharpf illustrated that measures taken to enhance market integration by eliminating national barriers to EU competition (negative integration) would diminish domestic problem-solving capacity in contiguous policy areas. A development that could obviously become a major threat if not countered by a considerable improvement of European policy-making:

> Europe will certainly fall behind if negative integration paralyses national and subnational problem-solving, while on the European level only unsatisfactory compromises can be reached after long and difficult negotiations. To succeed in the global economy, Europe depends on more effective European policy-making with better democratic legitimization (Scharpf 1996, 39).

But the most obvious solution of transferring autonomy to the European level proved impracticable since member states were particularly reluctant to give up

---

1   Wendler (2003, 6) links the concern about the consequences of the asymmetrical relationship between notably market-creating and market-correcting competences to the work of Leibfried and Pierson on the 'semi-sovereign welfare state'.

control over exactly those politically sensitive areas in which the competency gap is most critical. Against the background of an increasing need to bridge the distance between the different levels of governance in the European Union, diverse 'new forms of governance' have recently attracted significant attention. These methods, differing essentially from the traditional Community Method of 'regulation through legislation', can be seen as 'soft' forms of cooperation based on various combinations of common target development, the pooling of problem-solving experience, devolved decision-making, mutual deliberation, and benchmarking. Expectations are high with regard to these mechanisms, not only because of the alleged positive effect on learning processes and the diffusion of innovative policies, but also because of the perceived suitability for sensitive policy areas that require enhanced coordination but in which the applicability of the Community Method is limited and diversity is high.

One of the most significant new forms of European governance that reflects the main shifts suggested in the introduction of this book is the Open Method of Coordination (OMC). This form of experimental governance explicitly mentioned in the White Paper on European Governance (European Commission 2001), is considered an important tool for overcoming the existing impediments to transnational policy coordination. Although rapidly gaining ground, this new steering paradigm has been debated from a legitimacy perspective.

Like many of the governance practices discussed in the previous chapters, the OMC is characterized by an unleashing of 'governing' from the traditional institutions of representative democracy (Chapter 3 in this volume). This becomes most visible when we look at the role of the only directly elected European institution – the European Parliament –, which, in the case of the OMC, is considerably marginalized. Yet, it would be precipitate to conclude that the method, as such, contravenes the need for more democratic legitimization. After all, traditional mechanisms of democratic legitimization via the electorate are no longer considered to be the only way for the EU to secure legitimacy (Höreth 1998, 5).

Over the past years, the debate on European governance has become increasingly focused on the more participatory dimensions of democracy (De la Porte and Nanz 2004, 268). As such, it is interesting to note that the OMC has even been literally pointed out as an 'important tool to improve transparency and democratic participation' (De la Porte and Nanz 2004, 267).[2] Provided that a wide range of actors is involved in policy formulation, implementation, and evaluation across the various levels of governance, the OMC could be a valuable way to deal with substantial dilemmas related to the supposed European democratic deficit. It could, for example, enhance the representation of diverse perspectives, tap the benefits of local knowledge and hold public officials accountable for carrying out mutually agreed commitments. Some research mentions the OMC with regard to the debate

---

2   Original source: Council of the European Union (2000) 'The on-going experience of the open method of coordination', Presidency Note, No. 9088/00, 13 June.

about the search for ways to substitute traditional principal-agent democracy (Zeitlin 2003).

All in all, the OMC can be seen as an example of a broader shift in governance that is bound to affect the future of European cooperation. It gives an impression of one of the ways in which European and domestic actors are joining efforts to come to grips with 'the double requirement of effectiveness and legitimacy' with which the European Union is increasingly confronted (Eberlein and Kerwer 2001, 122).

In accordance with the theme of the book, we analyze the OMC from a democratic perspective. Hence, the central question that we address in this chapter is the following: 'How does the OMC as a new form of governance relate to the perceived necessity to improve the overall legitimacy of EU policy-making, and to what extent does the application of this method in the case of the EES actually live up to the core requirements to contribute to democratic legitimacy?'

In order to answer this question, we first look at the context in which the OMC was introduced. After shedding some light on the kind of shift in governance we are dealing with, we consider the OMC in terms of both the need for more democratic legitimization on the European level, and the notions on democracy put forward in the theoretical chapter by Bekkers and Edwards (Chapter 3). Combined with references to additional ideas about the sources of democratic legitimization from which the OMC could – in theory – draw, these notions will help to assess the extent to which the method could contribute to more legitimate policy-making in the areas in which it is applied. We pay special attention to determining the key requirements for the optimal functioning of the OMC from a legitimacy perspective. In the analytical section, subsequently, we address the extent to which these prerequisites are met in the case of the EES and assess whether the OMC actually lives up to its expectations. Finally, in our conclusion, we present an overview of the main findings in order to answer the central question formulated in the above.

1. The Development of the OMC: A Shift in European Governance

During the process of the completion of the internal market and monetary unification, the negative consequences of the asymmetrical development of the European Union described in the introduction became especially evident in the field of social and employment policy. Alongside the process of EU economic integration, national governments had given up a substantial part of their capacity to compensate for the negative effects of free market processes, as well as to influence growth and employment in their respective economies.[3] The augmented European interdependency showed 'how much the success of market-correcting policies did in fact depend on the capacity of the territorial state to control its economic boundaries' (Scharpf 1996, 16). Subsequently, as the awareness of the importance of the protection of their competitive position rose, EU member states became more

---

3 Except, of course, for a number of supply-side instruments such as further deregulation, privatization and tax cuts (Scharpf 2002, 46).

prone to the pressures and temptations of policy competition[4] (Scharpf 2002, 46–47; Corbey, 1999, 15; Groenveld 1999, 28–29).

In order to counter these difficulties and to secure both social cohesion and competitiveness, attempts were made to reach a higher level of European coordination in the field of social policy. However, this proved to be easier said than done. Mutual adjustment by means of the traditional Community method turned out to be extremely difficult – if not impossible – due to a severe lack of political support.[5] After all, the fact that the development of social policy had mainly taken place on the national level for a long period of time had resulted in an unmistakable institutional heterogeneity, as well as vast normative differences with regard to the division of responsibilities, the main goals, and the appropriate scope of welfare arrangements. Combined with the notion that social issues are traditionally closely tied to the core-responsibilities of the nation-state (Corbey 1999, 12), and given that member states already felt that their autonomy was being undermined, it is not surprising that there was great hesitance to give up what was left of domestic sovereignty (Borras and Jacobsson 2004, 190).[6]

'National governments, accountable to their national constituencies, […] could not possibly agree on common European solutions for the core functions of the welfare state' (2003, 51–52). Moreover, within the existing institutional framework 'effective solutions could not, at the same time, be uniform and consensual'; requirements both closely associated with the legitimacy of European policy-making (Scharpf 2003, 48–49).

In the search for a stable equilibrium between an effective level of European policy coordination and the maintenance of national autonomy, a combination of elements – partly derived from existing systems of multilateral surveillance and benchmarking – was finally found that would help to reach greater cohesion in the field of social policy, without endangering the variety of systems or putting the principle of subsidiarity at risk.

The resulting method – developed on the basis of the instruments aimed at the coordination of member states' economic policies established in the Maastricht Treaty (art. 98 and 99 TEC) – was first implemented in the light of the European

---

4   For example: 'The completion of the European internal market, reduces the freedom of national governments and unions to raise the regulatory and wage costs of national firms above the level prevailing in competing locations.' (Scharpf 1996, 17)

5   Moreover, the question arose if harmonisation would be desirable at all. For additional information on the arguments for and against the creation of a European social model see Corbey, 1999: 13–16; Bertozzi and Bonoli, 2002).

6   'The logic of EU harmonization by law clashed with the blatant reality of highly diversified welfare state models in Europe, and with a highly diversified understanding of the scope and forms of social protection. There was simply no political support for the further transfer of legal competencies to the EU in these areas' (Borras and Jacobsson, 2004, 190).

Employment Strategy (EES)[7] in 1997.[8] The new method immediately raised high expectations, and the EES-mechanism was placed in a broader perspective at the Lisbon European Council of 2000. Labelled the 'Open Method of Coordination', it was presented as one of the instruments that would facilitate the implementation of the EU's next strategic goal, namely 'to become the most competitive and dynamic knowledge-based economy in the world, capable of sustainable economic growth with more and better jobs and greater social cohesion' (Lisbon European Council 2000: Presidency Conclusions, § 5).

Designed as a 'means of spreading best practice and achieving greater convergence towards the main EU goal', as well as 'to help Member States to progressively develop their own policies, [the OMC] involves:

- Fixing guidelines for the Union combined with specific timetables for achieving the goals which they set in the short, medium and long terms
- Establishing, where appropriate, quantitative and qualitative indicators and benchmarks against the best in the world and tailored to the needs of different Member States and sectors as a means of comparing best practice
- Translating these European guidelines into national and regional policies by setting specific targets and adopting measures, taking into account national and regional differences
- Periodic monitoring, evaluation and peer review organized as mutual learning processes. (Lisbon European Council 2000: Presidency Conclusions, § 37).

Moreover, the Presidency Conclusions of the Lisbon European Council state that the implementation of the open method requires the European Institutions, national, regional, and local governments, as well as non-governmental actors such as the social partners and civil society to join forces in order to uphold a fully decentralized approach that does not contravene the principle of subsidiarity (Lisbon European Council 2000: Presidency Conclusions, § 38).

As a 'non-judiciable iterative policy process', the OMC is considered particularly suitable for areas in which the Treaty basis for Community action is generally weak (De la Porte and Nanz 2004, 267). Accordingly, its application has been extended to several other policy areas such as pensions, social inclusion, and information society. Moreover, the method has been recommended as a valuable instrument in several strategic European reports, for example those of the Employment Taskforce and the Lisbon Strategy High-Level Group chaired by the former Dutch Prime Minister Kok.

Central elements of the OMC, such as collective planning, benchmarking, target development, and multilateral surveillance, are frequently referred to as possible starting points for novel methods of policy-making. Another important aspect of

---

    7   Treaty basis for employment policy established in Amsterdam under art. 123–130 TEC.

    8   The Dutch RMO report explicitly links the introduction of the EES to the need to find a way to deal with structural unemployment within the EMU (2004, 231).

the OMC is its seemingly 'soft' character. Since no transfer of decision-making power takes place, the process of mutual cooperation is almost entirely reliant on a loose form of community-based control or peer pressure (Héritier 2001/14, 5). Furthermore, a strong focus is placed on the pooling of problem-solving experience. By identifying broad common goals and concerns – rather than specific programmes and/or instruments – national officials are enabled to map out a domestic strategy while sharing ideas and experiences with a wide range of partners in both the public and private realm. As such, the OMC combines common action and national autonomy in a way that is in line with the subsidiarity principle (Jacobsson and Vifell 2003, 6–7). The mentioned emphasis on decentralization is another element that is considered to contribute to the innovative character of the OMC. Although the European Commission takes on an important procedural role, the institutional design provides ample opportunity for considerably less hierarchical forms of cooperation than most classical governance mechanisms.

When trying to distinguish processes of open coordination from other mechanisms developed under the broad 'soft law' tradition in the EU, several more specific features draw our attention. First of all, the OMC has a stronger intergovernmental basis. In addition to the Commission, the Council generally has a substantial role in various stages of the coordination process. A related difference can be found in the political monitoring on the highest level. The Council plays a part in both the phase of policy formulation and how the entire process is monitored. Contrary to most traditional forms of soft law, OMC procedures are relatively well-defined. Moreover, the OMC's processes of deliberation and problem-solving are cyclical instead of sequential. This contributes to the possibility of steering on the basis of benchmarking and peer pressure. The systematic linking of issues across policy areas on and between the national and European level is a fourth quality often mentioned that underlines the innovative character of the OMC. In combination with the emphasis the OMC places on an active participation of social actors and the explicit aim of enhancing deliberation and mutual learning processes, this is probably one of its most interesting features (Borras and Jacobsson 2004, 188–189).

From this description of the main elements and distinctive features of the OMC, we can conclude that the method represents at least three of the shifts set forth in Chapter 2 of this book. First, the element of multi-level integration entails a shift that, at first sight, could be characterized as a movement away from the national level and toward the supranational level. This is, however, only partly the case because in the light of the OMC, no actual decision-making power is transferred from the member states to the EU. Moreover, the OMC stresses the importance of devolved decision-making and local implementation where possible. The method displays a second shift from attempts to reach greater cohesion by means of hierarchical steering to more voluntary horizontal coordination. Third, the emphasis placed on the inclusion and active participation of a wide range of stakeholders shows a shift towards interest aggregation, knowledge sharing, and the creation of public support via the participation of representatives of civil society.

After this description of the OMC, and having seen the types of shifts the method embodies, it is time to take a quick look at the actual need to enhance democratic legitimization on the European level. Subsequently, we will see how the OMC relates to this requirement from a theoretical perspective by placing it within the analytical framework on democracy that has been developed in Chapter 3 of this book. Finally, the next section identifies the most essential preconditions for the functioning of the OMC from a deliberative democratic perspective.

2. The OMC: A Way to More Legitimate EU Governance?

Dilemmas of European Democratic Legitimization

In the previous section we focused on the OMC as an example of the shifts in governance taking place on the European level. Once again, we have seen that a new form of governance has been developed from a desire to deal with the alleged crisis of the 'government' paradigm. Just like the new governance practices discussed in the previous chapters, the introduction of the OMC has raised questions with regard to how it relates to the requirement of democratic legitimization. Especially since the method has not been based on the more traditional mechanisms of representative democracy. In this respect, notably the OMC's soft character and the marginalized role of the European Parliament are often criticized. However, considering the increasing attention for other sources of democratic legitimization, as well as the specific focus of the European debate on the need for more legitimate policy-making, the OMC might just as well open up new possibilities.

In the ever-growing literature on the process of Europeanization, the so-called 'democratic deficit' of the EU is a grateful subject. Generally, three main problems are identified. First of all, the EU is confronted with the lack of a European 'demos', as well as with the absence of the intermediary structures traditionally considered essential for the functioning of a democracy (Höreth 1998, 14). These circumstances not only cause legitimacy problems on what Bekkers and Edwards refer to as the input-side, but they also reduce the legitimacy of the majority principle in decision-making processes and form a hindrance to sustainable accountability. As such, throughput and output legitimacy are affected as well.[9]

The second problem can be seen as a consequence of the development of the Union as a political system. Until well into the 1980s, consensual cooperation at the European level was not held to be inconsistent with democratic accountability

---

9 'Democratic legitimacy is, after all, not merely a question of the formal competencies of a parliament. Representation and majority rule will assure legitimacy only in the context of (a) the pre-existing collective identity of a body politic, which may justify the imposition of sacrifices on some members of the community in the interest of the whole; (b) the possibility of public discourse over which sacrifices are in fact to be imposed for *which purposes and on whom; and (c) the political accountability of leaders who are visible to the public and are able to exercise effective power'* (Scharpf, 1996: 26).

on the national level. The legitimacy of the process of European integration was largely based on the utilitarian support of the member states and their parliaments. Scharpf (1999, 25) refers to this as 'borrowed national legitimacy'. However, in the meantime, substantial political autonomy has been transferred to the European level. As a result, the EU crossed the boundary from intergovernmental cooperation to a more direct form of multi-level governance (Höreth 1998, 9). Consequently, indirect legitimization no longer appeared adequate (Jacobsson and Vifell 2003, 2): 'The more power over issues of core state sovereignty and redistribution was transferred to the European level, the more the Community was in need of its own sources of direct popular support' (Höreth 1998, 9).

The third problem has everything to do with the decline of output legitimacy discussed earlier in this chapter. After all, the legitimacy of the EU also depends on its capacity to achieve citizens' goals and solve their problems effectively (Höreth 1998, 6).

The lacking formal requirements for the functioning of a European democracy and the increased need for the EU to provide its own grounds for legitimacy, as well as to enhance the overall problem-solving capacity (Eberlein and Kerwer 2001, 122), gave rise to the notion of justification via the logic of instrumentality or functionality. The central idea behind this logic is that through effective problem solving, the EU will gain the trust of the European peoples (Jacobsson and Vifell 2003, 2). However, the general belief remained that a truly comprehensive approach aimed at increasing supranational legitimacy, should also provide a credible solution – or at least a way to place a counterweight – to the other dimensions of the democratic deficit discussed in the above. Consequently, participatory and deliberative structures gained salience, especially with regard to those areas in which the traditional forms of governance proved defective. Chambers (2003, 308) speaks of a movement from *vote-centric* to *talk-centric* democratic theory; a development that, in the discourse on European Integration, generally refers to a closer involvement of civil society and social partners in the policy-making process, rather than to direct citizen participation (De la Porte and Nanz 2004, 268).

Against this background, the OMC's objective of enhancing both effective problem-solving and responsiveness via the exchange of ideas and information among a wide range of stakeholders on the various levels of governance has led to 'a particular interest in this governance mechanism from the perspective of deliberative democracy' (De la Porte and Nanz 2004, 268).

> The OMC has been seen as a new and flexible instrument able to introduce more democratic parameters in decision-making, and to regain the lost popular confidence in the European integration project by inducing further political action complementing the Community method (Borras and Jacobsson 2004, 187).

Later in this section, we discuss the core preconditions the OMC needs to fulfill in order to contribute to the democratic quality of policy-making in the areas in which it is applied. First, however, we need to discuss how the method relates to different notions of democracy that go beyond the traditional notion of representative democracy. This will enable us to evaluate the democratic significance of the OMC more thoroughly.

Legitimacy and Democracy in Light of the OMC

Bekkers and Edwards quote Easton to indicate that politics is all about 'the binding allocation of values for society as a whole'. Focusing on the OMC, two elements of this citation stand out immediately. First, the OMC is indeed designed to reach a better coordination of the allocation of public goods, resources, and values. Although the guidelines formulated on the European level are not judicially binding, the process cannot be seen as entirely voluntary. The influence exerted by means of benchmarking and peer pressure should not be underestimated, especially considering the fact that the processes of open coordination take place under what has been referred to as the 'shadow of hierarchy'.[10]

Second, decisions are made on behalf of the citizens of the European Union; a community incomparable to the traditional idea of society found on the national and local level. This is especially interesting with regard to a specific element of how Bekkers and Edwards address the concept of legitimacy, namely as 'the expression of a recognition by a community'. In this respect 'a legitimate authority is one, which is recognized as valid or justified by those to whom it applies'. Yet, the above section has clearly shown that the areas in which the OMC is applied are generally characterized by a serious trade-off between the level on which policy-making could be conducted most effectively, and the level that is considered appropriate by the people ultimately affected by the decisions made. That this truly is a serious dilemma from a democratic point of view becomes even more clear when we consider the following thesis by Scharpf:

> '[D]emocratic legitimacy expands if decisions that were previously compelled by external necessity, or taken by non-accountable authority, become the object of authentic and effective collective choice. Conversely, legitimacy is reduced when policy areas that were previously the object of authentic and effective political choices in democratically constituted policies are pre-empted either by newly arising necessities or by coming under the control of politically non-accountable authorities' (1999, 26).

More specifically, in spite of the generally shared support for notions of distributive justice (Habermas 2001, 11; Scharpf 2002, 47), European citizens do not sufficiently experience the sense of belonging necessary for the creation of common social arrangements. At the same time however, social cooperation is held to be an important incentive for the development of a stronger public spirit (Corbey 1999, 16). Once again, *'legitimacy problems are made most visible in the acceptance of tension between general interests and particular interests'* (Bekkers and Edwards, this volume). Since the OMC explicitly seeks to combine common

---

10 For more information on what is understood by 'the shadow of hierarchy' see Börzel and Risse (2004).

action and national autonomy (Borras and Jacobsson 2004, 189), it is not surprising that it is considered a promising attempt to go round this problem and break the cycle. Simone Chambers (2003, 310) refers to the work of Habermas to underline the existential intertwinement of individual rights and popular sovereignty. This notion is especially interesting since it introduces another dimension necessary to reach a more comprehensive understanding of both the multi-layered character of the OMC, and how it is thought to contribute to the democratic legitimization of EU policy-making in sensitive policy areas. In order to secure the rights of the individual in a way that is perceived legitimate from a democratic point of view, close cooperation between the various stakeholders across the different levels of governance is held to be indispensable (Chambers 2003, 310). The participation of a wide range of stakeholders throughout processes of open coordination is equally important in view of the procedural justification of the decisions made during the various stages in the policy process. Bekkers and Edwards stress that legality and mere acceptance of the decisions made cannot be considered a sufficient indicator of democratic legitimacy. According to Daudt: '*Legitimization is* […] *the capacity to convince*' (Bekkers and Edwards, this volume). The fact that the OMC is explicitly based on persuasion rather than coercion (Borras and Jacobsson 2004, 187) could provide a source of both throughput and output legitimacy. The importance of a high-grade exchange of opinions brings us back to the discussion about the models of democracy reflected in OMC. In the above we have already seen that the European discourse relates new forms of governance such as the OMC to notions of deliberative democracy even though no citizens are directly involved. This is contradictory to the definition of deliberative democracy used by Bekkers and Edwards. In their terms the OMC would rather be considered a pluralist arrangement. One should note, however, that, as a 'soft' form of governance, the OMC is not so much about bargaining, but about the reasoned exchange of arguments and problem-solving experience between experts in order to reach better decisions and stimulate mutual learning. Against this background the method could be seen as a deliberative technocratic form of pluralism. The following sub-section will elaborate on the most essential prerequisites for an optimal functioning of the OMC from this perspective.

Promises and Prerequisites…

In the above discussion, we have come across several indications that the OMC could be a credible way of opening up interesting new possibilities for overcoming core hindrances to more legitimate European policy-making, be it in terms of input, throughput, or output legitimacy. The extent to which the method will show to full advantage is, however, largely dependent on both how it is implemented and the context in which it is implemented. A closer examination of the OMC against the background of the discussion of non-traditional forms of democratic legitimization and academic literature on deliberative and pluralist modes of decision-making provides insight into a variety of preconditions that are considered essential for the functioning of deliberative governance practices from a democratic point of view.

Although how these preconditions are formulated and labelled varies, they are by and large related to the stakeholders involved, the room for decision-making, transparency and accountability structures (De la Porte and Nanz 2004; Peters and Pierre 2001). In order to address at least the most central aspects, we have categorized the preconditions as follows:

- Qualitative representation
- Procedural 'openness'
- Transparency
- Public debate

The first two preconditions can be situated on the input side, whereas the two others relate to the throughput side (Bekkers and Edwards, this volume). Some publications in the field add learning and a sufficient level of responsiveness as separate preconditions for the democratic functioning of deliberative governance practices. In light of this chapter, however, these characteristics are considered elements of the democratic functioning of a deliberative governance practice instead of as preconditions. The presence of the prerequisites, i.e. representation, procedural openness, transparency and public debate, largely determine the extent to which these elements can be expected.

Qualitative representation   First of all, the lack of a European 'demos' could – under the right circumstances – be partly compensated by interest aggregation via processes of deliberation. However, as Bekkers and Edwards already indicated with regard to the notion of deliberative democracy: 'Input legitimacy is ... not negligible. At least a qualitative representation of all affected interests should be present in order to prevent that the agenda of the deliberation is biased to specific interests'. Although more direct involvement of a multitude of actors in the various stages of the policy process is often considered of great value – it can induce a sense of commitment and, as such, limit possible forces of opposition – this does not necessarily mean that all actors need to be directly represented in the various stages of the OMC process. Rather, it is important that the diverse perspectives and policy options are seriously taken into account.

Jacobsson and Vifell add that '[the deliberative tradition] focuses on the procedural aspects of policy-making and argues that the process needs to fulfill certain requirements for legitimacy to be obtained. ... It emphasizes that collective choices should be made in a deliberative way, and not only that those choices should have a desirable fit with the preferences of the citizens' (2003, 3). This brings us to the second precondition of procedural openness.

Procedural 'openness'   Both the desired quality of decision-making, and the creation of sustainable public support require sufficient room for deliberation. Neither the issues up for discussion, nor the possible outcomes of the deliberation process should be determined too strictly beforehand (Peters and Pierre 2001, 151–

152). The voluntary character of open coordination processes is in this perspective of great value. Conversely, the method's voluntariness also poses a risk. The absence of binding elements might lead to a too incrementalist approach. In this respect it is of great importance to circumvent a trade-off between the different dimensions of legitimacy. This is, however, easier said than done: 'The most idealistic assumption underlying the concept of democratic experimentalism is not that it works, but that (given some favorable circumstances) it can stand on its own feet and replace markets and hierarchies as forms for co-ordinating action' (Eberlein and Kerwer 2001, 134).

The eventual impact of a deliberative mechanism such as the OMC is largely determined by the extent to which the process induces learning and persuasion. To this purpose, the participants need to be open-minded and willing to listen to each other's ideas and preferences. Chambers (2003) argues that the absence of a sense of mutual commitment could, in this respect, just as well pose a threat to the functioning of talk-centric arrangements.

Transparency   In order for the central mechanisms – such as benchmarking and peer-pressure – to work, both the actors involved in the process and interest groups or citizens outside the arena need to have access to all the relevant information and documents at all stages of the process. This generally implies that: 'The EU institutions and member states must actively communicate about what the EU does in a way that is accessible and comprehensible to the general public.' (De la Porte and Nanz 2004, 272–273). If the condition of transparency is not sufficiently met, there will be serious consequences for the final prerequisite: an active public debate.

Public debate   A broad public debate about the topics under discussion in the deliberative process is of crucial importance for the formation of public opinion, as well as to ensure an adequate level of accountability via the imposition of reputational costs (De la Porte and Nanz 2004, 272–273).

We have discussed the need for improving the legitimacy of European policy-making in previous sections. Moreover, we have seen how the OMC relates to this requirement, as well as to the central ideas surrounding the concept 'legitimacy' put forward in the theoretical chapter. Finally, it became clear that – under the right circumstances – the OMC could, in theory, make a valuable contribution to the overall legitimacy of policy-making in the areas in which it is applied. Yet, the question remains of whether the OMC lives up to its expectations in practice. In order to answer this question, further inquiry is necessary. To this end, we have assessed the functioning of the OMC in the case of the EES. We pay special attention to the extent to which the prerequisites outlined above are met in the different stages of the OMC process.

3. Open Coordination in the Light of the EES: Mere Talk or More?

The Procedural Side of the Matter...

Before examining the EES in the light of the above-mentioned core prerequisites for the optimal functioning of the OMC from a deliberative/pluralist perspective, let us first take a look at how policy coordination is organized in this specific area.

As we have seen above, the EES was introduced to deal with the need to improve the effectiveness of EU policy-making in the employment sector. At the 1994 Essen European Council, attempts had already been made to reach a pan-EU strategy aimed at tackling unemployment by means of long range planning and better coordination, but the effectiveness of the initiatives remained limited due to the lack of a legal basis in the Treaty. Consequently, the Amsterdam summit gave birth to a new chapter in which employment was made a 'matter of common concern'. The starting-point of the new course would be a more coherent, pro-active approach aimed at ways of creating employment instead of dealing with unemployment. Against this background, the EES was introduced. As discussed in the above, a closer interlinkage of the different layers of governance and high-quality deliberation between the various stakeholders are important elements of the open coordination cycle.

The entire process starts with the Commission developing general ideas about the best employment strategy for EU member states to pursue. After a debate with high officials from the member states, the European social partners, and academics, these ideas are further defined in the form of guidelines proposed by the Commission. After the European Economic and Social Council (EESC) and the Committee of the Regions (CoR) have had the chance to comment on the draft guidelines, they are issued by the Council of Ministers of Social Affairs. In addition, a considerable number of indicators – ranging from basic economic figures (e.g. gross domestic product (GDP) growth and unemployment levels) to the availability of career breaks and child care, against which progress can be measured – is issued. These guidelines and indicators form the basis for the National employment Action Plans (NAPs) (Trubek and Mosher 2001; SEO 2002).

The NAPs are formulated by the individual member states in close cooperation with the trade unions and employers' confederations, as well as with local and regional authorities. In addition to a description of how a particular member state is planning to implement the guidelines, the results of the existing domestic employment policy and best practices that might serve as possible examples for other member states are included. Once submitted, the member states present their NAPs in a multilateral meeting with the Employment Committee; the official country examination. In order to rule out any possible misunderstandings, the countries additionally discuss the NAPs with the European Commission in a non-official bilateral meeting (SEO 2002).

The next step in the cycle is the preparation of the so-called Employment Package by the European Commission. The preliminary version of the package, consisting of a draft-version of the Joint Employment Report – including the analysis of the

NAPs, a proposal for country specific Council recommendations and the preliminary guidelines for the next round – is debated by the Employment Committee (EMCO). Next, political 'orientation' takes place in the Council of Ministers, followed by a second round of discussion in the Employment Committee. Finally, the Council of Ministers decides on the final version of the Employment Package. In the event that the European Commission sees room for improvement of a member state's employment policy, additional country specific recommendations can be proposed (SEO 2002, 5). After being discussed twice by the Employment Committee and agreed upon by the Council of Ministers, the recommendations are issued by the latter. The European Council also discusses the Employment Package and the recommendations, but has no decision-making power.

In order to intensify the effect of peer pressure, the European Commission also organizes peer reviews. During these sessions, countries that perform well on a certain issue are invited to give a presentation of their specific policy approach.

In this way, the Luxembourg process upholds a deliberative programme of yearly planning, monitoring, examination and re-adjustment. (Goetschy 2000; Trubek and Mosher 2001, 8; Overdevest 2001; SEO 2002, 5–6; SER 2000, 27–28.)

Legitimization through deliberation? The previous section provided a brief procedural illustration of the EES. Now it is time to examine the extent to which this application of the OMC actually fosters the most essential prerequisites for an optimal functioning of the method from a deliberative point of view.

First of all, it is interesting to see that all of the preconditions discussed above have, in one way or another, been mentioned in official documents on the implementation of the EES. A study of existing empirical research on the functioning and impact of the EES does, however, show that in practice some of the core conditions are not always fully met.

Qualitative representation With regard to the need for inclusiveness and active participation one should note that stakeholder involvement in the light of the EES is generally limited to the official social partners. Declining trade union density has led to critiques about the representativeness of these bodies. Another point of concern is related to the stakeholders' commitment to the broader process. At the time of the introduction of the EES, the call for closer involvement of stakeholders at the European level could not immediately count on great enthusiasm of the European social partners. Over the past years, the European representatives of the trade unions and employers' confederations have become somewhat more positive, but especially UNICE has long remained cautious (De la Porte and Pochet 2003a, 22).

Instead of relying on 'borrowed legitimacy' via the mandate of national parliaments, the OMC tries to gain the trust of key governmental and non-governmental actors on the various levels of governance. How the exchange of perspectives and the pooling of problem-solving experience are organised in the case of the EES differs both between the levels of governance, and from one member state to another (Borras and Jacobsson, 196–200; De la Porte and Pochet 2003a, 6).

On the national level, the implementation of the EES has, in most member states, encouraged coordination and consultation among domestic governmental actors and social partners (Govecor 2004, 11). Although some research shows that the participation of the social partners in the EES has improved since its implementation (De la Porte and Nanz 2004, 283), open coordination does not seem to have changed participatory patterns in a profound way (Radaelli 2003, 38). The degree to which stakeholders can actually influence the national strategy via processes of open coordination has remained limited (De la Porte and Nanz 2004, 238), and is strongly determined by – among other things – national traditions, the type of economy, and the member state's position on European cooperation (Radaelli 2003, 49). As such, the quality of social partner participation is vulnerable to political change (De la Porte and Nanz 2004, 280).

Irrespective of the level of governance, the actors involved in the EES can, by and large, be classified as experts. As such, their participation additionally forms a source of 'technocratic' legitimization (De Jonghe en Bursens 2003, 12). Shared theoretical frames of reference help to reach greater mutual understanding and raise deliberation to a higher level (Jacobsson and Vifell 2003, 19). This is especially important, since, for a large part, the legitimization of deliberative governance practices depends on the quality of the deliberation and the extent to which the ultimate strategy adds to the common good. Moreover, the participation of experts contributes to a crucial sense of commitment and procedural openness (Govecor 2004, 17). On the other hand, the fact that the stakeholders form a so-called 'epistemic community' seriously limits transparency and widens the gap with the general public. We briefly return to the latter later in this section.

Procedural 'openness'   In the field of employment, the non-binding character of open coordination has, as expected, proven to be an important precondition with regard to the participants' willingness to discuss a broad range of issues and options. This is of particular value with regard to the prerequisite of procedural openness.

When we look at the development of primary documents such as the National employment Action Plans (NAPs), the European focus is often hard to discern. The discussion rarely challenges or goes beyond the existing national strategy. In addition, in certain countries the drafting of the NAPs is considered 'homework' assigned by Brussels. Consequently, the NAPs are often largely controlled by the ministerial departments. National parliaments play a minimal role, as a result of which the visibility of the process is limited even further (De la Porte and Pochet 2003b, 8; Govecor 2004, 11). A final critique related to the development of the NAPs is often heard from the side of the social partners, who express their concern about the limited time they are given to prepare a proper response to the draft guidelines and indicators (SEO 2002, 23).

Transparency   The actual impact of the EES is largely dependent on the functioning of its central mechanisms, namely the underlying system of benchmarking and peer pressure. In addition, the overall process is – under the right circumstances

– intensified by its execution under the so-called European 'shadow of hierarchy'. These propelling mechanisms are clearly dependent on a sufficient level of transparency and public debate.

At first sight, it appears that with the implementation of the EES, ample attention has been paid to transparency, consistency and the development of yardsticks for systematic analysis. The benchmark and monitoring procedures allow for common evaluation criteria of policy performance (indicators) and descriptive analyses of policy change (SEO 2002, 28). However, the stages of decision-making and implementation have become blurred to such an extent that the responsibility can no longer be traced back unambiguously to one single source. Moreover, after closer investigation it becomes clear that the double requirement of volunteerism and transparency can cause a serious trade-off. On the one hand, due to the method's soft character, insufficient transparency might leave the EES too incremental to improve legitimacy via the output-side. On the other hand, too much emphasis on the disciplinary part of the system – based on the idea of reputation costs – undoubtedly makes the process less voluntary. As a consequence, benchmarking and peer review in the light of the EES are often hindered by symbolic action (Borras and Jacobsson 2004; SEO 2002, 33), which obstructs the necessary learning process altogether.

Public debate   A related point of discussion has to do with the limited possibilities for individual citizens to hold their representatives accountable. The limited *transparency* and fading of the separate stages in the policy process (Borras and Jacobsson 2004, 199), as well as the diffuse division of responsibilities and the absence of traditional intermediary structures stand in the way of an active public debate about the policy outcomes. In spite of this, some authors are very positive about the 'horizontal' accountability that could be stimulated by benchmarking and peer pressure, but this too will only work when all those concerned are actively involved and feel committed to the broader success of the process. In some member states, the EES provided an incentive to the national discussion on crucial issues in the field of employment. (SEO 2002, 28). However, the process of open coordination in the case of the EES is generally perceived as technocratic and relatively closed to both the broader public and other interested parties, such as executive agencies and actors at the sub-national levels (Govecor 2004, 79). Attempts to enhance the general awareness of the OMC and EES related topics have not been successful. The creation of a website on the EES has significantly improved the access to information and key documents pertaining to the development of European employment policy. However, the availability of information is not a sufficient condition to stimulate an active public debate (De la Porte and Pochet 2003a, 5), especially considering the declining media coverage (Radaelli 2003, 49; Meyer 2003, 143–144). As a result of the limited transparency, the actors involved are rarely called to account for their decisions, nor for the final policy outcomes (De la Porte and Nanz 2004, 277; Meyer 2003, 143). This, in its turn, links back to the first mentioned prerequisite of qualitative representation.

All in all, it becomes clear that – even though the most important prerequisites were taken into account during the implementation of the EES – practice is considerably more unruly. Certain preconditions are difficult to unite; others are just as dependent on certain intermediary structures as traditional mechanisms based on the idea of representative democracy. Such hindrances might, however, be overcome as time goes by. The functioning of the EES is periodically evaluated. Recent attempts to interlink the diverse applications of the OMC in various policy areas might improve the level of interdepartmental coordination. Moreover, additional attention is being paid to enhancing transparency and mutual learning (European Commission 2004, 5). Although it certainly is not a flawless alternative, the OMC could turn out to be a valuable means to complement more traditional ways of acquiring democratic legitimization. Striking the right balance will, however, continue to be very important.

4. Conclusion

In the introduction the following central question was suggested: 'How does the OMC as a new form of governance relate to the perceived necessity to improve the overall legitimacy of EU policy-making, and to what extent does the application of this method in the case of the EES actually live up to the core requirements to contribute to democratic legitimacy?'

The four key points addressed in all of the chapters of this book – namely the dominant objective of the new form of governance under investigation, the type of 'shift' it embodies, the legitimacy problems involved, and the model of democracy to be considered – have helped us answer the first part of this question.

The dominant objective of the OMC was to enhance the overall effectiveness of problem solving in sensitive policy areas. In an attempt to improve output legitimacy, the method entailed a shift from public government to deliberation among representatives of civil society. In addition, attempts to reach greater cohesion through hierarchical steering were replaced by horizontal coordination. Third, the OMC embodies a combined shift from national control to supra-national cooperation and devolved decision-making, which could be referred to as a form of multi-level governance.

Closer analysis of the legitimacy problems of EU governance from a deliberative/ pluralist perspective subsequently showed that any evaluation based on a strict observation of the formal requirements for democratic policy making would not do justice to the potential of the OMC. In addition to a partial solution to serious deficiencies on the output-side, the method could provide a way of dealing with the limited input and throughput legitimacy resulting from the lack of a European 'demos' and the limited potential of the intermediary structures.

Focusing on the basic democratic values identified by Bekkers and Edwards, the OMC is expected to stimulate legitimacy via the protection of popular sovereignty, free deliberation, increased responsiveness, and possibly even through horizontal accountability. In spite of the fact that direct participation of citizens is not to be expected, a combination of devolved decision-making and learning amongst a wide range of stakeholders could provide the checks and balances needed for the protection of weak interests and minority rights, among other things. However, in order for any of this to happen, applications of the OMC need to live up to a number of preconditions. In section 2, we identified four core prerequisites, respectively: qualitative representation, procedural 'openness', transparency, and an active public debate.

While the OMC may seem to be a panacea for the democratic flaws of EU policy-making in sensitive policy areas in theory, a closer examination of how the method is implemented in the case of the EES presents a somewhat different image. Although the major prerequisites for the effective functioning of this application of the OMC have been taken into account with regard to how the method is organized, certain preconditions are difficult to unite. Furthermore, in order to uphold other prerequisites the EES is just as dependent on principle intermediary structures as more traditional mechanisms based on the idea of representative democracy. Certain hindrances might, however, be overcome as growing pains are dealt with over time.

This chapter is meant to provide an illustration of a non-negligible shift in European governance. Of course extensive empirical research into the various policy areas in which the OMC has been, and is being implemented is needed to underpin this preliminary analysis of the OMC's potential to contribute to more democratic legitimization on the European level.

References

Bertozzi and Bonoli (2002), *Europeanisation and the Convergence of National Social and Employment Policies; What can the Open Method of Coordination achieve?* paper presented at the ECPR Joint-session, 22–27 March (Turin).

Börzel, T. and Risse, T. (2004), 'Public–Private Partnerships: Effective and Legitimate Tools of International Governance?' in Grande and Pauly (eds).

Borras, S. and Jacobsson, K. (2004), 'The open method of co-ordination and new governance patterns in the EU', *Journal of European Public Policy* 11:2, 185–208.

Casey, B.H. (2004), 'The Open Method of Coordination: how open is it?', Paper prepared for the International Conference on Democratic Network Governance 21–22 October (University of Roskilde).

Chambers, S. (2003), 'Deliberative Democratic Theory', *Annual Review of Political Science* 6, 307–326.

Corbey, D. (1999), 'Sociaal Europa: een inleiding', in C. Aarsen (ed.) *Sociaal Europa?* (Amsterdam: Instituut voor Publiek en Politiek), pp. 9–21.

De Jonghe, K. and Bursens, P. (2003), *The Quest for more Legitimacy in the European Union as a Multilevel Political System: a Conceptual Framework* Paper prepared for the ECPR Congress, 28 March – 2 April (Edinburgh).

Eberlein, D. and Kerwer, B. (2004), 'New Governance in the European Union: A Theoretical Perspective', *Journal of Common Market Studies* 42:1, 121–42.

European Commission (2001), *European Governance, A White Paper* (COM) .

European Commission (2004), Communication on Strengthening the implementation of the European Employment Strategy European Council (2000), *Presidency Conclusions* 23–24 March (Lisbon: European Council). <http://europa.eu.int/comm/employment_social/employment_strategy/key_en.htm

Grande, E. and Pauly, L.W. (eds) (2004), *Complex Sovereignty: On the Reconstitution of Political Authority in the 21ˢᵗ Century* (Toronto: University of Toronto Press).

Govecor (2004), *Self-Coordination on the National-Level: Towards a Collective 'Gouvernement Économique'* Final National Reports, www.govecor.org

Groenveld, K. (1999), 'Europa en de sociale zekerheid', in C. Aarsen (ed.), *Sociaal Europa?* (Amsterdam: Instituut voor Publiek en Politiek), pp. 22–33.

Habermas, J. (1996), *Between Facts and Norms: Contributions to a Discourse Theory of Law and Democracy*, (Cambridge: Massachusetts: The MIT Press).

Habermas, J. (2001), 'Why Europe Needs a Constitution', *New Left Review* 11, September/October, 5–26.

Höreth. M. (1998), *The Trilemma of Legitimacy, Multilevel Governance in the EU and the Problem of Democracy*, Discussion Paper C11/1998, Zentrum für Europäische Integrationsforschung (Bonn: Rheinische Friedrich Wilhelms-Universität).

Jacobsson, K. and Vifell, Å. (2003), 'Integration by Deliberation? On the Role of Committees in the Open Method of Coordination', Paper prepared for the workshop on *The Forging of Deliberative Supranationalism in the EU*, 7–8 February (Florence).

Marks, G., Scharpf, F.W., Schmitter, P. and Streeck, W. (eds) (1996), *Governance in the European Union* (London: Sage)

Overdevest, C. (2002), *The OMC, New Governance, and Learning; Towards a Research Agenda* The New Governance Project (University of Wisconsin-Madison).

Pierre, J. and Peters, B.G. (2000), *Governance, Politics and the State* (Houndmills: Macmillan).

Porte, C. de la, and Pochet, P. (2003a), *The OMC intertwined with the debates on governance, democracy and social Europe*, Research report prepared for Minister Frank Vandenbroucke, Minister for Social Affairs and Pensions, Research on the Open Method of Co-ordination and European Integration.

Porte, C. de la, and Pochet, P. (2003b), 'The Participative Dimension of the OM', paper prepared for the conference *Opening the Open Method of Coordination*, 4–5 July, (Florence: European University Institute).

Porte, C. de la, and Nanz, P. (2004), 'OMC – a deliberative-democratic mode of governance? The cases of employment and pensions', *Jounal of European Public Policy* 11:2, 267–88.

Radaelli, C. (2003), *The Open Method of Coordination: A New Governance Architecture for the European Union?* Report for the Swedish Institute of European Policy Studies (SIEPS), 20 February (Stockholm).

RMO (Raad voor Maatschappelijke Ontwikkeling) (2004), *Europa als sociale ruimte. Open coördinatie van sociaal beleid in de Europese Unie*, Advies 28, April (The Hague).

Scharpf, F.W. (1996), 'Negative and Positive Integration in the Political Economy of European Welfare Sates', in: Marks et al. (eds.), pp. 15–39.

Scharpf, F.W. (1998), *Governing in Europe: Effective and Democratic?* (New York: Oxford University Press).

Scharpf, F.W. (2002), 'Legitimate diversity: the new challenge of European integration', *Cahiers Européens de Science Po* 1: 2002.

SEO (2002), *Dutch experiences with the European employment strategy*, Research in commission of the Ministry of Social Affairs and Employment (Amsterdam).

Trubek, D.M. and Mosher, J. (2001), *New Governance, EU Employment Policy and the Social Model* (European Union Center: University of Wisconsin-Madison).

Wendler, F. (2003), 'Achieving democratic legitimacy through deliberative governance? The case of EU Social Policy', Paper presented at the 2nd ECPR Conference, 18–21 September (Marburg).

Zeitlin, J. (2002), *The Open Method of Coordination and the Future of the European Employment Strategy* Presentation prepared for the mini-hearing of the Employment and Social Affairs Committee of the European Parliament on the first five year evaluation of the Employment Guidelines, 8 July.

Zeitlin, J. (2003), *Opening the Omc: Employment and Social Inclusion* Presentation prepared for the Joint Saltsa, Observatoire Social Européen, University of Madison-Wisconsin Workshop, European University Institute, 4–5 July (Florence).

Chapter 14

Supranational Governance and the Challenge of Democracy: The IMF and the World Bank

Geske Dijkstra

The aim of this chapter is to assess the democratic deficit of two institutions that represent supranational governance, namely the International Monetary Fund (IMF) and the World Bank. The democratic legitimacy and accountability of these institutions has been questioned, as evidenced by the protests and riots that have accompanied annual meetings in recent years, and also by a debate in the literature on reforms of the governance of these institutions (Dahl 1999; Stiglitz 2003; Verweij and Josling 2003; Rapkin and Strand 2005). On the other hand, given the attention paid to these institutions in recent reports calling for more development aid for Africa and for achieving the Millennium Development Goals (Commission for Africa 2005; UN Millennium Project directed by Jeffrey D. Sachs 2005), the positions of the Word Bank and the IMF in the development community seem firmly established.

Democratic control of supra-national institutions is always a difficult issue. First, they are governed by *delegates* of member governments, which means that democratic representation and accountability can be indirect at most (Dahl 1999). And second, for reasons related to public choice theory, staffs of international bureaucracies tend to have even more power vis-à-vis politicians who are supposed to control them than domestic bureaucracies have (Frey 1991).

This paper argues that in the case of the IMF and the World Bank, this 'natural' democratic deficit of supra-national institutions has increased over time. In fact, both institutions have expanded in objectives and scope of activities. In contrast, decision making within IMF and World Bank is still largely as it was when the two institutions were established, implying that Central Bank Presidents and Finance ministers (in the case of the World Bank: Finance ministers and development cooperation ministers) of member countries make decision, while each countries' voting power is determined by the size of the countries' economies. Given the changes in mandate and tasks of the two institutions, this means that in fact, a majority of rich countries determines policies that mainly affect poor and middle income countries.

The chapter will show that the original democratic deficit was mainly a problem of input legitimacy, but that the changes and expansions of tasks have added substantial problems of throughput and output legitimacy, while also changing the nature of the input legitimacy problem. In response to growing criticisms, both institutions have taken measures to improve their transparency and accountability since the mid-1990s. The greater transparency is evident from the extensive websites of both institutions. Examples of increased accountability include the establishment of the World Bank Inspection Panel in 1995, and the creation of an Independent Evaluation Office (IEO) in the IMF.[1] Both institutions are also engaging more in public debate about their policies, including debates with international Non Governmental Organizations.

At the same time, while many proposals have been suggested to further increase legitimacy and accountability of these institutions, they have not been implemented (as of June 2006). While these proposals often involve fundamental changes in governance of the IMF and the World Bank, they tend to overlook the relationship between the nature of the democratic deficit of these institutions, and the practice of ever expanding tasks and responsibilities. I argue that this relationship is important and must be taken into account when assessing the possible effects of proposed changes in governance.

This chapter is structured as follows. In the next section, I describe the origins and aims of the two international financial institutions, as well as their evolution over time. In Section 2, I assess the democratic deficit and analyze the particular problems of legitimacy and accountability. In Section 3, I examine the consequences of the increase in tasks and responsibilities of the institutions, and the increasing legitimacy problems. In Section 4, I examine the changes implemented and their effects on reducing the democratic deficits, and the more radical proposals for improving input and output legitimacy that have not been implemented yet. Section 5 contains my conclusions.

1. Origins and Evolution of the IMF and the World Bank

Both the World Bank and the International Monetary Fund (IMF) were established in 1944 during a conference in Bretton Woods, USA. For this reason, they are also called Bretton Woods Institutions (BWI). The principle aim of the IMF was to secure the flow of international payments by guaranteeing exchange rate stability. This was motivated by the disastrous experience of the 1930s, when all countries sought their way out of the crisis by putting up trade barriers and by devaluing their exchange rates. In the end, this 'beggar-thy-neighbor policy' led to a negative spiral in the world economy and worsened the economic situation of all countries.

The International Bank for Reconstruction and Development (IBRD, or World Bank) was meant to be an international bank that would provide financing for the reconstruction of Europe after the Second World War. When the US government announced the Marshall Plan, this financing was no longer necessary and the Bank began financing investment projects in other parts of the world, mainly developing countries. The International Finance Corporation (IFC) that lends to the private sector

---

1   The World Bank already had an independent evaluation department, the Operations Evaluation Department (OED), recently renamed the Independent Evaluation Group (IEG).

of developing countries, and the International Development Association (IDA) that provides credit at very soft terms to the poorest developing countries also belong to the 'World Bank Group'.

The IMF and the World Bank were originally established by 39 countries, but membership has gradually expanded and by 2006, it includes 184 countries. Countries must be a member of the IMF before they can become a member of the World Bank Group. Members of the IMF must pay a contribution, called 'quota', which is based on the strength of a country's economy (Gross Domestic Product) and its share in world trade (exports and imports of goods and services). Members must pay 25 per cent of their quota in internationally usable currencies or Special Drawing Rights (SDRs),[2] and they may pay the other 75 per cent in their own currency.

Countries may draw on the IMF resources an amount of up to 25 per cent of their quota without any policy conditions. This is the so-called reserve tranche, but this borrowing seldom occurs. If they want to borrow more, the IMF sets policy conditions. Originally, countries could borrow up to 100 per cent of their quota. This was officially expanded to 300 per cent in the 1970s but in some recent crises – for example, Mexico in 1995 (Bakker 1996) – countries have been able to borrow up to 600 per cent of their quota. The policy conditions of the IMF are meant to warrant a good use of the IMF´s resources so that the money can be paid back. They are also meant to secure an orderly adjustment process with limited welfare losses, both for the country in need and the world at large (Guitian 1995).

In 1944, at the same Bretton Woods conference, a system of fixed exchange rates was set up with all currencies pegged to the US dollar. The dollar, in turn, would be exchangeable for gold at a fixed price. Devaluations or revaluations of exchange rates could only take place in situations of extreme balance of payments disequilibria and in consultation with the IMF. According to the Principles of Agreement by which the IMF was established, the IMF had three objectives (Riesenhuber 2001):

- Surveillance of the world financial system
- Provision of temporary balance of payments support
- Maintenance of a system of international trade and payments.

According to the original idea, the IMF would come into action in situations of both balance of payments deficits and balance of payments surpluses. Both deficit and surplus countries could be called upon to adjust so that equilibrium could be maintained. In practice, the IMF has only been active for deficit countries. The most important facility by which the IMF has provided this temporary balance of payments support is the Stand-By Arrangement. This can be given for 18 months and the annual interest rate is around 5 per cent.

In the years after the Second World War, most countries' currencies could not yet be purchased and sold on a free market, so international trade was still limited.

---

2   This is a currency created by the IMF in the 1970s. Its value is based on a basket of the five major currencies in the world.

This changed in 1961 when most European currencies became fully convertible for current account operations. The system as designed in the Bretton Woods conference became operational. Although capital movements were still not allowed, speculative capital flows came into being and gradually increased. They were based on expectations that exchange rates could not always be maintained and that the IMF would not be able to supply sufficient amounts to avoid changes in exchange rates. Speculative flows further increased as a result of the huge budget and balance of payments deficits incurred by the United States as a result of the Vietnam war in the 1960s. In 1971, several currencies began to float and the system finally collapsed when the US government announced that it would no longer maintain a fixed gold price in US dollars. This decision implied that not only the dollar, but all other currencies would begin to float.

For the IMF, this development meant that it lost most of its functions. There was no longer a need to provide short-term balance of payments assistance in order to maintain stable exchange rates or to achieve orderly and limited devaluations. Exchange rates would now adjust automatically in response to changing supply and demand for a currency. The surveillance function also became less important. As countries began to rely on private capital flows, their macroeconomic policies would be assessed by international private financial agents.

This could have led to the end of the institution, but the reality was different. Two years before the system of fixed exchange rates collapsed, it was already evident that world trade and capital movements were increasing so much that it was feared that there would not be sufficient international reserves available. The Board of Governors of the IMF therefore decided to create the Special Drawing Rights. However, the amount of SDRs was limited since decisions on the number of SDRs to be created depended on a 85 per cent majority vote and the rich countries feared that too much world liquidity would create inflation (Riesenhuber 2001).

In 1972 the Board of Governors decided to set up a Committee of 20 members in order to elaborate proposals for the reform of the international monetary system (Riesenhuber 2001). This Committee produced a report two years later, but there was no substantive proposal for reform. In contrast to the situation in 1944, countries had very different views on and objectives for international monetary policies. In addition, the world economic environment changed rapidly. In 1973 the oil crisis broke out, world inflation rose, and private flows of trade and capital continued to increase rapidly, thereby weakening the influence of governments or central banks on international monetary developments. Among the limited reform proposals that were also adopted were the creation of an Interim Committee of 24 countries represented by their central banks or finance ministries that would meet every six months, and the strengthening of the IMF's role in surveillance of national monetary policies. From that point on, the IMF would make annual or biannual assessments of monetary and macroeconomic policies of all members – not only the members in financial trouble.

Since there was no common agreement on abolishing the IMF or on a substantial reform of the institution, the staff managed to take advantage of changing world circumstances in expanding its tasks. The oil crisis produced large balance of payments deficits in developed countries, and many applied for support to the IMF. Since these problems could not be solved in the 18 months of the Stand-By Arrangement, the IMF created the Extended Fund Facility. This provided money for three years in order to solve more structural balance of payments problems. The debt crisis of the 1980s resulted in more countries approaching the IMF. Since the amount of support that the IMF could provide was too limited to solve the payment crisis in itself, the IMF began to negotiate with the banks on new finance and on restructuring debt payments while at the same time negotiating macroeconomic policies and structural reforms in the debtor countries. A program with the IMF in which a country promised to carry out policy reforms therefore became an official condition for debt rescheduling and forgiveness. Furthermore, an agreement with the IMF also became condition for official aid donors who wish to provide freely spendable funds, for example in the form of balance of payment support or budget support.

In 1986 a new IMF facility was created for the poorest countries with balance of payments and debt problems, the Structural Adjustment Facility (SAF). The IMF and World Bank began to work together in designing a program of structural reforms. In 1987, this facility was expanded with the Enhanced Structural Adjustment Facility (ESAF). An ESAF program is, in principle, for three years and countries can borrow up to 255 per cent of their quota (Bakker 1996). In 1999, the name of ESAF was changed into PRGF, Poverty Reduction and Growth Facility. Contrary to other IMF facilities, SAF, ESAF and PRGF carry very low interest rates (0.5 per cent). They are only available for countries that qualify for IDA credits, implying that annual GDP per capita must be below $895.[3]

In the aftermath of the fall of the Berlin wall and the collapse of the Soviet Union, the IMF again expanded its tasks. It was considered beneficial for the IMF to provide money and advice to these countries on how to reform their economies into market economies. The Systemic Transformation Facility was created, under which these transition countries could borrow up to 50 per cent of their quota (Bakker 1996).

The expansion of tasks and activities of the World Bank was of a slightly different nature. Over time, the amount of loans and credits by both the IBRD and IDA expanded enormously. However, in the early 1980s there was also a qualitative change. Until then, the Bank had provided loans for projects, often large infrastructural works but also projects for social infrastructure. With the developing country debt crisis, the Bank began to move into conditional lending. There was an increasing awareness that macroeconomic policies mattered for the success of individual projects. In addition, countries with debt problems needed large amounts of – freely spendable – balance of payments support with which to feed their populations and provide inputs for their production capacity. At the same time, absorption capacity for yet other investment projects was limited (Toye 1994). From then on, the Bank began to provide balance of payment support in the form of Structural Adjustment Loans

---

3   This is the amount in early 2006, based on 2005 GDP per capita.

or Sectoral Structural Adjustment Loans, on the condition that the country would carry out structural policy reforms. The Bank began to work together with the IMF on the formulation of these policy conditions. While the IMF, in principle, focused on fiscal and monetary policies that addressed the demand side of the economy, the Bank focused more on the structural policies that addressed the supply side of the economy. An IMF agreement was always a condition for the structural adjustment loans of the Bank. In 1999, the name of these programs was changed into Poverty Reduction Support Credits (PRSCs).

In the course of time, the nature of the policy conditions has changed as well. While structural measures like liberalization of domestic prices, abolition of subsidies, liberalization of foreign trade, privatization of state enterprise including public utilities, and financial liberalization and banking reform are still on the list (if applicable – that is, still due), other conditions have been added. There is increasing attention for governance-related conditionality, especially the more technical aspects of it, for example related to public finance management or fighting corruption. In addition, countries are expected to combat poverty. In order to qualify for the Heavily Indebted Poor Country (HIPC) initiative that was set up to solve the debt problems of the poorest countries, countries must write Poverty Reduction Strategy Papers and show that they implement these strategies.

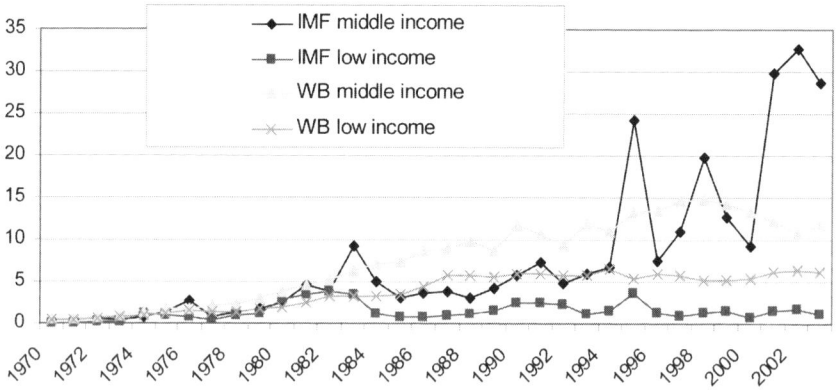

Figure 14.1 Gross disbursements of IMF and World Bank 1970–2003, to middle income and to low income countries, in US$ Billions
Source: World Bank, Global Development Finance 2005

In sum, both the IMF and the World Bank have vastly expanded their scale of activities in the course of time. Figure 1 shows that the amount of disbursements has steadily increased, with peaks for the IMF in the mid-1970s (oil crisis), in the early 1980s (debt crisis) and again in the 1990s and in 2001–2 (Mexico in 1995, then Asian crisis, and then large packages for middle income countries Brazil, Argentina,

Russia and Turkey). The scope of the policy conditions has also expanded far beyond the resolution of temporary balance of payments problems. They now include many structural policy reforms. While this had already been occurring for a long time with respect to low-income countries and countries in transition, it attracted broad attention and critique when the IMF also began to prescribe similar conditions to East Asian countries during the 1998 crisis (Wade 1998; Stiglitz 2002). The IMF was much criticized for the scope of its policy conditions, especially since these countries had experienced high growth for a long time and – according to many observers – only experienced a temporary loss of confidence. In practice, the objective of IMF programs has expanded far beyond fixing short-term monetary disequilibria such as inflation or a balance of payments deficit. As is also evident from the name of the facility recently created for poor countries (PRGF), economic growth has become the central objective of the IMF.

Another significant change is that since 1976, when Italy and the United Kingdom were the last developed countries to borrow from the IMF, no rich countries have drawn upon the IMF resources. All IMF finance has been directed to developing countries and countries in transition. This means that the equilibrium within the IMF has been distorted. It is no longer an institution in which all contributors may also be beneficiaries.

2. The Democratic Deficit

International institutions such as the IMF and the World Bank make decisions on behalf of the participating countries and their populations in order to promote the public good for which they have been created: stability of the international monetary system and financing development in less developed countries. The question is to what extent their decision making power and their decisions are legitimate. To what extent are these institutions accountable to governments of participating countries and ultimately to their populations?

In this book a distinction has been made between input, throughput and output legitimacy. Table 14.1 visualizes the distinction between these three. With respect to the IMF and the World Bank, there are legitimacy problems of all three kinds. In this section I first describe the governance structure of the two institutions and the accompanying, almost inherent, legitimacy problems as they existed when these organizations were created. Subsequently, the changes in the nature of the legitimacy problems will be analyzed. These changes are related to the alterations and expansions in the tasks of these institutions as described in the previous section.

Table 14.1   Forms of legitimacy

Input	Throughput	Output
Participants in decision-making	Rules and procedures for decision-making	Decisions

The governance structure of IMF and World Bank is broadly similar. The highest decision making body in the IMF is the Board of Governors, consisting of the Central Bank presidents or finance ministers of the member countries. This Board meets once a year. In practice, most power has been delegated to the Executive Board which meets several times a week. The chair of the Executive Board is the Managing Director of the IMF, who is also head of the staff. There are 24 Executive Directors, and in total they represent all member countries. The eight largest countries in terms of GDP and participation in world trade have their own Executive Director,[4] all other countries have formed constituencies: groups of countries that elect an Executive Director and an alternate. In practice, executive directors have an office in the IMF with a small staff originating from the member countries of the constituency. The Executive Board decides on the IMF facilities to be granted. These decisions are prepared by the Managing Director and his staff.

The World Bank also has a Board of Governors, but here the countries are represented by their finance ministers or ministers of development cooperation. The Executive Board also has 24 Directors elected by the same constituencies as in the IMF. The chair of the EB is the President of the World Bank who is head of the staff. The Managing Director of the IMF has always been from European origin, while the Bank's President has always been a US national. Staff of both institutions has expanded dramatically in the course of time. By 2006, the IMF has about 5,000 employees and the World Bank over 10,000, including more than 3,000 in offices in developing countries.

Decision making power within both institutions is based on membership contributions, so it is a system of weighted voting power. Contributions to the IMF are called quota. The quota allocation is decided upon by the Board of Governors and is based on the strength of the country's economy (GDP) and its participation in world trade (exports and imports of goods and services). Each member has 250 'basic votes', plus one vote for each 100,000 SDRs subscribed as quota. Many decisions of the IMF, however, including changes in the original articles of agreement but also the amount of quota for each member, have to be made with a qualified majority of 85 per cent of the votes. Since the US has almost 18 per cent of the total votes, the US has effective veto power.

A first general problem is that accountability of decision makers in these international institutions is at best indirect (Dahl 1999). There is no direct voting for the governing boards of these institutions. Governments send their representatives to make these decisions. To the extent that member countries have some kind of democratic system in which governments are elected by populations, populations can only indirectly, through parliaments, influence their representatives at international institutions. In practice, the policies of representatives in the Boards of governors and in the Executive Boards are prepared by staff in the ministries of finance, foreign affairs or development cooperation, and in Central Banks. Parliaments can discuss policies and actions of their countries' representatives in the Board of Governors

---

4   USA, UK, France, Germany, Japan, China, Russia and Saudi Arabia

(to the extent they are ministers), but cannot discuss directly with the Executive Directors. This means there is a lengthy accountability chain between decision makers and populations (Stiglitz 2003).

A second problem is the limited control of the member governments via their representatives in Board of Governors and Executive Board over the staff. The Board of Governors only meets once a year.[5] In these meetings the important policy decisions are made, such as quota revisions or decisions on new facilities. Daily operations of the institutions must be approved by the Executive Boards. Members of the Executive Board are employed full-time. In principle, this guarantees extensive oversight on behalf of member governments of the staff's actions.

However, in practice staff has substantial power vis-à-vis both Governors and Executive Directors. Politicians in general tend to have limited power over bureaucracies (Niskanen 1971). Staffs of government bureaucracies have a monopoly position with respect to politicians who control them. As a result of asymmetric information, bureaucracies will exaggerate the needs for their services as well as the resources needed to supply these services. This leads to a weakening in both allocative efficiency (the government supplying too many goods and services) and in X-efficiency (too large budgets for the amount of services supplied (Leibenstein 1966)). In a national context, however, politicians (ministers) also have a monopoly position with respect to 'their' bureaucracies and they have the power and the incentive to check their growth.

In international institutions both the *opportunity* and the *incentives* to control bureaucracies are more restricted (Frey 1991; Vaubel 1991). First, the possibility to monitor and control is weakened because it is more difficult to define and measure the output of international institutions as compared to the output of national bureaucracies. There are often conflicting views on the main objectives, and views on necessary activities and costs to meet these objectives are even more diffuse. This increases the information asymmetry between staff and controlling bodies. Second, the incentives to control are weakened because each member country only pays a small share of the costs of the organization. There is no incentive to be harsh to the organization since this would just mean a nasty conflict with other member countries, while the benefits for each individual member are small.

As a result of the lack of clarity of official objectives and desired outputs and their measurement, staffs of international institutions have only weak incentives to work for the official goals of the organizations. They tend to enhance their own goals and the goals of the bureaucracy itself. This means they are always trying to increase their tasks, activities and budgets. In the absence of measurable output, the organization also tends to confuse means with ends, implying that there will be a high degree of red tape and adherence to formal working procedures. For all these reasons, bureaucracies of international organizations tend to grow more than is warranted by increases in need, and they tend to have a high degree of X-inefficiency.

---

5   In practice they meet bi–annually; the other meeting is formally a meeting of the "Interim Committee" established in 1974.

This application of public choice theory on international organizations has also been confirmed empirically for the cases of the World Bank and the IMF. Vaubel (1996) found that personnel costs of the IMF and the World Bank increased faster than staffs in other institutions. In principle, personnel budgets can be expected to expand in proportion with increases in needs, in labor costs and in increases in X-inefficiency. For the IMF, need was operationalized by the size of current account deficits and by losses in foreign reserves, and for the World Bank by the number of new loans. As a measure for X-efficiency, the quota share of the ten largest countries was taken. It was assumed that the higher the share of the ten largest countries, the more incentive they will have to control the efficiency of the institutions. As the number of member countries expanded in the course of time, the quota share of the ten largest countries has shrunk over time. It turns out that the quota share is the only significant factor in a regression to explain the increase in staff budgets for the IMF. For the World Bank, labor costs also proved to be significant (Vaubel 1996). The variables used to measure need did not influence staff budgets at all. This means that the incentive to control is indeed a factor that influences the internal efficiency.

Vaubel (1996) also found that both institutions engage in 'hurry-up lending'. IMF lending significantly increases in the last year before the decision on quota revisions, which is done once in every five years. In the case of the World Bank, a similar development was visible with respect to the decisions on the IDA Replenishment Fund. These decisions are usually made once in the three years. In the year before that the volume of IDA credits always increases significantly (Vaubel 1996).

So far we have shown that the staff of both institutions is relatively powerful as opposed to the representatives of the member governments. This tends to reduce accountability in general, so implying an input legitimacy problem. It also tends to cause an expansion of tasks and activities of these institutions – more than is justified by objective needs.

In the case of the Executive Directors who, with their staffs, are supposed to act on behalf of participating governments, we can even question the extent to which they truly represent these governments. Their offices are located in the premises of the two institutions, where they occupy the highest and most luxurious floors, and their salaries are also paid by the two institutions. In fact, one can assume that their interests are very closely related to those of the staff: they also have an interest in expanding tasks and budgets, as they will directly benefit from that (Riesenhuber 2001). To some extent, this also holds for the relevant staff in the ministries and Central Banks within the member countries themselves. Their jobs, status and prestige are also related to the importance assigned to the international institutions, which they are supposed to control and influence. The more tasks and influence these institutions have, the better it is for those who prepare policies for them. This implies that the drive toward the expansion of tasks, budgets and activities of the two institutions is very strong and there are hardly any checks on the system.

Decision making rules and procedures within the institutions add to the legitimacy problem. Staff prepares the proposals for country programs in the case of the IMF, and for overall country lending strategies and concrete lending activities in the case of the World Bank. Internal disagreements among staff are resolved before they are brought to the Board (Woods 2001). Board meetings are secret, but it is generally known that voting hardly ever occurs. Although Executive Directors do make remarks and comments, the Executive Board usually 'rubber stamps' the decisions of the staff.

Similarly, IMF programs and World Bank loan proposals are only brought to the Boards once there is agreement between staff and recipient country governments. Staffs negotiate with governments of recipient countries on the policy conditions, but if the recipient country is in crisis or very poor, it is heavily dependent on an IMF program or a World Bank loan, and its position is weak. The substance of the policy conditions is never discussed during Board meetings, which means that recipient countries do not have the possibility of appealing through their representatives in the Executive Board (Riesenhuber 2001). This can be called a problem of throughput legitimacy. It further increases the power of the staff in relation to controlling bodies.

On the other hand, there is one exception to the rule that staff is more influential than representatives of shareholder governments. The United States as biggest shareholder has a direct influence on the staff. Staff will simply not bring any proposals to the Board if the US government opposes them. This has occurred, for example, with countries like Vietnam and Mozambique in the (1960s and) 1970s, with Nicaragua in the 1980s[6] and with Haiti during the more recent Aristide government.

3. How the Democratic Deficit has Increased since the 1980s

The changes and expansions in tasks and activities of the IMF and the World Bank have exacerbated the input and throughput legitimacy problems. At the same time, they have also created an output legitimacy problem.

Increased Input and Throughput Legitimacy Problems

The expansion in membership of the IMF has led to quota increases. But the current quota distribution and consequently voting power does not adequately reflect the strength of countries in the world economy (Kelkar *et al.* 2004). First, quota increases have not been accompanied by a change in the number of basic votes that each country has – the votes that are not proportional to the quota. In 1944, basic votes amounted to 11.26 per cent of total voting power but this share diminished to 3.02 per cent in 1995. As a result, the relative voting power of small countries has decreased. Second, quotas are calculated on the basis of variables that measure the country's economic strength (output measured by GDP), and variables that measure its potential need for resources, based on its openness to trade (exports, imports), the

---

6 Striking evidence of this is given, for example, in Leogrande (1996).

variability of its export receipts and its volume of international reserves. However, GDP is measured in a common currency, for example, the dollar, on the basis of prevailing market exchange rates. The disadvantage of market exchange rates is that they do not reflect variation in purchasing power parity of these exchange rates. As a result, the GDP of low and middle income countries is usually underestimated, which further reduces the voting power of these countries. Kelkar *et al.* (2004: 729) show that the relative voting power of small but rich countries like the Netherlands and Belgium is higher than that of India and Brazil, while even at market exchange rates, the GDPs of the latter countries are higher. If computed at purchasing power parities, they are much higher.

The relative reduction in voting power of low and middle income countries is in sharp contrast with the fact that, since 1977, all beneficiaries of IMF programs are precisely these countries. This means that a minority of rich countries decides on programs for poorer countries. Decision making power is concentrated among the creditors, and is very limited among the beneficiaries of the programs (Woods 2001).

The change in the objectives of IMF programs has created a further problem with input legitimacy. As long as the IMF focused on maintaining exchange rate stability and solving short-term balance of payments problems, it was justified that decision makers within the IMF came from central banks and ministries of finance. However, the IMF has shifted from being primarily a monetary institution to an institution that aims to foster growth and development. The dominance of central banks and ministries of finance has therefore become odd. The new tasks require other areas of expertise (Stiglitz 2003).

The original problem with respect to throughput legitimacy, namely that the contents of policy conditions is not discussed in Executive Boards, has been exacerbated over time as the volume and scope of conditions has increased. While a typical IMF program had six quantitative performance criteria in the 1970s and ten in the 1980s, it had 26 in the 1990s (Kapur and Webb 2000). This means that staff of the IMF has become ever more intrusive in recipient countries' policies.

In recent years, Executive Boards (EB) have attempted to improve their extent of control over the staff. They have demanded additional information on program countries, for example more extensive assessments of past programs in countries demanding new IMF assistance. However, since the EB's information processing capacity is always more limited than that of staff, this has led to more *formal* control but not always to more *actual* control (Cottarelli 2005). At the same time, the size of some recent IMF programs, the perceived non-technical nature of the conditions, and the criticisms of IMF effectiveness have led to a movement away from the Executive Board to the capitals in a few rich countries. While the United States has always been able to influence staff directly (see above), the Boards of Governors and Executive Boards are now often bypassed by the G7 meetings (Cottarelli 2005).[7]

---

7   For example, many high income non-G7 countries were unhappy with the 'announcement' of the 100 per cent multilateral debt relief proposal in the July 2005 G7

In conclusion, input and throughput legitimacy problems have been exacerbated as a result of the expansion of activities of the two institutions. Low and middle income countries have minimal voting power in the Boards while they are the principal clients, and the power of the Boards themselves has also been reduced.

Questionable Output Legitimacy

To some extent, output legitimacy may compensate for a democratic deficit on the input side. If the BWI deliver the intended international public goods effectively, there is less need to worry about input or throughput legitimacy. However, although space is lacking for a thorough analysis, there are many indications that output legitimacy is also problematic.

An overview of many empirical studies shows that IMF programs may have a beneficiary effect on the balance of payments – not surprising given that money is flowing in with a program – but that growth is often not forthcoming (Bird 2001). Several more recent studies have also shown that IMF programs have not succeeded in fostering economic growth (Przeworski and Vreeland 2000; Bird 2001; Dreher 2004; Butkiewicz and Yanikkaya 2005). Barro and Lee (2005) find that a higher use of IMF loans[8] reduces economic growth, even if corrected for the factors that led to IMF involvement in the first place. They focus on the use of Stand By Arrangements and Extended Fund Facilities, i.e. middle income countries. The negative effect on growth is stronger if all IMF programs are taken into account (Barro and Lee 2005).

These negative outcomes may be due to several factors: IMF conditions are not implemented, the amount of financing is too limited, IMF programs do not lead to the expected inflow of other, additional resources, or the IMF sets the wrong conditions, i.e. conditions that do not support growth. There is some evidence for all of these.

There is a large body of literature showing that IMF conditionality is not effective in insuring that prescribed policies are carried out. Programs are often interrupted for being 'off-track' (Killick 1995; Bird 2001) Countries do what they intended to do anyway, and other than this, they only implement cosmetically or with substantial delays (Killick *et al.* 1998; Dijkstra 2002). Domestic political economy factors are more decisive than IMF and World Bank conditionality (Dollar and Svensson 1998). In practice, IMF conditions are often not 'owned' by the country and are therefore not implemented.

The size of an IMF loan is usually relatively small in relation to the balance of payments deficit. It is expected that the existence of an IMF program with its accompanying conditions will work as the seal of approval that leads to capital inflows from other sources. However, IMF programs have proven to be unsuccessful

---

summit in Gleneagles.

8   Use of loans is defined as the fraction of months during a five-year period that a country participated in an IMF program.

in catalyzing private capital flows (Bird and Rowlands 2000). Given that IMF conditionality is ineffective, it is not surprising that the catalyst function does not work. It is not possible to 'buy reforms' and to have credible conditionality at the same time (Collier *et al.* 1997).

On the other hand, during recent currency crises, some middle income countries have received huge volumes of IMF assistance (East Asian countries, Russia, Brazil, Argentina, Turkey, see the peaks in Figure 1). In some of these cases, there have been accusations of political motives for the large lending volumes. Barro and Lee (2005) have empirically shown that countries with more intensive political and economic relations to the United States and large European economies receive larger and more frequent loans from the IMF (Barro and Lee 2005). These packages have also been criticized for their inducement of moral hazard among private creditors (IFIAC 2000). In fact, the IMF money allowed private creditors to get most of their money back during these crises, with negative incentive effects for future private investment decisions.

With respect to the contents of the conditions, the IMF programs and advices in countries in transition and in East Asia (before the 1998 crisis) have been criticized for their premature privatizations and liberalizations and lack of attention for institutions (Stiglitz 1998). The fact that the OECD and the IMF pushed for capital account liberalization in East Asia in the early 1990s is generally seen as a cause of the later crisis. The IMF has been called part of the Wall Street-Treasury-Complex, even by a prominent defender of free trade and globalization such as Bhagwati (Bhagwati 2004). When the Asian crisis broke out, criticisms were directed at the too restrictive fiscal policies that exacerbated the recession. In addition, in calling for substantive structural reforms, the IMF was screaming fire in the theatre which fuelled the outflow of foreign capital (Wade 1998; Stiglitz 2002).

In general, conditions of the IMF reflect the neo-liberal ideology of the rich countries, but this ideology is only pushed on low and middle income countries, while the rich countries themselves do not practice it. For example, during the 1998 Asian crisis, the IMF required an increased flexibility of labor markets that went far beyond what most industrialized countries accomplish in this area (Kapur and Webb 2000). Long before the Asian crisis, it was already evident that the IMF called for elimination of all trade barriers in developing countries so that rich countries could export their computers, machines, and commercial services, while there is no IMF pressure on rich countries to reduce protection for those sectors in which developing countries potentially compete, such as agriculture and textiles.

Another problem is that the extensive conditionality of the IMF and World Bank in many poor countries that are heavily dependent on aid tends to undermine domestic accountability processes (Verweij and Josling 2003). The IMF and the World Bank often require 'laws to be approved', for example on tax reform or on health policies. It will seldom be the case that parliament fully agrees with these laws. It may approve them if there is a lot of pressure, but the chances of implementation are low. These laws will not be owned by the country. In addition, this practice weakens domestic legal processes and public confidence in them, with potentially serious long-term consequences. This is one the 'paradoxes of conditionality' (Dijkstra 2002): donors push countries to have better governance and be more democratic, but they require the same countries to approve certain laws.

Finally, there is critique on the conflicting interests of the IMF in low-income countries. Poor countries with high debts need an IMF program in order to get debt relief and foreign aid. The IMF program is the seal of approval that opens the way to debt relief, grants and concessional loans. In this area of official and concessional finance, the catalytic function of the IMF is successful. But at the same time, the IMF is the creditor, and thus has an interest in a new program that brings in finance for repaying the old debts (White and Dijkstra 2003). The conflicting interest between the gatekeeper and the creditor role may lead to adverse selection: countries with worse policies receive more aid. Empirically, it has been shown that countries with higher multilateral debts receive more aid (Birdsall *et al.* 2003; Marchesi and Missale 2004).

As for the World Bank, the econometric evidence on the relationship between World Bank loans and economic growth appears to be more positive than that for the IMF (Butkiewicz and Yanikkaya 2005). However, the Meltzer report is very critical of the results of World Bank lending, concluding that there is a 55–60 per cent failure rate of projects (IFIAC 2000).[9] The same 'Meltzer report' established that the World Bank loans are directed to higher middle income countries that also have access to private credit markets.

The World Bank is also subject to criticisms on the proliferation of conditions and the large extent of non implementation due to lack of ownership (Mosley *et al.* 1991). In addition, some of the conditions that have been implemented have proven wrong. For example, state banks have been privatized before regulatory and supervisory frameworks were in place, and trade reforms have been carried out that led to great losses for the economy while the benefits accrued to other, less poor countries that did not carry out the same reforms.[10] For a long time, the World Bank has also been criticized for its lack of transparency, for negative social and environmental consequences of its projects, and for lack of attention of social and institutional factors in development.

4. Recent Changes and Reform Proposals

Since the mid-1990s and in response to the criticisms, both the IMF and the World Bank have introduced several changes in how they operate. These changes have been related, in particular, to improving throughput and output legitimacy. However,

---

9   The independent evaluation office of the Bank, OED (Operations Evaluation Department) generally concludes that one-third of projects is successful, one-third has satisfactory performance, and one-third fails.

10   The abolition of export taxes on raw cashew nuts in Mozambique, for example, led to the collapse of Mozambican cashew nut processing industries while India maintained these taxes and handsomely benefitted.

most of the implemented changes have only been carried out half-heartedly or cosmetically and have had limited real effects. On the other hand, far-reaching proposals have been suggested for changing internal governance in order to improve input legitimacy – but they have not been implemented so far. This section will first describe and analyze the changes that have been adopted, and then examine possible effects of the proposals that have *not* been implemented.

Changes Implemented

Both institutions have become far more transparent in their operations. Nowadays, the websites of both institutions give access to a huge amount of information on lending policies and actions. Subject to borrowing country approval, a large amount of information is also available on the developing country situation and on the nature of the institution's country program.

Both institutions but in particular the World Bank, have also opened up to debates with their critics, and in particular with local and international NGOs. In principle this is positive, but it also has some drawbacks. Some small developing countries complain that they have less influence on the Bank than the big international NGOs. Within borrowing countries, the activities of World Bank and other donors to stimulate civil society participation has induced politicians to 'moonlight NGOs' in order to have more influence (Woods 2003).

The increased exchange of views with NGOs has led to the establishment of several independent or joint Bank-civil society committees to review bank policies and enhance public accountability. These include the Structural Adjustment Participatory Review Initiative (SAPRI), the World Commission on Dams (to review the large number of dam projects of the Bank), and the Extractive Industries Review (similarly, in order to examine loans for oil and gas exploitation). These Committees came to critical conclusions and recommendations, but so far to very little effect (Bello and Guttal 2005).

The creation of the World Bank Inspection Panel in 1995 was another result of the increased pressure from international civil society organizations, particularly in the areas of environmental protection and human rights (Fox 2000). The Panel consists of high-level independent experts. Citizens of developing countries can apply to this Panel with complaints about environmental or social costs of Bank projects. Although this is an important step in promoting accountability, an assessment of the Panel's effectiveness results in a mixed judgment. While it raised the internal profile of the Bank's 'minimal safeguard policies',[11] it did not lead to sanctions in cases of non-compliance nor to changes in actual lending policies (Fox 2000).

In the same vain of improving throughput legitimacy, the IMF established its first Independent Evaluation Office (IEO) in 2002. So far, the IEO has produced several important reports and these have sometimes led to (small) changes in IMF policies

---

11 These are the policies about protecting the rights of people and of the environment.

(see below). But not all the recommendations have been implemented by Board of Governance or Executive Directors.

With respect to output, there have been some attempts to reduce the number and scope of IMF conditions, but on balance the results have been limited. When former Managing Director Horst Köhler took office in 2001, he announced that the IMF would return to its core business, i.e. examining fiscal and monetary policies only. However, in 1996, the Board of Governors required the IMF to include a concern about 'good governance'. In particular, the IMF was asked to 'promote good governance in all its aspects, which include ensuring the rule of law, improving the efficiency and accountability of the public sector, and tackling corruption, as essential elements of a framework within which economies can prosper'. This is certainly not the core business of the IMF. Yet, almost two-thirds of the Letters of Intent (the agreed upon conditions) concluded between January 2002 and April 2003 proved to include conditions related to good governance.[12]

In 1999, the adoption of the Heavily Indebted Poor Countries (HIPC) Initiative implied the obligation for these countries to elaborate Poverty Reduction Strategy Papers (PRSPs) with broad civil society participation. It was expected that these strategies would form the basis for lending and granting by all donors, so that no further conditions would be required. They would increase domestic and broad-based ownership in the recipient countries. Later on, the requirement of writing and implementing PRSPs was also attached to the new IMF facility for poor countries, the PRGF, and to the WB loans that replaced the earlier structural adjustment loans. However, in practice the earlier structural adjustment conditionality did not disappear (fiscal and monetary stabilization policies, structural reforms), so the requirement of elaborating a PRSP with participation implied an expansion of conditionality (Dijkstra 2002). In addition, the extent of actual participation in, and of national ownership of the PRSPs are not assessed favorably by the independent evaluation offices of both institutions (IEO 2004; OED 2004). In general, macroeconomic policies have not been discussed at all in the context of PRSPs and have been taken from earlier concluded ESAFs or PRGFs in which IMF staff has been dominant.

Since 2002, the IMF adopted a policy to 'streamline' conditionality, implying fewer conditions and a heavier focus on core conditions that are really needed to improve macroeconomic stability, thus leaving out the so-called structural conditions. But the evidence on practice is mixed. The number of structural conditions may have gone down slightly, but they have often been taken over by the World Bank (Bird 2005). On the other hand, core conditions still comprise only two-thirds of the total, and if conditions related to governance are excluded from this 'core', only 45 per cent (Martin and Bargawi 2005).

In September 2005, the complaints of the conflicting interests in the IMF role in low income countries led to the introduction of a new facility that separates the gatekeeping function from the lending function for low income countries. Countries

---

12 IMF Fact sheet 'The IMF and good governance', April 2003, downloaded from www. imf.org on 28 March 2006.

in need of a seal of approval but without balance of payments difficulties can apply to the Policy Support Instrument (PSI), implying the usual monitoring of macroeconomic policies but without any lending. By March 2006, it has been applied in two countries, Uganda and Nigeria.[13] It remains to be seen what the effects of this facility are. In countries without payment obligations to the BWIs, it may solve the conflict of interest but the gatekeeper role tends to be accompanied by tensions of itself: withholding the seal of good behavior has such severe consequences for the country (by losing access to budget support, in particular) that this will hardly ever been done.

The increased transparency, the WB Inspection Panel and the IMF's IEO are certainly important improvements. They can be seen as attempts to 'deliberately democratize' the institutions (Verweij and Josling 2003). But they have not brought an end to the demands for (further) improving legitimacy and accountability. Attempts to reduce the number and scope of IMF conditions have so far not been very successful.

More Fundamental Proposals

The proposals to fundamentally increase democratic legitimacy of the institutions can be broken down in two broad categories. The first group of proposals aims to improve the input legitimacy of the IMF and the World Bank by changing its internal governance. The second group focuses on the output side, and in particular aims at reducing the output of the organizations.

In line with the earlier criticisms of the low decision making power of the developing countries vis-à-vis the main shareholders, the most important proposals to improve input legitimacy include:

- Changing the quota system in the IMF so that poorer countries obtain more voting power (Woods 2001; Stiglitz 2003; Kelkar *et al.* 2004)
- Changing the distribution of executive directors so that more of them originate from poor countries, based on the idea that voice is surely as important as voting power (Woods 2001; Askari 2004)
- Leaving the quota system as it is, that is based on strength of the respective economies, but requiring a double majority for important decisions: one according to current voting rights, another based on member of countries (Rapkin and Strand 2005)
- Changing the area of expertise of the Governors in the IMF to include more individuals with expertise in development (Stiglitz 2003)
- Changing the rules and customs for electing the Managing Director of IMF and the President of the World Bank, so that they can originate from developing countries (Birdsall 2003).

---

13 Fact sheet and press releases downloaded 28 March 2006 from <www.imf.org.

The proposals that focus on the output side stress that the IMF has taken on too many tasks. It should restrict itself to its core business of resolving temporary balance of payments problems and currency crises. In these crisis countries, however, the IMF should refrain from extending the scope of its conditionality. Conditions should be limited to some core monetary and, if necessary, fiscal targets. According to Woods (2003), an independent agency is needed to monitor the already existing guidelines to streamline conditionality. Going back to the core business also implies that the IMF should no longer be involved in low-income countries with structural, development problems (IFIAC 2000; Birdsall *et al.* 2002; IOB 2003; White and Dijkstra 2003).

Analysis

The Under-Secretary of State Adams of the United States has said that the US will not give up its quota share and that an eventual redistribution towards fast growing emerging economies must come from the shares of other high income countries.[14] He suggested that the European Union countries consolidate their chairs in the Executive Boards, reducing the number of Directors from the ten that now represent the 25 European Union countries. This is unlikely to happen in the near future. Recent appointments of the Director of the IMF and the President of the World Bank have shown that rich countries are not willing to give up their priority position here, either. The call for representatives from other constituencies in the Board of Governors of the IMF is bound to conflict with the still dominant idea of the IMF as a monetary institution and not a development institution. The other proposals will also meet fierce opposition from the United States and other major high income countries.

But given the analysis above, one can doubt whether these proposed changes in internal governance would have much effect anyway. They are all related to formal decision making power in the Board, while it has been shown above that actual decisions are made by the staff and, in really important matters, by the governments of the major shareholders. The expansion of tasks of, in particular, the IMF, has to a large extent been the result of the lack of control of the member countries over the staff of these organizations. The Executive Board, which is supposed to exert this control on behalf of member countries' governments, is almost part of the staff: it has the same interest in growth of the organization. At the same time, we have shown that a coalition of staff and Executive Directors has succeeded in expanding the scale and scope of activities of both the IMF and the World Bank. In turn, this extension of activities has made the United States more concerned about exerting its influence on the institutions.

The IMF has become an instrument of the rich countries to impose policy conditions on low and middle income countries. The contents of the conditions reflects the neo-liberal ideology of the rich countries – more precisely, the neo-liberal ideology of central banks and ministries of finance of the rich countries. As Stiglitz

---

14 IMF Survey, 17 October 2005.

convincingly shows for the United States, there are checks and balances that prevent this ideology from dominating national policies within the rich countries (Stiglitz 2002). But in the context of IMF and World Bank, there are no checks and balances. The two institutions have a monopoly position towards countries in financial crisis and towards all low-income countries that are dependent on foreign aid. The strong position of the staff is enhanced by the procedural rule that the content of policy conditions is never discussed in the Executive Board. Recipient countries therefore cannot appeal to their representative in the Board in order to change these policy conditions.

This analysis implies that not much can be expected from changes in the composition of Executive Board members, voting power or the selection of the Director or President. The real power will continue to be exercised behind the scenes and will directly influence the actions of the staff. The democratic legitimacy problems will also continue to exist. For all these reasons, the proposals to substantially reduce the tasks of the IMF appear to be more effective for solving the legitimacy problems.

5. Conclusion

This chapter focuses on the democratic deficit of the IMF and the World Bank. While large bureaucracies always suffer from problems of input and throughput legitimacy, these problems are generally more severe for supranational bureaucracies. Democratic control can be indirect at best. Member countries have fewer incentives and fewer opportunities to control these big organizations. This usually leads to an expansion of tasks, and the chapter shows that the two BWI expanded the scale and scope of their activities enormously. The lack of effective control by the member states through the Executive Boards has facilitated this expansion. In fact, EB members and the constituencies in their home countries (staff working on the institutions in central banks and ministries of finance) had an interest in expanding the tasks and responsibilities of these institutions.

In turn, the expansion of tasks has exacerbated the democratic legitimacy problems of the two institutions. Relative voting power of low and middle income countries has diminished even though these countries have always been the only beneficiaries of World Bank loans and have now become the single beneficiaries of IMF programs as well. The expansion in conditionality and recently the enormous size of individual loan packages for middle income countries has led to an increased dominance of the United States and some few other major shareholders in decision making. This asymmetric decision making has influenced the contents of conditions and reduced their fairness. This has led to severe problems of output legitimacy. There is also increasing evidence of lack of effectiveness of, in particular, the IMF – especially with respect to the main aim that the institution has taken on in recent years, namely, promoting economic growth.

Both the World Bank and the IMF have become more transparent during the last ten years or so, and they have implemented some other changes in how they operate.

In particular, they are more open to debate with NGOs, the World Bank established an Inspection Panel to which citizens affected by projects can complain, and the IMF now also has an Independent Evaluation Office. In a way, the institutions have attempted to solve their democratic deficit by moving into a deliberative democracy model. However, the fundamental problems of input and output legitimacy continue.

Many proposals have been advanced for giving more formal voting power and influence to low and middle income countries in the Executive Boards. They are not likely to be implemented. More importantly, given the above analysis, they are unlikely to be effective in reducing the democratic deficit. In fact, real power is not with the Board of Governors or with Executive Boards, but instead with the staff and with the G7 or sometimes the G1 (the United States). All of this leads to the conclusion that the radical proposals for reducing the scale and scope of activities of the IMF are more likely to reduce the democratic deficit effectively.

References

Askari, H. (2004), 'Global financial governance: Whose ownership?', *Business Economics* April, 57–62.

Bakker, A.F.P. (1996), *International Financial Institutions* (London and Heerlen: Longman and Open University).

Barro, R. J. and Lee, J.-W. (2005), 'IMF programs: Who is chosen and what are the effects?', *Journal of Monetary Economics* 52:7, 1245–69.

Bello, W. and Guttal, S. (2005), 'Programmed to Fail: The World Bank clings to a bankrupt development model', *Multinational Monitor* 26:7/8, 23–9.

Bhagwati, J. N. (2004), *In Defense of Globalization*. (New York, Oxford University Press).

Bird, G. (2001), 'IMF programs: Do they work? Can they be made to work better?', *World Development* 29:11, 1849–65.

Bird, G. (2005), 'The IMF and Poor Countries: Towards a more fulfilling relationship', in J. J. Teunissen and A. Akkerman (eds) *Helping the Poor? The IMF and Low-Income Countries* (The Hague: FONDAD), 16–61.

Bird, G. and Rowlands, D. (2000), 'The catalyzing role of policy-based lending by the IMF and the World Bank: Fact or Fiction?', *Journal of International Development* 12:7, 951–73.

Birdsall, N. (2003), 'Why it matters who runs the IMF and the World Bank', Washington: Center for Global Development. Working Paper No.22.

Birdsall, N. and Claessens, S. and Diwan, I. (2003), 'Policy selectivity forgone: Debt and donor behaviour in Africa', *World Bank Economic Review* 17:3, 409–35.

Birdsall, N. and Williamson J. and Deese B. (2002), *Delivering on debt relief: From IMF gold to a new aid architecture* (Washington: Center for Global Development and Institute for International Economics).

Butkiewicz, J. L. and Yanikkaya, H. (2005), 'The effects of IMF and World Bank lending on long-run economic growth: An empirical analysis', *World Development* 33:3, 371–91.

Collier, P., Guillaumont, P. and Guillaumont, S. and Gunning, J.W. (1997), 'Redesigning Conditionality', *World Development* 25:9, 1399–1407.

Commission for Africa (2005), 'Our Common Interest: Report of the Commission for Africa' (London).

Cottarelli, C. (2005), 'Efficiency and legitimacy: Trade-offs in IMF Governance' (Washington, IMF: IMF Working Paper 05/107).

Dahl, R. E. (1999), 'Can international organizations be democratic? A skeptic's view', in I. Shapiro and C. Hacker-Cordon (eds), *Democracy's Edges* (Cambridge: Cambridge University Press), 19–36.

Dijkstra, A. G. (2002), 'The effectiveness of policy conditionality: Eight country experiences', *Development and Change* 33:2, 307–34.

Dollar, D. and Svensson J. (1998), 'What Explains the Success or Failure of Structural Adjustment Programs?' (Washington DC: The World Bank, Macroeconomics and Growth Group).

Dreher, A. (2006), 'IMF and economic growth: The effects of programs, loans, and compliance with conditionality', *World Development* 34:5, 769–88.

Fox, J. A. (2000), 'The World Bank Inspection Panel: Lessons from the First Five Years', *Global Governance*, 279–318.

Frey, B. S. (1991), 'The public choice view of international political economy', in R. Vaubel and T.D. Willett (eds), *The Political Economy of International Organizations: A Public Choice Approach* (Boulder, Co:Westview), 7–26.

Guitian, M. (1995), 'Conditionality: Past, Present, Future', *IMF Staff Papers* 42:4, 792–835.

IEO (Independent Evaluation Office) (2004), *IEO Evaluation Report on PRSPs and the PRGF* (Washington: IMF).

IFIAC (International Financial Institution Advisory Commission) (2000), 'Report of the International Financial Institution Advisory Commission', Washington: Report to the US Congress.

IOB (2003), *Results of international debt relief, with case studies of Bolivia, Jamaica, Mozambique, Nicaragua, Peru, Tanzania, Uganda and Zambia* (The Hague: Ministry of Foreign Affairs, Policy and Operations Evaluation Department (IOB)). IOB Evaluations 292.

Kapur, D. and Webb, R. (2000), 'Governance-related conditionalities of the international financial institutions', (Geneva: UNCTAD, Center for International Development Harvard University). G-24 Discussion Paper Series No. 6

Kelkar, V., Yadav, V. and Chaudhry, P. (2004), 'Reforming the Governance of the International Monetary Fund', *The World Economy* 27:5, 727–43.

Killick, T. (1995), *IMF Programmes in Developing Countries: Design and Impact* (London: Routledge).

Killick, T., Gunatilaka, R. and Marr, A. (1998), *Aid and the Political Economy of Policy Change* (London: Routledge).

Leibenstein, H. (1966), 'Allocative efficiency vs. 'X-efficiency'', *American Economic Review* 56, 392–415.

Leogrande, W. M. (1996), 'Making the economy scream: the US economic sanctions against Nicaragua', *Third World Quarterly* 17:2, 329–48.

Marchesi, S. and Missale, A. (2004), 'What does motivate lending and aid to the HIPCs?', Paper presented to the conference Debt Relief and Global Governance, Rotterdam, June.

Martin, M. and Bargawi, H. (2005), 'A changing role for the IMF in low-income countries', in J.J. Teunissen, J.J. and A. Akkerman (eds) *Helping the Poor? The IMF in Low-Income Countries* (The Hague: FONDAD), 68–126.

Mosley, P., Harrigan, J. and Toye, J. (1991), *Aid and Power: The World Bank and Policy-Based Lending* (London: Routledge).

Niskanen, W. A. (1971), *Bureaucracy and Representative Government* (Chicago: Aldine).

OED (Operations Evaluation Department) (2004), *The Poverty Reduction Strategy Initiative, an independent evaluation of the World Bank's support through 2003* (Washington: The World Bank).

Przeworski, A. and Vreeland, J.R. (2000), 'The effect of IMF programs on economic growth', *Journal of Development Economics* 62, 385–421.

Rapkin, D. P. and Strand J.R. (2005), 'Developing country representation and governance of the International Monetary Fund', *World Development* 33:12, 1993–2011.

Riesenhuber, E. (2001), *The International Monetary Fund under Constraint* (The Hague: Kluwer).

Stiglitz, J. (1998), 'More instruments and broader goals: Moving toward the Post-Washington Consensus' (Helsinki: WIDER, WIDER Annual Lecture 2).

Stiglitz, J. (2002), *Globalization and its Discontents* (London and New York: Norton).

Stiglitz, J. E. (2003), 'Democratizing the International Monetary Fund and the World Bank: Governance and Accountability', *Governance* 16:1, 111–39.

Toye, J. (1994), 'Structural adjustment: Context, assumptions, origins and diversity', in R. van der Hoeven, and F. van der Kraaij (eds), *Structural Adjustment and Beyond in Sub-Saharan Africa* (London/Portsmouth: James Currey/Heinemann), 66–89.

UN Millennium Project directed by 'J.D. Sachs (2005), 'Investing in Development: A practical plan to achieve the Millennium Development Goals' (New York).

Vaubel, R. (1991), 'A public choice view of international organization', in R. Vaubel and T.D. Willett (eds), *The Political Economy of International Organizations: A Public Choice Approach* (Boulder: Co, Westview), 27–45.

Vaubel, R. (1996), 'Bureaucracy at the IMF and the World Bank: A comparison of the evidence', *The World Economy* 19:2, 195–210.

Verweij, M. and Josling, T.E. (2003), 'Special issue: Deliberately democratizing multilateral organization', *Governance* 16:1, 1–21.

Wade, R. (1998), 'The Asian debt-and-development crisis of 1997–?: Causes and consequences', *World Development* 26:8, 1535–54.

White, H.N. and Dijkstra, A.G. (2003), *Programme Aid and Development: Beyond Conditionality* (London: Routledge).

Woods, N. (2001), 'Making the IMF and the World Bank more accountable', *International Affairs* 77:1, 83–100.

Woods, N. (2003), 'Unelected government: Making the IMF and the World Bank more accountable', *Brookings Review* (Spring), 9–12.

PART V
CONCLUSIONS

Chapter 15

Governance and the Democratic Deficit: An Evaluation

Victor Bekkers, Geske Dijkstra, Arthur Edwards and Menno Fenger

In the previous chapters we analyzed what kinds of shifts and modes of governance have occurred in the practice of public administration. These governance patterns can be defined as emerging political orders in which binding public decisions are made; political orders that are no longer organized (exclusively) around the state as ultimate source of authority and that go beyond the jurisdictions of (central) state authorities. Therefore, one may assume that the emergence of these governance practices could produce frictions in relation to their input, throughput and output legitimacy. From the perspective of representative democracy, these governance practices may result in a democratic deficit. The assessment of such a deficit should not only be based on the principles of representative democracy. Other democracy models should also be considered.

In this chapter, we compare the major outcomes of the case studies that have been conducted. Our case selection does not cover the whole range of (possible combinations of) shifts and modes of governance and models of democracy that are implied in our theoretical framework. Hence, we are reluctant to draw far-reaching conclusions. The case studies should be seen as in-depth illustrations of relevant shifts and modes of governance and their perceived legitimacy challenges. The emphasis in our comparison lies on the inductive interpretation of empirical findings in relation to the theoretical explorations that were set out in the beginning of this book, thereby looking for striking patterns of similarities and differences.

In the following sections, we follow the research questions as defined in the Introduction. First, we address the question what the case studies tell us about the nature of new governance practices and the motives behind them. Then we turn to their assessment in terms of democratic legitimacy. Is there a democratic deficit and how can it be understood? What other democracy models besides the dominant model of representative democracy are emerging in the slipstream of these new practices, and what strengths and weaknesses can be observed in relation to input, throughput and output legitimacy? These observations and insights may help us formulate appropriate democratization strategies, which is the topic of the final section.

1. The Nature of Governance

Two important observations can be made from the case studies. First, in practice, we see that a combination of shifts or modes of governance often occurs. The second observation is that most shifts and modes are induced by a desire to improve the effectiveness and responsiveness of public administration, so that it might be expected that at least these aspects of democratic legitimacy will be enhanced.

A Co-Evolution of Governance Practices

In many cases we see the occurrence of several shifts and modes of governance in combination. This process might be understood as the result of a process of co-evolution, and it might be related to the complex nature of the societal problems and political challenges that confront public administration. These problems and challenges could have an external origin, like fighting crime, or an internal origin, like improving the internal efficiency of public administration.

Central governments in various European countries are shifting problem-solving capacity towards other layers of government or towards the private sector. These shifts can be seen as a modernization strategy. In their comparison and analysis of the proposed shifts and modes of governance in the modernization programs of the United Kingdom, Germany, The Netherlands and Denmark (Chapter 5), Bekkers, Fenger and Korteland conclude that a shift towards self-government and self-regulation prevails, although this shift may be rhetorical. This shift becomes manifest in several modes of governance. First, the accompanying process of decentralization and deregulation facilitates governance at a distance. Moreover, decentralization is also viewed as a way to improve the quality of cooperation between different layers of government, leading to multi-level governance. Third, it facilities market governance, giving more liberty and autonomy – based on privatization and deregulation – to other quasi-government and private organizations. Fourth, it stimulates self-regulation and self-responsibility of citizens, thereby introducing forms of network governance and societal self- governance.

Due to increased public and political attention to local public safety and fighting crime, the police organization has been put under a lot of pressure during the last twenty years. This has led to various shifts in governance within the police system. Van Sluis and Cachet describe these shifts in the United Kingdom and The Netherlands (Chapter 6). In both countries they see a shift from a rather decentralized steering system towards more centralized steering, in which firm steering takes place on central input and output parameters. The emerging mode of governance is a hierarchical system of governance at a distance in which transparency of output and outcomes and accountability are important guiding principles. At the same time they see some striking other shifts. First, there is a downward shift in governance towards the local (municipal) level, stressing the importance of better cooperation between the police and the (law abiding) citizens and community policing. Second, there is a horizontal shift, leading to a proliferation of 'policing beyond the police' or 'grey policing' in which the private sector plays a vital role. Forms of market governance, for instance commercial police organizations, which are taking over traditional policing roles such as surveillance in neighborhoods and shopping centers have emerged. Furthermore, they see a horizontal shift towards network and societal self-governance. Especially in The Netherlands, citizens, companies, societal organizations and issue groups have become more involved in drafting local and integral safety programs; programs that are based on a shared understanding by relevant stakeholders about the causes of local safety problems and actions to be taken.

The emergence of governance at a distance in the British health policy and the education policy, analyzed by Hupe and Hill (Chapter 7), has led to more autonomy for hospitals and schools. However, autonomy also implies more accountability. The emphasis on accountability can be seen as a way to compensate the legitimacy of the throughput-side of governance, in which professionals make important decisions about how services are provided as well as about the quality of these services. Hence, it is important to look at how and in what kind of accountability relationships these decisions have been made. Hupe and Hill argue that improving accountability is not only a matter of governments that steer at a distance on the one hand and monitor and control the output and outcomes of the decisions made by the professionals on the other hand. Accountability is much more subtle than formal and vertical accountability systems would suggest. Horizontal mechanisms, controls from within the profession or directly by citizens affected, are observed as possibly compensating for deficits in the existing accountability regimes of representative democracy.

In the chapters grouped under network governance and societal self-governance, we also see combinations of different modes of governance. In his chapter on the Rotterdam Integrated Public Safety Program (Chapter 8), Marks observes vertical and horizontal shifts. First, the national public safety program had to be translated and (re) formulated into a municipal version, which subsequently served as a guideline for creating district safety plans. At the district level, a horizontal shift has occurred. The district safety plans are formulated in participative procedures in which residents, shopkeepers and other stakeholders are involved. In this case, we see that network governance at the district level is embedded in multi-level governance and governance at a distance.

The local environmental forums investigated by Edwards (Chapter 9) can be viewed as arrangements to involve residents as affected interests in environmental governance. In this way, the network of the primary stakeholders (businesses and regulatory agencies) is expanded with communities. In the cases he analyzes, there is a relation with multi-level governance because different governments are involved in the steering of regulatory agencies. The Local Development Commissions in Mozambique, investigated by Dijkstra and Lodewijckx (Chapter 10) are also embedded in multi-level relationships, but in this case a 'governance relationship', in terms of cooperation and pooling of resources, is clearly absent.

Multi-level governance refers to the cooperation between several layers of government: local, regional, national, and supranational. The cases analyzed in

Part four all deal with upward shifts of governance to higher levels, from municipal to regional or from national to European or global. Yet most cases also reflect combinations with other modes of governance. The chapter by Ruano de la Fuente and Schaap (Chapter 11) covers multi-level governance and network governance. The chapter deals with a rich diversity of empirical cases of supra-municipal government. They start with classifying two cases (Greater London and Greater Copenhagen) as consolidated regional government, and two other cases (ILEX near Madrid and Greater Hanover) as inter-municipal cooperation, but conclude in the end that both Copenhagen and Hanover are in fact hybrids with forms of inter-municipal cooperation co-existing with elected supra-municipal government bodies. In addition, Greater London and ILEX incorporate forms of network governance, allowing for policy co-production and co-implementation by citizens. In the case of Greater London, this also includes the private sector.

Two chapters analyze the democratic deficit of governance practices within the European Union. The monetary and fiscal policies dealt with by Van Nispen and Posseth (Chapter 12) are a pure case of multi-level governance. Zandstra (Chapter 13) examines the Open Method of Coordination (OMC) as a tool for enhancing European cooperation in employment policies. From the perspective of the European level, this OMC itself can be seen as governance at a distance in which some rules and procedures are set at the central European level but in which actual policy-making and implementation is still decentralized. The OMC also promotes network governance, at least, at the level of the countries. Dijkstra (Chapter 14) looks at governance within the IMF and the World Bank as cases of supra-national governance at the global level. It is interesting to observe some attempts at network governance by, in particular, the World Bank.

Strengthening the Effectiveness and Responsiveness of Public Administration

The second observation is that most shifts and modes of governance aim at improving two aspects of output legitimacy, namely the effectiveness and responsiveness of public administration. In relation to governance at a distance, we see that deregulation and decentralization strengthen the discretion of (semi-) public organizations to make binding decisions, presumably leading to more efficient and effective results; decisions and results that are also more responsive to the needs of citizens, groups, companies, societal organizations as well as other governments. The reduction of rather detailed rules and regulations makes it easier to develop tailor-made decisions and plans. Deregulation and decentralization can be seen as instruments for enhancing the quality of the decision-making process (throughput legitimacy) *in order to* produce better results, which in turn may contribute to a higher output legitimacy of governance practices. This line of reasoning can be found in chapter 5 in which the four modernization programs of the UK, Denmark, The Netherlands and Germany are analyzed. Furthermore, the existence of a general policy framework will also contribute to the legality of the collective decision-making process. General principles and rules must be followed, which could also improve the accountability for the results of policies. This is demonstrated in the chapters on the UK and Dutch police systems (Van Sluis and Cachet) and on accountability in the UK health and school system (Hupe and Hill).

In the chapters on network governance, a focus on output legitimacy is clearly visible in Marks' account of the Rotterdam Integrated Safety Policy. An important impetus to the safety policy was the electoral success of the late Pim Fortuyn and his local party Livable Rotterdam in 2002. The policy issues voters considered most important were fighting crime and ensuring safety. The new municipal executive embarked on a more fine-tuned and intensified public safety policy. Its focus on output legitimacy included not only effectiveness and responsiveness, but accountability as well. An extensive public information system was set up to monitor the development of safety at both the municipal and district level. In the cases described by Edwards, however, concerns related to input and throughput legitimacy go hand in hand with output concerns. The Residential Advisory Boards in the Rijnmond region aim to provide a channel for residents' desires and complaints (input), a forum for discussion about environmental issues (throughput) and for finding joint solutions (output). Likewise, the Environmental Committee in Cleveland was formed in response to residents' concerns and to help residents organize around environmental issues (input). The Mozambican case of promoting participation examined by Dijkstra and Lodewijckx is expected to enhance both effectiveness and democratization.

The chapters on supranational or regional governance examined in this book reflect a desire to improve the effectiveness of policies. This multi-level governance is based on the recognition that in order to effectively deal with certain societal problems or tasks, such as spatial planning or a stable international monetary and trading system, existing layers of government are not sufficient. Inter-municipal or international cooperation is expected to advance these regional or global 'public goods'. It remains to be seen, however, whether policy effectiveness really increases, and also to what extent responsiveness and accountability – the other two aspects of output legitimacy – are enhanced.

2. Assessing the Democratic Legitimacy of Governance Practices

In this section, we address our main research question: what are the consequences of new forms of governance for the democratic legitimacy of public policies? For each empirical chapter, we first establish which processes of collective will-formation and democratic feedback can be observed and to which model(s) of democracy they refer. Subsequently, we assess the democratic legitimacy of the governance practices.

Governance at a Distance and Market Governance

Looking at the realm of modernization in Denmark, Germany, The Netherlands and the United Kingdom, Bekkers, Fenger and Korteland suggest a relationship between self-regulation and accountability: more freedom and autonomy should imply more accountability for the output and outcomes of the decisions made. In order to strengthen accountability, they see the emergence of devices that draw upon the consumer model of democracy. This model, blended with ideas about New Public Management, can be seen as a complement to the existing order of representative democracy. In a consumer democracy, the wishes and preferences of citizens, companies and societal organizations as rational, competent and active clients of government services, are more effectively channeled to increase responsiveness. In this way the 'primacy of politics', which is crucial in the representative model of democracy, is strengthened. The idea is that if politicians know what citizens really want, it becomes easier for them to instruct bureaucracy.

However, the rise of governance practices that are oriented on improving the output legitimacy of public administration by introducing a consumer democracy may lead to one-sidedness in the evaluation of public administration. Bekkers, Fenger and Korteland identify several risks. First, the strong emphasis on efficiency could lead to a simplification of the nature of public administration and its legitimacy. The co-existence of different value-orientations and rationalities that are weighed against each other is essential for public administration when dealing with societal problems. Efficiency is not the only relevant value, but substantial values like security, liberty, equity and safety as well as procedural values like transparency, openness and accessibility are also relevant. The legitimacy of a governance practice is also determined by how these different values have been taken into consideration as well as by the quality of the decision-making process in which these different and very often competing values have been weighed against each other. Second, possible legitimacy problems occur if citizens are primarily perceived as consumers. It is assumed that citizens are capable of expressing their preferences at least in so far as their consumption of public services is concerned. It also implies a strong claim for having reliable and rather comprehensive information about service entitlements as well as about the means of enforcing those entitlements. Furthermore, as citizens are primarily defined as voters and consumers, there is hardly any attention for other roles of citizens, like the citizen as the involved *citoyen*, who wants to take up his or her responsibility in dealing with problems. However, the major strength of consumer democracy is that it can be seen as complementary to the existing democratic order. The political nexus of the representative democratic model is not fundamentally challenged. A consumer orientation on public services helps to effectively channel the wishes and preferences of citizens so that politicians can be more responsive to their needs.

The different shifts and modes of governance that occurred in the UK and Dutch police systems, have also led to the introduction of elements of other democracy models. Van Sluis and Cachet see elements of a consumer, deliberative and associative democracy. The emphasis on performance and accountability implies that citizens are considered the clients of the police. Performance management and accountability systems are used to show how the produced outputs and outcomes fare in accordance with the wishes and needs of citizens. Moreover, putting citizens in the centre of the attention also implies greater participation of citizens and other stakeholders in the agenda setting and policy drafting process. In a deliberative model of democracy, citizens and citizen groups are seen as important advisors or co-producers in the policy process, while in an associative model of democracy, neighborhood associations are viewed as co-producers of public safety policies. In both cases, participants are seen as important local sources of knowledge and experience, which could be used to enhance the responsiveness and effectiveness of safety programs.

The UK and Dutch cases show that the introduction of these new democratic elements is primarily viewed as a way to reinforce the existing representative model of democracy. At the same time, one of the interesting conclusions in both cases is that, in the end, the strengths of the additional measures that have been taken to improve the input and output legitimacy of the police governance systems are dependent on the quality of the institutions of representative democracy. Although the introduction of elements of the client, deliberative and associative models of democracy can be seen as a strategy to reinforce local representative democracy, the democratic embedding of the police system at the local level is still very weak because of the weak power of the local government. According to Van Sluis and Cachet, these democratization efforts will be in vain if the Dutch and UK local democratic institutions are unable to counter balance the centralization process, which is taking place in both countries. This centralization process, with its strong emphasis on performance management, tends to neglect local needs of citizens and other groups, and may ultimately result in a legitimacy deficit on the output side because the results of these safety programs are primarily local. Due to the local variety of safety problems and policy answers, it is important to formulate and implement policy programs that respond to the local needs and wishes of citizens. Another weakness is the fact that there is not always a plausible relation between police output and outcomes. Public safety is not only dependent on police output. An increase in the number of fines hardly tells us anything about the safety on the road or in neighborhoods. This could endanger the output legitimacy.

Does the focus on accountability in the UK health and school system lead to the emergence of new and additional models of democracy? Hupe and Hill conclude that the replacement of government by governance implies that democracy is conceptualized in a corresponding manner: away from only looking at the formal organs of representation. The authors show that the governance of accountability is not only a matter of using elaborated performance management and audit systems. They show that all kinds of other accountability systems are in use and are being developed. Horizontal mechanisms, controls from within the profession or directly by citizens affected, are observed as possibly compensating for deficits in the existing accountability regimes of representative democracy. The claim that these new societal or professionally based accountability regimes have a democratic deficit should be seen as political, expressed from a specific perspective, namely that of representative democracy. The importance of other models of democracy is that they provide a degree of legitimacy to the participation of societal actors (citizens and professionals), other than in their roles as voters. At the same time, Hupe and

Hill make the observation that the participation of citizens in assessing the quality of services is not enough. The delivery process cannot be improved by only taking the judgments of citizens (or clients) into account afterwards. Accountability can also be improved by giving citizens a position in the design of relevant policy and service delivery programs, thereby including more checks and balances in the process.

Network Governance and Societal Self-Governance

Network governance is steering focused on facilitating a shared understanding among the stakeholders of a policy network. The core of the notion of network governance is stakeholder participation, participation by actors who are interdependent in terms of resources. We have linked the notion of network governance with deliberative and associative democracy, models of democracy that also address citizens as bearers of (other) affected interests. We first address the question of whether practices of network governance fulfill the legitimacy norms from the perspective of deliberative democracy. We then return to the role of representative democracy. The co-production of policies in an interaction between stakeholders and other affected interests can be seen as a threat to the primacy of traditional 'politics'. How do we have to deal with the tensions between network governance and representative democracy, or can we approach this relationship also in a different way?

In his chapter on integrated public safety policy in Rotterdam, Marks describes how the Rotterdam municipal authority has tried to increase the democratic legitimacy of its policies by incorporating the Rotterdam citizens in the public safety policy process. The district public safety plans are explicitly formulated by going into dialogues with residents, local entrepreneurs and other stakeholders. Moreover, after the formulation of the district safety plans, the program is strengthened by a continuous feedback of information. By generating substantial information through population inquiries, the citizens as clients help strengthen the public safety policy. Marks observes that this new form of governance no longer solely fits into the representative model of democracy. A deliberative democracy model is present in formulating and implementing the district safety plans. Furthermore, the underlying democracy model takes on a client nature in the strengthening of the public safety program throughout the course of implementation. The representative democracy model, however, still has a strong presence because the municipal executive requires the public to render them accountable in the next election when they fail to make the city safer. Marks concludes that the Rotterdam policy has been successful in enhancing output legitimacy. The policy has been effective because the government is well on its way to reaching its goals for 2006. The decisions and outputs are in congruence with the (expressed) desires of the Rotterdam citizens. Furthermore, the municipal executive is held accountable to the public by, for instance, publishing the safety index and safety reports and by providing information through debates and contacts with the media. The political accountability to the council has also been enhanced.

The local environmental forums investigated by Edwards can be regarded as incipient forms of citizen participation to involve local residents in environmental governance. The analysis reveals that the forums fulfill important signaling and monitoring functions. Especially in their signaling function they enhance the input legitimacy of environmental decision-making. Although the assessment on the different input norms produced a mixed picture, the forums do provide a channel for citizens' concerns and wishes (openness of the agenda). However, the knowledge advantage of the companies and their lack of commitment to render accounts of their efforts to solve observed problems came out as two hindrances to meeting the legitimacy criteria on the throughput and output side. From this analysis, Edwards concludes that the deliberative arrangements themselves are not sufficient for providing the conditions for giving residents the needed leverage. The support of politicians and environmental organizations is indispensable. This underlines the importance of embedding deliberative arrangements in representative and pluralist democracy. With regard to the role of pluralist democracy, the American case is interesting. In Cleveland, the city in which the American case is situated, non-governmental organizations have initiated collaborative projects to enhance the availability of environmental information to neighborhoods, and to improve the capacity of community leaders to use this information in environmental decision-making processes. Linkages with representative democracy are twofold. First, elected officials are the politically responsible (co-) designers of public policies and the political administrators of public agencies that are involved in their implementation. Second, governments can fulfill a governance role as process manager. This role includes activities as facilitating and coordinating interactions, connecting actors and organizing research and information processes (Kickert, Klijn and Koppenjan 1997). In both roles, the backing of representative democracy is essential for providing the conditions within which deliberative forums can function as a check on decision-making by powerful stakeholders in network governance.

In their chapter on donor-induced participation in Mozambique, Dijkstra and Lodewijckx focus on the relationship between deliberative forums and representative democracy. They observe that the participation program succeeded in bringing villagers together to discuss their collective problems and to seek solutions for them. This is a major achievement in the context of Mozambique and it can be regarded as at least a potential enhancement of input legitimacy. However, severe limits are revealed when we turn to the throughput and output side. The authors point out that community members are confronted with authorities that interfere with all aspects of their life and are able to manipulate, mislead and seriously harm them. Decisions of these authorities are not made in public so cannot be checked. Local state authorities are only accountable to a higher hierarchical layer in the state apparatus. Because they report themselves, they can interpret everything in their own interest. The research shows the limits of participation in this 'façade democracy'. The lack of separation of powers (checks and balances) at the local level, and the lack of transparency and accountability structures severely limit the chances of success of the participation program. This study sheds new light on the issue of a possible tension between deliberative democracy and representative democracy as it is often posed in the context of established democracies. The study suggests that the existence of a legitimately elected and representative legislative body is a necessary condition for the success of deliberative forms of policy-making, rather than a complication or a redundancy. The presence of institutions of a representative democracy enforces accountability and offers bottom-up initiatives a fair chance.

We can conclude that the (Dutch) local environmental forums, analyzed by Edwards and the Local Development Commissions analyzed by Dijkstra and Lodewijkckx provide opportunities for residents to express their wishes and concerns, and to discuss their collective problems. This is a gain in terms of input legitimacy, but the throughput and output legitimacy suffered from a lack of transparency, of appropriate checks and balances, and of accountability structures. In fact, due to these weaknesses these forums and commissions can hardly be regarded as forms of deliberative democracy. We reach the interesting conclusion that in real life settings of network governance, incipient forms of citizen participation can only reach the status of deliberative democracy if they have the backing of representative and pluralist democracy: strong representative political institutions and a vital civil society. This is a conclusion that can be overlooked in abstract accounts of deliberative democracy that are proposing this model as a fully-fledged alternative for representative democracy. Marks' chapter supports this conclusion, since in the Rotterdam case the deliberative arrangements were set up 'under the shadow' of the municipal executive's decision to connect its own fate to the safety issue in the subsequent election.

Multi-level Governance

Ruano de la Fuente and Schaap examine, in particular, the input and throughput legitimacy of four different cases of supra-municipal cooperation in different European countries. If anything, the chapter shows that one cannot draw general conclusions on differences between consolidated regional bodies on the one hand, and forms of inter-municipal cooperation on the other. Different aspects of input legitimacy and throughput legitimacy vary across the four cases. One of the two regional bodies, Greater London, has a directly elected government, while the other, the Greater Copenhagen Authority, does not. This implies that there is only indirect representation of general citizenship. The government of Greater London also offers more opportunities for consultation and cooperation to specific groups of citizens than greater Copenhagen. In Greater London, the representative model is complemented by incipient forms of deliberative democracy. However, the agenda for these consultations is mainly set by the politicians, the discussions take place behind closed doors and the ultimate decision can be taken by the Mayor without involvement of an elected Assembly. Throughput legitimacy is therefore limited. In Greater Copenhagen there is also some influence of the central government, providing a check and balance to decision making within this regional body. Democratic legitimacy in Greater Copenhagen therefore fully relies on the model of representative democracy but this representation is only indirect: through elected governments from the participating provinces, on the one hand, and through elected national governments, on the other.

The two forms of inter-municipal cooperation examined, ILEX in Spain and Hanover association in Germany, also proved to be widely different with respect to the different aspects of input and throughput legitimacy. In fact, for Hanover and its 20 neighboring municipalities a new regional body was created with a directly elected assembly and president. The Spanish cooperation relies on indirect representation since decisions are made by representatives of elected governments of the four participating municipalities. On the other hand, ILEX has advanced more with participatory democracy models. It created forms of citizen consultation and participation in the form of focus groups on specific services jointly provided by the four municipalities, implying the introduction of a consumer or client democracy. Demands of specific groups, such as elderly and immigrants, are taken into account. Citizen participation is absent in the Hanover area. With respect to decision making processes, ILEX works by consensus, which guarantees the influence of all participating municipalities and secures checks and balances: throughput legitimacy, at least at the level of the participating municipalities, appears to be guaranteed. At the same time, the effective veto power of all municipalities may lower effectiveness (output legitimacy). In the Hanover region, the allocation of responsibilities between the participating municipalities and the regional body is not clearly defined, which may hamper effectiveness and accountability (output legitimacy).

Van Nispen and Posseth examine the democratic legitimacy of macroeconomic governance in the EU, in particular, the common monetary policy and the fiscal policy. European monetary policy is in the hands of the European Central Bank governed by a council of national technocrats. National governments and their representatives in the Economic and Financial Affairs Council have very little to say, nor has the European Parliament. Nevertheless, democratic legitimacy of the common monetary policy proves to be quite high. European populations are generally in favor of the Euro and also agree with the central objective of the common monetary policy, namely price stability. This, in turn, requires an independent European Central Bank. So far, the ECB has been rather successful, which implies a high degree of output legitimacy.

European populations also prove to have a high degree of trust in the objectives for the fiscal policy, namely low fiscal deficits, but much less in the agency that coordinates this policy, the Economic and Financial Council (ECOFIN, consisting of ministers of Finance). This weakens input legitimacy. Furthermore, the involvement of national parliaments proves to be limited, both in preparing the discussions of the ECOFIN, and in holding the ministers accountable. In recent years, effectiveness also seems to be reduced given that several countries violated the 3 per cent target of the Maastricht treaty. The European Parliament is not involved at all. All this reduces throughput legitimacy but also output legitimacy. The technocratic nature of these two policy areas makes it unlikely that other and new democracy models can be applied. Representative democracy is the dominant model, but most representation is indirect and in monetary policy there is hardly any representation at all. However, the democratic legitimacy is mainly derived from the outputs of the policies, and to some extent also from the trust in the agencies implementing the policies.

While European coordination is strong in monetary policies especially for the Euro currency area, and reasonably strong in fiscal policies, it is weak in employment policies. Yet, the coordination of national employment policies and other structural economic policies is increasingly seen as necessary for the success of the common monetary policy. However, national governments and parliaments are not eager to give up their autonomy in this area, nor are national employers' organizations and unions. In order to overcome obstacles to coordination, the Open Method of Coordination (OMC) has been developed. It is expected to establish a non-directive but effective way of improving coordination, while at the same time leading to better input and throughput legitimacy of European policies by involving more stakeholders. This means that an attempt is made to apply pluralist and deliberative models of democracy along with the representative model. Zandstra examines the practice of the OMC for the European Employment Strategy. Countries are expected to formulate National employment Action Plans in cooperation with trade unions and employers' associations. They are also expected to incorporate EU guidelines and to submit their plans for discussion in various European discussion forums. Peer pressure is expected to lead to changes in the direction of more coordination and more application of best practices. However, in practice the level of stakeholder participation in the elaboration of the plans has been more determined by earlier practices within countries than by the recommendations of the OMC. Although countries comply with the requirements to elaborate plans and their accompanying monitoring systems, and some increased transparency of policies is achieved, Zandstra concludes that to a large extent, these are symbolic actions that do not lead to real changes in participation, to improved public debates or to more responsiveness and accountability. Moreover, the European influence on national policies is also still limited. While the OMC was meant to enhance input, throughput and output legitimacy of European policies, in the area of employment policies so far the results are limited. It proved impossible so far for the European Union to introduce deliberative and pluralist democracy models in countries with no tradition in these forms of democracy.

The IMF and the World Bank examined by Dijkstra belong to the family of United Nations institutions but have a kind of independent status and have a different governance structure: decision-making does not follow the 'one country, one vote' model as in the UN, but voting rights depend on economic power. The chapter shows that the indirect representation of elected country governments has caused problems of input and throughput legitimacy as well as of accountability (an aspect of output legitimacy) from the beginning. But these problems have exacerbated over time due to the ever increasing tasks and responsibilities of the two institutions, and due to the increasing asymmetry in their operation: a minority of economically powerful countries decides on loans and policy conditions for a majority of low and middle income countries. Contrary to the case of monetary and fiscal policies of the EU, there are also more doubts on effectiveness, and thus there are problems of output legitimacy. It is widely recognized that changes in governance are needed, and in fact many proposals for changes have been advanced and some of them have already been implemented. The latter include attempts to introduce deliberative democracy models, for example, improving transparency and openness and expanding the involvement of civil society. However, so far this does not seem to have led to real changes in decision-making processes or in output, so the democratic deficit continues to exist.

In sum, the democratic deficit of these supra-municipal or supra-national forms of multi-level governance is often related to the indirect representation of citizens in regional or international bodies. If there is direct representation such as in Greater London, Hanover area, or the European Parliament (EP), responsibilities of these elected bodies are limited (EP, Assembly of Greater London) or are not clearly defined (Hanover). Output legitimacy in terms of effectiveness and responsiveness is strong in some cases but weak in others, while accountability is almost always weak. The one case that shows the introduction of consumer or client democracy on a limited scale (ILEX) appears to be successful. The limited successes of introducing deliberative models of democracy at either the supra-municipal level (Greater London), the European level (the case of the OMC) or the global level (the World Bank) may have a similar cause as observed in the cases of network governance: the lack of a strong representative body that supports these attempts. In Greater London the elected Assembly has limited decision making power, the World Bank lacks a representative body altogether, and neither the European Commission nor the European Parliament have sufficient authority and power to promote national deliberative decision-making processes.

3. Democratization Strategies

A Democratic Deficit?

Do the new governance practices have a 'democratic deficit', and if so, how can it be understood? We concluded above that the examined governance practices are combinations of different modes of governance, and that in most cases representative democracy is supplemented by elements from other models of democracy. As a result, the empirical picture reveals 'less democratic deficit' than we would expect on theoretical grounds. As commonly understood, the democratic deficit in governance practices is a result of the unleashing of governing from the institutions of representative democracy. Of course, we have to bear in mind that governance modes are always embedded in representative democracy to a certain extent. This implies that there are always some checks and balances based on constitutional rules. From our research we can conclude that in many of the examined practices, the democratic deficit is also partially compensated for by other democratic devices. This picture does *not* refute the proposition that there is a democratic deficit as commonly understood, because the initial mechanism is that the input and throughput legitimacy of governance (and accountability at the output side) are weakened by the loosening grip of representative democracy on acts of governing. Moreover, if we look more closely at the new arrangements we do observe some important weaknesses and risks in legitimacy, which led to specific democratic deficits.

First, we observe that in the domain of governance at a distance and market governance, consumer democracy tends to be used as the primary additional mechanism for democratic will-formation and feedback. However, in Chapter 3 we argued that client or consumer democracy has little to contribute to input and throughput legitimacy. Second, in the cases of network governance, we found (incipient) forms of citizen participation but their performance was mixed in terms of our legitimacy criteria. We argued that forms of citizen participation can only develop into full-fledged forms of deliberative democracy if they have sufficient backing from representative and pluralist democracy: strong supportive representative institutions and an active civil society. Apparently, this backing was in several cases (almost) absent. In sum, in the domains of governance at a distance, market governance and network governance, 'new' democratic deficits can be identified in terms of inadequate or insufficient 'compensation' of the initial democratic deficit as understood in the governance literature. Third, in the domain of multi-level governance, the classical notion of the democratic deficit comes most clearly to the fore. Representative democracy is weakened. Input and throughput legitimacy, as well as accountability, are based on borrowing the legitimacy of institutions at other levels, such as municipal councils and national parliaments.

What kind of strategies can be discerned to overcome the democratic deficits? In general, we have to distinguish between democratization strategies that aim to improve the functioning of representative democracy by introducing specific elements of other models of democracy, while still maintaining the traditional primacy of politics, and strategies that introduce fully-fledged arrangements derived from those other models of democracy. In the latter case, we have to deal with the interrelations and possible tensions between representative democracy and other democracy models.

Democratizing Governance at a Distance

Our comparison shows that governance at a distance is a mode of governance that in essence does not conflict with representative democracy. We have shown that using elements of a consumer democracy may strengthen the output legitimacy of these governance practices. However, the strong emphasis on improving the output legitimacy may lead to a possible neglect of the input side. That is why it could be interesting to strengthen the input and throughput legitimacy side of governance at a distance by introducing elements of deliberative and associative democracy. Citizens and (other) stakeholders can be seen as possible sources of additional information, knowledge and experience, which can be mobilized by politicians when determining the relevant (input and output) parameters. This does not challenge the primacy of politics in the representative model. A more fundamental tension will occur if strong versions of deliberative or associative democracy are introduced, in which citizens and (other) stakeholders are co-producers of the decisions to be taken.

Another flaw in the legitimacy of governance at a distance occurs in relation to the use of decentralization. Decentralization can be seen as a system of delegated legitimacy, which affects the throughput and output legitimacy of organizations that have acquired more power and discretion. Citizens or companies have to rely on the quality of the decision-making process of these organizations. If these are municipalities this is probably no problem. A municipality is embedded in a system of democratic participation and control. In other cases, for instance other public or semi-public agencies, these democratic mechanisms do not prevail. In these cases, the introduction of a consumer, deliberative and associative democracy model may enhance the legitimacy of the black box of the decentralized process of decision-making.

Democratizing Market Governance

In this mode of governance, the market mechanism is used to produce outcomes that reflect the desires and wishes of the consumers of public services, like citizens or companies. One could expect that the output legitimacy of this mode of governance is rather high. Providers that do not produce services that reflect the wishes and needs of the consumers (in terms of price and quality), would not survive in a market. In order to produce responsive services, it is necessary that providers create possibilities for participation, for instance of consumers, in the design of new services or the redesign of existing services. One could argue that a perfect market automatically implies a consumer democracy. However, the daily practice of many market governance practices is that it has been rather difficult to create a well functioning and transparent market. The development of general rules of the game in which weak interests are protected and conditions are formulated to secure equal access of all citizens to market-based public services, and the introduction of a capable regulatory or supervisory body to guarantee the compliance to these rules is a necessary condition for the legitimacy of market governance. Up till now only the institutions of representative democracy can be seen as the most powerful democratic institutions which are capable of defining a fair 'level playing field'. This implies that market governance should be embedded in a system of checks and balances in which the introduction of consumer democracy is combined with the use of the institutions of representative democracy as a possible watchdog.

Democratizing Network Governance and Societal Self-Governance

The strategy for democratizing network governance and societal self-governance is twofold. First, fully-fledged forms of deliberative democracy have to be introduced. The notion of network governance includes the participation of stakeholders in a process of negotiation and dialogue. However, in the practice of network governance openness to the interests of lay people, residents, and minority and disadvantaged groups is not self-evident. In contrast, the notion of deliberative democracy is based on the inclusion of all affected interests in public decision-making. Second, forms of deliberative democracy have to be embedded in representative and pluralist democracy. Deliberative procedures require guarantees for openness of the agenda and for an unconstrained dialogue. The procedures should also have some political prominence, in that the results must be formally taken into account in the final political decision-making.

These conditions can only be guaranteed by binding rules, which implies that forms of deliberative democracy are dependent on the backing of representative democracy. At the same time, giving deliberative procedures some prominence in terms of final decision-making creates certain tensions between deliberative and representative democracy. Against this backdrop, elected representatives have to perform a balancing act and to reinvent their political roles. We propose that a primary role of representative politics in network governance and societal self-governance is procedural, aimed at the creation and maintenance of conditions for openness, the quality of representation, the quality of participation, checks and balances, transparency and accountability procedures. Moreover, politicians should support deliberative procedures by a consistent policy of self-binding their decision-making to the results of the procedures. This does not mean that politicians have to retreat completely from making substantive choices. As suggested by Klijn and Koppenjan (2000), politicians can establish some substantive terms at the start of the process, allow for feedback to these terms during the process and make selections and combinations of attractive policy proposals at the end.

Democratizing Multi-level Governance

It is difficult to secure effective institutions of representative democracy at the supra-national or supra-municipal level. Decisions are often made by coordinating bodies in which representatives of national or municipal elected governments participate. This reflects, at best, an indirect representation of citizens' interests, and our cases show that national parliaments and municipal councils tend to give little attention to what happens in these coordinating bodies. On the other hand, if elected bodies at the supra-municipal or supra-national level exist, they tend to have little power (Greater London's Assembly, the European Parliament), which in turn reduces citizen's interest in (voting for) them.

In theory, this weakness of representative democracy is a perfect basis for introducing elements of other democracy models. In ILEX, Spain, it proved possible to involve citizens as clients or consumers of services jointly provided in inter-municipal coordination. The Open Method of Coordination aims to improve policy coordination within the EU while at the same time opening up space for participation of citizens and stakeholders in decision making. Although it has not fulfilled all expectations so far, it may contribute to more legitimacy of policies in the future. IMF and the World Bank have made their actions more transparent and increased consultations with NGOs. All these attempts to introduce elements of deliberative democracy were not very successful so far, and we concluded an important reason is that they lacked support from effective representative institutions that could force executives to take the outcomes of consultations seriously. Nevertheless, some democratization strategies can be suggested. In those cases where elected regional bodies exist, such as in Greater London and in Hanover area, more powers can be given to these bodies. The Greater London Assembly should for instance obtain the right to approve the spatial plans for the London area. Dependent on the role to be played by the councilors, this might contribute to opening up agendas and improving the effectiveness of citizen consultations.

Van Nispen and Posseth suggest that the legitimacy of fiscal policy coordination can be improved by giving the European parliament a role in holding the ECOFIN (Economic and Financial Affairs Council) to account. They also propose minor improvements in democratic legitimacy of the ECB, especially in the area of accountability. More and more easily accessible information regarding inflation and inflation forecasts could be made available.

For the case of the IMF and the World Bank, Dijkstra argues that the only way to improve democratic legitimacy of these institutions is to radically reduce their tasks and responsibilities.

4. Conclusion

Our research has highlighted that in the slipstream of the examined governance practices new democratic arrangements are emerging from other models of democracy besides the dominant representative model. However, in many of the examined practices this 'compensation' for the 'original' democratic deficit that resulted from the unleashing of governing from representative democracy proved to be insufficient in terms of the legitimacy norms that we have proposed.

The finding of these new and specific democratic deficits is the first major outcome of our research. The second outcome is that our research lends strong empirical support for the notion that well-functioning representative institutions are a necessary condition for the performance of other democratic arrangements.

In the literature, the relation between representative democracy and other sorts of democracy is often analyzed in terms of tensions. These tensions do exist. Further democratized modes of governance are in conflict with the traditional idea of the political primacy of politicians. However, in the last instance, modes of governance are always more or less embedded in the institutions of representative democracy. These institutions, together with a strong civil society, are the ultimate sources for the necessary checks and balances in governance practices. The search for relations of mutual reinforcement between different models of democracy, on the basis of the inherited representative institutions, is an important task for the theory and practice of public administration.

References

Kickert, W.J.M., Klijn, E.H. and Koppenjan, J.F.M. (eds) (1997), *Managing Complex Networks* (London: Sage).

Klijn, E.H. and Koppenjan, J.F.F.M. (2000), 'Politicians and interactive decision-making: institutional spoilsports or playmakers', *Public Administration* 78:2, 365–387.

Index